UNDER A BLOOD RED SUN

UNDER A BLOOD RED SUN

The remarkable story of PT boats in the Philippines
and the rescue of General MacArthur

JOHN J. DOMAGALSKI

Philadelphia & Oxford

Published in the United States of America and Great Britain in 2016 by
CASEMATE PUBLISHERS
1950 Lawrence Road, Havertown, PA 19083, USA
and
10 Hythe Bridge Street, Oxford OX1 2EW, UK

Hardcover Edition: ISBN 978-1-61200-407-5
Digital Edition: ISBN 978-1-61200-409-9

A CIP record for this book is available from the Library of Congress and the British Library

Printed and bound in the United States of America

For a complete list of Casemate titles, please contact:

CASEMATE PUBLISHERS (US)
Telephone (610) 853-9131
Fax (610) 853-9146
Email: casemate@casematepublishers.com
www.casematepublishers.com

CASEMATE PUBLISHERS (UK)
Telephone (01865) 241249
Fax (01865) 794449
Email: casemate-uk@casematepublishers.co.uk
www.casematepublishers.co.uk

MIX
Paper from
responsible sources
FSC
www.fsc.org FSC® C011935

CONTENTS

Prologue: War Comes to the Philippines   viii

PART I: VOYAGE TO THE ORIENT

Chapter 1	3
Chapter 2	13
Chapter 3	22
Chapter 4	29
Chapter 5	37
Chapter 6	46

PART II: THRUST INTO THE FIRE

Chapter 7	57
Chapter 8	64
Chapter 9	72
Chapter 10	80
Chapter 11	92
Chapter 12	102
Chapter 13	109
Chapter 14	116
Chapter 15	122
Chapter 16	129
Chapter 17	137
Chapter 18	144
Chapter 19	155
Chapter 20	164
Chapter 21	173
Chapter 22	181

PART III: EVACUATION

Chapter 23	191
Chapter 24	202
Chapter 25	212
Chapter 26	219
Chapter 27	229
Chapter 28	237

PART IV: SCATTERED

Chapter 29	249
Chapter 30	257
Chapter 31	263
Chapter 32	273
Chapter 33	277
Chapter 34	286
Chapter 35	297
Chapter 36	305
Chapter 37	311
Chapter 38	323
Chapter 39	330

Epilogue	337
Appendix 1: MacArthur's Evacuation Mission	341
Appendix 2: Motor Torpedo Boats Squadron Three	
Final Disposition of Boats	343
Notes	344
Bibliography	368
Index	380

MAP LIST

Map 1: The Philippines, 1941   24
Map 2: Manila Bay Area   31
Map 3: Attack on the Philippines   74
Map 4: Retreat to Bataan   133
Map 5: Bataan and Corregidor   139
Map 6: Attack on Binanga Bay   146
Map 7: DeLong's Escape   157
Map 8: *PT-41* Subic Bay Action   175
Map 9: *PT-32* Action off The Points 177
Map 10: Last Visit to Subic Bay   183
Map 11: MacArthur's Escape Route   204
Map 12: Southern Philippines   221
Map 13: Sea Battle off Cebu   265
Map 14: Mindanao   288

WAR COMES TO THE PHILIPPINES

A ringing telephone pierced the night-time silence in the officer's quarters at the Cavite Navy Yard. The largest American naval base in the Philippines was positioned on the very end of Stanley Point—a small finger of land that jutted out into Manila Bay from the mainland. About 8 miles across the water to the northeast was Manila, capital of the American Commonwealth and a majestic city long known as the Pearl of the Orient.

A sleepy Lieutenant John D. Bulkeley turned on a bedside lamp. The young officer had been in the Philippines for less than three months. He commanded Motor Torpedo Boat (MTB) Squadron 3. The unit comprised six small wooden torpedo boats, commonly known as PT boats, and about eighty men.

A glimpse at his watch revealed it was a few minutes after 3:00 am. Bulkeley picked up the receiver to the sound of an excited voice. "We're at war!" the caller exclaimed before continuing with some stunning news. "The Japs have just bombed Pearl Harbor. The Old Man wants you to get down here, right away."[1] Bulkeley knew exactly what it meant. The Old Man was Rear Admiral Francis Rockwell, commander of the Sixteenth Naval District. Rockwell oversaw an assortment of naval bases in the Philippines and some local defense forces.

Bulkeley was now wide awake. He shook one of his officers, Ensign Anthony Akers, and told him the news. Akers though it was a joke.

"This is a hell of a time to be declaring war!" he mumbled, and rolled over.[2]

The start of the war came as no surprise to Bulkeley, who like most servicemen in the Pacific knew tensions between the U.S. and Japan had reached a boiling point, but where it began was a shock. He thought the first shots would be fired somewhere near where he was in the Far East. It was December 8, 1941 in the Philippines. Over 5,100 miles to the east and a day earlier, due to crossing the International Date Line, the Japanese had launched a surprise attack on the Pacific Fleet in Pearl Harbor, Hawaii, with planes from aircraft carriers. The biggest American naval and air facility in the Pacific had been taken by complete surprise. The fleet sustained serious damage as the United States was abruptly thrust into World War II.

Bulkeley ran out to a jeep after quickly putting on some clothes. He then began making his way to the Commandantia. The old thick-walled fortress of a building from Spanish colonial days served as Rockwell's headquarters on Stanley Point.

Rockwell was notified of the start of war by his immediate superior. Admiral Thomas Hart, Commander in Chief of the United States Asiatic Fleet, was the first high-level American leader in the Philippines to receive news of the Pearl Harbor attack. Hart was in command of all naval forces in and around the Philippines. Marine Lieutenant Colonel William Clement had called Hart, telling him to "put some cold water on your face." He arrived at the admiral's residence in Manila a short time later carrying a simple plain language message from the Navy in Hawaii. "Air raid on Pearl Harbor. This is no drill."[3]

Sitting on his bedside, Hart drafted a brief message for Clement to immediately send out to all units of the Asiatic Fleet. "Japan started hostilities. Govern yourselves accordingly." The dispatch went out at 3:27 am.[4] He did not, however, send the message to the army command in the Philippines, although he later dispatched his chief of staff to army headquarters.

It did not take long for Bulkeley to reach the Commandantia. He rushed into the headquarters to find Admiral Rockwell fully dressed along with his chief of staff, Captain Harold Ray. Dawn was just beginning to break over Manila Bay. The grim-faced Rockwell was calmly staring at the sky. "They ought to be here any minute," he said, referring to the Japanese bombers he was certain were en route.[5] The admiral did not want the PT boats to stay at Cavite as it was too risky in the event of an air attack. He ordered Bulkeley to get his boats ready for sea and then go across Manila Bay to Mariveles Harbor.

At about the same time Bulkeley was leaving the Commandantia, a ringing bedside telephone awoke General Douglas MacArthur. The general commanded all American army and army air force personnel in the Philippines. He resided in a lavish penthouse suite at the opulent Manila Hotel in the downtown area of the capital city. MacArthur picked up the receiver to hear the voice of his chief of staff, Major General Richard Sutherland, who told him the war had started.

The Army learned the news not from the Navy, but when an enlisted signalman picked up an electrifying flash news bulletin about the Pearl Harbor attack from a commercial radio station in San Francisco. "Pearl Harbor!" MacArthur exclaimed in disbelief. "It should be our strongest point!"[6]

The telephone rang again as the general rushed to get dressed. This time it was Brigadier General Leonard Gerow. The chief of the Army's war plans division was calling from Washington, D.C. to confirm the news bulletin. The general was ordered to execute the prearranged war plan. "I wouldn't be surprised if you get an attack there in the near future," Gerow warned.[7] MacArthur replied that his forces were on alert and ready for action. However, the coming days would call into question this statement. He then read the bible for ten minutes, as he customarily started every morning, before heading out to his headquarters.

MacArthur arrived at his office to a chaotic scene. Officers and staff members were trying to gather accurate information from Pearl Harbor and determine Japanese movements in order to ascertain the true situation in the Pacific. The question was not if an attack was coming, but when. The Japanese were certain to strike the Philippines by air, sea, or both. It would be up to MacArthur alone, however, to determine how to respond to the impending action.

The PT boats under John Bulkeley's command were among the Navy's fastest and newest weapons. So new, in fact, that formal operational tactics had not yet been developed. The squadron commander knew he would be creating the tactics as he went along, in wartime conditions.

The stay at Rockwell's office was short. Bulkeley returned to his boats. His men were by now awake and alert. He calmly began issuing orders for the sailors to get the PTs ready for action. He took some precautions, perhaps also expecting Japanese planes to appear at any time as Rockwell had warned. One of the boats was sent to cruise nearby waters, while the five remaining PTs were separated about a hundred yards apart along the shore.

Preparing the boats for action was a painfully slow process that would take most of the day. Boxes of machine-gun ammunition were hauled aboard by crewmen. Food supplies of all types—anything that could be found on base—were collected for use on the PTs. The list included cans of corned beef and Vienna sausage, canned vegetables, fresh fruit, and coffee. Torpedoes, the main weapon of the PT boats, required some work before they could be fired in combat. Live warheads needed to be attached to each underwater missile and armed.

Rumors of enemy movements began circulating among the sailors almost as soon as the news about Pearl Harbor broke, and continued to build into a crescendo as the day progressed. The falsehoods took various forms, including that a Japanese invasion fleet was sitting just off the coast and part of the Philippines was already under enemy control. None proved to be accurate.

The expected Japanese air attack never came during the first day of the war. Some planes, however, flew high over Manila Bay around noon, prompting the boats to quickly get under way. The aircraft were likely friendly, but drew some sporadic antiaircraft fire from nervous gunners none the less.

Bulkeley decided to divide his boats into two groups of three as some PTs neared a state of readiness. At about 3:00 pm he ordered his second in command, Lieutenant Robert B. Kelly, to take three boats to Mariveles and report to a submarine tender for more torpedoes and water. He gave Kelly explicit instructions: "Remain on the alert and attack anything I order you to attack!"[8] The boats took off at 6:45 pm.[9]

The voyage of slightly more than 25 miles took Kelly's boats southwest across Manila Bay. Positioned on the west side of the Philippines' largest island of Luzon, it was well recognized as one of the finest natural harbors in the Far East. From a modest 12-mile-wide entrance with mountainous terrain on both sides, the bay expands to a broad 30-mile width. The Bataan Peninsula marks the west side of the bay. American commanders had long considered the mountainous finger of land to be an ideal defensive position to protect Manila Bay in the event of an enemy invasion.

Kelly's PTs were pointed towards the southern end of Bataan as the trio of boats sped through Manila Bay. Situated at the extreme southern tip of the Peninsula, Mariveles Harbor was an excellent anchorage and home to a small naval base. The boats, however, were not going directly to Mariveles. Kelly first had to drop off some passengers on the small island of Corregidor, located about two miles off the coast of Bataan.

The rocky, tadpole-shaped island measured 3½ miles in length and one 1½ miles at its widest point. Heavily fortified with a variety of large guns, defensive positions, and even a system of underground tunnels, Corregidor symbolically stood guard over the entrance to Manila Bay. A couple of smaller, but equally well-defended islands were in close proximity.

Darkness was falling by the time Kelly pulled away from the dock on Corregidor. He thought about how quickly things had changed in the last 24 hours. He had been enjoying a full steak dinner at the Army-Navy Club in Manila only the night before. Now he was leading the first wartime voyage of his squadron's boats.

Several minefields were near the entrance to Mariveles Harbor. The underwater weapons, along with Corregidor, were part of a defensive network protecting the opening to Manila Bay. The PT sailors had passed through the minefields many times before—even at night—but never in the blackout conditions now required by war. The minefield lights were off and the boats were unable to turn on their lights. It made for a precarious situation, with a thick air of tension coming over every sailor aboard the boats.

The PTs slowly edged through the mines as tense crewmen nervously waited for an explosion. The boats made it safely through with no detonations, but the passage was not without incident. The roar of the boat motors was echoing against the mountains on Bataan. Jittery soldiers could hear the noise, but not determine from where it was coming. Searchlights suddenly began to flicker across the area, scouring the sky for Japanese planes, as a cascade of antiaircraft batteries opened fire.

The boats made it into the harbor without damage from mines or friendly artillery. Kelly had no sooner moored his PTs alongside the submarine tender as directed when the ship's commanding officer notified him that he had orders to leave the area for an unknown destination far to the south. The tender would be gone before daylight.

Kelly was left to contemplate how the torpedo boats would operate remotely from Mariveles Harbor with no support. John Bulkeley remained back at Cavite with the remaining three boats. Both must have been nervously wondering about the immediate future. War had finally come to the Philippines.

MacArthur, Rockwell, Bulkeley and the rest of the American servicemen in the Philippines would soon have plenty to be worrying about. Bulkeley and his men, in the United States only four short months before, were now on the front lines of the war. The world had dramatically changed since the group set sail for the long voyage to the Philippines.

PART I

VOYAGE TO THE ORIENT

CHAPTER 1

Daylight was on the horizon when three tugboats gathered around *Guadalupe* as she slowly entered the Brooklyn Navy Yard. The New York City skyline loomed in the distance across the East River. The new Navy tanker had been in service for less than two months and had spent the last six weeks transporting oil from Texas to New Jersey.[1] Workers quickly began to tie down mooring cables after the tugs gently nudged her into a berth along sprawling Pier G.

The expansion of the Navy was making the Brooklyn base a busy place. Five large warships and two small coast guard vessels had been launched in the last five years alone. With war already under way in Europe and tensions mounting in the Pacific, the orders for new ships kept coming. The massive 45,000-ton battleships *Iowa* and *Missouri* were in the early stages of construction just across the yard.[2]

Morning light marked the start of August 16, 1941. The day promised to be full of activity for *Guadalupe*. Lieutenant John Bulkeley and his fellow officers of a new PT boat squadron boarded the ship just after 6:00 am.[3] Bulkeley's stocky and muscular body stood 5 feet 8 inches tall. He had thinning black hair and penetrating eyes infused with shades of blue and gray.

The ship would serve as Bulkeley's home for the next six weeks. She was the means of transporting his squadron halfway around the world. Bulkeley, his boats, men, and associated supplies were about to undertake a long voyage to the Philippines.

Activity on the tanker began in earnest when yard workers came aboard to make her ready for the special cargo. The work began when the tug *Penobscot* brought an ammunition barge along the starboard side. A crane then began transferring over the ordnance almost immediately.

A 350-ton Hammerhead crane towered over *Guadalupe* from Pier G. It was an iconic image known throughout the yard as a symbol of power and might. The crane sprang into action just after the noon hour, hoisting the first PT boat onto the tanker's deck. The work continued throughout the day, with tugs twice shifting the position of the tanker to better align with the crane. All six of the PTs were aboard by 8:30 pm.

Yard workers returned the next morning to secure the PTs to the tanker's deck. Three boats were positioned on each side of the ship. All of the boats were on the well deck, an area in the middle of the ship that was positioned slightly lower than the deck forward and aft. The workers began to install machine guns on each boat. A total of 656,400 rounds of ammunition—mostly 50-caliber bullets—were now safely aboard.[4] A variety of spare parts rounded out the PT supplies.

Tuesday, August 19 was Bulkeley's 30th birthday. It was also the day for *Guadalupe* to depart the Brooklyn Navy Yard. The yard workers left the ship for good late in the night after completing nearly three days of hard labor. The tanker and her cargo were now ready to set sail.

The silence of the dark morning hours was broken when the ship tested her siren and whistle at 2:00 am. She was under way 15 minutes later. Commander Harry B. Thurber conned the vessel down the East River and past the southern tip of Manhattan. The Statue of Liberty faintly appeared off the starboard side as she continued to follow the Hudson River towards the open ocean. Speed increased to 16 knots as the tanker paralleled the eastern seaboard by following a southerly heading for a full day of sailing. The setting sun found *Guadalupe* in international waters about 145 miles southeast of Virginia Beach, Virginia.

John Duncan Bulkeley was born on August 19, 1911 in New York City to Elizabeth and Fredrick Bulkeley.[5] His father's side of the family had a long history with the United States Navy going all the way back to the Revolutionary War, when a distant relative served under John Paul Jones aboard the famous warship *Bonhomme Richard*. Fredrick also served a stint in the Navy, contracting a tropical disease while on a port call in Panama. He later married a hospital nurse, settled in New York City, and became a successful businessman.

The younger Bulkeley grew up with a great fascination with the sea. He decided at an early age that he wanted to attend the United States Naval Academy in Annapolis, Maryland. The elder Bulkeley, sensing his son's nautical interest, signed him up to become a seaman aboard the S.S. *Baracoa* of the Colombian Steamship Line. The younger Bulkeley spent three consecutive summers, starting at the age of 12, learning about seamanship from an international crew as the ship plied the waters of the Caribbean. He was paid 30 dollars a month for his work. Bulkeley later recalled it to be a "fantastic amount for doing what I dearly loved."[6]

Bulkeley was unable to gain the required congressional appointment to the Naval Academy from his home state after graduating from high school in Hackettstown, New Jersey in 1928. He scored high enough on the entrance exam to be considered as an alternate, available to enter the school only if one of the chosen candidates withdrew. Luck, however, did not work in his favor and no spots from New Jersey opened up.

The young man was undaunted. He decided to travel to Washington, D.C. to personally lobby members of congress who might still have appointments available. Bulkeley made little progress until he walked into the office of Representative Morgan G. Sanders of Texas. All of Sanders' candidates for both the navy and army school had failed the entrance exams.

The congressman became intrigued when Bulkeley mentioned his father owned land in Sanders' district. Impressed by his determination and initiative, Sanders offered Bulkeley his choice of an appointment to either the Naval Academy or the Army equivalent at West Point.[7] Bulkeley chose the Navy, passed the entrance exam a second time, and entered the school the following summer.

Like all first-year students at the Naval Academy, Bulkeley was forced to suffer cruel hazing at the hands of upper classmen. The acts, including physical beatings, were designed to weed out those unable to endure the physical and psychological rigors of military life. Bulkeley survived the hazing, but it left him with bad feelings about the academy that lingered throughout the remainder of his long naval career.[8]

Bulkeley graduated in the lower half of the class of 1933. President Roosevelt attended the commencement and personally handed him a diploma. The country, however, was in the mist of the Great Depression and the hard times also extended to the Navy. Budget constraints led to extreme measures. Only the top half of the graduating class became commissioned naval officers.

In the unusual position of having graduated from the Naval Academy, but not formally entering the service, Bulkeley searched for something to do with his life. He was accepted as a flying cadet by Army Air Corps and reported to San Antonio, Texas in the fall of 1933 to begin pilot training. He knew aviation was the future, and thought it would be a good opportunity to get into the fast-growing field. Bulkeley, however, was not destined to become a pilot. Crashing at least one plane, he did not make it through the training. Bulkeley was luckily able to cheat death, walking away from the aborted flight training with no serious injuries.

A breakthrough with the Navy came the following year when Roosevelt recalled the recent graduates to active duty. Bulkeley was formally commissioned an ensign, the lowest-ranking naval officer, on June 19, 1934.[9] His first assignment was to serve aboard *Indianapolis*. Bulkeley served as a junior officer after reporting aboard the heavy cruiser at Cape Cod, Massachusetts. He became a qualified turret officer for the warship's 8-inch main battery guns before rotating among the various functional departments.

The new officer's first great naval adventure occurred while *Indianapolis* was visiting Norfolk, Virginia. It began innocently enough with a few days of leave. Bulkeley boarded a coastal steamer bound for Washington. While aboard the small vessel he noticed several Japanese men, one of whom was identified as the Japanese Ambassador to the United States. He thought the men were acting suspiciously and wondered why diplomats would be near the bastion of American naval power on the Atlantic.

Bulkeley decided—on his own accord—to delve into the world of espionage and intelligence. He used the cover of darkness to swipe the ambassador's briefcase and then immediately plunged overboard. Keeping the case above water, he swam to shore and hitchhiked to Washington. A couple of days later he presented the unopened briefcase to a startled individual who answered the door at the Office of Naval Intelligence.

Bulkeley was sent to see the captain shortly after returning aboard *Indianapolis*. The commanding officer did not want to know any details of his exploits, but simply directed him to resolve his affairs aboard the cruiser immediately and report to the transport *Chaumont*. The ship was moored nearby and promptly sailed for Shanghai, China two days later.

Making the long voyage across the Pacific gave Bulkeley time to put the Japanese ambassador's briefcase caper behind him and focus on the next stage of his naval career. He was assigned to the old gunboat *Sacramento* in December 1936, soon after arriving in China. Entering service before the start of World War I, the vessel began her China duty in April 1932.[10] Her mission, in conjunction with a small group of other warships in the area, was to protect American interests in the region. A variety of duties awaited Bulkeley aboard *Sacramento*. The junior officer stood watches and spent time in engineering and gunnery.

China was soon a nation ravaged by war with Japan. A biographer later wrote that Bulkeley, already suspicious of the Japanese, quickly developed a deep hatred for them after hearing and seeing the many cruelties—rape, murder, torture of various kinds, and even public beheadings—being inflicted on the Chinese people. His extreme dislike flourished after Japanese planes sank the American gunboat *Panay*, allegedly by accident, on the Yangtze River near Nanking in late 1937. Bulkeley became convinced the United States and Japan would someday be at war.

The officer sought revenge in various ways for the *Panay* incident. He failed to sound the alarm as required by duty when Chinese torpedo boats sped past *Sacramento*. The small craft later torpedoed a Japanese warship. He again tried his hand at espionage work, dressing as a civilian to take pictures of military forces with a hidden camera. The ploy unraveled when he was taken into custody after refusing to bow to a Japanese sentry. Bulkeley was released after reluctantly writing the phrase 100 times, "I must bow before sentries who represent the Imperial Majesty the Emperor of Japan."[11]

A chance meeting in the coastal city of Swatow during the fall of 1937 again changed Bulkeley's life. He was among a small group of American officers invited to attend a farewell party aboard H.M.S. *Diana*. The British warship was preparing to depart for a long voyage to England. She had been operating near *Sacramento* in the area about 180 miles northeast of Hong Kong. Bulkeley was waiting to climb aboard the vessel when a group of British civilians arrived. One particular young lady caught his eye. It was Hilda Alice Wood.

Known to her family and friends as Alice, she held a degree from Hong Kong University and lived with her parents in the Swatow area. Her father worked for Lloyds of London as a harbor pilot. "On our first meeting, I saw a rather boyish looking young man with a zest for life and terrific drive, with the navy blue and gold running through his veins," she later recalled.[12]

The two began dating and romance soon flourished. The couple was married in a simple civil ceremony by a U.S. judge in Shanghai on November 10, 1938. Circumstances did not allow for a more formal event.[13] The newlyweds took a launch back to *Sacramento* and dined aboard ship with other officers. The couple spent then their wedding night apart, as John was required to stand watch aboard ship. He took his bride to a nearby abandoned house along with some marines for protection. She slept alone on a cot with her husband's pistol nearby and guards patrolling outside. She was now a navy wife.

The decrepit *Sacramento* received orders in December 1938 to return to the United States for some badly-needed overhaul work. She first moved from China to the Philippines. The gunboat left the Philippines on January 12, 1939 bound for New York, via the Mediterranean. The five-month journey spanned nearly 18,000 miles and featured many ports of call, including Singapore, Bombay, Egypt, Naples, and Gibraltar.[14]

Alice Bulkeley was not yet formally an American citizen even though she was married to an American naval officer. Immigration rules forced her to stay behind in China until her husband arrived in the United States and sent for her. The couple then set up home in Long Island City, New York.

Promoted to a lieutenant (junior grade) while in China, Bulkeley was aware that his naval career was moving at a slow pace as he waited for his next assignment. However, new orders came in January 1940 with a directive to report to one of the Navy's largest vessels, the aircraft carrier *Saratoga*. Bulkeley traveled across the full width of the country to board his new ship in Long Beach, California. Life aboard the big ship was far different than on the small *Sacramento*. He was assigned to be a second division officer, a position of great responsibility aboard such a large vessel. The assignment allowed him to stand deck watches and to observe flight operations.

Seeing the planes take off and land rekindled Bulkeley's interest in becoming a pilot. Captain Albert Reed, *Saratoga's* spit and polish commanding officer, took a special interest in the aggressive junior officer. An accomplished aviator himself, Reed soon recommended Bulkeley for naval flight school. Bulkeley was quickly accepted. He set out for Pensacola, Florida in early 1941 for what he thought was the start of a future career in naval aviation.

Fate would have it that Bulkeley did not travel a direct route to Pensacola. His trip from the carrier *Saratoga* on the west coast to naval flight school required an intermediate stopover in Washington, D.C. It was during the short visit to the nation's capital that he first learned about the Navy's new PT boat program. The burgeoning service was looking for aggressive junior officers to join the ranks. It was an enthralling opportunity that offered the possibility of a command. Bulkeley quickly jumped at the chance. "Whatever in the hell these PTs were, [they] captured my imagination anyway," he later recalled of the decision. "I couldn't wait to sink my heart and soul into the program."[15]

Bulkeley arrived at the Brooklyn Navy Yard to begin his new duty less than a week after volunteering for the PT service. He assumed command of Motor Boat Submarine Chaser Squadron 1 on February 20, 1941.[16] The squadron was due to take delivery of 12 new Elco 70-foot boats in March. All would be identical to the PTs, except that the torpedo tubes were replaced by depth charges and the boats were given a PTC (Chaser) designation. Eight of the new boats, however, were soon earmarked for transfer to the British under the Lend-Lease Program, leaving Bulkeley with only four boats.

Using small motorboats to hunt submarines was an unproven concept. The four PTC boats under Bulkeley's command were fitted with sonar equipment and sent to Key West, Florida for testing. The voyage south served as a shakedown cruise for the new squadron.

The trip to the warm currents of the Caribbean was a welcome change from the cold waters around New York. The boats moored along a sea wall close to tennis courts and an officer's club. Just about everything in town was in easy walking distance. Boat exercises typically lasted three or four hours after starting at the comfortable hour of 10:00 am.[17] The squadron leader received word of a promotion while enjoying the southern sunshine. Bulkeley attained the rank of full lieutenant on April 1, 1941.[18]

Sonar uses echoes from underwater sound waves to pinpoint the location of submarines. The equipment was commonly installed on larger warships, such as destroyers. Early testing at Key West revealed the equipment did not work well with the motorboats. When the PTCs moved at full speed, the noise of the boat engines drowned out the echoes. If the boats stood still in anything but completely calm waters, pitches and rolls then interfered with the sound waves. The PTCs had no way to find submarines without workable sonar.

Ordered back to New York, Bulkeley decided to make much of the trip at full throttle to see how the boats handled at high speed in the open ocean. The four boats pulled into Norfolk for refueling and unknowingly moored next to the quarters of Admiral Earnest J. King. The commander in chief of the Atlantic Fleet was known to be a stern disciplinarian. Wearing dirty clothes, Bulkeley's tired and unshaven men were eating sandwiches on deck when King's flag lieutenant suddenly appeared in dress whites. "Admiral King wants you to report to him immediately—in the uniform of the day."[19] Bulkeley knew the ominous request meant trouble and quickly departed the area at high speed bound for New York.

The PTC concept was declared a failure. The only positive feature to come out of the test was the boats' handling in the open sea. The craft did extremely well on their high-speed return trip to New York through rough and choppy Atlantic waters and only needed two refueling stops. The squadron was decommissioned on July 17, 1941. The four boats were earmarked for conversion to gunboats and eventual transfer to the British.[20]

The end of the PTC program left Bulkeley temporarily without an assignment. It did not last long, however, as he shortly learned a new PT squadron was about to be formed and he would be given the command. The unit was earmarked for duty in the Philippines, information that Bulkeley kept secret. What Bulkeley now needed the most was people.

The squadron commander had a good idea of the type of men needed for PT boats. It was not a job for just any sailor. The men needed the endurance to be able to ride the small boats in bumpy waters—very different from the smooth sailing of larger vessels. He began talking up the opportunity to men from his former PTC squadron, noting they would be deployed to a faraway location. "Such a prospect was exciting to most of us and it didn't take long to put together ten officers and 60 crewmen for the newly commissioned Squadron 3," recalled Ensign Henry Brantingham.[21] The squadron personnel eventually increased to 12 officers and 68 enlisted men.

Motor Torpedo Boat Squadron 3 was formally commissioned on August 12, 1941.[22] It consisted of only six boats: *PT-31* through *PT-35* and *PT-41*. Bulkeley selected the 41 boat to be his flagship. All were of a new Elco variety and represented a slight upgrade from the PTCs taken to Key West. The PTs had entered service in July.

Only a short time existed for Bulkeley to get his squadron ready to depart for the Philippines. A litany of tasks needed to be accomplished, including assigning officers and crews to individual boats, procuring spare parts, and obtaining ammunition—not to mention the building of camaraderie that has to happen with a new team. Some of the work was undertaken before the delivery of the boats.

Exactly one week passed between the commissioning of the squadron and its departure aboard *Guadalupe*. Bulkeley did not reveal the squadron's ultimate destination to his men until the voyage was well under way. "We didn't know where we [were] going until we got through the Panama Canal," recalled Machinist's Mate First Class John Tuggle.[23]

The commander told the group they were going to the Philippines and that it would be a dangerous mission. He also added a stipulation. "If we didn't want to go then, we could back out then," Tuggle remembered. The long voyage would take the sailors halfway around the world.

CHAPTER 2

The PT boats under John Bulkeley's command were the latest product of a U.S. Navy program that was still in its infancy. The rise of torpedo boats came about in the late nineteenth century with the invention of the self-propelled torpedo. The underwater missile was originally developed in Britain in 1866 as a defensive weapon to be fired from land.[1] Naval planners immediately saw the potential of the torpedo for combat at sea, but it took decades of work to turn it into a deadly ship-launched weapon capable of sinking or seriously damaging large warships in a single stroke.

The first variants were propelled by compressed air and suffered from the dual drawbacks of slow speed and short range. Improvements came in the form of motors and gyro-stabilizers to increase speed, extend range, improve stability, and enhance accuracy. The concept of the torpedo boat was born when small craft were developed to serve as launching platforms, allowing the weapon to become seaborne.

Numerous countries began to develop motor torpedo boats—some for coastal defense and others in place of big ships deemed unaffordable. A larger variation of the vessel eventually became the destroyer, but interest in the smaller version remained strong and the developments rapid. The United States, however, was anything but an ardent proponent of the little boats.

The American Navy grew in size and importance as the country slowly emerged as a world power in the early twentieth century. Battleships dominated as the weapon of choice in the minds of top American naval leaders. The big-gunned warships represented status and power, and were capable of taking the fight across the two large oceans separating the country from many potential enemies. The small torpedo boats, largely confined to coastal waters due to their short range, were considered unimportant.

World War I marked an important milestone in the development and use of torpedo boats. The conflict began in 1914 and soon engulfed all the major European powers. With the exception of the Battle of Jutland in 1916, the large battle fleets mostly avoided major confrontations. A variety of small craft—including torpedo boats—were used to fill the void.

The vessels were produced quickly and cheaply by many of the warring nations, allowing the craft to be rushed into action. Britain and Italy took a leading role in deploying the small boats for a variety of duties beyond torpedo attacks, including coastal patrols, mine laying, antisubmarine operations, and rescuing downed pilots. The Italian Navy carried out a series of daring raids against Austrian naval units in 1917–18, sinking a light cruiser and battleship with torpedoes in the Adriatic Sea.[2]

The operational success continued after the war, when British torpedo boats sank or damaged three large Russian ships and two destroyers in the Baltic Sea during a limited naval operation related to the Russian Revolution. The British and Italian strikes served as a strong reminder to naval leaders that torpedo boats were lethal weapons. European navies continued to make design improvements in the decades after World War I, most notably Britain, Germany, and Italy.[3]

American interest in a large-scale torpedo boat program remained lethargic until the late 1930s. Rear Admiral Emory S. Land was among the first high-ranking officers to urge Navy officials to explore the possibility of adding the weapon to the fleet. The request came in the form of a letter sent to the chief of naval operations on December 5, 1936. He recommended the start of an experimental program, citing the continued development under way by various European navies and the successful use of the boats during World War I.

Land did not, however, feel the boats would be used for offensive operations by the United States. He believed the small craft to be best suited for the protection of coastal areas to free up larger vessels for overseas operations in the event of war. The request was forwarded to Secretary of the Navy Claude A. Swanson. He turned the topic over to the general board for further consideration.

The Navy General Board was an advisory body that typically comprised senior officers, often near the end of their careers. The group was to "deliberate selflessly and objectively on matters ranging from strategy to ship characteristics."[4] The group studied the topic in greater detail and found it to be worthwhile.

In a report back to Swanson, the board recognized the boats offered less initial value for the American Navy than for European powers due to the different strategic situations. The countries in Europe were positioned closely together with an abundance of coastal areas, while the United States was protected by two oceans. The board did, however, believe the boats could play an important role in a long war. It noted "future situations can occur under which it would be possible for such small craft to be used on directly offensive missions—as is no doubt contemplated in certain foreign navies."[5] Members even envisioned mining and antisubmarine work in addition to the standard torpedo-boat operations. The report recommended "the inauguration of an experimental development program on a moderate scale."

Evidence suggests Douglas MacArthur may have played an important role in the board's decision. Working on the development of military forces in the Philippines at the time, the general foresaw the potential of the small boats in the defense of the islands. MacArthur presented his ideas to the board in what can be considered as tremendous farsightedness.[6]

Swanson formally endorsed the board's recommendation on May 7, 1937. A little more than a year later, Congress appropriated a sum of $15,000,000 for use by the Navy. The funding was to be "expended at the discretion of the President of the United States for the construction of experimental vessels, none of which shall exceed three thousand standard tonnes displacement."

The plan was to develop a variety of craft, including a 70-foot and 54-foot motor torpedo boat. The efforts of Assistant Secretary of the Navy Charles Edison, son of the famous inventor, helped push the funding through the congressional system. President Roosevelt, who once held the same post and was well known to be a strong Navy supporter, may have also helped the program along.[7]

The Navy quickly sponsored a design contest for the torpedo boats. It was looking for original American designs to be based on a set of specific criteria. Requirements for the larger torpedo boat included a length of about 70 feet (but not to exceed 80 feet), trial speed of 40 knots, and an operational radius of 550 miles at cruising speed with a minimum radius of 275 miles at top speed. Minimum armament requirements were two torpedoes, four depth charges, and two machine guns.[8]

Additional steps were taken to help foster a good turnout before the September 30, 1938 proposal deadline. A prize of $15,000 was offered for the winning design of each type and a sum of $1,500 was to be awarded to all finalists. Additionally, all plan submissions would be kept confidential to ensure the contest was not dominated by large companies.[9]

A total of 37 torpedo boat concepts was submitted. The Navy selected eight finalists, three of the 54-foot boat and five from the 70-foot version. Each was invited to submit detailed plans. Winners for each category were announced on March 21, 1939. Sparkman and Stephens won the larger boat category. The naval architects were best known for their sailboat designs. Professor George Crouch, whose plan was submitted on behalf of yacht builder Henry B. Nevins, Inc., was the winner in the 54-foot class.[10]

Contracts were issued to three ship builders to construct six torpedo boats based on the winning plans. A few of the boats would have slight design modifications put in place by Navy planners. Additionally, two more boats were ordered based on a Navy plan that was developed separately from the design contest. The Navy was now using the term "patrol torpedo boat" to describe the new vessels. It was soon shortened to simply a "PT boat." Each would be assigned a hull number, not a name, as was common with larger warships. The new boats were designated *PT-1* through *PT-8*.

The American torpedo boat program took a radical turn when the experimental boats were still about a year from completion. Soon to be named secretary of the Navy after Claude Swanson's untimely death, Charles Edison wanted to add a British-built torpedo boat into the mix. He felt the addition offered a host of benefits, including having an established design on hand for comparison purposes, a backup plan in case the experimental boats proved unsuitable, and, at the same time, accelerating the speed of the program.

Edison conferred with the Navy General Board. The group agreed, noting "Inasmuch as said design is known to be the result of several years' development, the General Board considers it highly advisable that such craft be obtained as a check on our own development." President Roosevelt also supported the idea. It was thought, however, to be politically unwise for the United States Navy to purchase a warship from a foreign country.

Edison arranged to have Henry R. Sutphen, an executive of the Electric Boat Company (commonly known as Elco), to travel to England at his own expense in February 1939 for the purpose of evaluating and procuring a British motor torpedo boat. Originally incorporated in 1892, Elco had decades of experience in building small boats—including constructing 500 80-foot long gunboats for the British Navy in World War I.[11]

Sutphen reviewed several boats while in England. He returned in early September aboard S.S. *President Roosevelt* with a British torpedo boat strapped aboard as deck cargo. World War II in Europe was just days old when the liner pulled into New York. The 70-foot-long craft was designed by renowned British speed-boat racer Hubert Scott-Paine. She was powered by three Rolls-Royce engines and armed with torpedoes and three light antiaircraft guns.[12] Sutphen had not only purchased the boat, but also procured the rights to duplicate it in the United States. The boat impressed Navy officials in a series of tests conducted off Elco's submarine construction facility in Groton, Connecticut. The craft was later designated *PT-9*.

Edison then made a highly controversial decision to swiftly move the PT program from experimental to operational reality. Acting with presidential approval, he used the remaining $5,000,000 of the original funding for experimental boats to award Elco a contract to build 23 PT boats based on the British design.[13] Edison was confident of Elco's production ability due to the company's vast experience in building small boats. If the new boats proved suitable, the Navy would then have a single design that could be mass-produced. The contract was finalized on December 7, 1939.[14] Elco would build 11 torpedo boats (*PT-10* to *PT-20*) and 12 additional boats whose armament was modified for antisubmarine operations.

Finding the British plans to be incomplete, Elco engineers were forced to use the Scott-Paine boat as a working model to develop a new set of blueprints. The length of the boats remained at 70 feet and American armament was added. The Rolls-Royce machinery was replaced with a new engine of American origin.

The standard power supply for all American PT boats going forward was the supercharged Packard engine. The design originated with the 1925 Liberty aircraft engine. It was later modified for use in speedboats through variety of enhancements.[15] The motor was rated at 1,200 horsepower. The Packard engine eventually proved to be one of the most reliable components of the PT boats.

Production took place at the Elco's new Bayonne, New Jersey plant. When the assembly run was completed, the Navy would have enough boats to operate two squadrons of 12 PTs (including *PT-9* and the experimental boats), plus those planned for antisubmarine work. For simplified administration purposes, the Navy would only commission squadrons, not individual boats.

The first group of the new 70-foot Elco PTs entered service in November 1940, along with several of the experimental models from the design contest. The boats, however, were already determined to be inadequate. All had been designed to carry 18-inch diameter torpedoes—vintage World War I relics still in abundance. American torpedo technology had since advanced to a 21-inch version. The Navy wanted all new PT boats to be armed with the larger torpedoes.

Elco engineers modified the design of the last boat to meet the new requirements. The length was increased to 77 feet to accommodate four 21-inch torpedo tubes. The Navy promptly used funds from a new appropriation bill for additional construction. Dated September 17, 1940, the contract ordered 24 boats from Elco. PTs 20 to 44 were to be constructed based on the new design. With most of the smaller boats eventually sent off to the British as part of the Lend-Lease Program, the initial group of the 77-foot boats—including those under John Bulkeley's command—were destined to be the first American PT boats to face the Japanese in combat when the Pacific War erupted.

The new boats measured 77 feet in length and had a beam (width) of nearly 20 feet. Each displaced 33 tons. Three Packard engines, using 100-octane aviation-grade gasoline, allowed a maximum speed of 39 knots. A total range of 550 miles could be achieved at cruising speed.[16] The crew typically consisted of two officers and about ten enlisted men. The commanding officer of each PT was known as the boat captain.

The boats had the sleek lines of speedboats with a bow that protruded higher above the waterline than the stern. A small charthouse jutting up from the deck served as the nerve center of the boat. The area was commonly known as the conn. An undersized life raft was often lashed to the forward deck.

The main armament consisted of four 21-inch torpedo tubes, mounted two per side. Each tube carried one Mark VIII torpedo. The vintage World War I-era design was initially created for destroyers and first used in 1914. It spanned just over 21 feet in length and weighed 3,050 pounds. The weapon could travel a distance of 16,000 yards at a speed of 26 knots.[17] Although later versions of the weapon would have a larger explosive charge, Bulkeley's torpedoes carried only 300 pounds of TNT.[18] The Mark VIIIs were slower and packed less of a punch than torpedoes used later in the war, but were the only ones available for the PTs at the time. As Bulkeley and his men would soon discover, the torpedoes were plagued by a variety of problems when used in combat.

Additional armament was limited to light guns. Two twin 50-caliber machine guns were mounted in small gun tubs in the middle of the craft. Packing a slightly lighter punch were two Lewis 30-caliber machine guns mounted on free-standing pedestals just forward of the chart house. The boats were painted gray when received from the Elco factory in New Jersey, with a lighter shade on the hull and a darker tone used on the topside.[19]

Various types of wood were the main materials used to construct the boats. The keel was fashioned of Alaskan spruce and the stem of oak. The hull was made of two layers of mahogany planking laid diagonally, with a sheet of glue-impregnated aircraft fabric nestled in between.[20] The arrangement provided for a sturdy watertight hull. Other parts of the PTs, including the charthouse, were constructed of plywood. There was no armor plating to protect the boat's critical components and crewmembers.

The last months of 1941 found the United States Navy's torpedo boat program still in the early stages of development. Even as Bulkeley's boats arrived in the Philippines and the country stood on the eve of World War II in the Pacific, the small craft seemed to be a work in progress. Many of the boats coming off the Elco production line did not have complete armament due to material shortages.

Only three PT squadrons existed—including Bulkeley's Squadron 3. Squadron 1 was getting ready to ship out to Hawaii for duty with the Pacific Fleet. The boats were in Pearl Harbor the day of the Japanese attack. All of the PTs survived, with some firing on the attacking planes. The squadron initially stayed in the eastern Pacific after the start of the war. Squadron 2 was awaiting the delivery of some new boats in New York and would later be sent to Central America to guard the approaches to the Panama Canal.

Much of the Navy's work on PTs up to this time had focused on design, production, and experimentation to determine the boats' capabilities and limitations. Little documentation existed in the way of specific strategy and tactics. In fact, the Navy's formal book of tactical orders and doctrine for PT boats was almost a year away from release.[21] In case of combat, it was presumed the boats would simply attack larger enemy warships with torpedoes and, hopefully, rely on speed to get away. As the only squadron deployed to a forward operating area, Bulkeley and his men would literally have to write the book on operational tactics when the war started.

CHAPTER 3

Morning light was still hours away when *Guadalupe* entered the Pedro Miguel Locks just before 2:00 am on August 25, 1941.[1] The move signified her slow trip through the Panama Canal was nearing the final stretch. She set a course to the northwest after entering the Pacific Ocean. Her bow was pointed towards California as she followed the west coast of various Central American countries and Mexico.

The sighting of Catalina Island's East End Light indicated the tanker's arrival off the Los Angeles area early on September 1. She entered San Pedro Harbor and docked at the Standard Oil refinery in Wilmington. Her stay in California, though, would be short.

Workers began pumping 100-octane aviation gasoline into one of the tanker's cargo bunkers shortly after her arrival. The same fuel was then added directly into the tanks of the PT boats sitting on deck. Additional cargo was taken aboard in the form of standard Navy fuel oil. All of the loading was completed by the early afternoon of the following day. The vessel put to sea late in the day on September 3 bound for Hawaii.

The long voyage across the Pacific proved uneventful. Diamond Head loomed in the distance as *Guadalupe* approached the island of Oahu during the late morning hours of September 9. She followed the southern coastline past the city of Honolulu. The tanker docked adjacent to the Hickam Army Airfield near the entrance channel to Pearl Harbor. The area had undergone extensive expansion since the Pacific Fleet had arrived from California more than a year ago. The base was a major naval operating center with repair facilities, fuel storage, airfields, and troop barracks.

Over the next four days, the tanker unloaded her gasoline cargo and shifted the remaining fuel oil payload to better balance the ship. Bulkeley decided to take advantage of his stay to have the squadron's supply of torpedoes offloaded for charging and maintenance. *Guadalupe* departed Pearl Harbor for the final stretch of the voyage to the Philippines on September 13. It was the second time the young officer in charge of the PT boats made the lengthy journey to the Orient.

For the first time since departing New York, *Guadalupe* was not traveling alone when she pulled out of Pearl Harbor during the middle of September. The backdrop of mounting tensions with Japan, and concerns about the possible activity of German surface raiders operating in the area, caused top Navy officials to see a significant threat to military cargo in the Pacific area. The Navy accordingly implemented a policy of providing armed escorts for voyages to the Orient.[2] The tanker was joined by two other vessels just hours after departing Pearl Harbor. The three ships together formed Task Force 17.

The transport S.S. *President Coolidge* was an American President Lines ship operating under military control. She was packed full of reinforcements bound for the Philippines, including an artillery battalion, 53 tanks, pilots, and supplies.[3] The heavy cruiser U.S.S *Astoria* served as the escort.

The Philippines are over 5,000 miles from Pearl Harbor across the vast central Pacific. The task force took a direct route, passing through the Mariana Islands. *Astoria* led the other vessels in a tight column formation. The ships were separated by 1,000 yards as the group plodded west.

The lengthy journey proved uneventful for the PT sailors. Many of the men passed time reading, playing cards or writing letters. Few actual drills were held, but Bulkeley conducted regular meetings to discuss strategy and tactics as *Guadalupe* slowly steamed towards the Philippines.[4]

It took 12 days to reach the eastern approaches to the American Commonwealth. The force entered the San Bernardino Strait during the midday hours of September 25.[5] The narrow passageway allowed

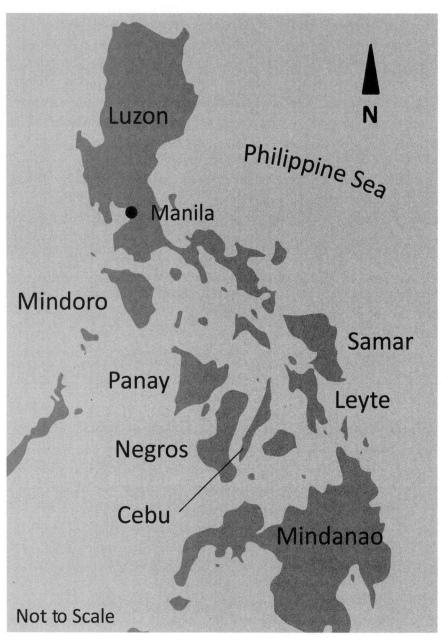

Map 1: The Philippines, 1941

the ships to maneuver through various waterways and around numerous islands while moving through the Philippines from east to west. The ships turned north once safely through the maze of islands.

A small patrol boat arrived just before noon on September 26. She took a position at the front of the formation as the task force approached Manila Harbor. She would ensure the ships passed through the various defensive minefields sown in the area without incident. *Guadalupe* dropped anchor in Manila Harbor at exactly 2:00 pm. Her mission was accomplished in good order, with the cargo of fuel oil, six PT boats, associated personnel, and supplies having been safely delivered to the Philippines.

The anchor chain on *Guadalupe*'s starboard side slowly began to rise out of the shallow water in Manila Harbor during the midafternoon hours of September 26. The tanker began moving and was soon securely moored along Pier 7. Capable of simultaneously docking multiple large vessels, the covered pier jutted out from Manila's teeming waterfront district.

Yard barges and workers arrived the next day to begin the job of unloading a PT boat squadron. A large floating crane hoisted each PT boat from *Guadalupe*'s deck before carefully placing the craft into the water. John Bulkeley's sailors began to leave the vessel, marking the end of a long six weeks, mostly spent at sea. The unloading of supplies and ammunition to a barge began the following day.

The long process was not fully completed until the morning of September 30.[6] The tanker then made preparations to move to the navy yard. The PT sailors were now ready to set up shop in the Philippines.

The majority of officers disembarking from *Guadalupe* were hand-picked by their commander. Bulkeley had been able to select most of the key officers who would become members of his new torpedo boat squadron prior to departing for the Philippines. It was an advantage rarely afforded to ship or unit commanders. Many of his selections had experience in small boats, with some having been along for the PTC trip to Key West.

Bulkeley's able choice for second in command was Lieutenant Robert B. Kelly. The executive officer was tall and slender, with sandy colored hair. Kelly was born in New York City on June 9, 1913 and attended high school in New Britain, Connecticut.[7] He was appointed to the United States Naval Academy from Connecticut, entering the school in the summer of 1931.

Kelly was commissioned an ensign upon graduating from Annapolis on June 6, 1935. He spent the next two years serving on *Tennessee* in keeping with the common naval practice of sending newly minted officers to battleships. The vessel was part of the Pacific Fleet, with San Pedro, CA serving as home port. Peacetime service aboard a battleship involved regular training, maintenance, and readiness exercises, including an annual fleet problem. The large-scale war game, involving most of the United States Fleet, pitted two teams of vessels against each other in a variety of strategic and tactical situations.[8]

The young sailor spent the next several years aboard the destroyers *Edsall* (engineering and communications officer) and heavy cruiser *Quincy* (radio officer). Kelly then had a brief stint of land duty in Florida. He was promoted to lieutenant (junior grade) in June of 1938.[9]

Kelly moved to smaller boats in 1941. He commanded Motor Torpedo Boat Submarine Chaser Division 1 from February to July. It was during this stretch that he came into contact with Bulkeley. The failure of the small boats in the antisubmarine role soon left the officer looking for a new job. He joined Motor Torpedo Boat Squadron 3 shortly after its inception in August.

The executive officer would serve the new squadron well. Kelly became known as a tough, hardworking, and aggressive officer. He would be Bulkeley's right-hand man, assisting in all aspects of the squadron's operations. Additionally, Kelly was selected to serve as boat captain of *PT-34*.

The remaining squadron officers were a cross section of America. The men were a mix of Naval Academy graduates and reserve officers. Lieutenant Edward DeLong came from Santa Cruz, California. Lieutenant (junior grade) Vincent Schumacher called Kalamazoo, Michigan home.

Along with Ensign Barron Chandler, they would spend time as boat captains and executive officers of the various PT boats.

Henry Brantingham held the rank of ensign, having graduated from the Naval Academy with the class of 1939. A native of Arkansas, he served aboard the heavy cruiser *Minneapolis* and two old destroyers in his short naval career before joining Bulkeley's PTC squadron for the trip to Key West. He was quick to join the new PT squadron after hearing about the opportunity from Bulkeley. Brantingham was assigned to be the boat captain of *PT-33*.

Two naval reserve officers—George Cox and Anthony Akers—would come to play important roles within the squadron. Ensign George Cox was good-looking with yellowish hair. Cox was born in Niagara Falls, NY and grew up in upstate Watertown. The young man gained valuable small-boat experience as a speedboat pilot running races on the St. Lawrence River. He attended the University of Rochester and Earlham College before deciding to go overseas.

Cox volunteered for the American Volunteer Ambulance Corps and was soon on his way to France. The organization was founded in World War I to help get wounded Allied troops off the front lines and into hospitals. The American was in country when the German Army smashed into France during the spring of 1940. He was still in France when the nation surrendered to Germany on June 22, 1940.

Although supporting Great Britain, the United States was technically neutral in the European conflict and Cox was able to slip unnoticed into Spain. He was released after a brief internment by Spanish authorities.[10] Cox immediately joined the Navy after returning to the United States. He received the French Croix de Guerre for service to the nation. The military medal was commonly awarded to foreigners allied with France.

Cox was one of the few members of the torpedo boat squadron to see war first-hand prior to arriving in the Philippines. He would spend much of his time as the boat captain of *PT-41*. The duty put him in regular close contact with the squadron commander.

Ensign Anthony Akers was a tall, soft-spoken Texan standing 6 feet 4 inches. He was born near San Antonio as the seventh of 13 children.

Akers wanted to join the military after attending the University of Texas. All branches of the service, however, initially rejected him due to his height.[11] He was able to enter the Navy in June 1940 and was commissioned an ensign on December 12 of the same year. Bulkeley assigned him to *PT-35*.

Most of the men in the unit had never been to the Philippines before. The sailors quickly settled in to their new environment before taking time to become acclimatized to their new boats. The squadron members, however, would have only a short time in their new home before being thrust into war.

CHAPTER 4

Arrival in the Philippines put Bulkeley and his sailors in what had long been one of the most sought-after duty stations for United States servicemen. The territory offered an expansive list of amenities. Among the many perks available were nice apartments, servants, golf courses, beaches, tennis courts, restaurants, and an abundance of drinking establishments. Plenty of off-duty leisure time was common. With an exchange rate of two Filipino pesos for one American dollar, even lowly enlisted men could live a lifestyle only available to the wealthy back home.[1]

The warm and tropical environment made the surroundings even more pleasurable. "It's a lovely place filled with a floral display that would knock your eyes out," a young American soldier wrote of the area in a letter home. "Palm trees, coconut trees, thousands of vari-colored flowers and big bushes of gardenias."[2] The benefits were so enticing it was not uncommon for servicemen to spend time on a lengthy waiting list or even accept a temporary reduction in rank to get an assignment in the Philippines.[3]

Manila was now a fully Americanized city, slowly molded as such after decades of rule by the United States. Its downtown featured wide streets, lavish hotels, and a scenic waterfront. First-run movies were common in theatres. Fine restaurants and night clubs were plentiful, as were attractive Filipino girls. The backdrop made for a vibrant nightlife greatly enjoyed by American personnel who were stationed thousands of miles from home.

By late 1941, however, change was permeating the tropical air. The military build-up was plainly evident. The growing possibility of a war with Japan was a common topic of conversation. American dependents and civilians were starting to head back to the United States. Bulkeley and his men would have only a few short months to enjoy the tropical paradise.

Relations between the United States and the Empire of Japan had been near a breaking point for months by the time the PT boats arrived in Manila. A review of geography in late 1941 revealed the Philippines to be an isolated American outpost in East Asia, strategically positioned to be in the epicenter of any conflict.

Formidable Japanese airbases dotted Formosa (presently Taiwan) only 300 miles off the northern tip of the Philippines. The large island, located just off China's coast, had been under Japanese rule since 1895. The French colony of Indochina, including modern-day Vietnam, was about 750 miles west across the East China Sea. It was also under Japanese control. The vast Pacific Ocean, abutting the eastern coast of the Philippines, provided only a mirage of protection. The area was home to the Marianas, a chain of islands formerly administered by Germany, but taken over by the Japanese during World War I. The Marianas blocked the direct east-west route between the Philippines and Hawaii—the closest sizable American possession.

The area to the south, the Dutch East Indies, was of greatest concern to the American commanders. Abundantly rich in oil and a variety of minerals, the region was likely a prime target for Japanese conquest. The parent nation of the Dutch colony had fallen to Germany more than a year earlier in the European side of the war. The Philippines were perilously located directly between the home islands of Japan and Dutch oil fields.

Although the situation in the Far East rapidly deteriorated in 1941, ultimately resulting in the outbreak of war, the roots of the conflict stretched back decades. It began with America's last war fought in the Pacific.

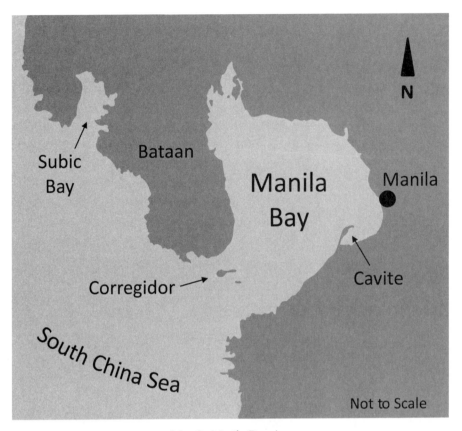

Map 2: Manila Bay Area

The crushing naval victory by American warships under the command of Commodore George Dewey over a Spanish fleet in Manila Bay on May 1, 1898 marked the beginning of a new chapter in the history of the Philippines. The land had been under Spanish influence or outright control since the late 1500s. Spain lost much of its remaining colonial empire when the Spanish-American War officially ended with the signing of the Treaty of Paris in December 1898. The United States gained control of the Philippines, plus additional territories in the Caribbean and Pacific, for the sum of $20 million as part of the settlement.[4]

The acquisition of the Philippines was not without controversy in the United States. Those in favor of the move argued it was needed to keep the land out of the hands of another European power or Japan, while distracters decried it as raw American colonialism. The U.S. Senate ratified the peace treaty by the slim margin of only one vote.[5] The Philippine government was initially set up under the direction of a commission, but power soon moved to a governor general appointed by the president of the United States.[6]

America's new Pacific territory was an archipelago comprised of almost 7,100 islands stretching just over 1,000 miles from north to south. The entire land area encompassed about 115,800 square miles—roughly equal to the land area of the state of Arizona. The majority of the population, however, resided on two large islands—Luzon in the north and Mindanao in the south. The capital city of Manila was located on the west central portion of Luzon. It represented the center of culture and commerce under Spanish rule and would remain the same as the country was slowly Americanized.

The geography of the Philippines features plenty of mountains, with numerous coastal plains, beaches, and an abundance of thick jungle vegetation. Forests cover about 60 percent of the total land area. The tropical climate features a rainy season, the timing and length of which varies by region. The population of the Philippines would steadily grow under American rule, with the islands eventually becoming home to just over 12 million people by the early 1930s.[7]

The American military quickly established a presence on the island nation after the end of the Spanish-American War. It went into action to quell a bloody insurrection between 1899 and 1902 by Filipino insurgents seeking immediate independence. The military began to build permanent facilities in 1904 and eventually settled in with a garrison of about 10,000 men. Even with the rebellion defeated and established bases in place, the United States had no intention of keeping the territory long term.

Congress promised the Philippines self-government in 1916, but it did not become official until 1934 with the passing of the Tydings–McDuffie

Act. The law created the Commonwealth of the Philippines and granted a transitional period leading to full independence by 1946. The act also allowed for American military forces to operate in the region during the transitional time and put control of Filipino armed services under the American president.[8] The law and transition time guaranteed the two nations would be closely connected for the near future.

Manuel L. Quezon was elected the first president of the Philippines Commonwealth in 1935. He immediately set out to prepare the country for future independence. Among his many areas of focus was to build a modern armed forces. Quezon would later have help in the endeavor from a famous American general.

The acquisition of the Philippines was only one small step in the process of putting the United States and Japan on a slow road to war. The European powers of Britain, Holland, France, Germany, and Russia had already carved out spheres of influence—or outright territories—across East Asia. China was the largest country in the area. However, it was a fragmented state, with various warlords competing with the national government for control of different regions. Japan stood almost alone as an independent country. The national interests of all of these nations would eventually lead to conflict in the Pacific.

Japan at the dawn of the twentieth century was a country in the process of modernizing. Japanese leaders strongly believed their nation should be the sole power in the region, with influence extending over China and Southeast Asia. The nation's chance to expand its authority came in 1905 with the surprise ambush and stunning defeat of a Russian fleet in the Tsushima Straits between Korea and Japan. It was the decisive battle in a larger conflict between the two nations over the control of key ports in northeastern China and the domination of Korea.

It was the first time an Asian country had defeated a major European nation in modern history. Japan's prestige in the international community rose immensely, while Russia was relegated to a European rather than a world power. Japan quickly expanded, gaining influence over parts of northern China and taking control of Korea. The great victory later helped fuel the belief among Japanese military leaders that their forces could defeat any of the industrialized nations.[9]

America's global reach was also expanding during the early 1900s. Its leaders sought to maintain free and open trade with China. The policy was in direct conflict with Japanese desires for expansion.

World War I found Japan on the side of the Allied powers of England and France. Japanese leaders viewed the European conflict primarily as a means to consolidate their power in the Pacific.[10] By the end of the war, Japan had control of German assets in China and various island holdings in the central Pacific. The United States and European nations, weary of growing Japanese power, tried to curb the expansion of her military through several postwar naval treaties. None proved effective over the long term.

The 1920s was a time of great political unrest in Japan. Military leaders saw the attempts of the west to limit their military power as treachery and as a betrayal of national security.[11] The decade ended with the military exerting considerable influence over Japanese foreign policy. In the next ten years, the nation withdrew from naval limitation treaties and began an intensive shipbuilding program.[12] With the country slowly turning into a totalitarian state, the stage was set for continued Japanese expansion and greater instability in Asia.

Japanese leaders had long sought to gain control of China. The nation invaded Manchuria in 1931. The newly added territory in northeastern China served as a staging area for a wider war in the summer of 1937. The Chinese were unable to stop advancing Japanese forces when they struck south, taking control of many large population centers. The Japanese targeted civilians throughout the conflict, inflicting horrible atrocities of torture, rape, and murder on untold thousands. At least 250,000 civilians were thought to have perished just in the city of Nanking.[13] The Japanese advance later bogged down as various western nations provided aid to China.

The United States initially reacted with condemnation, but was not ready to go to war with Japan to stop the aggression. Then World War II began in Europe on September 1, 1939. The situation in Europe began to rapidly deteriorate in the middle of 1940. Germany took control of France, Holland, and Belgium in a series of lightning attacks starting in May. Great Britain soon stood alone and was fighting for survival.

Japan used the sweeping German victories to make additional moves in the Pacific. The government announced its intention to create the Greater East Asia Co-Prosperity Sphere, with a goal of having the region under Japanese control free of Western colonialism and influence. In September it forced weak French authorities to allow Japanese military bases in the northern part of French Indochina. During the same month Japan signed the Tripartite Pact with Germany and Italy, formally creating the Axis Alliance. Japanese militarists hoped the agreement would deter the United States and Great Britain from interfering with their expansion plans in Asia by the prospect of having to fight a two-front war against fascism.[14]

American countermoves were quick to come in the Pacific. President Franklin D. Roosevelt ordered the Pacific Fleet west to Hawaii from its home port in California. The move put America's most powerful weapon about 2,000 miles deeper into the Pacific. He then initiated a series of embargoes against Japan, beginning in July 1940. By January 1941 the list of prohibited materials included strategic minerals, chemicals, scrap metal, and aviation fuel.[15] Shipments of American oil to Japan—the most important ingredient to an industrialized economy and war machine—were ultimately curtailed after Japan took control of the remaining part of French Indochina in July 1941. The Panama Canal was closed to Japanese shipping as a further restriction to trade.

As an island nation largely dependent on imports, Japan could not survive without a continuous flow of essential raw materials. Almost all of its oil was purchased from the United States. Reserves would only allow the military to operate for about two years. The nation began diplomatic negotiations with the United States, while also planning for war at the same time. An internal debate among Japanese leaders over whether to attack north into Russia or south towards the Dutch East

Indies effectively ended when Japan and Russia signed a neutrality pact on April 13, 1941.

Japan was now free to strike south. Leaders knew the move would inevitably result in war with the United States and Great Britain. England was preoccupied with the struggle in Europe and likely could only spare limited resources for the Pacific. America, though, represented a serious and powerful threat.

The Japanese war plan was to deliver a decisive knockout blow to the American Pacific Fleet at its main base in Hawaii, followed by a series of fast attacks on British and Dutch possessions in Southeast Asia. Additional territories had to be quickly secured to build a defense perimeter around the empire. Any American counterattack would then have to fight through layers of defenses to get to Japan.

War planning became more formalized during the second half of 1941. The Japanese Navy trained and prepared for the bold plan to attack Pearl Harbor. At the same time troops and air units for the strike south covertly moved into positions at various locations, including Indochina and Formosa.

Negotiations with the United States were still continuing, with little progress, but abruptly ended with the surprise attack on Pearl Harbor. The sudden onset of hostilities could not have begun at a worse time for the servicemen in the Philippines. The rush to build up the defenses of the Philippines was still in progress. At the forefront of the effort was an American general whose name will forever be associated with the nation—Douglas MacArthur.

CHAPTER 5

Douglas MacArthur's long and illustrious military career began when he graduated at the top of his class from West Point in 1903. His father was a Civil War Medal of Honor winner who later rose to the rank of general in the Army and spent time as military governor of the Philippines. The younger MacArthur spent time at various posts in the Philippines, Central America, and United States before going to Europe with the American Expeditionary Force during World War I. He served with distinction during brutal trench warfare in France and was promoted to brigadier general in June 1918, becoming the youngest American general ever to command a division.

MacArthur's career continued to rise in an upward trajectory after the conflict. He held a series of commands through the 1920s, each with increasing levels of stature and importance. His duty included time in the Philippines.

MacArthur rose to the pinnacle of American military power as the new decade of the 1930s dawned. He served as army chief of staff for nearly five years, starting in November 1930. It was a difficult time to be the nation's most senior uniformed army officer, due to severe budget constrains in place as a result of the Great Depression. Accomplishments during his reign included emphasizing deficiencies in personnel and materiel, devising plans for industrial mobilization and manpower procurement, and establishment of a headquarters for the burgeoning Army Air Force.[1] During this time he often clashed with politicians, even to the point of causing Roosevelt to later view MacArthur as a potential political rival.

The 56-year-old general was contemplating retirement as his term as chief of staff was nearing an end in 1935 when he suddenly received an offer he could not refuse. Philippine President Quezon was looking to hire a top-notch military leader to oversee the commonwealth's growing armed forces. MacArthur was an old friend of Quezon, the two having first met in 1903, and was the Philippine president's top choice for the leadership position. MacArthur became military adviser to the Quezon government. President Roosevelt readily consented to the move. MacArthur was initially granted a leave of absence from the U.S. Army under a special arrangement approved by Congress. He retired from the service in 1937.

The general's new role was to build a strong Philippine military capable of defending the nation from outside threats. It was a position that was both challenging and financially rewarding. MacArthur negotiated a salary equal to the Philippine president ($18,000 per year) plus a hefty expense account.[2] Quezon then crowned his new advisor a field marshal—a rank that did not even exist in the American Army. He was also given broad powers to fulfill his duties, including direct access to the U.S. Secretary of War and army chief of staff.

MacArthur took up residence in a luxurious penthouse suite atop the Manila Hotel in the downtown area of the city. He set up headquarters in the nearby walled city, the centuries-old seat of Spanish colonial power. Operating with a small group of mostly U.S. Army assistants, including Major Dwight D. Eisenhower, MacArthur devised a strategy to fulfill his mission. Eisenhower later transferred back to the United States and was eventually replaced by Richard Sutherland. The autocratic and protective chief of staff would stay with MacArthur for the rest of the war, rising to a general's rank.

Building up the Philippines military was not an easy task, as the United States had protected the nation for three decades. The general's plan called for the Philippine Commonwealth to have a small regular army and air force backed by a conscription system and robust reserve force. An undersized navy, limited to small vessels for coastal defense, rounded out the intended military forces. All units were to be fully functional by 1946, the year of planned full independence. MacArthur confidently believed the Philippines armed forces would be capable of successfully opposing "any conceivable expeditionary force" capable of threatening the nation by that time.[3]

The development of the Philippines military, however, proved to be painfully slow during the remaining years of the 1930s. Inadequate funding, coupled with insufficient and outdated equipment, resulted in an under-manned and ill-trained force. Quezon became discouraged. By the end of the decade he was even entertaining thoughts of relieving MacArthur and pursuing a course of neutrality in the region.[4]

The situation in the Philippines began to dramatically change with the start of the 1940s. American-Japanese relations were rapidly deteriorating. Many Filipinos were convinced their nation would be in the front lines of any upcoming conflict. It was no surprise to American leaders. The United States had been planning for a war with Japan for decades. Up until the late 1930s the strategy was commonly known as War Plan Orange, due to a color-coding scheme used to identify potential enemies for strategic planning purposes, Japan having been assigned orange.

Strategists envisioned a conflict beginning with a strong Japanese offensive against American possessions in the western Pacific. Most would not be able to withstand the onslaught, but some could buy valuable time while the American military mobilized. The holding of the Philippines as a whole was deemed infeasible, with some American leaders considering the island chain to be indefensible due to the vast amount of coastline. Defense of the territory was to be centered on Manila Bay, the nearby Bataan Peninsula, and the adjacent fortified island of Corregidor. American and Filipino forces were to fight a delaying action until help could arrive.

The Navy maintained a long-standing policy throughout the early 1900s of not basing battleships in the Philippines, believing the fleet could rapidly deploy to the area in the event of crisis.[5] War planners envisioned the battle fleet leading a counterattack across the Pacific to isolate and defeat the Japanese. Manila Bay was seen as a valuable anchorage to be used as a forward operating base for staging additional offensive actions as needed.

By 1939 it was apparent that the color-coded war plans, originally drafted on the basis of the United States fighting only one potential enemy at a time, were no longer valid based on the current world conditions. The outbreak of war in Europe changed everything. American planners began work on a new series of Rainbow war plans, based on the United States and allies fighting a coalition of enemies on different continents. War Plan Orange was replaced with Rainbow Three. The basic strategy in the Pacific remained about the same. However, the internal debate about the desirability of trying to defend the Philippines was again rekindled in light of the worsening relations with Japan.

The urgency of the situation in the Pacific compelled President Roosevelt to issue an executive order that would dramatically alter events in the Philippines. MacArthur was recalled to active duty in the United States Army on July 26, 1941 with a rank of lieutenant general.[6] He was put in charge of a new command in the Philippines to be headquartered in Manila. The U.S. Army Forces in the Far East (USAFE) included all American and Filipino army units currently stationed in the Philippines and any additional forces to be sent there. The Philippine Army was absorbed into the U.S. Army under MacArthur's unified command. The combined force was to be increased over time to a strength of 200,000.

Still one of the most experienced and best-known senior American military officers, MacArthur's recall may have been intended to impress the Japanese by signaling the seriousness of the conditions in the Far East and to bolster the morale of the Filipinos.[7] Although a capable leader, the general was seen by many as overly ambitious. Some historians describe him as someone who carried a high level of arrogance and was a constant seeker of publicity.

MacArthur put in motion a plan to mobilize ten Philippine Army divisions. Leaders in Washington promised to send reinforcements. MacArthur's list of needed materials and supplies was lengthy.

He requested everything from tanks, artillery, and modern planes to new steel helmets and rifles. The general planned to have his force at full strength by the early part of spring 1942.

As MacArthur returned to active duty, American war planning was again undergoing a revision. With Europe in conflict and Japan allied with Germany and Italy, the shape of the next war was now very clear. Discussions between senior American and British leaders identified Hitler as the most dangerous enemy—with his vast army and mighty industrial machine—and the one to be defeated first. The final war plan update, Rainbow Five, endorsed what became known as the "Germany first" strategy. The majority of resources during a conflict were to be directed to Europe, while more of a defensive posture was to be maintained in the Pacific. The plan assumed the likely loss of various American possessions in the Pacific, including the Philippines.[8] It became the primary policy guideline for the United States in World War II.[9]

MacArthur, however, wanted no part of what seemed to be simply presiding over a doomed territory. He viewed the current American strategy related to the Philippines as defensive and defeatist. The general argued to leaders in Washington that all of the Philippines could be successfully protected. He developed an aggressive plan to defend the Philippines at the beaches. Any invader would be met head on at the point of landing and pushed back into the sea. The plan required approval from superiors in Washington, reinforcements, and the movement of materials and supplies, as most stores had been positioned around Bataan and Manila. It was a radical departure from the long-standing plan to focus on only defending Manila Bay.

Opinions in the War Department began to change in the months following MacArthur's reinstatement. More leaders were convinced of the need to defend the Philippines. Even President Roosevelt was advised to take action, with Secretary of War Henry Stimson urging "all practical steps should be taken to increase the defensive strength of the Philippines."[10] At least two decades' worth of pessimistic views by American military leaders about holding the Philippines were about to be reversed. "By the fall of 1941 there was a firm conviction in Washington and in the Philippines that, given sufficient time, a Japanese attack could be successfully resisted," wrote army historian Louis Morton.[11]

The defense of the Philippines suddenly became an urgent mission in the latter part of 1941. MacArthur was informed by leaders in Washington that he would receive substantial reinforcements. Army Chief of Staff General George C. Marshall bluntly told his immediate staff, "It was the policy of the United States to defend the Philippines."[12]

Among the forces sent to MacArthur's command were B-17 Flying Fortress bombers and modern P-40 fighter planes. Originally designed to defend the American homeland from enemy invasion fleets, the B-17 was the Army's newest four-engine bomber. The plane could carry a heavy payload, had a range of 1,000 miles, and was equipped with the sophisticated Norden bombsight.

The B-17 added a new dimension to the defense of the Philippines. It gave MacArthur an offensive capability previously unavailable to American forces in the Far East. Many leaders in Washington hoped the B-17s would serve as a deterrent to further Japanese expansionary moves. Some even felt the bombers, if delivered in sufficient numbers, could turn the Philippines into a self-sustaining fortress capable of blockading the South China Sea.[13] The Army allocated over 240 fighters, 52 dive bombers, and 165 heavy bombers for delivery to the Philippines by March 1942.[14] However, the process of getting the planes to the Far East would prove to be a slow one.

What MacArthur and the Philippines needed most was time. The month of April 1942 was commonly accepted as the critical end date when a Japanese attack could be expected and the moment that all American-Filipino forces needed to be fully trained and ready.[15] The United States was not yet on a war footing. The country simply did not have the funds, equipment, manpower, industrial capacity, or shipping to reinforce the Philippines on short notice.[16] It was unclear if the reinforcement process and in-country training could be completed prior to the start of a conflict.

The most serious setback in the supply chain was the shortage of available shipping. The scarcity of transports made it difficult to get men and equipment from the United States thousands of miles across the Pacific in a timely manner. Shipments increased tremendously, however, during a three-month span in late 1941. A total of 14 small task forces or individual supply ships arrived in Manila from September through the end of November.[17] The vessels brought much-needed fighter planes, cannons, troops, and all types of supplies. B-17 bombers flew from the United States to the Philippines via Hawaii. More men and materials gathered in San Francisco waiting for transportation west.

Time, however, ran out for the Philippines. The start of war with the attack on Pearl Harbor abruptly ended the supply operation when it was far from complete. MacArthur commanded almost 100,000 men by early December, with the U.S. Army garrison alone swelling to 31,095—an increase of over 8,500 since the end of July.[18] The overall numbers represented a dramatic expansion since MacArthur's recall to active duty, but the number was deceptive. A large portion of the force comprised undermanned Philippine Army divisions. The infantry units lacked basic training, modern equipment and weapons, uniforms, and even adequate rations.[19]

The Philippine Scouts represented the most reliable infantry troops under MacArthur's command. Part of the regular American Army and commanded by American officers, the force comprised tough and experienced Filipino soldiers. It was considered a high honor to serve in the unit and many of the men had decades of service.[20] It was, however, a relatively small group that was low in total numbers.

The army operated from three main bases—all located on Luzon—although some smaller outposts existed elsewhere in the islands. Fort Stotsenburg was about 50 miles northwest of Manila. Fort William McKinley was just outside the capital city, and the island of Corregidor stood near the entrance to Manila Bay.

The ground portion of MacArthur's army was directed by a trio of subordinate generals. Major General Jonathan Wainwright, Major General George Parker, and Brigadier General William Sharp were each assigned to defend a geographic area of the Philippines. Combat troops were divided among the commands with additional units held in reserve.

Wainwright was a career cavalryman whose name will forever be associated with the fall of the Philippines. He commanded the majority of Luzon from Manila north. His group, known as the Northern Luzon Force, was responsible for defending the most important region of the archipelago, including Manila Bay and the Bataan Peninsula. Wainwright's men would likely face the brunt of a Japanese invasion under MacArthur's beach defense plan. The force included three Philippine divisions and a cavalry regiment of Philippine Scouts.[21]

Sharp oversaw a large swath of geography representing the southern half of the Philippines. His command was known as the Visayan-Mindanao Force. It included a large number of small and medium-sized islands plus Mindanao. The general controlled four Philippine divisions.

A narrow band in the middle was to be defended by Parker's South Luzon Force of three Philippines divisions. An assortment of other ground forces was held in reserve near Manila. The group included two American tank battalions—MacArthur's only large armor force—two additional Philippine Scout units, some artillery, and the only infantry regiment in the commonwealth composed entirely of American soldiers.[22]

The Army Air Force component of MacArthur's command included airplanes, early warning systems, and antiaircraft weapons. The need for modern airfields was recognized by MacArthur early in the process of building the Philippines military. Most of the initial focus was on the large island on Luzon. A total of six army airfields were operating within 80 miles of Manila by 1941. However, most were only suitable for fighter planes. The exception was Clark Field northwest of Manila. It was the largest of all the air bases and capable of operating heavy bombers. A few other scattered fields were primarily used for dispersal purposes.

More capacity was needed to accommodate the expected influx of planes. MacArthur allocated almost $10 million between August and October 1941 for airfield development. Much of the funding went towards work on Clark and Nichols Fields, the latter just southeast of Manila. MacArthur decided in the middle of November to establish a heavy bomber base at Del Monte on the southern island of Mindanao. The existing small runway could land B-17s, but could not operate a large group of the bombers. Unlike the bases on Luzon, Del Monte was beyond the range of Japanese bombers on Formosa. Work began immediately at a rushed pace.

As MacArthur's air force continued to grow in its number of planes, two critical areas remained inadequate. Both early warning systems and antiaircraft defense would become victims of the shortage of time and materials. Although MacArthur's plan to develop an air warning service had been approved by officials in Washington by the middle of September, much of the men and equipment did not arrive in time to take part in the fighting.

There were seven radar sets in the Philippines when the war started, but only two—one near Manila and the other at Iba on the western coast of Luzon—were set up and operational. In place of the modern technology was a primitive warning system that relied on native air spotters to telephone or telegraph plane sightings to a central station at Nichols Field for relay to other command posts.

Plans to bolster the number and quality of antiaircraft guns were in motion right up until the final days of peace. However, none of the planned reinforcements arrived in time. The limited number of anti-aircraft units possessed an assortment of antiquated weaponry including 3-inch cannons, 37-millimeter guns, and 50-caliber machine guns. Japanese medium bombers were capable of flying higher than the range of all these weapons.

Overseeing the air force buildup was MacArthur's new air commander, Major General Lewis Brereton. Although USAFE could boast a total of 277 aircraft by December 1—more than were stationed in Hawaii at the time—less than half were modern warplanes suitable for frontline combat.[23] Only 35 B-17 bombers were in the Philippines at the start of hostilities.

MacArthur is often viewed as having had supreme control over all military units in the Philippines during the years leading up to World War II. The general, however, only yielded direct control over ground and air units. His command did not extend to the Navy. The newly arrived PT sailors began a period of intense training as the rush to reinforce the Philippines continued around them.

CHAPTER 6

A naval reserve officer was among the few members of the squadron who were already in the Philippines when Bulkeley arrived aboard *Guadalupe*. Twenty-three-year-old Ensign Iliff Richardson was already an accomplished world traveler in spite of his young age. He was fated to remain in the Philippines for the bulk of World War II.

The brutal trench fighting of World War I was still raging in Europe when Richardson was born in Denver, Colorado on April 9, 1918. His father was a Methodist minister and his mother a teacher. He was their only surviving offspring. Richardson's father died when Iliff was three years old. For the next 11 years the young child moved among various Colorado towns as his mother Velma taught Latin and music. He also spent time at his grandfather's ranch in Springview, Nebraska.

Velma used her inheritance to move to California after Richardson's grandfather passed away. The pair eventually settled in the Los Angeles area, spending time in the communities of Bell and Maywood. Both were small cities south of downtown Los Angeles. The young Richardson learned valuable skills as a member of the local boy scout troop—skills he would put to good use decades later in the Pacific during World War II.[1]

Richardson entered Compton Junior College in suburban Los Angeles after graduating from high school in June 1936. He took classes for two years, earning an associate's degree in June of 1938. He then decided it was time to see the world. Richardson went overseas using the money earmarked for the last two years of college. For the next 21 months he traveled through Europe, Scandinavia, the Middle East, and North Africa, visiting a total of 43 countries.[2] The war in Europe abruptly started while he was abroad.

He was convinced it was time to join the service after returning home to California in the middle of 1940. "I had been in Europe for two years, and I knew that America was going to be in the war," Richardson later recalled. "I felt very sorry about that."[3] He enlisted in the Navy on July 29, 1940, and less than two months later was enrolled in a brand new officer training program.

The U.S. Navy sought to expand its officer corps beyond what could be provided by the Naval Academy as the nation edged closer to war. The result was officially known as the V-7 United States Naval Reserve Midshipmen's School. The program was initiated in June 1940 and administered through three universities. Although it was later modified to accept only four-year college graduates, the school was initially open to men who had attended college for only two years—allowing Richardson to join.[4]

Appointed candidates were designated midshipmen. The students took accelerated courses on gunnery, navigation, engineering, and seamanship to get ready for navy life.[5] Graduates attained the rank of ensign, the lowest officer rank, in the naval reserve upon successful completion of the program. Richardson's V-7 appointment was officially dated September 16, 1940.[6] He was soon traveling to Chicago on orders to report to the midshipmen's school at Northwestern University. Classes began in October at the university's lakefront campus in downtown Chicago. The program was scheduled to last three months.

Richardson met Coma Noel of Houston, Texas during his stay in Chicago. She was a student studying at a local university. The soon-to-be naval officer made a strong first impression, taking her to see *Aida*. "How many first dates will take you to the opera?" she recalled years later.[7] The two dated as Richardson continued his coursework. He wanted to get married, but she preferred to wait until he fulfilled his duty with the Navy.

The onset of the cold Chicago winter marked the end of officer training. Richardson successfully completed the required coursework. The first class of midshipmen from Northwestern—337 new officers in all—graduated during a ceremony on December 16, 1940. The commencement speaker was Rear Admiral Chester Nimitz.[8] Almost a year later, the admiral was thrust into the forefront of World War II in the Pacific as the new commander in chief of the Pacific Fleet in the immediate aftermath of Pearl Harbor.

Many graduates were immediately called up for active service. Richardson volunteered for duty in the Philippines. "I felt that [to be with the Navy in] the Philippines—at that time it was called the Asiatic Fleet—was the place to be," he later remembered. "Besides, I hadn't seen China."

The newly minted officer received a set of orders to go west after acceptance of his commission as an ensign. He was to proceed to San Francisco, California to board the S.S. *President Cleveland* for the voyage to Manila. He was to report for duty at the Sixteenth Naval District upon arrival in the Philippines. The liner was scheduled to depart on January 10, 1941.

It was to be another trip halfway around the world for the seasoned international traveler. Coma stayed behind in Chicago. She eventually returned home to Texas and later graduated from the University of Houston.[9]

Richardson arrived in the Philippines to waiting orders after enduring the long trip across the Pacific. "Your orders of November 29, 1940, are so far modified that upon arrival of the S.S. *President Cleveland* at Manila [Philippines], on or about February 1, 1941, you will disembark and report to the Commanding Officer, U.S.S. *Bittern*, for duty," the memo read.[10] He was assigned to a minesweeper.

The aged *Bittern* was launched in early 1919. She sailed for the Philippines less than a year later and would remain in the Far East for the rest of her naval life.[11] She was among the smallest boats serving in the commonwealth at the time of Richardson's arrival.

The next nine months found Richardson fulfilling a wide variety of duties aboard the vessel in rapid succession. His functions included second division officer, watch officer, commissary officer, first lieutenant, navigator, communications officer, and executive officer. "Proficiency in the above listed duties has been impossible to attain due to insufficient time, frequent changes, and additional assignments," Richardson wrote at the time.[12] The experience did however give him a good working knowledge of the ship.

Commanding officer Lieutenant Lynn C. Petross gave Richardson good marks in a standard officer evaluation dated September 18, 1941. He noted the officer was doing excellent work aboard the vessel. "He will improve with more experience," Petross wrote. "He has a good personal and military character."[13] In the same evaluation, Richardson listed his next duty preference as a light cruiser in the Atlantic or the Third Naval District (New York City). The circumstances of war would prevent him from doing either. He would, instead, be serving aboard PT boats.

Richardson first caught sight of the small craft during a routine taxi ride along the Manila waterfront. Although officially known as PT boats, the vessels were called a variety of nicknames, including "mosquito boats," due to their small size and fast speed. He had previously heard about the new PTs, but knew few details of the small boats.

The taxi was passing near the Pasig River in the center of the Manila waterfront district when something caught Richardson's eye. "At this point the forward parts of the newly arrived Mosquito Boats projected out of the marine sheds originally designed for the [Filipino] Q boats," he wrote at the time. "The sleek graceful outline of the bow and cockpit seemed freshly painted the usual navy gray."[14]

He decided to take a closer look and asked the taxi driver to stop at the gate. A sentry at the guard post directed him to John Bulkeley, who was standing nearby in the center of a small group of officers. He approached and introduced himself as "Ensign Richardson from the minesweeper *Bittern*." After a round of introductions, Richardson told the squadron commander he heard the unit was looking for some more officers and would like to apply.

A PT boat engine suddenly fired up with a quick whine and explosive sound, followed by a steady roar. The conversation then had to continue at a yell to be heard. Bulkeley warned that life aboard a PT boat was sometimes rugged. "I was asked to look the boats over and if I liked them to make my request through official channels," Richardson later wrote.

The visitor already knew one of the PT boat men. Anthony Akers was Richardson's classmate at V-7 school back in Chicago. The prospective officer was allowed to board Aker's *PT-35*. The pair walked down a narrow catwalk before stepping aboard the stern of the boat. "The crew were busy with routine work so I only took a superficial look around," Richardson wrote of the moment. He was struck by the compactness and sleek lines of the boat, along with the powerful looking torpedo tubes. "In short, without looking any further, I was sold."

Richardson was introduced to a trio of ensigns just after stepping off the 35 boat. George Cox, Cone Johnson, and William Plant were all officers aboard other boats. "So [you're] crazy and want to keep from growing old by joining the suicide squadron," Johnson remarked with a laugh. "With ten thousand dollars' worth of life insurance, I'm probably worth more dead than alive," Richardson replied with a chuckle. A transfer request soon went up the chain of command and was approved through official channels.

New orders cut on October 22 brought an end to Richardson's time aboard *Bittern*. He was directed to "regard yourself detached from duty on board that vessel and from such other duty as may have been assigned you; report to the Commander Motor Torpedo Boat Squadron Three for assignment to duty."[15] He had to wait for *Bittern* to return from patrol before reporting for the new duty. Richardson officially became a member of the PT squadron on October 30, 1941.[16] "Upon arrival I was assigned duties as executive officer, [*PT-33*] under Ensign Brantingham, commanding officer."

The newly arrived PTs were initially assigned to operate from the Manila Yacht Club while preparations were made to receive the boats at the Cavite Navy Yard. The boats regularly docked in covered sheds near the waterfront. "We immediately commenced maneuvering exercises in an effort to 'shake down' my boats and crews," Bulkeley recalled. He wanted to get his officers used to working with each other as well as himself. The squadron commander insisted on precision while maneuvering at sea and meticulous maintenance when the boats were docked. "I'm sure they each thought during the first two weeks of exercises that I was a 'flaming nut,'" he added.[17]

Bulkeley had a chance encounter with Admiral Thomas C. Hart, commander of all American naval forces in the Philippines, shortly after returning from exercises at sea on a rainy afternoon. Many of the PT sailors were shirtless due to the heat and humidity. It did not sit well with the admiral. Hart advised the soaking-wet Bulkeley that it was a health risk to be operating in such conditions with a possible war approaching. He directed all PT sailors no longer to live aboard their boats, but to take up accommodations in a local hotel. The men were to eat hot meals prepared by the hotel staff and get plenty of rest, with the Navy picking up the bill.

The PTs conducted a few joint exercises with three Philippine Q boats while in the Manila area. The small torpedo boats of British design were designated for coastal defense. Bulkeley soon learned that Hart had assigned his PT boats the same role. The squadron leader, however, felt the PTs were a viable weapon better suited for operations with the main battle units of the fleet.

About a month after his first encounter with Hart, Bulkeley sought a meeting with the admiral to personally discuss the arrangement. The request followed a series of failed attempts to work on the issue with the admiral's staff. Bulkeley proceeded to the Marsman Building in downtown Manila. Following about an hour of respectful banter, Hart agreed to conduct a test of the torpedo boats' effectiveness during fleet exercises. It was to take place the very next evening.

The light cruiser *Marblehead* was sent about 50 miles offshore with six destroyers acting as screens. The ships observed darkened conditions and radio silence to create a realistic scenario. The PTs were to attack the warships using Very pistols with green flares to signal the actual torpedo firing. The ships were similarly to fire flares to simulate the detection and attack on the torpedo boats.

Luck was riding with the small craft—or perhaps it was the squadron commander's training. Approaching the warships under the cover of a slightly overcast night, Bulkeley was aware the "enemy" lookouts would likely be honing in on the ferocious roar of his boat's engines. Following a prearranged plan, and correctly guessing the course changes of the warships, the PTs cut to idling speed on one engine and drifted through the destroyer screen completely undetected. The boats opened fire with the Very pistols about 300 yards from *Marblehead* to score a surprise victory. "After 'firing' had ceased, my squadron reformed on my command," Bulkeley noted. "We gave the unbelieving onlookers a taste of our maneuverability and headed home."[18]

The torpedo boats did not escape the victorious night unscathed, however. *PT-34* hit a buoy while departing the area. The heavy iron object was low in the water and the PT struck it almost head on, puncturing the wooden hull in two places. Robert Kelly guided his wounded boat towards port, proceeding independently at a slow pace. Although the holes were small, each about the size of a hand, moving at high speed invited a torrent of inflowing water.

Richardson remembered the incident. "Almost as soon as the 34 tied up a tug was there pumping out the bilges," he wrote. "This prompt action undoubtedly saved much of the equipment in the engine room that would have been damaged by the action of salt water had it raised any higher." The boat was hauled away for repairs on a marine railway the same day she made port. She returned to service after undergoing extensive hull repairs. Richardson spent some time aboard the 34 boat as cross training.

Aside from the damaged boat, the mock exercise allowed Bulkeley to prove the worth of his new weapons. The PTs were no longer considered coastal defense craft. Hart, however, remained skeptical of the small boats.

The time operating from the Manila Yacht Club was soon over and the squadron moved south. Although Manila was the headquarters of the naval forces in the region, the Cavite Navy Yard served as the operations center. Years of American investment had transformed Cavite from an old Spanish naval base into a modern station with repair shops, an ammunition storage depot, docking facilities, and fuel storage.[19] The base was situated on a small finger of land, adjacent to Canacao Bay, jutting out into Manila Bay from a narrow peninsula ending at Stanley Point. The city of Cavite stood in close proximity to the facilities. A large number of local Filipino residents were employed at the base.

Bulkeley reported to Admiral Rockwell, who then became his immediate superior. The squadron's 12 officers and 68 enlisted men moved into living quarters at the naval base. Also arriving with the unit was a cadre of spare parts, machine-gun ammunition, and 24 torpedoes.

The supplies included ten spare engines—the only extra motors available to the PT boats. These critical components were needed to keep the boats running. Bulkeley considered the engines so important he eventually ordered the units dispersed to various locations for protection, including some hidden in secret sites around Manila.

The training continued into November. Word was passed one day for all boats to get under way in five minutes. The group was to head out into Manila Bay for antiaircraft practice. "Light off," Brantingham told Quartermaster First Class Clayton Beliveau.[20] The engines of the 33 boat started with a wail followed by a steady rumble. A deafening roar quickly permeated through the area as the other boats fired up their motors almost simultaneously.

Bulkeley's flagship *PT-41* was the first to back away from the slip, followed in rapid succession by the others. All six boats were soon under way, moving in a column formation at 10 knots. A signal to increase speed then came from the flagship. "The signal was acknowledged and on the next signal to execute, Brantingham pushed the throttles forward a little and in a flash the 33 leaped forward with a corresponding increase in exhaust blast and the production of a huge wake astern," Richardson wrote of the moment. "Making 30 knots, we rapidly reached the rendezvous."

Machine gunners were manning their weapons as the subject of the exercise soon appeared off the starboard beam of *PT-33* in the form of an Army P-40 Warhawk fighter. The plane sped past while flying only 300 feet above water. The gunners took aim and followed the plane while simulating fire.

Later during the same day, the boats made practice torpedo runs on unsuspecting merchant ships maneuvering through the waters of Manila Bay. "The crews of the merchant ships stood with mouths agape and watched large fast speed boats peel off from the group of six boats, come directly at them at very high speed, then turn abruptly around and retreat in the same manner," Richardson recalled. The boats occasionally fired live torpedoes at targets and conducted night maneuvers in the open sea.

Bulkeley's letters home to Alice in late 1941 showed he expected war was very close. "I don't think it will be too long before we get into war for keeps—we have certainly prepared ourselves the best we can," he penned in a letter dated November 6. He shared some more ominous remarks only three weeks later. "The situation is tense out here—and no fooling! Our decks are cleared. If Japan wants war, we are ready. It sure seems very close."[21]

The squadron commander was correct in his predictions. Bulkeley, Richardson, and the rest of Motor Torpedo Squadron 3 were soon thrust into action as World War II suddenly erupted around them.

PART II

THRUST INTO THE FIRE

CHAPTER 7

Although commonly accepted as the top American military commander in the Far East, General MacArthur's authority did not extend over the ocean. The naval forces assigned to the defense of the Philippines were part of the United States Asiatic Fleet. The unit existed in some form, often as a small squadron of vessels, for nearly a century dating back to 1835. It was expanded to fleet status in 1902.[1] The fleet's main duties were to protect American interests in China and provide security for the Philippines. Ships of the fleet regularly made courtesy calls to major Far Eastern ports, including Tokyo, Hong Kong, Singapore, and Hanoi.

Relations with Japan were already strained when Admiral Thomas C. Hart assumed command of the Asiatic Fleet on July 25, 1939.[2] The admiral was well respected within the Navy as a good administrator and student of strategy. He was also known as a strict disciplinarian. Much of the 1930s found Asiatic Fleet activities focused on China, with the unit maintaining headquarters in Shanghai. Hart decided to move his center of operations to the Philippines and did so in late 1940 over State Department objections that a "retreat" from China would only encourage more Japanese aggression.[3] The admiral later established permanent headquarters in the Marsman Building near the waterfront in downtown Manila. Rear Admiral William Purnell served as Hart's chief of staff.

The main naval facilities in the Philippines were an operating base at Olongapo in Subic Bay on the west coast of Luzon and the Cavite Navy Yard near Manila. Some smaller facilities existed, including a station at

Davao on the island of Mindanao in the southern part of the islands. Hart's command had full fleet status. Operating independently of the Pacific Fleet at Pearl Harbor, he reported directly to the Chief of Naval Operations, Admiral Harold Stark.

Military and political leaders in Washington discussed sending major naval reinforcements to the Asiatic Fleet in late 1940. The force was to include the new aircraft carrier *Yorktown*, four heavy cruisers, and an assortment of smaller vessels. The plan was never made formal and was eventually negated by President Roosevelt.[4]

In the end, there were few reinforcements in the way of surface ships available to Hart as he set out to prepare his fleet for a possible war with Japan. Admiral Stark did, however, authorize the deployment of Bulkeley's PT boats to the Philippines. Unsure of the real value of the small craft, Stark told the Asiatic leader he "hoped that the PTs will be of real service to you. The British think they are fine."[5] Six additional torpedo boats were earmarked for the Philippines, but the PTs never made it across the Pacific prior to the outbreak of war.

The bulk of Hart's battle strength consisted of the heavy cruiser *Houston*, two light cruisers, and 13 outdated World War I-era destroyers. *Houston* served as Hart's flagship. Also attached, but not necessarily as a permanent member of the fleet, was the light cruiser *Boise*. She arrived as a convoy escort in early December 1941 and was still in the area when the war started. Hart certainly welcomed her extra firepower.

The undersea component of the fleet was the only area to receive substantial reinforcements before the start of hostilities. Most of the submarines available to Hart prior to end of 1941 were small outdated S-Class boats. The arrival of 12 large submarines in November, along with the tender *Holland*, increased the number of underwater boats to 29. An assortment of support ships, coastal gunboats, minesweepers, and Bulkeley's PT boats rounded out the sea force.[6] A total of 11,125 Navy personnel were in the Philippines by the first week of December.[7]

Hart's jurisdiction also included the Sixteenth Naval District. Based at the Cavite Navy Yard, the district oversaw local defense, logistics, and administrative matters for the geographic area of the Philippines.[8] Rear Admiral Francis Rockwell assumed command of the district in late

1941. The final components of the fleet were Patrol Wing 10, containing Catalina PBY seaplanes along with the associated support vessels, and a regiment of marines recalled from duty in China shortly before the hostilities started.

The Asiatic Fleet was anything but a powerful force during the last days of peace in the Pacific. American naval leaders recognized that Hart's ships would be no match for the powerful Japanese Fleet in battle. The broad strategy of Rainbow Five charged the Asiatic Fleet with supporting the defense of the Philippines in the event of war for "as long as that defense continues."[9] Prewar strategy, however, authorized Hart to move his larger surface forces out of the Philippines as the situation demanded until the Pacific Fleet arrived in the area.[10]

Hart was able to do plenty to ready his force for battle, even without major reinforcements. All units of the fleet were recalled to the Philippines. The major ships of the fleet began extensive operational training in January 1941. The exercises took place in the waters south of the Philippines and continued until October. During the extended time, the ships only returned to the Manila area for supplies, fuel, and maintenance as needed. Defensive minefields were laid in Manila and Subic bays to help keep Japanese surface ships out. A new operating base was built at Mariveles on the southern tip of the Bataan Peninsula. Regular reconnaissance flights of PBY seaplanes began in July 1941.

Hart organized the majority of his surface fighting ships into a strike force, designated Task Force Five, as a final preparation for war. Rear Admiral William Glassford, Jr., was put in command. The admiral had been overseeing a small group of American gunboats still in China and arrived in the Philippines just days before the conflict.

Glassford's force was free to move south when war came to begin operations against the Japanese, presumably in conjunction with British and Dutch warships in the region. No formal arrangements, however, had been made with those nations for such operations.[11] The remainder of the fleet, including submarines, PT boats, local defense warships, and patrol planes, would remain in Philippine waters to engage the Japanese directly.

The Hart and MacArthur commands, unfortunately, did not coexist in unity. The two leaders clashed on strategy and had harsh exchanges over each other's specific duties in the event of conflict.[12] MacArthur vehemently disagreed with the Navy's plan to move the surface ships out of the Philippines during war conditions. The general belittled Hart by portraying him as a big admiral with a small fleet.[13] The two commanders rarely coordinated on planning and strategy, even though they lived in the same hotel and worked nearby.

Hart sought to deviate from the prewar strategy of moving his big ships south in the weeks leading up to the war. He proposed concentrating his force in Manila Bay, citing the protection that could be provided by the growing air force. The request, however, was denied on November 20 by Secretary of the Navy Frank Knox.[14]

The start of hostilities found the major units of the Asiatic Fleet scattered among the Philippines and areas to the southwest. Two of the big ships were well south of Manila—*Houston* at Iloilo and *Boise* at Cebu. The light cruiser *Marblehead* and five destroyers were at Tarakan off Borneo. Four destroyers and the tender *Black Hawk* were further south at Balikpapan. Many of the smaller warships, submarines, and support ships were split among Manila Bay, Cavite, and Olongapo.

A series of warnings about potential hostilities began emanating from Washington in late November as negotiations with Japan faltered. An alert sent to Pacific commanders on November 24 warned the chances of a negotiated settlement with Japan were slim and mentioned the possibility of a surprise attack on one or more territories, including the Philippines. A more ominous message from the War Department to all commands three days later stated "Japanese future action unpredictable but hostile action possible at any moment."[15] A follow-up note from the Navy Department to its commanders in the Pacific contained even stronger words and noted it should be considered a war warning.

Adding further to the tensions in the Pacific during the first week of December were reports of a Japanese convoy on the move off Indochina. The ships were thought to be headed towards Malaya. At the same time unidentified planes, presumably Japanese, were spotted flying over parts of Luzon.

MacArthur, Hart, and Francis B. Sayre, U.S. High Commissioner to the Philippines, met to discuss war preparations following the November 27 warning. Reconnaissance flights, already under way by both army and navy planes, were intensified and extended further out. Hart recalled the last remaining naval units from China.

Admiral Rockwell was also making preparations at the Cavite Navy Yard. Ammunition and drums of fuel were moved to a newly completed dump. Long-scheduled routine maintenance work on ships was suspended so that vessels already in the yard could be made ready for a quick departure.

The chief of Great Britain's Far Eastern Fleet, Admiral Sir Tom Phillips, arrived in Manila on December 5 to confer with Hart and MacArthur on joint plans for regional defense. The battleship H.M.S. *Prince of Wales* and the battle cruiser H.M.S. *Repulse* were on the final leg of a voyage to Singapore. The two large warships represented Britain's last-ditch effort to deter further Japanese aggression in the Pacific. Little was accomplished at the meeting of leaders in Manila before reports of Japanese ship movements sent Phillips rushing back to Singapore.

MacArthur ordered Wainwright's Northern Luzon Force to be ready to take up beach-defense positions on short notice. The general reported the situation to military leaders in Washington. "Within the limitations imposed by present state of development of this theater of operations, everything is in readiness for the conduct of a successful defense."[16]

The final days of peace in the Philippines were drawing to a close. Sailors, soldiers, and airmen went about their normal business on December 7 (local date and time). Many eagerly awaited the arrival of the Pan Am clipper. The plane flew a regular trans-Pacific route and brought mail to servicemen. The tropical paradise was about to be quickly engulfed in war.

The bombs had barely stopped falling on Pearl Harbor when Japanese forces lashed out across the Pacific in a series of preplanned and well-coordinated attacks. The speed and number of the strikes took many Allied leaders by surprise. The targets were various American and British possessions, including Wake Island, Guam, Hong Kong, Malaya, and the Philippines.

The conquest of the Philippines was largely a sideshow for the Japanese military. The main thrust south was to secure the oil and minerals of Malaya and the Dutch East Indies. The archipelago represented a bastion of American power—one that could potentially disrupt the lines of supply and communications if left unchecked. The Philippines had to be neutralized and its military forces destroyed as a safeguard to prevent the possibility of its use as an advanced base for future American operations against Japanese interests. The Philippines were of no significant importance to Japan in terms of resources aside from the possible exception of some copper. The value of the nation was largely strategic.

The Japanese plan to attack the commonwealth incorporated elements of surprise, overwhelming force, and air superiority. Planners assumed American naval and air power in the region, although believed to be substandard, would be fully deployed in the protection of the territory.[17] The Japanese thought the main American defense would be centered on Manila and envisioned a large land battle near the capital to decide the fate of the nation. The invasion plan was for a pincer movement to divide American land forces, with attacks on the capital from both the north and south.

The initial air attacks emanating from Formosa were to be strategically focused on knocking out American air and naval power. Japanese Army fighters lacked the range to reach most of the large air bases on Luzon. Navy medium bombers and long-range Zero fighters could hit the area, but not points further south. These forces were called upon to carry out the initial strikes. The Japanese Navy's large aircraft carriers were all committed to the Pearl Harbor operation and could play no part in the invasion plan.

Tactical air attacks and preinvasion bombardments on shore objectives were eliminated to help keep hidden the actual location of the main landings.[18] An overwhelming force of surface ships was assigned to protect the invasion fleet. The cruisers and destroyers could quell any interference from the Asiatic Fleet. Japanese commanders, however, remained wary of the American submarine force stationed in the Philippines and made sure plenty of escorts were on hand for protection.

The land forces assigned to spearhead the ground attack on the Philippines were members of the Japanese Fourteenth Army. The force was based in Formosa under the leadership of Lieutenant General Masaharu Homma. Some of the units under the general's command had combat experience in China. In addition to two infantry divisions and one mixed brigade, Homma had the support of two tank regiments, field artillery, engineers, and a variety of support units.[19]

The initial landings were planned to secure airstrips in the far northern portion of the island. The move would allow land-based army planes to be quickly put into action, extending air coverage over much of the Philippines. The various attack elements were coordinated down to precise times to be synchronized with the attack on Pearl Harbor. The plan called for the first strikes targeting American air power to take place at dawn on the first day of the war, after the invasion convoys were already en route.

The Japanese were confident of a swift victory over MacArthur's forces. Imperial leaders gave Homma 50 days to complete his conquest of the Philippines. The confident general believed his mission could be accomplished in 45 days.[20]

CHAPTER 8

News of the Pearl Harbor attack spread quickly among the American servicemen in the Philippines throughout the early morning of December 8 (local time). It was common knowledge among all levels of rank by breakfast time. There was no immediate large-scale attack on the Philippines, but uneasiness quickly spread across the islands.

The news of war, so expected for months, brought acceptance and little in the way of outward emotion from many of the military men in the commonwealth. Most knew a conflict with Japan was not something that was going only to affect others. There was no ocean to protect them from the enemy, as was the case for those back in the United States. The war was going to be front and center, with them right in the middle of it. One army officer later recalled a "grim, thoughtful silence" falling over the islands after the war news broke.[1]

The army and navy headquarters in Manila were full of activity throughout the morning hours. Staffers sought information on Japanese force movements and damage to the American fleet at Pearl Harbor. Reports soon began to flow in from all across the Pacific—Japanese planes over Singapore, Guam attacked by air, and enemy ships steaming towards Wake Island. There was no let up in the frantic reports.

Search planes were dispatched to scour nearby waters for any sign of an approaching invasion force. War plans were initiated. Army troops were ordered to battle positions. Japanese planes, however, did not appear over Manila at dawn as many had feared.

The opening shots of the battle for the Philippines came not on Luzon, but on the southern island of Mindanao. The seaplane tender *William B. Preston* had recently set up a small base in Malalag Bay near Davao. Morning light found one of her three PBY seaplanes out on patrol. The other two, fueled and loaded with bombs, were moored in the water awaiting further instructions.

There was little time for crewmembers to react when 13 dive bombers and nine Zero fighters suddenly attacked without warning. The planes came from the light carrier *Ryujo* operating in the open waters to the east. Several bombs fell dangerously close to the tender, but she escaped damage. Both PBYs, however, were destroyed. Ensign Robert G. Tills, a pilot, was killed trying to get his plane airborne to become the first American casualty in the Philippines during World War II.[2] The vessel immediately departed the area for safer waters to the south.

Five hundred miles north of Manila, a thick fog blanketed the Japanese airfields on Formosa, preventing the main attack force of Navy planes from taking off for the scheduled morning attack on the Luzon airfields. The clouds started to arrive after midnight to create an unforeseen delay in the operation. Air commanders waited in nervous anticipation for a break in the weather, knowing that the element of surprise was gone.

The Americans had certainly heard of the Pearl Harbor attack and were likely alert and prepared for action. The Japanese were also well aware of the presence of the B-17s and of the bombers' capabilities. The possibility of an American attack on their airfields could not be discounted. Some worried Japanese, fearful their aircraft could be caught on the ground, donned gas masks and waited for the arrival of American planes after an intercepted radio message was misinterpreted to indicate an attack was on the way. Hoping they would be able soon to leave Formosa, some pilots half expected to pass B-17s traveling in the opposite direction while en route to the Philippines.[3] The delay did create a short window of opportunity, but the Americans were unable to take advantage of it.

The situation unfolding at the American Army headquarters in Manila remains cloaked in controversy to this day, with various accounts offering different versions of events. General Lewis Brereton's staff car came to a sharp stop shortly after 5:00 am at One Calle Victoria. The address, inside of Manila's walled city, was home to MacArthur's command center. The air commander was unaware the Japanese planes were grounded as he raced up the stone stairs.

Brereton was agitated and nearly out of breath as he entered the wooden building. He sought permission to carry out a daylight attack with B-17s on Formosa. Japanese airfields, transports ships, and warships were all high-priority targets, with the air bases at the top of the list. His intentions and concept was good—hit the enemy forces that would be spearheading the attack on the Philippines as soon as possible.

The general's 34 B-17s, mostly based at Clark Field, were the largest concentration of the powerful bombers anywhere in the American arsenal. The planes were originally sent to the Philippines as a deterrent. Now it was time for action.

Brereton knew the only individual who could authorize such an attack was MacArthur. His request to see the leader, however, was blocked by Richard Sutherland. MacArthur's domineering chief of staff reported that the general was unavailable. He advised Brereton to begin making the necessary preparations, but to stand by for further orders. The disgusted air commander returned to his office at Nielson Field just outside Manila.

The air commander made a return trip to the army headquarters about 7:15 am, but was again told by Sutherland to stand by for orders. One concern apparently raised was the need for adequate preattack target information, since the data on file was thought to be outdated. Brereton later wrote that reconnaissance missions to gather details of the Japanese installations on Formosa were forbidden by MacArthur before the war.[4] A basic plan for such an attack, however, was already on file, containing an outline of objectives but lacking calibrated bomb target maps and aerial photographs.[5] Although not fully detailed, an intelligence officer serving on the air staff recalled it as "complete enough" to have proceeded with the mission without delay.[6]

Preparations were made to send three B-17s to southern Formosa on a photographic reconnaissance mission—an operation approved by Sutherland. There was some high-level discussion about proceeding with an attack once the results were known. The planes were fueled, but could not depart until extra cameras arrived from Nichols Field.[7] As events unfolded in the coming hours, however, the mission was never carried out.

At about this time Brereton received a call from General Henry H. Arnold in Washington. The chief of the Army Air Force explained how the American planes at Pearl Harbor were destroyed on the ground. He did not want the same to happen in the Philippines.[8]

Unconfirmed reports of Japanese aircraft en route to Luzon now arrived at Manila, sending fighters airborne. At about 8:00 am. the B-17s at Clark Field were ordered to take off—without bombs—to avoid being caught on the ground during an air attack. A small number of Japanese Army bombers had managed to take off from Formosa at daybreak as planned and attacked military installations in northern Luzon. The targets were Camp John Hay, an army outpost, and a small airfield containing no planes. Japanese pilots were astonished when they arrived and departed unmolested by American fighters. The details of this strike, however, were slow in getting to the American command in Manila.[9] No planes approached or attacked Clark Field.

News of Japanese planes over the Philippines prompted Brereton to pick up the telephone at about 10:00 am. "I personally called General Sutherland and informed him that hostile aircraft were operating over Luzon and that if Clark Field was attacked successfully we would be unable to operate offensively with the bombers."[10] His luck on the phone was no better than in person—Sutherland's directive to stand by remained the same. The decision left Brereton seething with anger.

In a surprise turn of events, MacArthur called Brereton directly a mere 14 minutes after the air commander spoke with Sutherland. "If you feel offensive action is in order, Lewis, the decision is yours," MacArthur told his subordinate.[11] The one sentence changed everything.

Brereton quickly assembled his staff. By 10:45 am the group had a working plan for the two squadrons of bombers at Clark to attack airfields on southern Formosa before the end of the day. Additionally, the B-17s at Del Monte Field on Mindanao were to be moved north to Clark under the cover of darkness for additional operations the following morning.

The bombers returned to Clark Field at about 11:30 am after an all clear was sounded. The planes had circled the area for hours. The B-17s parked in neat rows and most of the airmen went to lunch. Ground crews immediately began the long process of refueling and loading bombs to ready the planes for the attack mission. The fighters also landed for refueling. The preparation work on the B-17s was still ongoing less than an hour later when Japanese bombers suddenly appeared overhead.

The fog over Formosa had lifted enough for the Japanese Navy planes to take off at 10:15 am. A group of 108 twin-engine bombers and 84 Zero fighters headed south. The fighters were specially modified to allow for the extended range. The target of the attack force was two important American airfields—Iba and Clark.

Reports of approaching Japanese planes began trickling into the Air Warning Center at Nielson Field at about the same time the B-17s were landing at Clark. The center served as a clearinghouse for information on approaching threats from the air. The flow of reports, arriving by telephone, telegraph, and from the limited radar early warning stations, soon turned into a flood.

Colonel Alexander Campbell was the officer in charge. It was now very clear that a large group of Japanese planes was arriving over Luzon. The enemy formation seemed to be pointing directly at Clark Field. Campbell sent a Teletype warning the base, but the message did not make it through. He was equally unsuccessful when trying the radio. The operator at Clark was apparently out to lunch. Campbell was finally able to get through by telephone. A junior officer promised to relay the information to the base commander as soon as possible.

For reasons that are unclear, the warning either did not make it to the right people or was not transferred in time and no immediate action was taken. Air raid sirens sounded on all airfields around Luzon—except Clark—at 11:56 am.[12] The alarm sent fighters racing into the air at the various other bases.

The first Japanese planes appeared over Clark Field to find all but one of the B-17s still neatly lined up. Eighteen refueled P-40 fighters were parked on the edge of the field, with pilots awaiting orders to take off. Most would never make it off the ground.

With the news of the Pearl Harbor attack more than nine hours old and the morning fog delaying their departure, the Japanese pilots did not expect to find the American planes on the ground.[13] A flight of 27 bombers suddenly materialized in a V formation, just as the Clark air raid sirens finally sounded. The planes flew at a height of almost 25,000 feet dropping bombs on aircraft and buildings. Among the structures quickly destroyed was the communication center, temporarily cutting off Clark Field from the outside world.

The force of explosions rocked the ground with increasing frequency and intensity. Billowing black smoke rapidly engulfed the entire area. Shells from the outdated American antiaircraft guns fell far short of the attackers. After a second group of bombers made a similar run with equally devastating results, Zeros swooped in for a low-level strafing attack.

The sound of the wailing warning siren sent American airmen racing out from the mess hall only to witness a stream of cascading bombs falling from the sky. Ground crews and pilots alike acted heroically in defense of the base, but it was a hopeless cause. The Japanese achieved complete tactical surprise during the attack. Only three American fighters made it airborne and could do little to stop the hour-long assault.

The experience of B-17 navigator Lieutenant Edgar Whitcomb was common among the airmen who went through the attack. After a morning full of activity, he had eaten a quick lunch at the mess hall and rushed back to the squadron headquarters awaiting further war developments. He was waiting to take off for an attack on Formosa and did not understand why such a mission was not already under way. The sudden scream of "Here they come" announced the abrupt arrival of Japanese bombers.

Whitcomb ran for a nearby trench. "Then, as I hit the bottom of the trench, there was a terrible explosion, followed by another, another, and another," he later recalled. Bombs seemed to be raining down all around him. "When I was finally able to stand up I wiped the sand out of my eyes and ran over to the end of the headquarters building to see what happened. There, across the field, we could see our beautiful silver Flying Fortresses burning and exploding right before our eyes as we stood completely powerless to do anything about it."[14]

He and others "stood silently as at a funeral" for a short period of time watching their planes burn before the sound of machine-gun fire sent them scurrying back into the trench. Surveying the carnage after the attackers departed, he did not think there was one American plane left untouched. The destruction was complete.

A torrent of wounded servicemen flooded into the army hospital at nearby Fort Stotsenburg. Some were suffering from horrible burns. The small facility was soon overwhelmed, necessitating the transfer of patients to a larger hospital in Manila.

Iba Field was also hit by a large group of Japanese planes at about the same time. The base was located about 40 miles west of Clark on the coast of Luzon. It was primarily used for fighters. Zeros ambushed and destroyed a flight of P-40s attempting to land in the opening minutes of the assault. Other planes attacked the base facilities, demolishing buildings, equipment, and the precious radar station. Ten of the twelve P-40 fighters stationed at Iba were destroyed.

The attack on American air power was devastating. Only three of the 17 B-17 bombers based at Clark Field survived. Fifty-three P-40 fighters and 30 other American aircraft of various types were lost. Japanese losses amounted to a mere seven fighter planes.[15] Two important air bases were completely wrecked. MacArthur's air force had been dealt a crippling blow in one definitive strike.

The events of the debacle were never fully reconciled. Few written records survived the Japanese occupation of the Philippines. The principal decision makers—Brereton, Sutherland, and MacArthur—contradicted each other in their postwar statements and writings. The conversations were laced with accusations and denials.

Brereton blamed Sutherland and MacArthur for delaying his recommended attack on Formosa. It is unclear, however, what impact such a strike, if executed, would have had in slowing the Japanese onslaught. Sutherland in turn held Brereton responsible for the loss of the bombers by failing to move the planes south to Del Monte as previously ordered by MacArthur.[16] The southern airfield was not yet completely ready and was earmarked to be the future home of a group of bombers scheduled to arrive from the United States. MacArthur later claimed Brereton never recommended an attack on Formosa and that "the overall strategic mission of the Philippines command was to defend the Philippines, and not to initiate outside attack." He added such an attack "would have had no chance of success."[17]

The assignment of blame for the debacle was never solved, but some amount of fault clearly lies with all of the key players. Astonishingly, General MacArthur, who shouldered a fair amount of responsibility for the calamity, escaped the severe consequences that befell the leaders in charge of Pearl Harbor at the time of the surprise attack. A long list of items—including poor planning, inexperience, indecision, miscommunication, incompetence, and some just plain bad luck—had all conspired to help defeat the American air forces in the Philippines.

The loss of about half of the modern aircraft on the first day of the war all but eliminated MacArthur's air force as an effective fighting unit. The Japanese would have air superiority for the entire campaign. The defense of the Philippines was off to a bad start.

CHAPTER 9

John Bulkeley remained near the Cavite Navy Yard with three torpedo boats as the drama unfolded at the army headquarters in nearby Manila and later over Clark Field. No planes attacked Cavite. With the squadron commander were PTs 31, 33 and 35.[1] Bulkeley stationed one PT at the Stanley Point buoy. The boat was to act as a plane guard to rescue any pilots—friendly or enemy—shot down over Manila Bay.

The other two PTs were moored to buoys in Canacao Bay off Stanley Point as an added safety measure to guard against a surprise air attack. A distance of about 75 yards separated the two boats. The craft never came to the nearby wharf together as an additional precautionary measure. Bulkeley's three boats spent the next couple of days on short patrols and running messages as work continued on preparing the PTs for combat.[2]

Aboard *PT-33*, Iliff Richardson remembered the relentless movement of the boats during the first two days of the war. The PTs would get under way in a hurry every time the base air raid siren sounded. "Instead of going into the slips bow first, the boats backed into the slips, which made getting out much faster," he later wrote. Bulkeley did not want his PTs caught at the piers during an air attack. "Once under way, all boats proceeded out into Manila Bay on divergent course from the others, spreading out in such a manner that it would be unlikely we should lose [all] boats in case of [an aerial] attack."[3]

The constant rumbling of the PT engines soon caused a high level of uneasiness in the immediate area. "The exhaust blast from the engines of PT boats is very similar to that of aircraft and this similarity proved to be a big moral deterrent," Richardson wrote. "Civilians were sure that the sound of the boats represented a squadron of enemy bombers." The fears became heightened after the attacks on the Clark and Iba air bases.

The Cavite area had been full of activity ever since the first news of the war brought Admiral Rockwell rushing to the Commandantia during the early morning hours. He sent a radio message to all American merchant ships to "Proceed [to] closest U.S. or friendly port immediately."[4] The process of destroying classified documents began as a precaution. Various reports of approaching enemy planes and Japanese movements around the Philippines filtered into the command on a regular basis. Most proved inaccurate, including a naval intelligence report from a Japanese citizen under arrest that four Japanese battleships were scheduled to arrive at Davao very soon.

Admiral Hart ordered Cavite to maintain blackout conditions during night-time hours. Marine guards were doubled and antiaircraft batteries were notified to expect an attack. Air-raid sirens were commonplace.

Sensing an attack on Cavite was imminent, Rockwell took steps to protect the civilian population in the immediate area. He reduced the number of civilian workers on base to the bare minimum and worked with the mayor of Cavite to begin a partial evacuation of the city. The admiral was uneasy about the stockpile of fuel around Stanley Point and the safety of the modern naval hospital at Canacao.

Rockwell directed 5,000 drums of high-octane gasoline be moved to Mariveles to better address the fuel situation. In a Herculean effort, led by the admiral's flag lieutenant Malcolm Champlin and involving about 200 men, the heavy drums were loaded on barges to be sent across Manila Bay. The action would have a far-reaching impact on PT boat operations in the coming months. Other fuel stores were broken into smaller caches around Stanley Point.

The admiral believed the hospital was vulnerable to destruction due to its close proximity to the navy yard. He ordered all medical supplies divided into thirds, with one transferred to Manila and another to Mariveles. Rockwell later decided to transfer all 185 patients currently at

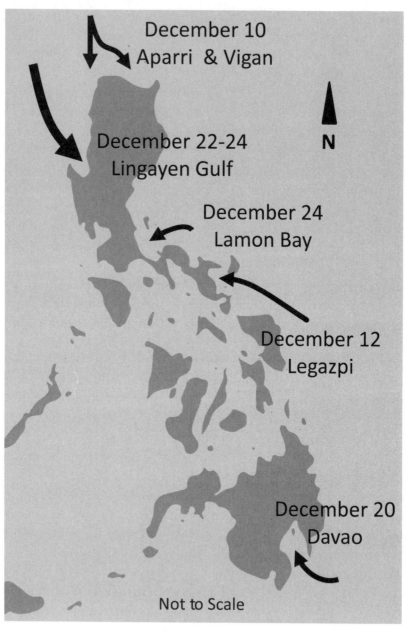

December 10
Aparri & Vigan

N

December 22-24
Lingayen Gulf

December 24
Lamon Bay

December 12
Legazpi

December 20
Davao

Not to Scale

Map 3: Attack on the Philippines

Canacao to an army hospital in Manila. The process began immediately, with the ferry *San Felipe* providing the transportation. The hospital staff was to stay at Canacao with the remaining supplies, to be ready to accept new patients as needed.

At the same time, Robert Kelly was dealing with a host of problems across Manila Bay at Mariveles Harbor. He left Cavite under Bulkeley's orders late in the day on December 8 with PTs 32, 34 and 41 to rendezvous with a submarine tender. He arrived safely, after navigating a minefield at night and avoiding jittery gunners, who mistook the sound of his boat motors for Japanese planes only to find the tender was departing the area for waters to the south.

Kelly's boats were low on gas and his sailors had limited rations. The PTs typically needed to operate from a land base or a larger ship due to their small size. The departure of the tender left him with no base of operations. The three PTs ventured out to reconnoiter the southern tip of Bataan on the morning of December 9. It was during the short voyage that Kelly found Sisiman Cove. The small inlet, just east of Mariveles Bay, seemed to be a good place for a temporary PT base. It could be used in addition to or in place of Cavite should something happen to the navy yard. The new remote base would soon become the epicenter of PT boat operations in the Philippines.

Kelly next found a supply of fuel in an unlikely place—aboard barges in Manila Bay. The two barges, each loaded with barrels of the high-octane gasoline needed by the boats' Packard engines, were the end result of Rockwell's dispersal order. Both barges had been towed into the bay for safekeeping. It was a wise decision due to the likely prospects of enemy air attacks. If kept moored to a pier, the explosive cargoes could quickly engulf the entire area in flames with a single bomb hit.

The PT boats were not the only vessels of the Asiatic Fleet active during the first days of the war. The heavy units of Rear Admiral William Glassford's Task Force Five were scattered around various points south of Manila. The admiral left the capital by plane during the late morning of December 8 to rendezvous with his flagship *Houston* at Iloilo in the central Philippines. The light cruiser *Boise* soon arrived from Cebu.

That night the aircraft tender *Langley* and two destroyers slipped out of Manila Bay to join the group.

Glassford proceeded south to Borneo on orders from Admiral Hart. He planned to fuel up in the Dutch territory before assembling the remaining ships of his force. The warships encountered no Japanese on their voyage south. The main fighting power of the Asiatic Fleet was out of Philippine waters by December 10, leaving behind Bulkeley's torpedo boats, an assortment of small craft, and submarines for local defense.

The start of the war found the majority of the fleet's submarines in Manila Bay. Hart ordered eight of the boats to hunt Japanese shipping off Formosa and Indochina. Eight additional submarines were sent to patrol various key points around the Philippines to be on the lookout for an invasion force. The remaining boats stayed near Manila for quick deployment as the situation dictated.

Admiral Hart met with Rockwell and Captain Frank Wagner amidst all of the activity. Wagner was the commanding officer of Patrol Wing 10 at Stanley Point. The unit's PBY seaplanes had been busy flying reconnaissance patrols around Luzon. The planes also conducted a few attacks on vessels mistakenly thought to be Japanese. Hart ordered the group's fuel supply to be dispersed for safekeeping, as air attacks were undoubtedly expected to continue.

A thick fog returned to blanket Formosa again on the morning of December 9. It prevented large-scale Japanese air operations for the day. The enemy air commanders had hoped to continue their success against the Philippines with further strikes against airfields and naval installations, the latter having been untouched.

A small number of Japanese bombers managed to take flight, striking Nichols Field just outside of Manila. The attack destroyed various buildings, but the runways and grounded fighter planes amazingly survived intact.

American planes continued reconnaissance flights throughout the day. The scouts scoured the waters northeast and northwest of Luzon looking for any signs of an approaching invasion force. None of the numerous sighting reports flowing into Manila proved to be valid.

General MacArthur promised an air raid on Formosa in the aftermath of the devastating air losses the day before. One B-17 was dispatched on a reconnaissance mission at about 8:00 am, but later turned back due to mechanical problems.[5] The attack mission never materialized, but the day was full of activity on the ground. Crews worked at a furious pace to clean up the damage and repair planes at Clark Field. Thirteen B-17s moved north to Luzon from Mindanao. Some spent the bulk of the day airborne, fearful of being caught on the ground in another attack.

Steps were taken throughout the day to strengthen the air defenses in the greater Manila area. An antiaircraft battery stationed on Corregidor was redeployed to the capital to provide added protection near the port area, oil-storage facilities, railroad yard, and Nichols Field. About 500 airmen from Clark were reorganized into a new air defense unit and sent to Manila.[6]

The lack of radar continued to seriously hamper the efforts of an effective air defense. The radar set at Iba Field was perhaps the most valuable piece of equipment lost during the recent air attacks. With the only set covering the northern approaches to the Philippines gone, visual contact would have to be the early warning system when the Japanese struck next.

The temporary lull in action proved to be short lived. As December 9 drew to a close, the American disposition in the Philippines was faltering. The main naval firepower, with the exception of the submarine force, was en route to safer waters in the south. The air force had taken a terrible blow, with almost half of its modern warplanes destroyed. The situation was about to become much worse.

A break in the morning mist during the early hours of December 10, 1941 revealed the presence of Japanese ships off northern Luzon. It marked the start of the third full day of war in the Philippines. The day would prove to be a decisive one in the American defense of the islands. The Japanese assault from the air was scheduled to continue with the same fury seen during the previous two days. The campaign, however, was about to enter a dangerous new phase with the landing of the enemy's first ground troops on Luzon.

Three Japanese task forces had slipped out of Formosa ports under the cover of darkness during the evening hours of December 7 (Tokyo time)—the night before the Pearl Harbor attack. The departures went unnoticed as the vessels sailed south. The groups—termed surprise attack forces by the Japanese—represented the vanguard of the ground assault on the Philippines.

The Japanese invasion of the territory actually began at dawn on December 8—even before the opening air attacks—when one of the task groups sent a force of 490 naval combat troops accompanied by air corps men ashore on tiny Bataan Island. The minute speck of land, halfway between Luzon and Formosa but considered part of the Philippines, was seized for a small airstrip. Workers quickly upgraded it to handle army fighters, but additional work was required to make the field suitable for large-scale operations. The landing was unopposed and the American command appeared to be unaware of the operation.[7]

The success of the initial attack on Clark Field made upgrades to the airfield unnecessary. The planned runway expansion was quickly canceled. Japanese forces on Bataan moved south to establish a seaplane base on Camiguin Island, only about 35 miles off Luzon. The operations on the two small islands were merely cautious stepping stones for larger landings yet to come.

The next stage of the Japanese amphibious operations commenced at dawn on December 10, when the two remaining surprise attack forces appeared off Aparri and Vigan on the northern portion of Luzon. The goal of the operation was to gain additional airfields for fighter operations over the Philippines. The attack groups had miraculously escaped detection since departing Formosa until that very morning, when one was spotted by an American reconnaissance plane.

Two companies of Japanese troops landed unopposed at Aparri on the northern tip of Luzon in poor weather conditions. The remainder of the 2,000 men came ashore about 20 miles to the east. The second part of the operation came under attack by American planes when two squadrons of P-40 fighters and five B-17s struck Japanese ships.

The only vessel damaged was a minesweeper. She became a total loss after her depth charges exploded, forcing the small warship to beach herself. The landing continued at a rushed pace, but was otherwise unhindered. Japanese troops were soon in control of two airfields in the Aparri area. When both proved unsuitable for bomber operations, the troops advanced 50 miles south to capture a third air strip.

A second amphibious operation took place simultaneously near Vigan, a coastal city facing the East China Sea. An American P-40 sighted the approaching invasion force early in the morning, allowing planes to stage several attacks throughout the day. An assortment of fighters and bombers managed to sink a minesweeper and damage two transports to the point of beaching.[8] The attacks marked the last large-scale coordinated efforts by MacArthur's air force.[9]

Poor weather conditions also plagued these landings. Only a small portion of the troops earmarked for the operation was able to make it to land. The remainder successfully came ashore the next day a few miles to the south. Japanese troops quickly consolidated before moving inland, capturing an airfield.

Most of General Wainwright's troops allocated to beach defense were deployed around Lingayen Gulf, a large inlet on the west coast of Luzon. American commanders correctly assumed the enemy landings in the north were minor operations and the main thrust was yet to come at Lingayen. As a result, Wainwright had no forces further north to oppose the landings, but moved troops into position to block the enemy movement south. The general's thinly stretched and poorly equipped Filipino troops, however, were unable to hinder the Japanese advance in the days that followed. The enemy quickly had a firm foothold on Northern Luzon.

CHAPTER 10

Fog again caused problems for Japanese airmen on Formosa during the early morning hours of December 10, but unlike the previous two days, the situation rapidly improved. The Imperial Navy, with its long-range fighters, was again taking the lead role in the air attacks for the day. A large group of naval planes took off at about 10:00 am. The force consisted of about 52 Zeros and over 80 bombers.[1] Their target was the greater Manila area.

The first reports of approaching planes reached the Air Warning Center at Nielson Field at about 11:15 am. Fighters at Clark Field, refueling after the morning attacks on Aparri and Vigan, were immediately scrambled and directed to cover Manila Bay, Bataan, and the port of Manila. A total of 35 P-40s were eventually airborne.

The impending air battle was anything but a fair fight. The untested American pilots were up against seasoned Japanese veterans, most with combat experience over China. A comparison of the two planes revealed additional disadvantages for the Americans. The Zero outclassed the P-40 in the crucial areas of speed and maneuverability.

Attempts by the fighters to engage the enemy bombers were thwarted by swarms of Zeros. The American fighters could do nothing to protect the airfields or hinder the bombers while they were involved in a series of swirling dogfights over the greater Manila area. Some became low on fuel and were shot down while attempting to land.

The Japanese air armada divided into two groups somewhere north of Manila. One continued towards the capital, while the second was pointed in the direction of Cavite. Bases around Manila were under attack about an hour after the initial warning. Del Carman, Nielson, and Nichols Fields, along with Camp Murphy, an army base just outside of Manila, were all targets.

The same method employed two days earlier in the attack on Clark Field was repeated, with equally devastating results. High-level bombers appeared first over the airfields to hit buildings and hangers. Zeros then came in low for devastating strafing runs.

Army Doctor Ralph Hibbs watched the attack unfold from the relative safety of a foxhole. "I could see the bomb bay doors open, then the bombs glistened in the sun," he later wrote of the attack. "They seemed to tumble wildly. Soon, as if on command like puppets, they lined up in the sky in perfect formation, plunging earthward with a spine-chilling crescendo."[2]

Fighters then swooped in for a low-level strafing attack, destroying planes, people, and facilities of all types. There was little effective antiaircraft fire. Zero pilots found 15 obsolete P-35 fighters, recently returned from an attack on one of the Japanese landing sites, lined up on the ground at Del Carman Field. Ten were quickly destroyed and the remainder damaged—an entire squadron eliminated in a single instance.[3]

A cluster of 54 Japanese bombers proceeded unimpeded towards Cavite as the air bases around Manila were pummeled. Half the planes veered off to attack ships in Manila Bay, while the remaining 27 bombers went directly to the navy yard. A variety of vessels were in the bay at the time, including two British destroyers, two American submarine tenders, and some submarines. The British ships had just arrived after making an escape run from Hong Kong. The pair was planning to make a short refueling stop before departing for Singapore. An assortment of more than 40 merchant ships was also in the area; many were seeking haven from the war in the American port.

The American naval bases in the Philippines had thus far escaped the rain of bombs that befell the army airfields, but the Navy's luck was about to run out. Although commonly referred to as the Cavite Navy Yard, Stanley Point was home to an array of naval facilities that served as the operations center for the Asiatic Fleet. In addition to the yard for ship maintenance and repairs, the area included machine shops, a radio tower (the largest the Navy had in the Philippines), fuel storage, ammunition storage bunkers, a seaplane base, and administrative buildings. A variety of wood and metal buildings stood packed closely together.

The day found the navy yard full of activity. The gunboat *Mindanao* arrived from China during the morning, with some Japanese prisoners picked up en route from a trawler in the South China Sea. Two old four-stack destroyers were moored at Central Warf. The pair had been involved in a collision a few days earlier. Submarines *Sealion* and *Seadragon* were tied together along with Iliff Richardson's former ship *Bittern* at the very next pier. The large submarine tender *Otus* was nearby. Other vessels in the area included the minesweeper *Quail*, submarine rescue ship *Pigeon*, patrol yacht *Isabel*, and destroyer *John D. Ford*. The latter arrived during the late morning for a quick refueling.

Burning of the remaining secret documents at Cavite's war plans office was completed at noon. Reports of enemy planes en route to the area had already reached the base. The piercing sound of the navy yard's air raid siren began to wail at 12:35 pm.[4] False alarms were commonplace since the start of the war, but this time it was for real.

The piercing sound of the siren sent Marines racing to man their antiaircraft guns. The air defenses guarding Cavite were meager at best. Nine obsolete 3-inch antiaircraft guns, a few machine guns, and shipboard guns were all the weapons available to protect the area.

Across the bay near Mariveles, Robert Kelly's three PT boats were alongside a minesweeper taking on fresh water when word arrived around noon of Japanese planes heading towards Manila. The boats quickly pulled away and made for open water. About 15 minutes later, several large groups of twin-engine bombers came into view. Kelly estimated the planes were flying at 25,000 feet. The neat and tight formations reminded him of a parade.

The boat captain waited for American fighters to tear into the enemy, but none came. The bombers eventually faded out of sight over a mountain range. Distant rumblings soon began indicating the start of an air raid. Kelly wondered about the targets—airfields, Manila, Cavite or all of them? He just did not know.

John Bulkeley was also waiting for the arrival of American fighter planes. The squadron commander did not want to risk having his three PTs caught at Stanley Point during an air raid. He moved PTs 31, 33 and 35 out into Manila Bay after hearing enemy planes were on the way. It was a process that had been repeated many times over the past few days. The weather was clear with almost unlimited visibility, affording the PT men a good view as the bombers approached Manila.

Iliff Richardson was aboard *PT-33* as she raced towards the center of Manila Bay in advance of the attack. An overhaul of the boat's torpedoes had been completed the day before at Cavite in what can be considered extraordinary good timing. She took aboard food and water before relieving the 31 boat at the Stanley Point buoy.

The approaching planes were soon spotted in the cloudless sky. "The silver colored bombers could be seen against the blue sky background with an occasional glint from the sunlight hitting one of the shining surfaces," Richardson wrote. "Over to the east, a smaller dark colored pursuit or dive bomber was made out commencing a nearly vertical dive. This plane dove several thousand feet then pulled out and immediately afterwards came the flash of an explosion as the plane's bomb hit Nichols Field."[5]

Bulkeley was aboard *PT-35* when he saw bombs slowly fall from the bellies of planes towards targets in Manila Bay before gradually picking up speed while descending from hundreds of feet in the air. Explosions in the water sent up large geysers that glistened in the sun like the ends of a rainbow. The resulting mist made it difficult to see the targets, though he thought most of the ships escaped damage. He then saw a formation of planes heading towards Cavite.

Admiral Rockwell had much to be worried about as the Japanese bombers bore down on his base. He was most concerned, however, about the naval ammunition dump. It was positioned in the heart of the base and loaded with 700 tons of high explosives. "It was truly an aviator's dream of a perfect target for fragmentation and incendiary bombs," he later wrote.[6]

The Japanese planes were on their final approach when a battery of 3-inch guns opened fire on a low-flying aircraft coming from the direction of Manila. The bullets hit home, sending the plane down into the bay. Unfortunately, it was a P-40 piloted by Lieutenant Jim Phillips. He became a victim of mistaken identity while attempting to engage a Japanese plane. Phillips survived the incident and was pulled to safety by a rescue party from the navy yard.

By 1:00 pm the bombers were directly over Stanley Point. Flying at an altitude of over 20,000 feet made them immune from the small black puffs of antiaircraft gunfire erupting below. Various accounts indicate the initial group of planes did not drop any bombs during the first pass. Circling around gave the Japanese bombardiers time to take careful aim at the narrow target below before releasing a stream of bombs. The rain of destruction then began in earnest.

A second group of bombers soon joined the attack. The assailants passed back and forth in a leisurely fashion, dropping their deadly cargo at will with no opposition. The bombers most likely flew in nine-plane formations owing to the narrow scope of the target.[7]

Fires started almost immediately, quickly spreading with vigor. Oil storage tanks ruptured, producing flames and billowing black smoke. "Practically all bombs (including many fragmentation and incendiary) fell within the navy yard limits, and direct hits were made on the power plant, dispensary, torpedo repair shop, supply office and warehouses, signal station, commissary store, receiving station, barracks and officers' quarters, and several ships, tugs, and barges along the waterfront," Rockwell reported.

Some of the vessels around Stanley Point were able to break free of their moorings and move into the more maneuverable waters of Manila Bay. Others, such as *Sealion*, were not as fortunate. The submarine was hit by two bombs causing extensive damage. She flooded immediately and would never again put to sea. The heat from fires and explosions was so hot it scorched the hull of neighboring *Seadragon*, causing paint to blister. The submarine, however, survived and went on to have a long and decorated battle career during the war.[8] Although not directly hit by bombs, *Bittern* was heavily damaged from fire, near misses, and flying debris. She was later scuttled in Manila Bay.[9]

Four PBY Catalina seaplanes, each loaded with a torpedo and two bombs, were bobbing at moorings as the attack began. The planes were sitting ducks in their current location. Crewmen raced to get engines started, knowing their only hope to escape destruction was to get airborne.

Richardson had a front-row seat for the unfolding events while aboard *PT-33* in Manila Bay. His attention quickly turned to the motion of three Catalinas moving to take off. The first seaplane was on track to pass close above the 33 boat with a Zero close behind. The pair passed almost directly over the PT. "The gunners on the PBY returned the fire of the Japanese pursuit plane, but both planes passed by so quickly that we were unable to fire," he remembered of the frantic moment.

A lone American P-40 fighter suddenly appeared from the east to attack a Zero. The sailors aboard the 33 boat watched the ensuing dog fight as the planes tangled almost directly over the PT. "Although we did not see either plane fall into the sea, the low-flying PBYs made good their escape while the famous Zero fighter was very busily engaged."

One PBY, under the command of Lieutenant Harmon T. Utter, was attacked by several Zeros soon after takeoff. In a gallant duel, bow gunner Chief Boatswain Earl D. Payne was credited with shooting down a Japanese plane, the first to be accomplished in air-to-air combat by the Navy in World War II.[10]

Admiral Rockwell was among the many to take cover in a shelter ditch during the raid. "The water level prevented digging even slit trenches deeper than two or three feet," he recalled. Two Filipino yard workers were in close proximity during the attack. One was killed and the other wounded. "Both of these men were calm and in their assigned places for the air raids."[11] Rockwell escaped unharmed.

Explosions and flames rocked Stanley Point from one end to the other. A bomb hit a warehouse full of torpedoes, resulting in a spectacular explosion—and a tremendous loss for the PT boats. Fires reached a building storing small arms and ammunition, igniting a string of sporadic flare ups. Even the docks were on fire.

The men aboard *PT-33* watched helplessly from their location in the bay as various groups of Japanese planes attacked the airfields around Manila, ships in the port area, and the Cavite Navy Yard. The PT boat was about three miles from a group of merchant ships when the vessels came under attack in spectacular fashion. "Over an area of three-quarters of a mile arose almost instantaneously a forest of tall white trees of water extending one hundred feet into the air, and in some cases almost obscuring the ships," Richardson wrote. "The trees melted away almost as quickly as they had formed, leaving a dense mist of smoke and spray." A series of tremendous explosions followed, but most of the merchant ships seemed to have escaped serious damage.

The role of spectator abruptly ended for the sailors when five Japanese planes suddenly headed straight for the boats. A shout of "Here come the bastards" came from someone aboard *PT-35*, the boat carrying John Bulkeley.[12] The sailors thought the planes looked like dive bombers, but they were more likely Zeros carrying bombs, as the single-engine dive bombers did not have the range to reach the area from Formosa.

It was to be the first real action for the PTs in the Philippines, and Bulkeley knew there was no textbook strategy for what was about to happen. The attackers leveled off at about 1,500 feet. The red circles were plainly visible on the fuselages. Every sailor knew the situation—a single bomb hit would blast the little wooden boats out of the water.

The three PTs increased speed and began a series of evasive maneuvers. Tactics to defend against air attacks would be perfected by American sailors in the South Pacific later in the war, but for Bulkeley's men it truly was a baptism under fire. The helmsman aboard each PT watched for the bomb to be released just as a plane closed on a boat to make a final run, before swinging the wheel hard to make a sharp turn. The result was a bomb exploding harmlessly in the water, sending a spray over many of the sailors.

The planes made multiple passes, but were unable to land a bomb on any of the torpedo boats. The enemy regrouped in the distance, then came roaring came back for a strafing run. The attack, however, was thwarted by heavy machine-gun fire.

Machinist's Mate Second Class Joseph Chalker and Torpedoman's Mate Second Class John Houlihan each manned a 50-caliber machine-gun mount on *PT-35*. Both gunners concentrated their fire on the plane leading the formation. Bulkeley felt the pair maintained a calm, but angry, demeanor as they fired away at the attacker. Chalker continued to fire until the barrels of his gun became red hot. In only a matter of moments the plane began to trail smoke and quiver. It eventually went down in Manila Bay. Cheers quickly erupted to mark the first small victory scored by the PT sailors during the war.

Two additional Japanese planes were shot down before the attack subsided. Bulkeley gave credit to *PT-31* for the kills, but all the boats poured fire into the enemy formation. With heavy gunfire coming from various areas in the bay, however, other vessels likely contributed to the shoot downs.

A group of planes later passed almost directly over *PT-33*. A single bomb fell towards the small target, but landed in the speeding boat's wake almost 300 yards behind. Richardson momentarily thought it would have been a hit had the PT been going at a slower speed. "The rest of the afternoon was spent dodging formations and observing the various bombings in a mobile ringside seat," he explained. At one point, the boat had to make a radical turn to avoid hitting the periscope of an American submarine.

All of Bulkeley's boats survived the air raid intact. After the Japanese planes departed, an eerie silence seemed to fall upon Manila Bay. The sailors, however, could plainly see the huge plume of black smoke rising from Stanley Point.

Admiral Hart had watched the attack unfold from the top of the Marsman Building in downtown Manila. He was in a helpless position. The admiral was unable to intervene and could now only stare at the rising smoke. The loss of Cavite was the worst-case scenario for his Asiatic Fleet.

The attack on the Stanley Point naval facilities lasted for almost two hours. The entire base and a part of the adjacent city of Cavite was a continuous wall of flames when it ended. The burning conflagration produced clouds of billowing black smoke visible from miles around. The naval ammunition dump, which had so worried Rockwell, had miraculously escaped a direct hit. There was a high risk, however, that the fires could cause it to explode.

The base and adjoining streets were littered with dead bodies. About 1,000 Filipinos were thought to have perished in the raid. Marine Private First Class Thomas Wetherington became the first of many in that branch of service to lose his life in the defense of the Philippines.[13]

The valiant effort of American personnel and Filipino yard workers was not enough to contain the raging fires. "Every effort was made to keep the fires away from the naval ammunition depot and the few buildings which were still standing (including the Commandantia) but frequent shifts of wind, lack of equipment, loss of the power house, and fire mains made this impossible," Rockwell wrote. A blood-stained uniform later revealed the admiral's personal involvement in the effort to help the wounded.

Robert Kelly's three PTs were still at sea near Mariveles, far from the devastation across Manila Bay. The sound of cursing sailors permeated his boat as the executive officer looked skyward to see the Japanese bombers departing the area in the same tight formations. It looked to him as if not a single plane was missing. Kelly was seething as he still wondered what had happened to the American fighters. The rising black smoke was plainly visible from the area around Cavite. A sickening feeling overtook him as he thought about the outcome of the raid.

Bulkeley cautiously brought his three boats back to Stanley Point after the air raid ended, dodging flotsam and floating dead bodies in the process. It was a hellish scene of fires, carnage, and devastation. The destruction was so complete it seemed almost unbelievable.

With the screams of rescuers and the moans of the grievously wounded serving as a macabre backdrop, the squadron commander and his men made their way through twisted wreckage and grisly scenes of bodies and body parts. The smell of death permeated the air. Bulkeley caught a brief glimpse of Admiral Rockwell working feverishly to direct the recovery effort.

The PTs were soon turned into floating ambulances as men loaded wounded aboard their boats for transportation to area hospitals. "We could hardly keep on our feet, for blood is as slippery as crude oil—and the aprons of the hospital attendants were so blood-spattered they looked like butchers," Bulkeley recalled.[14] The rescue work took much of the afternoon.

The PT sailors learned their living quarters were completely destroyed in the attack. All of the squadron's men, including those of the base force, were thought to have survived the raid. "However, everything insofar as personal effects that was not on the boats was destroyed or plundered," Richardson wrote. "This applied to officers as well as men, with few exceptions." The sailors had no choice but to go forward with the limited supplies they had on the boats.

Efforts to control the raging fires at Cavite continued into the evening hours. Rockwell still feared the fires would ignite an explosion at the ammunition depot. He gave the order to abandon the navy yard and surrounding area at about 9:00 pm. All personnel departed the immediate area, with orders to gather at a nearby school. An armed guard was posted to prevent unauthorized return to the base.

Daylight on December 11 found the fires still burning uncontrollably, revealing the full scope of the destruction. The base facilities were practically demolished. "Cavite was wiped off the map," Commissioner Sayre later wrote. "The Commandantia was burned to the ground."[15] The largest American naval base west of Pearl Harbor was gone.

From the burning flames of Cavite came some sobering realizations from Admiral Hart. After later reviewing damage reports and conferring with Rockwell, Hart reported to officials in Washington that Manila was untenable as a naval operating area due to the destruction of Cavite and complete Japanese air superiority. He ordered as much equipment and supplies as possible to be salvaged and dispersed among various locations.

Hart also made some important decisions regarding the Navy's role in the campaign. He ordered additional ships to head south to safer waters, but vowed to keep up the defense of the Philippines as best he could with the remaining resources. "[I] am still resolved to operate submarines from here as long as possible with primary objective of damaging important enemy ships," Hart wrote.[16] He doubted, however, that the submersibles would be able to seriously disrupt the Japanese invasion. An assortment of small vessels, including Bulkeley's PT boats, was to stay in area for local defense.

The destruction of Cavite would have far-reaching effects for the operations of Motor Torpedo Boat Squadron 3. Gone were 233 spare torpedoes and thousands of gallons of high-octane fuel.[17] "With the bombing of the Cavite Navy Yard … all spare parts were destroyed," Bulkeley wrote.[18] The losses included one of the squadron's ten spare engines and all of the smoke generators. The latter had just arrived and had not yet been installed aboard the PTs.

With Cavite finished as an operating base, Bulkeley made ready to depart the area for Mariveles. After their work of transferring the wounded was completed, he directed his men to collect any useful items that could be found to put aboard the boats, including food supplies. Rockwell declined an offer to leave with the PTs, saying it was his job to stay behind.

Richardson remembered many of the passengers aboard *PT-33* were happy to be departing. "The base force was particularly glad to be away from the navy yard, and gave us a graphic description of the wholesale bombing and burning of the navy yard," he recalled. The trio of torpedo boats then set out to cross Manila Bay, leaving the carnage and still-burning base behind. "The largest and fiercest fire was the navy yard and immense volumes of black smoke billowed slowly into the air; it was then carried by the wind as a low hanging cloud which was visible stretching over an area of 20 or 30 miles."

Bulkeley's boats were to join up with those of the executive officer. The PTs were journeying to a new home and an uncertain future.

CHAPTER 11

A steady flow of bad news about the war kept streaming into General MacArthur's headquarters in Manila as each day of the conflict progressed. The Japanese struck two sizeable blows to the Allied cause in the Pacific on December 10, 1941—the very day Admiral Hart's naval facilities at Cavite were destroyed.

The first blow came about 1,500 miles to the east at Guam. The closest American territory to the Philippines fell to Japanese invaders. The token force of fewer than 500 defenders, armed with nothing larger than 30-caliber machine guns, surrendered after a short fight.[1] The loss severed the most direct supply route between Manila and Hawaii. The Philippines were becoming more isolated by the day.

An even larger catastrophe befell British naval forces about 1,500 miles to the southwest. Admiral Sir Tom Phillips departed Singapore with the battleship *Prince of Wales*, battle cruiser *Repulse* and four destroyers at the onset of hostilities to search for a Japanese convoy reported off Malaya. The Royal Navy force was without air cover when it was attacked by a swarm of Japanese planes. Phillips was among the many sailors to perish when both of the large ships were sunk.

The news was not much better elsewhere as time advanced further into December. Hong Kong was under attack by air and land. The British territory would surrender on Christmas Day. The enemy was moving against Malaya in great force. An attempted Japanese invasion of Wake Island was repulsed on December 11, but a follow-up attack was expected at any time.

The American defenders back in the Philippines were coming to grips with their situation after suffering a series of tremendous setbacks after only three days of conflict. Japanese troops now had a foothold on northern Luzon and a bigger amphibious attack was expected soon. Enemy naval forces were consolidating positions around the islands, preparing to block any supplies or reinforcements.

American airpower was largely decimated, with Clark Field, the largest base, deemed unsuitable for bomber operations. All of the remaining B-17s, except for one, were ordered south to safer surroundings at Del Monte Field on Mindanao. Only 30 operational fighters were left. The small number was unable to provide adequate air cover for any military unit or facility. The decision was made to use the planes chiefly for reconnaissance purposes.[2] American air operations began to dwindle as Japanese superiority in the sky took a firm grip over the Philippines.

John Bulkeley's three PT boats pulled into Mariveles Harbor after leaving behind the inferno of fire and destruction at Cavite. The sailors were exhausted from the arduous work of evacuating the wounded. A putrid odor of blood still permeated the boats, reminding the men of the ordeal.

The boats later moved to nearby Sisiman Cove. The secluded small inlet on the southern tip of the Bataan Peninsula, originally found by Robert Kelly, was to be the torpedo squadron's new operational base. Kelly showed the cove to the squadron commander soon after he arrived.

The area was home to a native fishing village that was largely abandoned, except for a few remaining families who had chosen to stay. The PT men constructed the base themselves, making do with the limited resources the area had to offer. It was a functional outpost, but quite different than the comfortable accommodations back at Cavite.

Nipa huts served as the sailors' new accommodations ashore, although it was common for the men to stay aboard the boats to be ready in case of an air attack. The small single-room structures, standing 4 or 5 feet above the ground on stilts, were made of bamboo with a thatched straw roof. A small sand box in the corner provided a place for a cooking fire, with the smoke wafting out though the open windows. About 20 such huts were in the immediate area.

An empty goat slaughterhouse measuring 100 by 30 feet with a concrete floor was cleaned up and made into squadron headquarters. The smell never entirely went away, but it was habitable. An old fishing pier was available for use by the boats as needed. Fresh water was piped in from a spring somewhere further inland. A wooden plank transformed into a makeshift sign dubbed the area Sisiman Bay Yacht Club.

Iliff Richardson remembered the mooring arrangements as "One boat was stationed at the pier to maintain communications with Corregidor by telephone and the rest of the boats anchored out in the bay, spread 75 to 100 yards apart for protection; visual communication connected the anchored boats with the one at the pier."[3] Bulkeley wanted the PTs to be able to operate at the fastest possible speeds. He ordered each boat to move any unnecessary equipment to the beach. "Radios, electric fans, rubber mats, electrical cooking equipment, excess spare parts, and personal equipment were then immediately taken off the boats and stowed ashore," Richardson wrote.

The burdensome task of hauling in the boat's anchor by hand every time PT-33 needed to get under way was quickly solved using old-fashioned ingenuity. The anchor was firmly set on the bottom of the sea and an empty 5-gallon can attached to the other end of the line. "Thus, we merely threw the can over the side to get under way, and fished it in with a boat hook when we returned," recalled Henry Brantingham.[4]

All six of Bulkeley's PT boats were now operating together for the first time since the hectic initial day of the war. Edward DeLong came by to give Kelly the details of the attack on Cavite. It was only then that the executive officer learned the full extent of the destruction.

Even though the squadron now had a new base, the men still had to contend with a host of problems. All of the spare parts were destroyed at Cavite, along with the personnel effects of the sailors. Only nine spare engines, scattered around the Manila Bay area for safe keeping, remained available. The remoteness of the Sisiman Cove base meant it did not have the necessary winches and equipment needed to make large repairs, such as changing an engine.

The PT men soon uncovered a serious problem with the fuel supply. The primary source of fuel for the boats was the two barges that had been moved from Cavite to Mariveles during the first days of the conflict. The pair was subsequently moved away from land as a precaution. The gasoline was in large drums. The slow process of transferring it to the boats was tedious and strenuous work.

The critical supply of gas was sabotaged. Bulkeley wrote it "was found to contain a soluble wax deposit in large quantities. This foreign substance clogged gas strainers and carburetor jets to such extent as to cause most unreliable operating, necessitating the cleaning of carburetors and strainers hourly."[5]

Bulkeley and Kelly immediately took a boat out to the barges after the problem was brought to their attention. The two Filipino guards who had been hired to protect the supply were searched by several sailors. Kelly discovered blocks of paraffin wax when he overturned some bags of rice the guards had brought aboard. "Turn these two bastards over to the military police," Bulkeley barked, suggesting he should just shoot them himself.[6] American guards were soon watching over the precious fuel supply.

The gasoline problem would hamper PT boat operations for the remainder of the campaign. "It was never known when a boat engine would stop," Bulkeley added. "It eventually became necessary to open the gas tanks and thoroughly clean [each tank] with the limited means available."

Each boat used whatever materials were available to deal with the fuel problem, with crewmen spending untold hours cleaning equipment. An old felt hat aboard *PT-33* was used to filter the fuel as it was poured into the boat's tanks. It was dangerous and laborious work, as any small spark or static shock could cause an immediate explosion. Kelly equated it to playing with dynamite.

Amidst all of the other problems, the sailors soon learned they would be eating less. Navy officials already foresaw a coming food shortage and cut rations down to two meals a day. It went into effect on December 16.[7]

Admiral Rockwell gave Bulkeley a set of standing orders to check in with him on a daily basis. Various naval functions under the admiral's command were scattered around the bay area as a result of the destruction at Cavite. As Bulkeley went to visit Rockwell or his chief of staff Harold Ray, the boat crews performed maintenance work or went on scavenging missions. The men were looking for food, gasoline or anything else that could help them survive and keep the boats moving.

The boats were assigned a variety of duties. "In general, operations were divided into two parts: (1) Offensive operations and (2) Auxiliary services," Bulkeley wrote.[8] The latter entailed escorting submarines and merchantmen in and out of Manila Bay. It also included using the boats to provide a messenger service between Bataan, Corregidor, and Manila. "In this manner commands could be kept in closer contact and secret correspondence [sent] with greater security and speed," Richardson added. He remembered one boat was eventually stationed at the navy landing in Manila and another at Corregidor.

The offensive portion of operations involved regular patrols. "Routine patrols by single boats on the east and west coast of Bataan and in Verde Island Passage, alone or in company with an inshore patrol ship for communication purposes," Bulkeley explained. The patrols were needed to fill the reconnaissance void created by the dwindling number of available planes.

Prior to the start of the war, it was a common practice for PTs to patrol in groups of two or three boats to be able to provide mutual assistance should one run into trouble. The plight of Bulkeley's squadron, with only six boats and gasoline in short supply, often allowed for only a single boat available for patrols. A coastal craft or one of the three small Filipino patrol boats usually accompanied a PT. The old destroyers *Pillsbury* and *Peary* also participated in the patrols before departing the area for southern waters.[9]

One night a false alarm sent all of the available boats out on a voyage to search for Japanese ships reported in the vicinity of Subic Bay. The crack and roar of starting engines shot through Sisiman Cove as the PTs raced out. "The boats were steaming in battle condition, with all hands on the lookout for a black form on the dark horizon," Richardson remembered. It was a moonless night. The crewmen aboard *PT-33* seemed eager to get a chance to attack the Japanese.

The black night allowed Richardson to take in an interesting phenomenon. "In tropical seas, millions of small phosphorescent glowing fish swim near the surface of the water and at high speed the action of the ultrafast spinning propellers excite these little organisms so that they turn on their little lamps to full brilliance," he wrote. "This luminous wake directly behind the boat rises several feet in the air depending upon the speed the boat is making and the illuminated spray goes much higher."[10]

The glowing wake at times seemed to become more vivid or would slightly dim based on the concentration of the small fish. Richardson worried it would help the enemy find his boat. "At times it is bright enough to be seen for some distance and, coupled with the roar of the engines, would direct the eyes and ears of the enemy to our actual position." It did not, however, play any role in the outcome of this particular voyage.

The patrol yielded no sign of the enemy. The boats rendezvoused at daybreak as per the prearranged plan before returning to base as a group. The PTs spent much of the morning taking aboard fuel. The boats were again ready for action in the early afternoon. The string of fruitless patrols continued.

One morning Bulkeley received orders to report to Admiral Rockwell in Manila as soon as possible. Robert Kelly joined him as the 34 boat departed for the voyage across the bay. The PT had just cleared the minefields when the pair noticed an armada of ships—vessels of all types and sizes—rushing out into the bay from the Manila harbor area. Bulkeley quickly saw the reason for the mass exodus as he looked up to see an approaching formation of Japanese bombers. Much to his astonishment, two more formations followed the initial group.

No American fighters appeared to challenge the enemy. The sailors were finally accepting the idea that any planes spotted in the future were probably always going to be Japanese. *PT-34* changed course to keep a safe distance from the attackers. She then slowly made her way around the perimeter of the bay to get to Manila.

Bulkeley and Kelly arrived safely at the Marsman Building. Once inside, they spotted Rockwell through an open door in conversation with some officers. A map of Luzon and the surrounding waters was posted on the wall. Rockwell had summoned Bulkeley because he was considering using three of his boats to stage an attack on Japanese ships off the west coast of Luzon. It would be a dangerous mission. The admiral had since, however, changed his mind, dismissing the attack as a suicide mission.

The trip, though, was not a complete waste of time. The 34 boat was sent away with a load of files and records. The naval headquarters was getting ready for a move to Corregidor.

The next few days were somewhat quiet for the PT sailors. From their position in Sisiman Cove, they routinely watched Japanese bombers move across the sky to hit unknown targets out of sight in the distance. Bulkeley managed to scrounge up some basic supplies—such as shirts, underwear, and toothpaste—to replace the items lost when the crew quarters burned at Cavite. Each boat was also given two razors for shaving.

Nothing unusual was recorded as having taken place at the PT base in Sisiman Cove on the night of December 16. In a matter of only a few hours, however, some members of the squadron would be thrust into the midst of a maritime tragedy. Passengers were piling aboard the S.S. *Corregidor* across the bay on the Manila waterfront. She was the fastest ship of a small group of inter-island steamers operating in the Philippines. The vessel had a long life behind her, including participating in World War I as the British seaplane tender *Engadine*.

She pulled away from the dock at about 8:00 pm bound for the southern Philippines. The vessel was under the control of an experienced captain who had previously made multiple trips through the bay. An accurate record was not kept as to the number of the passengers aboard for the voyage, but it is thought to have been between 1,200 and 1,500.

Most were civilians hoping to escape the war in the north. The total, however, included some Filipino soldiers. Artillery pieces and ammunition bound for army units on Mindanao were also on the ship.

The first hours of December 17 found *Corregidor* passing her namesake island near the entrance of Manila Bay in moonless conditions. She was now dangerously close to the defensive minefields that had been in place since the summer. The vessel, however, had not been properly cleared for departure. As a result, an electronic mechanism to temporarily deactivate the mines was not working.[11]

The steamer was suddenly rocked by a large explosion on the starboard side near her stern—she had struck a mine. At the time she was passing near La Monja Island, almost directly south of Sisiman Cove and west of Corregidor. The overcrowded vessel began to sink immediately.

Mr and Mrs Elton "Jack" Fee were among the seven Americans thought to be aboard.[12] The pair was returning to Mindanao, where he was a manager for the Standard Oil Company, from a business trip to Manila. "We picked ourselves up, put on our life belts, and in the utter darkness left our cabin and hurried to the deck above," Dode Fee later wrote. "There was chaos—no chance of getting into a life boat." The Fees made it topside, where the couple became separated, and then jumped into the darkness below like hundreds of other passengers. Searchlights from nearby Corregidor were soon plying the waters, trying to determine what was happening.

The explosion attracted the attention of the sleeping sailors at Sisiman Cove. Iliff Richardson remembered the sound as "a powerful muffled explosion followed by a second explosion two seconds later." The men could only make out a faint outline of a ship and some flickering lights on the surface. Bulkeley immediately ordered three boats ready to get under way. PTs 32, 34, and 35 set out into the bay to investigate. The boats were approaching the edge of the minefield when the water abruptly became thick with fuel oil. Bobbing survivors then suddenly began to appear.

Bulkeley was aboard *PT-32* and recalled entering a literal sea of people. Cries for help seemed to be coming out of the dark night from all directions. The sailors quickly jumped into rescue mode, rigging ladders and tossing lines over the sides. About ten or 12 Filipinos grappled for every line tossed over the side.[13] The PT men worked until the point of exhaustion pulling oil-soaked survivors aboard their boats.

The small craft, designed to operate with only about a dozen men aboard, were quickly filling up with rescued passengers. Many of the survivors had been sleeping when the ship began to sink and were clad only in night attire. A Filipino woman in need of clothes was pulled aboard one boat. She was given a clean white navy uniform and sent below with some other passengers to rest. A crewman later gave her a slap on the back, thinking she was a fellow PT sailor taking a comfortable nap while the others were engaged in the grueling rescue work. He quickly left the dimly lit compartment, however, after seeing his mistake.[14]

Dode Fee had been in the water for about three hours when a PT approached. A rope was quickly tossed in her direction. "I was so tired and cold, but I hung on and they grabbed me and hauled me aboard," she wrote of the experience. "I was their first survivor, and what a surprise I must have been, [a] tall American woman covered in fuel oil and a life belt and not much else." Mr Fee also survived the sinking. The couple, along with their young children, made it through the war as civilian internees of the Japanese.

The search and rescue continued until daylight revealed there were no more survivors in the water. Many of the passengers were delivered to Corregidor, but some were transferred to the freighter S.S. *Si Kiang* in Mariveles Harbor.

The three PT boats pulled aboard a total of 296 *Corregidor* survivors, of whom seven perished. "This was done over a minefield and [we] were the only boats engaged in the rescue work," Bulkeley wrote of the operation. "*PT-32* rescued 196 survivors in one boat, in addition to her crew."[15] The total number of those lost in the *Corregidor* disaster has never been accurately established.

The boats returned to Sisiman Cove during the early morning hours. There was no time, however, for the exhausted crewmen to rest. Many areas of the PTs, including the decks, passageways, and below-deck compartments were splattered with oil from the survivors. Clean-up work began immediately.

Robert Kelly did not participate in the rescue operation. He was, however, at the hospital on Corregidor when the survivors began to arrive. Many were severely burned and in terrible agony.

Kelly had been nursing a sore index finger ever since making the initial trip over to Mariveles. He snagged it on a piece of equipment aboard his boat during the voyage. Kelly saw a Navy doctor after it became painfully swollen and infected, but had resisted any additional help. Bulkeley finally ordered him to visit the hospital on Corregidor, where he was admitted as a patient.

The facility was located underground in a tunnel on the fortified island. An army doctor gave Kelly sulfur pills and warned he could lose his arm due to the delay of getting to the hospital. Additional treatment included packing the arm in hot-water bottles and bed rest.

Kelly conversed with various wounded soldiers during the hospital visit. He later heard first-hand accounts of the fighting from tankers and pilots. As the only Navy man in the ward, he was also at the receiving end of some pointed questions of why the Navy had not been able to deliver reinforcements. He of course did not have the answer.

Kelly also met army nurse Beulah "Peggy" Greenwalt during his hospital stay. The two soon became friends, seeing each other frequently. Kelly later accompanied Greenwalt to a dance put on for the nurses, even though she was dating an army officer at the time. She later dined with the PT officers at the Sisiman Cove base.

The executive officer would be sidelined for about a month. He would be sorely missed by his squadron mates as they struggled to begin operations against the enemy. Ensign Barron Chandler temporarily took over as the boat captain of *PT-34*.[16]

CHAPTER 12

The Japanese assault on the Philippines continued unabated while Bulkeley and his men were getting acquainted with their new base. Air raids persisted throughout the month of December against feeble American resistance. Japanese planes were in complete control of the sky. Roaming aerial marauders attacked any target deemed suitable—both on land and at sea.

The naval station at Olongapo in Subic Bay was struck after enemy fighters shadowed a group of PBYs returning from patrol. Seven of the seaplanes were destroyed, prompting Admiral Hart to order the remnants of the squadron south. A small number of the damaged seaplanes, four of which were capable of flying, stayed behind. The primary means of naval reconnaissance was now gone. Olongapo was subsequently abandoned as a base, with all personnel transferred to Mariveles. The area was then mined to prevent the Japanese from using the harbor.[1]

Japanese forces struck from another direction on December 12. Troops came ashore at Legaspi on the far southeastern coast of Luzon. The landing was near the strategic San Bernardino Strait, where large ships could transverse the Philippines from east to west. The operation was unopposed—the nearest American and Filipino troops were about 150 miles away.[2] Japanese soldiers quickly moved inland and took control of an airfield. American defenders now had to contend with enemy forces on both ends of Luzon.

Japanese bombers paid a return visit to Stanley Point on December 19, pounding the already heavily damaged naval facilities. Bombs fell over a wide area to cause even more destruction. Admiral Rockwell noted "12 Marines were killed, most of the aviation gasoline, which had been dispersed in drums, was destroyed, the water supply and mains broken up, the high-power radio station completely put out of commission (one tower knocked down, direct hit on the power plant), and most of the houses burned." The fires from the gas and oil became so fierce it was decided to simply attempt to hold them in check instead of trying to extinguish the inferno.

The radio tower loss was a critical blow to the already reeling Philippine defenders. It left the Americans with only unsecure short-wave radio capabilities for communications around Manila Bay. The fast messenger service provided by Bulkeley's PT boats suddenly took on added importance.

The next day Admiral Hart directed Rockwell to move his headquarters to Corregidor. Rockwell left behind a captain to oversee Stanley Point until it became time to evacuate the area. A second officer was designated to take command of Mariveles.

The long-awaited main Japanese amphibious assault began during the early morning hours of December 22, when 85 transports under heavy escort steamed into Lingayen Gulf. The large body of water on Luzon's west coast was an ideal landing point. The Japanese hoped to advance inland onto the central plain of Luzon and then drive south directly to Manila about 125 miles away.

The American submarine *Stingray* sighted the invasion fleet the night before, but failed to attack. Hart quickly rushed six additional undersea boats to the area. Only *S-38*—a single American submarine—managed to sink a Japanese ship.[3] *Hayo Maru* was torpedoed just before 8 am during a tense string of action in the gulf. The shallow waters of the area offered natural protection to the invading ships, while faulty torpedoes likely contributed to the poor performance of the submarines.

A series of minor air attacks—all that could be mustered by the decimated American air groups—caused no damage. The invasion continued unhindered. Thousands of Japanese troops were soon swarming ashore at multiple points on the east side of the gulf.

General MacArthur's land commanders correctly assumed Lingayen Gulf would be the site of the main Japanese invasion. With the enemy already ashore in the far northern portion of Luzon, MacArthur directed General Wainwright to focus on defending the area from Lingayen Gulf south. Two Filipino infantry divisions—poorly trained and lacking modern equipment, firepower, and communication gear—had moved into the area in an attempt to stop the expected assault.

At only one beach did Japanese troops come under fire from Filipino forces waiting for their arrival with one 50-caliber and a few 30-caliber machine guns. The latter weapons fell silent early in the action, probably owing to faulty ammunition.[4] The gunfire initially caused heavy casualties, but the Japanese soldiers pushed forward. The Filipino units quickly withdrew after the invaders gained a firm foothold ashore. The landings were unopposed at the other sites.

MacArthur's plan to stop the Japanese at the beaches had completely failed. Enemy units pushed inland after consolidating their positions near the landing areas. Filipino forces fell back as the enemy advanced. Japanese forces were moving south on Route 3 in a matter of only a couple days. The hard-surfaced two-way road, heading south directly to Manila, was in excellent condition. The enemy had to be slowed—and quickly—or the Americans would soon be facing a full-fledged rout.

General MacArthur initially estimated he was facing close to 100,000 Japanese soldiers in the battle for the northern part of Luzon. The number, however, was greatly overstated. Although his assessment was inaccurate, the general still faced a formidable enemy force. Just over 43,000 Japanese landed during the span of about a week. The soldiers were members of well-equipped army units, enjoying the full support of artillery, tanks, and almost complete control of the sky.[5]

Wainwright's forces in northern Luzon seemed incapable of stopping the advancing invaders. His over-matched and outgunned troops were quickly in full retreat south. MacArthur's aggressive plan to meet an enemy invasion with offensive action at the point of incursion remained unchanged in the initial days after the Lingayen landing, even as Japanese troops were swarming ashore and advancing inland.

MacArthur then suddenly seemed quickly to lose confidence in the ability of his forces to stop the enemy advance. If Luzon fell into Japanese hands, then all of the Philippines would be lost in short order. The general knew that something fast and dramatic was needed to stem the rising Japanese tide.

On December 23, the general abruptly decided on a revision of strategy. MacArthur abandoned his hard-hitting beach defense plan. He instead chose to withdraw his Luzon forces into the Bataan Peninsula and the fortified island of Corregidor. He notified all commanders with the simple message "WPO-3 is in effect."[6]

The plan was an updated version of the longstanding War Plan Orange concept approved in April 1941. It was incorporated into the larger set of Rainbow 5 plans calling for the primary focus of the war effort to be against Germany, with a more defensive posture in the Pacific.[7] WPO-3 was well known to all American commanders who had been in the Philippines prior to the start of the war. The old plan, representing the original American contingency for military forces in the Philippines during a war with Japan, was to withdraw into the Bataan Peninsula and wait for help to arrive. That help, however, could only be provided by the now crippled Pacific Fleet.

Army headquarters and the Philippine national government could not stay in Manila under the new strategy. Both would have to move to Corregidor as soon as possible. MacArthur had previously notified President Quezon about such a possibility, advising him to be ready to move there on four hours' notice.[8] Departing the capital city did not come easily to the Americans and Filipinos alike. MacArthur, Quezon, and Commissioner Sayre, along with staff and family members, arrived at Corregidor on December 24.[9]

MacArthur was faced with a new crisis only one day after making the decision to change strategy. Lingayen Gulf was only the first of two large Japanese landings planned for Luzon. The amphibious forces struck again at Lamon Bay on December 24. The area on the southeast coast of Luzon was much closer to Manila than Lingayen Gulf, but required an overland trip through mountainous terrain to reach the capital.

About 7,000 Japanese soldiers came ashore at three different points after making a long voyage from islands near Japan. The enemy troops faced stiff resistance at only one of the landing points. As with the Lingayen Gulf invasion, the Filipino defenders were incapable of stopping the enemy. A small number of American planes joined the action, but were unable to make any impact on the invasion. A Japanese pincer movement was now advancing on Manila from the north and south.

Further north, General George Parker was put in charge of the newly formed Bataan Defense Force. He was given two Filipino infantry divisions to augment the soldiers already in the area. Parker's orders were to build up defensive positions on the peninsula in advance of the retreating Luzon defenders.

The plan for withdrawing forces from the north and south into Bataan involved difficult movements and precise timing. The movements of various units had to be coordinated to provide mutual cover. "The hazardous timing of this movement was its most notable feature," MacArthur later wrote of the retreat: "one slip in the coordinated maneuver, and the motor columns from southern Luzon would have been cut off and cornered in Manila."[10] If one group was to arrive at Bataan before the other, or the Japanese captured a key road or bridge, the result could be a complete disaster.

The most critical task of slowing the enemy advance initially fell on the Northern Luzon Force. Wainwright turned to a regiment of the 26th Cavalry for help. The unit was part of the well-trained Philippine Scouts. It was considered one of the best units in the islands. The force, however, lacked artillery support and many of its armored cars.

Poor coordination, however, plagued Wainwright's forces as the chaotic events unfolded. A group of light tanks, capable of providing mutual support, were not properly synchronized with the scouts. The armor was not even under Wainwright's control, but reported to a separate tank commander.[11]

The Philippine Scouts were only able to temporarily delay the advancing enemy. It was long enough, however, to allow the retreating

Filipino forces to cross the Agno River. From there it would be nearly 150 miles to get to Bataan. The waterway was the first in a series of predetermined defensive positions on the road south labeled D1 through D5. MacArthur's troops had practiced manning these lines before the war. The main goal was to delay the Japanese long enough for the escape of the forces in southern Luzon. It was also to buy time to allow as many supplies as possible to be transferred to Bataan.

The first four defensive lines could only provide token resistance as a result of the rapid Japanese movements. Wainwright's troops delayed only long enough to force the enemy to stop and prepare for a major attack. The defensive position was then abandoned as troops fell back to the next line.

Defenders prepared for a more determined stand at the southern-most line, D5, taking advantage of some mountainous areas and other favorable terrain, including impassable swampland. The line was positioned east-west across Luzon just north of the entrance to the Bataan Peninsula, stretching for about 20 miles. It included the main army base Fort Stotsenburg. It was critical that the position be held to allow the forces from the south to pass through the narrow corridor into Bataan. Once the southern troops moved behind the D5 line, it would swing south to close like an iron gate across the top of the peninsula.

The hasty change of strategy created major problems in the American supply chain. Although MacArthur enacted the old Orange War Plan, the supply situation no longer reflected the strategy. Under the general's prewar scheme to defend all of Luzon supplies were moved out of Bataan, as had been required under the Orange plan, and scattered among various forward locations close to the beaches. Now it was critical that the same supplies be moved back to Bataan quickly.

Officials scrambled to get stores from various points around Manila Bay onto Bataan by any means. In the forward areas, however, it was difficult to impossible. Filipino transportation workers fled ahead of the advancing Japanese or abandoned their posts altogether. Some truck drivers simply took off in the stampede to get to Bataan—with empty trucks.

Filipino laws prohibited the movement of foodstuffs from one province to another. MacArthur and Quezon insisted the laws be enforced in what can only be considered a blundering move.[12] Much of the supplies from central and northern Luzon never made it to Bataan.[13] MacArthur's soldiers would pay dearly in the months to come as a result of the supply shortage.

MacArthur was determined to save Manila, the city he so cherished, not from the Japanese but from complete devastation. Retreating forces from the south were to simply pass through the city on their way to Bataan. The general notified his staff that Manila would be declared an open city.

CHAPTER 13

The daily routine for the PT sailors continued without much change as MacArthur's army units were in headlong retreat across Luzon. "All boats were confined to patrols at night, both inside the bay and outside along the coast, in addition to duties at Corregidor as fast messenger-passenger boats. Each PT was relayed so that we should get one night patrol and one night rest (with variations for special missions)," Iliff Richardson wrote. "The daytime was spent in upkeep, overhauling carburetors, fuel pumps and gas strainers, and refueling from the gas drums."[1] The duties quickly became dull and repetitive.

False sightings of enemy vessels near the Bataan coast, many originating from jittery lookouts, increased with the Japanese successes on the battlefield. The result was many futile patrols where the sailors searched for an imaginary enemy.

An exception seemed to have finally come toward the end of December. A report from the army of three unidentified ships off the Luzon coast near Bataan reached Admiral Hart's headquarters at about 9:00 pm on December 21. The exact origin of the sighting is unclear, but troops had been moved to the area as a precaution. The admiral directed Bulkeley to immediately send three PT boats out to investigate and attack anything sighted. It proved to be just another false alarm.

Night patrols into the Verde Island Passageway became commonplace late in December. American commanders could not discount the possibility of a seaborne attack on Manila Bay as Japanese forces on northern

Luzon rapidly advanced towards Manila. Any such move coming from the south would require enemy ships to pass through the Verde Island Passageway. Located about 50 miles south and slightly east of the entrance to Manila Bay, the narrow waterway separated Luzon from the adjacent island of Mindoro.

A four-stack American destroyer often accompanied the PT boats on the voyage south. Richardson remembered one such patrol. "At sunset on the 22nd of December the PTs 31 and 33 got under way in company with the destroyer *Pope* and proceeded south to Verde Island Passage," he wrote. Richardson felt it was a considerable advantage to be operating with a destroyer, especially for the extended range the vessel provided. "The destroyer's wake provides waves which make it possible, with proper PT boat handling, to be constantly before the next crest of a wave and as a consequence always going downhill like a surf board."

The small force split apart upon arrival in the assigned patrol area. The destroyer remained in the center of the passageway, while the PT boats split up to cruise through the northern and southern areas. "Radio communications were set up with the destroyer in case of our discovery of enemy ships," Richardson continued. "The sea was very calm, being protected by the coast." Lookouts on all the boats carefully plied the water looking for any sign of movement.

It proved to be an uneventful night. No enemy activity was sighted during the patrol. "At daybreak the 31 and 33 boats proceeded back to Mariveles independently of the *Pope*."

The PT men tried to keep up on the latest updates on the progress of the war. Some of the information came all the way from the United States. "We use to listen to broadcasts from San Francisco as war news from the Pacific came over the air," Henry Brantingham later wrote. He remembered hearing regular updates as to how many Japanese planes were shot down over Corregidor, with the total eventually reaching over a hundred. "Although I watched every day, and although Sisiman Cove was only a few miles from the action over Corregidor, I never saw one plane go down." The numbers did not seem to make sense. "Perhaps the broadcasts were good for the morale of the folks back home," he concluded.[2]

Watching the steady stream of enemy bombers became predictable, but the sight of so many Japanese planes was anything but good for morale. "They seemed to use this cove as a navigational checkpoint," Brantingham recalled, after repeatedly seeing the planes fly almost directly overhead.[3] It was only a matter of time before the bombers hit Mariveles. It happened just before Christmas, with the S.S. *Si Kiang* as the target.

The Free French freighter was bound for Indochina with a load of gasoline and flour when she was requisitioned by American authorities, most likely due to her valuable cargo, and sent to Mariveles under control of a marine guard. She was moored about 50 yards offshore. The unloading of her cargo during daylight hours may have attracted Japanese attention.

Several PT boats were in the immediate area when the attack occurred. Richardson spotted nine Japanese bombers passing over Mariveles Harbor from his position aboard *PT-33*. It appeared as if the planes were making a trial run. Looking through binoculars, he could distinctly make out the solid red circles against the backdrop of the silver fuselages. The planes circled to the west. "It first appeared as though they were going to bomb Corregidor Island, but on the second lap around, the bombers again flew directly in line with the *Si Kiang*, which was 400 yards from the PT-boats," Richardson remembered. "When these medium bombers were at an angle of about 40 degrees relative to the *Si Kiang*, through the binoculars we could see the bomb-bay doors in the nine planes open."

A stick of bombs was suddenly unleashed from each plane. "The planes closed their bomb doors and began again to circle to the right to avoid the small black bursts of antiaircraft shells appearing in front of them." A whistling sound could be plainly heard as the bombs seemed to pick up speed. Richardson could see the attackers were aiming for *Si Kiang*. He thought the freighter would soon be in for a bad time.

Pillars of water shot up all around the vessel as the sound of explosions cracked through the air. "Almost immediately the zi-ing plop of bits of bomb fragments hitting the water around the 33 was seen and heard by all on aboard." It was a new experience for those aboard the boat. "This was the first bombing the 33 had seen at close range, and when the bombs start to fall everyone has a feeling that he wants to do something, anything—but at least something." Boatswain Mate Second Class Ernest Pierson did do something—he jumped into the water. "It was necessary to take a boat hook and haul him back aboard," Richardson remembered.

The freighter miraculously survived the crescendo of bombs. The planes, however, were not yet through. The group circled around for another pass. "This time they were flying at an altitude which exceeded the effective range of our antiaircraft guns," Richardson continued. Two bombs squarely hit the freighter, setting her on fire. PTs 31 and 41 went alongside the stricken vessel almost immediately to render aid and take off the wounded for transfer to Corregidor. Two men were killed and three wounded in the attack.

The fire was brought under control, but the freighter was later abandoned. She eventually settled on the bottom of the harbor. The valuable fuel had already been removed, but the load of flour was lost with the ship.

Admiral Hart was preparing to leave the Philippines altogether while Bulkeley's PT boats were conducting fruitless patrols. The big ships of the fleet were already out of the area. His remaining forces had thus far done little to hinder the Japanese onslaught. The fleet's main weapon still in the area was the submarine force.

The undersea boats, fated to play such an important role in winning the Pacific War, had thus far failed to make a difference in the defense of the Philippines. Crew fatigue, faulty torpedoes, and a lack of good aerial reconnaissance all combined to hinder the submariners' efforts.

The boats operated from Manila Bay with the tenders *Canopus* and *Pigeon* providing maintenance and support. The larger of the two vessels, *Canopus*, was moored to a dock in Manila with a layer of camouflage nets providing protection. Japanese control of the air required submarines returning from patrol to lie submerged in the bay during the daytime hours, surfacing only at night for repairs and replenishment. It made for exhausting work for both the submariners and support personnel alike.

Admiral Rockwell arrived at his new headquarters at Corregidor on December 21. The cramped quarters, located inside a tunnel, were anything but ideal. It did, though, put him in contact with various army officials with whom he would be working closely during the next few months. "Communications, however, were in a sorry state as the one telephone line was overcrowded and unreliable, no two of us seemed to have the same code books, and the voice radio was being used both by the air warning net and the inshore patrol," he wrote of the conditions.[4]

Hart held a final conference among his senior staff on December 24 in Manila. Rockwell remembered "the Marsman Building was bombed three times" during the meeting. MacArthur failed to inform Hart of his plan to declare Manila an open city. The admiral, however, learned the news by chance a couple of days earlier.[5] The proclamation went into effect at noon on December 26.[6] The timing left Hart with only a short window of time to evacuate his remaining personnel and materials from Manila.

Hart notified the staff of his decision to depart the Philippines to join the major units of the fleet further south. The admiral felt he could provide the most benefit operating in that capacity. "I was in complete agreement with this decision, for once having lost all use of the facilities of the City of Manila, in addition to all control of the air, it would no longer be possible to operate the fleet from that area until control had been restored," Rockwell wrote.

A flurry of directives followed the announcement of Hart's pending departure. Submarine operations would remain in Manila Bay for as long as possible. The naval headquarters in the Marsman Building was to be abandoned. Personnel were to move as quickly as possible to Bataan.

Rockwell was appointed to take command of all of the remaining naval units in the Philippines. His authority went into effect at noon on December 25. "A letter was prepared for me to present to General MacArthur advising him of my authority, that I would inform him when Admiral Hart had reestablished his headquarters, and that the Marines would be turned over to the Army Command as already agreed upon

[in] conversations previously held on the topic," Rockwell recalled. He reported for duty to General MacArthur on December 26.

Hart then gave Rockwell verbal instructions to proceed with the evacuation and destruction of all naval facilities in Manila, Cavite, and Stanley Point. A rush of activity followed as navy personnel scrambled to get as much supplies and equipment as possible moved over to Bataan and Corregidor. Anything unable to make the trip had to be destroyed.

Rockwell dispatched a trusted subordinate on a special mission. "Lieutenant (jg) Champlin was sent to Manila to carry out the very important and very difficult mission of destroying all bulk oil, diesel oil, and aviation gasoline without setting fire to the city or pumping it into the harbor—he accomplished this in a highly satisfactory manner by a display of initiative, tact, and resourcefulness far beyond that which could be expected of an officer of his rank and experience," Rockwell wrote.[7] Nothing of value could be left for the Japanese.

The destruction of facilities at Cavite and Stanley Point, or what remained of it after the devastating Japanese air attacks, began at once. The area was again bombed at the beginning of the work, but little additional damage was caused. Any vessel in operating condition still there was moved across the bay, along with all of the remaining confidential documents.

Sailors destroyed the aircraft shop, including a PBY then under repair, and spare aviation engines. Unusable munitions, such as mines and aerial depth charges, were loaded aboard a lighter. The small boat was sunk after being towed out to a deep area of the harbor. Among the items lost were 550 drums of high-octane gasoline, part of a dwindling fuel supply available to Bulkeley's PT boats.[8]

The submarine *Sealion*, heavily damaged in the first bombing of the navy yard, could not be moved or repaired under the circumstances. She was ordered to be scuttled. Workers removed all salvageable equipment before hauling aboard depth charges. The explosives were ignited, sending the boat to the bottom of the harbor in a tremendous blast.

The work was largely completed by the end of the day on December 26. Personnel then left the area by boat or truck soon afterwards. A small contingent, however, returned a few days later to finish off a few overlooked items.

Hart planned to depart the area in one of the three remaining fly-able PBYs. The plan, however, was thwarted when two planes were destroyed by the enemy shortly after the other had already departed with an advanced party. He instead boarded the submarine *Shark*. She pulled out of Manila Bay at 2:00 am on December 26.

Rockwell was left with a miniature navy for coastal defense. The force included three river gunboats, three minesweepers, four tug boats, two converted yachts, two submarine tenders, Bulkeley's squadron of PT boats, and associated support personnel. The primary mission of the small armada was to support the ground forces on Bataan by pro-tecting the approaches to the area against possible Japanese amphibious operations.[9] The destroyers *Pillsbury* and *Peary*, along with the remaining submarines, also fell under Rockwell's command as long as the vessels remained in the area. For the submarines, however, the stay was not long.

The deterioration of the situation around Manila resulted in the early departure of the submarine force. Rockwell wrote "it was decided—due to the increasing danger and difficulty of service in Mariveles, shortage and limitation of fuel and total lack of rest for personnel between patrols, as well as the likelihood of the Japanese blocking Manila Bay entrance—that basing of submarines in this area was no longer practicable." The move was to happen quickly.

The submariners were to "proceed south as soon as the submarines, then in port, could be made ready for sea." The tenders *Canopus* and *Pigeon* would remain in the Manila Bay area. "Appropriate authorities, including General MacArthur, were informed of this decision and the reasons therefore," Rockwell concluded.

It had scarcely been two weeks since the start of the war. Admiral Hart was gone, along with his big warships and submarines. Rockwell was now on Corregidor pondering how to best use his small fleet to help the defense of Bataan.

CHAPTER 14

The sequence of events leading up to the first boat loss for the squadron began on the night of December 24, 1941. PTs 31 and 33, accompanied by the destroyer *Pillsbury*, ventured out for an evening voyage. The group traveled south from Manila Bay under orders to patrol the Verde Island Passage.

Henry Brantingham was the boat captain of *PT-33*. He recalled the force was to look for enemy submarine activity in the passage. Iliff Richardson was serving as the boat's executive officer. He remembered instructions to attack any vessel encountered, as it would be Japanese because no friendly ships were operating in the area.

The voyage was proceeding as planned until 8:30 pm, when the engines of *PT-33* suddenly stopped just prior to reaching the designated patrol area. The 31 boat and *Pillsbury* quickly disappeared into the distance. The culprit was most likely dirty gasoline.

The lull, though, was only temporary. "At 8:35 pm the engines were started, and an attempt was made to rejoin formation, using the formation's probable intentions as the best immediately useful information," Brantingham reported.[1] Richardson remembered the boat took off at maximum speed. "This speed was needed to regain the formation ahead," he later wrote. "It was already dark at the time, and although we proceeded at high speed for several minutes, keeping a sharp lookout all the while, we failed to see either the ships or their wakes."[2]

The PT continued on the dead reckoning course "until a flashing light, construed to be signals, was seen on the port bow," Brantingham continued. "*PT-33* then headed in that direction, known to be Point Santiago." The boat captain suddenly sighted something phosphorescent off the port bow. He hoped it was the wake of *PT-31*, but did not discount the possibility it could be an enemy submarine. It turned out to be a shallow coral reef.

The 33 struck the underwater hazard just after 9:00 pm. She came to an abrupt stop with a thunderous thud. Brantingham remembered it as a sickening sound. "At this moment, I was thrown violently into the cockpit and my head [struck] against the sharp corner of the windshield," Richardson recalled. "The roar of the engines again stopped. We were hard aground, set on at maximum speed." He estimated the momentum carried the boat almost 60 feet onto the reef. The PT was about 1,600 yards off the coast of Luzon, about 5 miles north of Point Santiago.

None of the crew was injured in the sudden stop. Richardson grabbed a flashlight to check for damage. The hull seemed to be intact. "No part of the hull itself was seriously damaged," Brantingham reported. "One slight crack was found in the lazarette bilges. Screws, shafts and rudders were badly bent."

After consulting with the tide tables it was determined the area was now in high tide. "This was unfortunate in this case, [as] because of the relatively shallow draft of PT boats, the normal difference between high and low tide will often be enough to make them waterborne," Richardson wrote of the situation. "At any rate, all hands immediately got into the water and we tried in vain to rock the 33 and push her off. After 15 minutes everyone climbed back aboard and into dry clothes." The boat was firmly stuck.

The sound of engines soon broke the silence of the night as *PT-31* came into view. "We assembled on our stern, showed lights and yelled at the top of our lungs," Brantingham later wrote. "Finally, *PT-31* heard our warning and stopped nearby."[3] Edward DeLong was the boat captain of the 31. Brantingham later learned the men aboard the other PT had nearly mistaken them for the enemy.

DeLong's boat came dangerously close to joining the 33 on the reef. "It was only by frantic signaling and screaming we were able to keep the 31 from going aground in precisely the same manner as we had," Richardson remembered. "The 31 stopped about 100 feet in front of the coral shelf."

It was possible *PT-31* would be able to pull her sister boat free. High tide seemed to be the best time to try. DeLong sent over towing cables before slowly revving his engines. It was not to be—the tow lines parted, leaving *PT-33* in place.

The 31 boat eventually set out for base to notify the squadron commander of Brantingham's predicament. Daylight the next morning—Christmas Day—found *PT-33* still stranded. "The whole boat rested on one place on the false keel forward, and on the propellers aft," Richardson wrote of the situation. "The coral formations were like soft limestone and could be cut and cleared to some extent; this we started to do in an effort to make a channel to deep water, during low tide." Anything was worth a try to get the boat free.

The work, however, soon came to an abrupt halt when bullets started splashing around the boat. Filipino troops ashore had mistaken the torpedo boat for a Japanese vessel. Richardson quickly fired off a Very pistol in an effort to alert the Filipinos that they were a stranded friendly boat. It did not work. The flare may have had the opposite effect, in fact, with the troops ashore thinking the signal was a call for reinforcements.

Crewmen next raised up the American flag to the highest point possible on the boat. It was either not seen owning to the distance, was perceived as a Japanese flag, or was simply ignored. A few bullets hit the PT, with one striking the mirror in the crew's head. Fortunately no sailors, torpedo warheads, or fuel tanks had been hit—so far.

Just then Ernest Pierson, one of the tallest men on the boat, grabbed a white sheet and stick. He began to slowly walk across the reef towards shore, carefully meandering in an attempt to stay out of the direct line of fire. "We watched Pierson for some time through the binoculars and then a small native boat came out from the shore to the reef, as the reef did not extend to the shore," Richardson recalled. Pierson stayed with the party for over half an hour as the anxious sailors aboard the PT wondered what was happening.

There was some speculation that the Filipinos may not have believed the sailor's story. Richardson then decided to venture out to join the group himself. He found an army officer who spoke good English. The officer told him a local mayor had called an army post to report a Japanese invasion after seeing lights and hearing engine noises during the night. A detachment of troops arrived the next morning. The men opened fire at the urging of the mayor, who had ordered residents to evacuate, disrupting their Christmas holiday. Whether the story was true or not was unclear, but at least the shooting stopped.

Crewmen aboard two other PT boats were enjoying a Christmas meal on deck while anchored in Mariveles Harbor when word arrived of the stranded boat. The sailors, however, were soon faced with a more urgent crisis when a barge loaded with mines was spotted adrift and moving towards the boats. "Through the work of the two crews of the two boats, the lighter was secured about three feet from the bows of the boats, saving damage," Chief Quartermaster DeWitt Glover recalled.[4] The boats were now free to help their stranded sister PT.

At about midday, *PT-31* returned, along with John Bulkeley and *PT-41*. The squadron commander quickly reviewed the situation. He directed the torpedoes to be fired off and other items such as ammunition to be transferred off in an effort to lighten the stranded boat. A joint attempt was then made by the 31 and 41 boats to pull *PT-33* free. It also failed. Bulkeley ordered the 33 boat to be scuttled by burning, after a final attempt yielded no progress.

The end of *PT-33* came at about 8:30 am on December 26. A dejected Brantingham set out to destroy the only boat he had thus far commanded in his navy career. His first step was to see that "all possible useful removable material was removed from the boat prior to burning." The crewmen were then transferred to *PT-41* via small boat, leaving only the boat captain and Richardson aboard. The flagship stood back at a safe distance.

A pile of combustible materials, including an assortment of wood and flammable cloth items, was assembled below deck in the forward crew compartment. The pile was then doused with gasoline. Richardson moved to a small boat stationed just off the stern. He grabbed a hold of a deck cleat and the back of a torpedo tube. "My head extended just above the deck so that I could see what was going on forward," he later wrote of the moment. Brantingham felt it was best to set off the inferno with the help of a broom. Setting it on fire topside in the cockpit, he ventured back down below deck to toss the flaming stick into the pile. The result was a tremendous explosion.

The force of the blast blew the boat captain back up topside. He was momentarily knocked out and suffered some minor burns, but miraculously was not seriously injured. Richardson thought he was at a safe distance in his position off the stern. "I heard and saw the explosion and the deck over the forward compartment of the 33 rise instantaneously about 75 feet in the air," he wrote of the event. "My immediate concern was, as I gazed at this aerial deck, a piece of this deck falling in such a manner as to hit the spot where I was now standing." He hastily bailed out of the small boat with only seconds to spare. "As I hit the water, a piece of the 33's decking, 2 feet by 3 feet, hit the gunnels of the punt I had just recently vacated and rested there like the deck it had been."

Richardson climbed back into his boat after pushing off the decking. He was looking for his boat captain, but could not see him. Richardson was about to go back aboard the 33 when Brantingham finally appeared. Brantingham slowly regained his stamina and saw small fires radiating out from the large blaze in the forward area. The flames were heading towards the stern—and the gas tanks. He stumbled towards the back of the boat to join Richardson.

The pair was soon on board the small boat rowing towards *PT-41*. "I cast off without delay and commenced paddling with an improvised paddle about 2 inches wide, at a speed that would have made a rowing coach stand up and cheer," Richardson recalled. "The thought uppermost in my mind was that if 1¾ gallons of 100 octane gasoline fumes would make that explosion, what would happen when the brightly burning fire reached the main gasoline tanks." There fortunately was no second explosion.

The initial progress of getting away from the flaming boat, however, was hindered as the duo began rowing in circles. "My [executive officer], in his enthusiasm to leave the burning wreck before its gas tanks went up, was taking about two strokes to my one," Brantingham later wrote. The pair was soon able to synchronize their effort to move in the right direction. They were soon safely hoisted aboard the 41 boat. Bulkeley gave the boat captain a welcoming slap on the back, mentioning how he thought he was not going to make it off the burning PT.

The vivid orange fire and billowing black smoke slowly faded away as the 41 led *PT-31* out of the area. Bulkeley reported the loss to Admiral Rockwell during the early afternoon. His squadron was now down to five boats.

The sailors from the lost boat were given new duties aboard the other PTs, in many cases based on their own choosing. Brantingham went to the 32 boat. "I reported aboard the *PT-34* for officer duties," Richardson wrote. "The 34 was called the Lucky 34 because three and four always make the lucky seven, winning number with the galloping dominos." Only time would tell if luck would follow the boat into battle.

CHAPTER 15

The American retreat into Bataan was tenuous at times, but for the most part was working as planned during the final days of 1941. The move took Japanese army commanders by surprise. General Homma's orders from Imperial Headquarters were to capture Manila under the assumption that the largest confrontation of the campaign would take place around the capital.

Japanese air and ground forces had not aggressively attempted to cut off the American and Filipino troops moving towards Bataan, nor had pressed hard on General Wainwright's D5 defensive line north of the peninsula. Operational plans had not considered a battle for Bataan. Homma's main striking force was moving towards Manila as a result.

A frenzied situation existed behind the American front lines. The roads leading into Bataan were clogged with vehicles of all types, including trucks, cars, buses, and tanks. In some areas there were bumper-to-bumper backups stretching for several miles. Columns of people, mostly civilian, walked alongside the roads. Japanese planes failed to significantly attack this inviting target. Nor had enemy bombers attacked the Calumpit bridges north of Manila. The vital spans remained open. The position, however, was soon threatened from the ground.

Although the D5 defensive line was holding firm in the area directly north of Bataan, a large enemy ground formation was advancing east of the position. It could not outflank the line due to a large area of impassable swamp, but was moving towards the Calumpit bridges. The long twin spans were the only way for the remaining forces coming from Manila to move west to Bataan. The troops would be trapped if the bridges fell into enemy hands. Such a calamity could then allow the Japanese to use the strategic Route 3 road to move behind the defensive line guarding the entrance to Bataan.

Filipino infantry units set up positions near the town of Baliuag in an attempt to stop the Japanese advance. General Albert Jones sent in the only armored unit available when a column of enemy tanks were seen approaching the town at about 1:30 pm on December 31. Two platoons of light American tanks of the 192nd Tank Battalion, a federalized National Guard unit, supported by a handful of cannon-equipped halftracks, moved forward to attack. A fierce battle erupted within the town as the tanks fought on city streets amongst buildings and Nipa huts. The Japanese tanks lacked armor-piercing shells, giving the Americans a key advantage.[1]

The attack was a complete success. Eight Japanese tanks were destroyed in the fighting against no American losses. The enemy advance had been stopped short of its objective.

The Calumpit bridges remained open for the last Filipino troops to safely cross as the final hours of 1941 expired. General Wainwright could not wait any longer, as the enemy came closer. He gave the order to "Blow the bridges." as the sounds of distant rifle fire crackled in the background.[2] The two spans suddenly disappeared in the crash and flash of a small explosion. It was 6:15 am on January 1, 1942.

All the movements of the southern Luzon units were now completed. The D5 line began to fall back towards Bataan. Japanese commanders now realized the main battle would be for Bataan, not Manila. The capital city, however, still had to be occupied.

The last days of Manila before the Japanese occupation were marked by utter chaos. General MacArthur's open city proclamation went into effect on December 26. The announcement was communicated by all newspapers and radio stations throughout the day. "In order to spare the metropolitan area from ravages of attack either by air or ground,

Manila is hereby declared an open city without the characteristics of a military objective," MacArthur's message began.[3]

Fear quickly spread among the city's residents as they came to grips with the meaning of the declaration. Many businesses immediately closed their doors. Streets were jammed with military trucks as soldiers from the south passed through on the way to Bataan. Rumors began circulating of MacArthur massing troops north of the city for a decisive battle on the central plain of Luzon. The gossip was quickly dispelled as false. The mandatory blackout was lifted, although reluctantly by some residents, resulting with the city bright with lights during the night hours—a first since the start of the war.

Reporter Clark Lee stepped out of his downtown hotel expecting to see the American National Guard unit from New Mexico, who had been manning antiaircraft guns out front. Everything was gone, to his great surprise. All that remained were the empty fox holes. The army troops were not the only ones leaving the city. "The roads back into the hills were black with people striving to reach their native villages before the murderous armies overwhelmed them," Lee wrote. "The few trains still running into the provinces were literally jammed to the car tops."[4]

Things were especially chaotic at the waterfront, where military personnel had been working around the clock. Piles of hastily assembled supplies and equipment sat on the docks waiting for transport across the bay. Any vessel unable to leave was to be sunk in place to avoid capture.

Boat captain Anthony Akers was sad to be leaving Manila. He had been stationed at the waterfront from December 13 onwards as the Manila arm of the PT boat courier service. With Admiral Hart's departure, and Admiral Rockwell's move to Corregidor, the service was no longer needed. "We slept aboard the boat, and when the bombs started down, we were supposed to get away from the wharf and out into the bay," he recalled. "Sometimes people used to stow away, to get away from the bombs."[5]

Akers marveled at the morale of the Filipino people. No matter how bad the situation was becoming, there seemed to be a strong belief that somehow the Americans would come through to turn the tables on the Japanese. He knew, however, the sullen faces at the Army-Navy Club told a different story. Akers headed back to Sisiman Cove, reluctantly leaving behind a Filipino girl from a well-to-do family he had recently met.

Akers later made one last quick trip to Manila to pick up some remaining items. With his boat low on gas, he was able to get in and out about 12 hours before the Japanese arrived. The entire capital city would soon be overrun by the Japanese.

Other PT boats helped in the evacuation of the city. George Cox brought a boat into Manila Harbor after it had been declared an open city. Looking around the harbor, he saw ships of all sizes scattered about the immediate area on fire and sinking. Japanese bombers dotted the sky above, yet there was no antiaircraft fire of any type.

Cox knew the Japanese were not far from the edge of town. The streets seemed largely deserted. A big church was burning in the distance. During a short stint ashore, he found Filipino storekeepers "would give me anything we Americans needed without either money or a voucher—just sign a paper that was all. They trusted us."[6]

It was initially unknown as to how the Japanese would react to the open city announcement. Radio Tokyo acknowledged hearing the broadcast from Manila. The Americans assumed it meant no military action would be taken against the city. It was not the case, however, as Japanese bombers struck again on the very next day with successive waves of planes hitting the port area and the walled city. Three ships were sunk in the harbor. Additional attacks on shipping took place the following day.[7]

All American and Filipino military forces were to be out of Manila no later than December 31. MacArthur had already left with his staff and family. The civilian government of the country had also moved to Corregidor. President Quezon, who had recently been re-elected to a second term, was officially sworn in during a brief ceremony held on the island December 30.

Brigadier General Richard Marshall, a member of MacArthur's staff, stayed behind to head up the American rearguard. He was to supervise the removal of supplies, oversee the shutdown of the headquarters, and see that the last remaining troops departed.[8]

Medical personnel did everything in their power to help the wounded under treatment in the city. All 87 American Army nurses were safely transported from Manila to Corregidor, along with every moveable patient from Sternberg Hospital. A small group of navy nurses, however, were left behind. The group later became Japanese prisoners.

Perhaps the most dramatic escape was the inter-island steamer *Mactan*. She was converted into a makeshift hospital ship. Her skipper agreed to try running the Japanese blockade to Australia. About 300 of the most seriously injured patients were loaded aboard, along with supplies for a 30-day trip. The small vessel braved heavy seas, the threat of attack by the Japanese, and a boiler fire during the perilous voyage. Good luck and adroit seamanship combined miraculously to allow *Mactan* safely to reach her destination.[9]

The last American forces pulled out of Manila on New Year's Eve. Billowing smoke from various burning military installations wafted across the sky, providing an eerie backdrop as a foreboding feeling of terror descended on the city. A large white banner with the words "Open City" hung on the front of city hall.

The disheartened capital, though, was still ready to celebrate the New Year. Hotels and bars opened for a subdued party. A New Year's Eve dance was held at the elegant Manila Hotel, with some women donning fine gowns for the first time since the start of the war.[10] The evening festivities ended with many bartenders dumping out their remaining liquor to keep it from falling into Japanese hands.

The reality of the war quickly returned with the start of the New Year. Uncollected garbage was piled on the streets and looting began. The remaining military stores in the port area were opened to the public. Throngs of people responded, grabbing whatever supplies they could find.

What had only a month ago been a pristine city now seemed unrecognizable. On January 1, 1942, enemy ground forces stood 12 miles north and less than 10 miles south of the city, but did not enter the capital. Japanese troops first entered the city at 5:45 pm the next day.[11] The setting sun later marked the end of an era for the city—40 years of American rule was over.

John Bulkeley and *PT-41* were using the cover of darkness to silently slip into Manila Harbor one last time during the evening hours on the day the enemy first came into town. The move was unknown to the

Japanese occupiers entering the capital at the very same time. The boat moved at a slow speed with her engines muffled. Darkness concealed the extent of the damage in the port area. The PT men may not have been able the see the blackened piers and charred walls marking the locations where buildings once stood.

Looking ashore, the squadron commander made out a haze of smoke hanging over the city. The sky seemed to have a faint glow in the reflection of burning buildings. The streets were mostly deserted except for an occasional cyclist and a fleeting glimpse of a Japanese infantry column. Sporadic distant gunfire was occasionally heard in the direction of Nichols Field.

Bulkeley could see the Army-Navy Club as the boat moved further into the harbor. It had long been a popular hang out for American servicemen. The building was closed and darkened at first, but the building later started to light up. He sadly concluded it was the Japanese entering for the first time to take it over.

Bulkeley and his men were on a special mission to destroy any vessels not already scuttled to prevent their capture and use by the Japanese. The sailors dared not to go ashore. Crewmen jumped into small boats as the PT slowly moved through the harbor. They then used axes to knock out the bottoms. Larger vessels required special work—demolition charges with time-delayed fuses.

The work had been completed by 3:00 am. The 41 moved out of the harbor, setting a course for the southern tip of Bataan. It had been only three months since Bulkeley and his men first entered the city after the long voyage from the United States. It would almost certainly be their last visit—at least as free men.

Robert Kelly was still in the army hospital on Corregidor when Manila was evacuated. His swollen arm and finger were resisting the various treatments. The executive officer was down on himself for not healing fast enough to rejoin his PT boat squadron. "Alone in the evening after sunset I walked out to the mouth of the tunnel and sat down, to watch the twilight of the old year die away," he said.[12] Kelly was by himself. The sound of music coming from an officers' party softly resonated in the distance. It was an event some of the army officers were holding for the nurses. Kelly assumed his friend "Peggy" Greenwalt was there, as he heard the officer she was seeing had just returned from Bataan.

A nurse named Charlotte then sat down next to him. She had to go on duty soon and was not able to go to the dance. Charlotte tearfully told him that her boyfriend had been wounded on the battlefield. Just then another person sat down on the other side of Kelly. It was Nurse Peggy. She had not gone to the dance after all.

The two managed to cheer up Charlotte, who departed for duty, but not before securing two bottles of beer for Kelly and Greenwalt to celebrate. The beer, along with some apples and marshmallows, made a New Year's Eve feast that Kelly thought "couldn't have tasted any better."

The strain of continuous operations was beginning to show on Bulkeley's PT boats and men. Admiral Rockwell took notice in late December. "Motor torpedo boats are rapidly deteriorating due to lack of spare parts and bad gasoline," he recorded in his war diary. "Because of emergency trips and patrol duties their crews are becoming exhausted and the boats are in poor operating conditions." The admiral decided to abandon the long patrols in the Verde Island Passage due to "lack of results, loss of *PT-33* by grounding, and the exhaustion of personnel."[13] The PTs, instead, were to be "made available as dispatch boats and for attack on vessels in the immediate vicinity."[14]

The destroyers *Pillsbury* and *Peary* would also no longer be available to assist in PT boat operations. The target of numerous air attacks during recent days, Rockwell decided on December 27 to send the ships south. The pair departed under the cover of night for the voyage to Java.

The admiral later established some PT patrols around the local area. The year ended with the boats operating inside Manila Bay.[15] For John Bulkeley's PT sailors—and the rest of the Philippine defenders—the prospects for 1942 seemed grim.

CHAPTER 16

Captain Norman Scott's heavy cruiser *Pensacola* had not yet reached the International Date Line on the morning of December 7, 1941 when word came of the Japanese attack on Pearl Harbor. The warship was escorting a group of eight vessels en route to Manila via the South Pacific. The ships were passing through the Phoenix Islands, almost 2,000 miles southwest of Hawaii, after departing Pearl Harbor on November 29.[1]

Packed aboard the four transports and three freighters were reinforcements bound for General MacArthur's Philippine defenders. The cargo included planes, field artillery, a large amount of ammunition, supplies of various types, and soldiers. The tender *Niagara* rounded out the group.

The sudden outbreak of war threw Scott's mission in peril. The group was directed to make port at Suva, Fiji without delay until a decision could be made about its final destination. Thus began the vexing American debate as to whether, and how, to reinforce the Philippines now that the war was under way.

MacArthur began requesting urgent help from Washington as soon as the fighting began. He continually urged assistance of any type be sent to his forces. Troops, planes, ammunition, food, and medical supplies were needed most. The general was critical of Admiral Hart for moving the big warships of the Asiatic Fleet south at the onset of the fighting. MacArthur felt the move only made sending reinforcements a more difficult undertaking.

Reinforcing the Philippines posed a complex problem for leaders in Washington. Many officials were concerned about the defense of Hawaii, Alaska, and even the West Coast of the United States in the aftermath of the Pearl Harbor attack. With the Pacific Fleet crippled and the "Europe first" strategy already firmly in place, limited resources were stretched even thinner. Some high-ranking military officers believed the Philippines were a lost cause. They argued against committing additional forces to an unwinnable situation.

The *Pensacola* convoy was sent to Australia in the hopes it could somehow eventually make it north to the Philippines. Orders were issued for two transports in San Francisco to be loaded with fighter planes and ammunition for a voyage to Australia. A command was set up on the Allied nation with the directive of helping to get supplies to the Philippines. A sum of $10,000,000 was immediately made available to help get the process started.

General Marshall notified MacArthur in late December that the War Department "is proceeding with utmost expedition to provide necessary supplies at base with early emphasis on most critical items."[2] Hope among the defenders for help surged when President Roosevelt issued a communiqué on December 28, 1941. "I give to the people of the Philippines my solemn pledge that their freedom will be redeemed and their independence established and protected. The entire resources, in men and in material, of the United States stand behind that pledge."[3]

MacArthur in turn rallied his troops to hold out. "Help is on the way from the United States," the general told his men in a message. "Thousands of troops and hundreds of planes are being dispatched. The exact time of arrival of reinforcements is unknown, as they will have to fight their way through."[4] It could not have been further from the truth.

By early 1942, the American public was beginning to view MacArthur and his beleaguered men as a symbol of resistance against a seemingly unstoppable enemy.[5] Public support for sending help to the Philippines defenders was widespread and growing. The War Department in Washington, with the support of President Roosevelt, was determined "to make every effort to reinforce the United States Army forces in the Far East ... and to make endeavor to provide these forces with additional munitions and supplies."[6] The pledge stood in the face of the deteriorating situation on the battlefield.

The aid, however, never arrived. Plans to send a convoy north from Australia were officially scuttled in early January.[7] The men and supplies packed aboard Admiral Scott's ships, once earmarked for the Philippines, remained in the South Pacific. The decision came after great debate among top military and political leaders. The Japanese were rapidly expanding in the area south of the Philippines. The United States simply did not have the naval and air power available to fight all the way through to MacArthur.

Many refused to give up hope, clinging to the idea of reinforcements suddenly arriving. Soldiers, sailors, and airmen alike looked for any sign, no matter how small or even imaginary, that help was on the way. Barron Chandler thought he discovered the sign while his PT was patrolling the dark waters off Bataan in early January 1942.

Lookouts sighted an unidentified vessel, prompting the PT to quickly send out a challenge signal. The reply eventually came—it was the American ship *Ranger*. Chandler was elated, for he knew *Ranger* was an aircraft carrier and that the warship was not previously stationed in the Philippines.

Upon returning to Sisiman Cove, he rushed to tell John Bulkeley that help had finally arrived. The squadron commander knew it was not the case. "I don't know what you saw or thought you saw, but I want you to understand this," Bulkeley calmly said. "Our air force has been wiped out, our ships and submarines have left. No help is coming. Do you get the picture, Barron?"[8]

Chandler did actually find *Ranger*. However, it was not the aircraft carrier, but a broken-down old tugboat bearing the same name. No American reinforcements ever made it to the Philippines. MacArthur's men would have to hold out with what they had.

In the end, only a small amount of supplies made it to the Philippine defenders, with just a trickle reaching Bataan. A handful of blockade runners and an occasional plane succeeded in reaching the southern

Philippines, but inter-island steamers were only able to deliver a limited amount of the cargo north.

Submarines made a greater number of trips to the Philippines throughout the campaign, with some going directly to Corregidor. The number of boats available for the task, however, was few and cargo capacities were small. One of the largest supply drops occurred when the submarine *Sargo* delivered one million rounds of 30-caliber ammunition in February. The trickle of supplies was not enough to sustain the defenders.

The American defense of Bataan officially began on January 7, 1942, when the final elements of the 26th Cavalry moved from rearguard positions south into the peninsula.[9] Behind were the Japanese forces that had chased the defenders from Lingayen Gulf in the north and through Manila from the south and east. All of Luzon, except for Bataan and Corregidor, was now essentially Japanese territory.

American and Filipino forces had successfully escaped the death trap of the Japanese pincer. Speed, luck, determination, and tremendous bravery among some of the ground forces under General Wainwright combined to make the withdrawal a success. MacArthur had nothing but admiration for his men. "No trained veteran divisions could have executed the withdrawal movement more admirably than did the heterogeneous force of Filipinos and Americans," he later wrote.[10]

The Japanese Army General Staff later praised the operation as "a great strategic move."[11] Had the enemy attacked Wainwright's final defensive line more aggressively or better deployed their airpower, the retreat to Bataan could have been turned into an American rout. The Japanese Army leaders, instead, were now faced with flushing an enemy out of a fortified peninsula. The operation could take months, and would tie down valuable forces needed for conquests further south.

Bataan was an ideal defensive position, bordered by Manila Bay on the east and the South China Sea to the west. It was, however, small and narrow, measuring just 25 miles in length and 15 miles wide at the center.

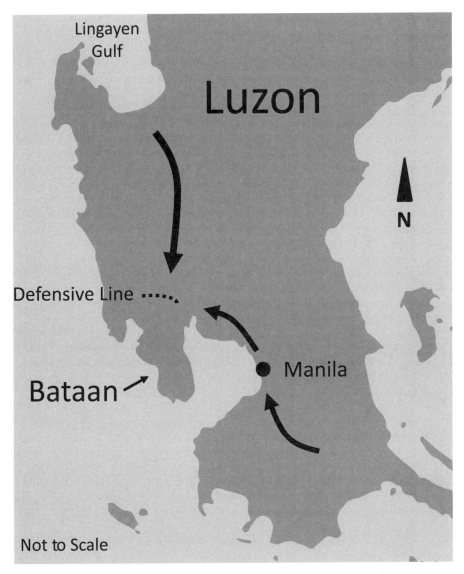

Map 4: Retreat to Bataan

The geography featured a mountainous interior with a coastal plain along each coast. The shore line had both steep cliffs and sandy beaches, with the western coast heavily indented with a variety of small bays and inlets. The area contained a predominantly jungle vegetation, giving the defenders a potential advantage unavailable in the areas of Luzon where they previously battled the Japanese. The number of main roads was limited to only two going north–south, each running parallel along one of the coasts, and one east–west road traversing the interior.

The front line was a defensive boundary known as the main battle position. It stretched from west to east across the peninsula, broken only by the towering Mount Natib. American commanders assumed the 4,222-foot peak was impassable. As a result it was not covered by the defense line, but was regularly patrolled.

Eight miles behind the main battle position, and roughly paralleling the only east–west road on Bataan, was a second line of defense stretching uninterrupted across the peninsula. Although envisioned as the main defensive line by prewar planners, it served only as a fallback position during the current campaign. Preparations along the line, now known as the rear battle position, were still under way during the first week of January. Troops were also stationed along the coastal areas to guard against an amphibious assault.

MacArthur divided Bataan into three command areas. The two defensive lines were split into an east and west zone. Wainwright commanded 22,500 troops of the I Corps in the western half. General Parker led about 25,000 soldiers of the II Corps defending the eastern area. A third zone, known as the Service Command Area, covered the southern portion of Bataan. It was primarily for support personnel and reserves.[12]

Nearly 80,000 soldiers and 26,000 civilians were now packed into the Bataan Peninsula.[13] It was a formidable number on paper—many more than were envisioned by prewar planners—but was elusive in reality. MacArthur's men lacked the basic essentials needed to put up an effective long-term defense.

The headlong retreat across Luzon had resulted in the loss of a substantial amount of supplies. In one instance alone, retreating soldiers left 50 million bushels of rice untouched north of Manila at the government depot in Cabanatuan.[14] The amount of food available to feed the army was critically low. Fresh meat and fruit were already gone. There were only limited stocks of canned fruit and other nonperishable items. Soldiers were cut to half rations almost immediately. Medical supplies, drugs, blankets, mosquito netting, and clothes were among the growing list of items running dangerously low. Many of the defenders were exhausted from days of movement. Some Filipino soldiers arrived at Bataan without shoes, their footwear having literally been worn out during the long retreat. It did not take long for the defenders to begin falling victim to a host of tropical diseases under these difficult conditions. Soldiers fell ill with malaria, scurvy, dysentery, and beriberi. The situation only became worse as the campaign progressed.

The fortified island of Corregidor, just off the southern tip of Bataan, was the nerve center of the American defense. It had been serving as a post for the protection of Manila Bay since the Spanish colonial days. The tadpole-shaped island was about 4 miles long and measured just over a mile at its widest point. Millions of American dollars and decades of time were required to build it into the fortress that existed at the start of the war.

A variety of coastal gun batteries and mortars were in place to defend against invaders from the sea. Other facilities—including a power plant, railroad, small airfield, barracks, and water desalination plant—made it a virtual standalone city. Two landing areas, known as the North Dock and South Dock, were available for use by small vessels.

The centerpiece of the island, though, was the Malinta Tunnel. The labyrinthine system of tunnels and laterals was completed in 1932. It featured MacArthur's main command center, a modern hospital, supply stores, and Admiral Rockwell's headquarters. A system of blowers brought in a supply of fresh air, while reinforced concrete walls, floors, and arches made the facility nearly bomb proof.

The fortifications earned the island the nickname "Gibraltar of the East," after the British fortress in the Mediterranean.[15] The weak link in the bastion was the inadequate antiaircraft system made up of primarily 3-inch cannons and machine guns. The decimated American air forces could provide little in the way of fighter protection. The Japanese bombardment of Corregidor started at once with airplanes. Heavy artillery guns later joined as the ring around the defenders tightened.

MacArthur and his staff directed operations from Corregidor. The general began his only known trip to front lines late on January 9 by traveling from Corregidor to Mariveles before driving in a four-car caravan north along the east coast of Bataan. He was met by Wainwright and other officers upon his arrival the next morning at the II Corps headquarters.

The general spent time touring battle positions and conferring with commanders. When Wainwright suggested they go a short distance to see a 155-millimeter howitzer, he declined saying "I don't want to see them. I want to hear them."[16] MacArthur was back on Corregidor by evening, with the entire trip lasting about ten hours. He then reassured President Quezon about the ability to hold back the Japanese for months, noting "there was no reason for immediate worry."[17]

The Japanese ironically selected the same day as MacArthur's Bataan visit to make a demand for his surrender. In the message, air dropped behind the front lines, General Homma told the American leader that he was doomed and the end was near. MacArthur did not respond.

CHAPTER 17

The operational home for Bulkeley's torpedo boats remained Sisiman Cove as the retreat into Bataan by the ground forces concluded. There were no large machine shops or base facilities to support the boats once Cavite was destroyed. Help came from the submarine tender *Canopus* and floating dry dock *Dewey*.

The aged *Canopus* moved from servicing primarily submarines at Manila to Mariveles Harbor—close to the new PT base—on Christmas Day. Although subsequently damaged by Japanese air attacks, she was disguised as an abandoned hulk by her clever commanding officer. The ruse included a list, disorderly cargo booms, and smoky fires burning in smudge pots. Her crew continued to provide vital support for various small vessels while working mostly at night.[1]

Dewey had seen nearly 40 years of service, having been constructed in 1905. Spanning just over 500 feet in length with a beam of 100 feet, she was capable of servicing vessels up to the size of battleships.[2] She had been towed to Mariveles Harbor ahead of the Japanese advance from her normal operating station in Subic Bay. The dry dock was used by the PT men for any type of hull repairs or cleaning. *Dewey* was flooded to become submerged during the day to keep hidden from the Japanese.[3] An assortment of smaller vessels also occasionally helped the sailors keep their boats running.

Admiral Rockwell directed the squadron commander to begin local-ized patrols in the immediate area right after the start of the New Year.

"Established night patrol by two motor torpedo boats, one inside Manila Bay from a point 3,000 yards east of Caballo Island to 4 miles from Manila, the other outside the entrance to Manila Bay," was recorded in the admiral's war diary on January 2, 1942. The patrol inside the bay was later deemed unnecessary.[4]

The PT boats had occasional brushes with enemy planes, now that Japanese bombers were focusing on Bataan and Corregidor. The morning of January 5 found Vincent Schumacher's *PT-32* moored at the pier in Sisiman Cove. The calm was suddenly broken at about 7:45 am. "Heavy machine-gun fire was heard in the vicinity of Mariveles Harbor and immediately thereafter, two enemy aircraft passed directly overhead in an easterly direction," he reported.[5] The speeding planes banked to the south and west, allowing gunners on the boat to fire off some quick machine-gun bursts. "No hits are believed to have been scored."

About half an hour later, a third enemy plane came into view to the east of Sisiman. "It was apparently maneuvering to make an attack out of the sun upon Mariveles Harbor," Schumacher noted. The aircraft flew along the eastern shore of the cove, passing within 200 yards of the boat. It was just enough time for all of the guns on *PT-32* to get into action. "Numerous hits are believed to have been scored on this last aircraft." The boat expended about 400 rounds of ammunition in the short action.

Iliff Richardson's *PT-34* was later involved in what he thought was an enemy air attack. "The squadron commander made reveille optional for the boats, with the condition that all boats must clear the dock before [7:00 am]," he later explained. "On the 34, all hands were up in the morning at 6:00 am."[6]

One morning, though, found PTs 32 and 34 still in Sisiman Cove when the familiar sound of aircraft propellers and machine guns came from the direction of Mariveles Harbor. "We on the 34 were in the process of manning our guns when in a flash the plane was flying over us about 100 feet from the water," Richardson continued. "One of the 30-calibers was not being manned, so my part in the fray was a very few shots at a fast retreating plane."

The aircraft flew some distance from the boats before making a wide turn. It was soon speeding back directly towards the PTs with the bright

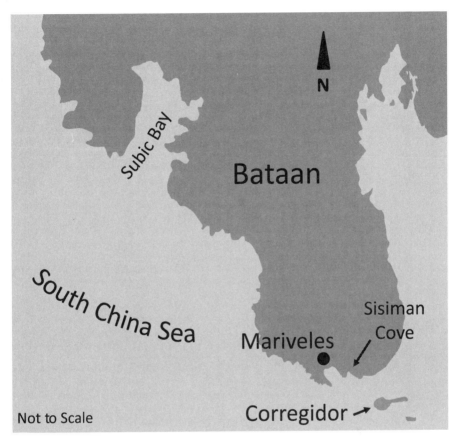

Map 5: Bataan and Corregidor

morning sun at its back—a well-known trick used by enemy pilots to blind the gunners on ships. "I had put a new pan of ammunition on the gun in the meantime and at a distance of 1,000 yards, I opened fire on the plane," Richardson recalled. "The other guns on both boats started firing at about the same time. Such a blaze of tracers converged on the plane that the pilot altered course." The action was over almost as soon as it started.

About a day later, Richardson learned the plane was an American P-40 fighter. The fuselage had been riddled with bullets. The pilot complained to army commanders about friendly fire, noting that most of the damage came from two PT boats. Nothing further ever came of the incident.

Army officials soon banned PT boats from operating around Manila Bay during the late morning and early afternoon hours. The noise of the boat engines was mistaken for the sound of enemy aircraft on a regular basis. As a result, it was not uncommon for the PTs to be stuck in place next to the fuel barge during the midday hours—at the same time Japanese bombers were often roaming the area. It began to cause a high level of apprehension among the sailors. The boats had previously put to sea immediately when Japanese planes arrived so as not to be a sitting target—or near the floating fuel dump.

The new policy put Richardson in the middle of one of the first large air attacks—a real attack by Japanese planes—on Corregidor. "The 32 and 34 were moored alongside the North Dock of Corregidor waiting to be sent on some mission when the planes arrived at 12:30 pm," he later wrote. "In this case we were unable to get under way." Even worse was the boats could mount no air defense, as the machine guns on the PTs were unable to reach the heights of the approaching bombers. Boat captains Barron Chandler and Vincent Schumacher quickly concluded it was unwise to stay with their craft. They ordered everyone to the air raid shelter.

The sailors were forced to rely on their ears once inside the shelter. "First came the drone of the bomber engines," Richardson recalled of the terrifying experience. "Then the explosions of the antiaircraft guns and their bursts; the whistle of the bombs increasing in velocity." He likened the latter to the sound of heavy rain hitting a tin roof. Then the bombs hit with "the concussion in the air raid shelter whipping our pants and shirts." The sailors cautiously peered out during any break in the bombing. "If we saw that the path of the bombers was not directly overhead, we would watch the fall and burst of the bombs," Richardson wrote.

Ensign Cone Johnson had forgotten his helmet aboard *PT-32* in the rush to get to the air raid shelter. He decided to retrieve it during one of the brief lulls, even though the boat was about 300 yards away. "One of his crew asked him to bring back a package of cigarettes,"

Richardson remembered. "He arrived at the boat just in time to see an approaching squadron and, although being a little heavy set, he made it back in record time: the explosions of the fallen bombs and Johnson arrived at the same time." The entire episode lasted only two minutes. Cone, however, did not produce the cigarettes, saying he "had smoked them all on the way back."

The PT men ventured back to their boats after the last of the bombers departed. Dead fish floated around the North Dock, victims of the bombs hitting the water. Neither of the PTs was damaged, but Richardson found spent shrapnel covering the decks of *PT-34*, indicating bombs had exploded nearby.

Wear and tear, accidents, and the lack of spare parts continued to plague the torpedo boat squadron. The 35 boat limped into Sisiman Cove on the morning of January 13 after hitting a partially submerged object during an otherwise an uneventful patrol. Two of the boat's propellers were damaged. Bulkeley noted she "cannot be repaired without spares and docking. Accordingly the port wheel has been removed, giving the *PT-35* two screws with which she can make 30 knots."[7]

The number of operational PTs was reduced to four after the 32 boat suffered an accidental gasoline explosion. The blast took place while the boat was in Sisiman Cove. The cause was thought to be related to the ongoing problem of impurities in the fuel supply.

Henry Brantingham was serving as *PT-32*'s executive officer at the time. "The explosion ripped open the above water portion of the after (rear) third of the boat," he recalled. "Our ship's cook, who was standing on a part of the deck which had been reinforced for a gun mount, was thrown 30 feet in the air, landing unharmed in the water astern."[8] A small fire in the engine room was quickly put out with a fire extinguisher, but several crewmen were injured.

PT-34 was among the other boats in the cove at the time. The incident reminded Richardson of the explosion he had observed when his former 33 boat was recently scuttled. "The 31 arrived on the scene before the 34 and commenced towing the 32 into the water dock, while the 34 picked up various [pieces of] equipment floating in the water," he later wrote.

The damaged PT required extensive repairs. "We hastily repaired and reinforced the stern sections, but the aftermost torpedo tubes had to be discarded so that the weakened stern section would stand a better chance of survival," Brantingham recalled. She returned to limited duty later in January.[9]

The American and Filipino defenders had barely settled into Bataan when the Japanese launched an assault on the east side of MacArthur's main battle position. The attack began on January 9 and quickly strengthened to involve three Japanese regimental combat teams. Heavy fighting developed, with powerful artillery barrages on both sides followed by a series of fierce attacks and counterattacks.

There was no decisive battle during the first wave of fighting. Japanese forces, however, were able to exploit a weakness in the main battle position by moving through the mountainous interior of Bataan—territory previously thought to be impassable by American commanders. A renewed Japanese attack began on January 22 with a thunderous artillery barrage. Effective use of airpower limited the response from American guns. General Parker's soldiers, short of rations and basic supplies, were pushed back.

The action was not limited to the east side of the peninsula. Japanese forces moved south by land and sea from Olongapo on Subic Bay to strike the coastal city Moron on January 16. Wainwright's troops were running low on food and ammunition, but put up a determined resistance before having to fall back after heavy fighting. The combat included the last known horse-mounted charge of World War II by the 26th Cavalry Regiment of the Philippine Scouts.[10]

MacArthur ordered a retreat when it became clear the main line could no longer be held on either side of the peninsula. Units began to move south during the evening of January 23. The rear battle position, stretching continuously across Bataan without interruption, offered a better line for the defenders to make a determined stand.

Japanese commanders hoped to immediately capitalize on the American retreat by attacking the new line during the last days of January. Enemy troops managed to breach defenses in two places. The exhausted Japanese, however, could not advance further. General Homma's troops had suffered heavy casualties in battle and were beginning to wilt under the strain of a variety of tropical diseases. The general ordered his units to disengage while he reluctantly requested reinforcements from Imperial headquarters. It was an embarrassing move for the leader, who had been hoping to take control of the Philippines on a short timeline.

Leaders in Tokyo approved Homma's request for reinforcements on February 10, but time was needed to transfer a full division from Shanghai, China. Additional heavy artillery units, though, were rushed to the Philippines from Hong Kong and Malaya. More air units were also dispatched to the front. Homma would use the new weapons to hammer away at the defenders on Bataan and Corregidor while he waited for more soldiers to arrive.

The weary American and Filipino forces were in no position to launch a counterattack. The defenders shored up their defensive line while waiting—and hoping—for reinforcements that most knew would never come. An eerie lull settled across the Bataan battle line by early February as a result of the stalemate situation. The action for Bulkeley's PT boats, however, was just beginning.

CHAPTER 18

John Bulkeley followed his usual routine on the morning of January 18, 1942, arriving early at Admiral Rockwell's headquarters on Corregidor. He reported for duty, just as he had done every day for nearly a month, perhaps expecting nothing further than more orders for the monotonous patrols his boats were running around the Bataan area. Bulkeley soon found, however, that the day would be different. Rockwell had decided to send the boats on an attack mission.

Bulkeley was handed a written order from Rockwell's chief of staff, Harold Ray. It was labeled secret. "Army reports four enemy ships in or lying off Binanga Bay," the short memo began. "Force may include one destroyer, one large transport. Send two boats [to] attack between dusk and dawn."[1] The enemy vessels were thought to be landing troops and providing gunfire support for land forces.

The squadron commander now had what he had been waiting for—an offensive operation. He knew it was going to be an extremely dangerous mission. Bulkeley's boats would have to venture into Japanese-held waters alone, without support from any other vessels or aircraft.

Binanga Bay was also commonly known as Port Binanga. It was nothing more than an inlet on the northwestern coast of the Bataan Peninsula. The small anchorage, slightly more than a mile across at its widest point, jutted straight east into Bataan from Subic Bay. Up until recently the bay had been home to a small American naval base at Olongapo, but the area had been completely abandoned during the retreat into Bataan. No American vessels had ventured into the vicinity of Subic Bay since.

Bulkeley quickly put together a plan of attack. The use of two PTs seemed sufficient for the mission, especially since the squadron currently only had four operational boats. PTs 31 and 34 were selected for the operation after they were deemed to be in the best operating condition among all the boats.

The pair was to proceed together to the mouth of Subic Bay. The boats would then split apart for reconnaissance sweeps through the immediate area. *PT-31* was designated to reconnoiter the eastern side of the entrance to the bay and the 34 boat would pass through the western side. The plan called for the boats to rendezvous half an hour later at the entrance of Binanga Bay for the attack. If one of the boats failed to make the meeting, the other was to continue the operation independently. Lastly, the pair was to make a final rendezvous at dawn near Corregidor just outside of the defensive minefields.

Barron Chandler, still substituting for the ailing Robert Kelly, was the boat captain of *PT-34*. Bulkeley accompanied Chandler and was in overall command of the operation. He not only wanted to be part of the action, but also desired to see how his men performed during the attack. Edward DeLong commanded *PT-31*.

Much of the day was spent making sure the two boats were in the best possible operating condition. "We tested everything—tuned the motors, greased torpedoes," Bulkeley recalled.[2] A sharp crack pierced Sisiman Cove when the boats' Packard engines rumbled to a start. The evening darkness was slowly covering the area.

Iliff Richardson was aboard *PT-34* as the boat's executive officer. He suspected the mission offered the first chance for real action after many false alarms. "Reports had come in before of various ships seen during the daytime, but it was not learned whether or not these ships were anchored or even in the area still, and unless their approximate anchorage is known the surprise attack is reduced to a fruitless search along the coastline pregnant with small bays and coves suitable for anchoring," he wrote. "In view of these facts, the squadron had not been called out."[3]

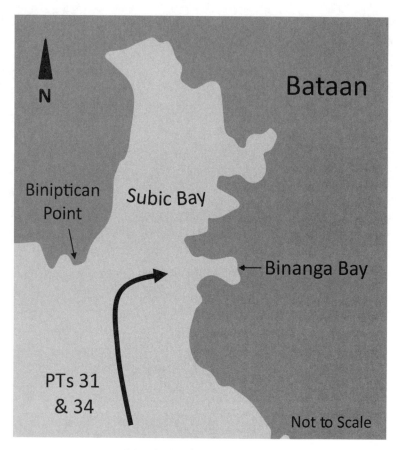

Map 6: Attack on Binanga Bay

The boats departed the Sisiman Cove with the 34 in the lead. "The *PT-31* took her station off our starboard quarter," Richardson recalled. "The two boats proceeded at idling speed and were soon past the mine-field channel entrance and sufficiently far out to sea to test the machine guns. Each machine gun on both boats fired a short burst and was found to be in good working order." The pair rounded the bottom tip of Bataan before turning north to approximately parallel the west coast of the peninsula.

The waters were rough as the boats sped along at a speed of about 30 knots. Bulkeley and his sailors were facing many unknowns as they ventured north. Were there more Japanese ships in Subic Bay than had been reported? Could the PTs become easy targets for land-based guns? There were no answers.

The boats arrived at the entrance to Subic Bay shortly after midnight on January 19. The pair then separated, according to plan, to make the reconnaissance sweeps. Visual contact between the PTs quickly ceased. "The night was particularly dark, so much so that the horizon could hardly be distinguished," Richardson recalled. "The weather was good and the seas were calm." A cool light breeze was blowing.

Chandler's boat was pointed northeast as she entered Subic Bay. *PT-34* was suddenly challenged by a signal light off the port beam. The light was emanating from Biniptican Point on the western shore of the bay, about a mile away. "It won't be long now," commented Chief Machinist's Mate Carl Richardson, wondering when the enemy would open fire.[4]

The boat turned slightly east to avoid a confrontation. "Speed slowed from 18 knots to ten knots," Bulkeley reported. A single cannon then opened fire from land somewhere to the east. It seemed to be coming from just south of the entrance to Binanga Bay. "This field piece could have been fired at *PT-31* as no splashes were seen around *PT-34*."[5]

The challenges were to become commonplace as the night progressed. "Suddenly, out of the blackness of the mainland to the right, appeared an orange signal gun which blinked out the Japanese code recognition challenge—dash-dash-dash-dot," Richardson recalled of another instance. Another enemy lookout was trying to determine if the PT was a friend or foe. "Inasmuch as we did not know the answering signal, all that could be done was to change course a little to the left, which would take us further from the coast—and ignore the challenge. In all, there were five different stations that challenged us that night and none of them received any reply."

The 34 continued in an easterly direction, only to be challenged again by light a short time later from what appeared to be a small vessel. "Course was immediately changed directly towards this boat to investigate her, but she was not clearly made out, and course was again changed to 110 degrees [heading southeast] and speed was reduced to eight knots to be at the north entrance of Port Binanga at 1:00 am, at which time

PT-31 would be on the south entrance and a joint attack would be made," Bulkeley wrote. Apparently the small vessel was thought to be not worthy of expending a torpedo.

Two more searchlights lashed out into the darkness as *PT-34* continued towards Binanga Bay. One came from Grande Island, a small land mass in the middle of Subic Bay, about a mile to the north. The second light originated from a point just south of Binanga Bay. A rattle of machine-gun fire soon followed from the latter direction. It was quickly joined by shells from larger cannons, with a few heard whizzing overhead. Bulkeley had earlier taken over the wheel from Chandler. He steered the boat further seaward to avoid the gunfire.

No shells landed near the 34 boat. The gunfire, however, provided the valuable benefit of helping the sailors to find the shoreline in the darkness. The sailors were able to discern their location in spite of the mountainous backdrop behind Binanga Bay. "In the darkness of the night, a mountain range 15 miles away appeared only as a black outline against the sky," Richardson explained.

"Damn nice of them," Chandler commented on the enemy's actions. "It's a hell of a lot easier to see where we're going with all this light—as long as they keep looking and shooting in the wrong direction."[6]

The men aboard *PT-34* were filled with anxiety. On top of the gunfire and searchlights, Bulkeley sighted a strange red light emanating from a nearby mountain. It could be seen from all across the bay. The Japanese seemed to know something was amiss off the coast.

The 34 arrived at the rendezvous point on time at 1:00 am. Bulkeley steered the boat in circles at slow speed waiting for *PT-31* to arrive. Ten minutes passed, then 20. He became increasingly concerned when DeLong's PT did not appear.

PT-31 was not going to make the rendezvous. DeLong's boat ran into engine trouble early in her sweep of the eastern side of Subic Bay's entrance. She would play no role in the forthcoming Binanga Bay attack.

It was now 1:30 am. Half an hour had passed since *PT-34* arrived at the rendezvous point. Bulkeley finally decided to venture forward alone for the attack. "*PT-34* then entered the bay on two engines at idling speed," he wrote. He noticed the area was quiet—no guns were firing, unlike the situation outside the bay.

The entire crew was at battle stations. Bulkeley donned a pair of binoculars as he manned the torpedo director in the small conn area. The rudimentary device was used to help aim the torpedoes. Boat captain Chandler stood ready at the torpedo firing keys. "My station was the steering wheel—and throttles," Richardson wrote. A feeling of tension gripped the sailors, including the officers, as the boat quietly moved forward at a speed of eight knots.

"At first nothing was visible but the black outline of the surrounding hills," Richardson recalled. "Right a touch," Bulkeley said, while carefully peering through his binoculars.[7] Richardson repeated the command as he nudged the wheel right. "Steady," Bulkeley then said, as he alternated between looking through his binoculars and the torpedo director.

The PT was no more than 500 yards into the bay when the faint outline of a two-mast freighter suddenly came into view. Bulkeley, Chandler, and Richardson all saw it. "No other ships were sighted," Bulkeley reported. "Preparations were made to fire."

Two torpedoes were ready to go when a searchlight on the target abruptly switched on, flashing an identification signal. The dazzling beam of light momentarily engulfed the torpedo boat—*PT-34* had been spotted! A scant ten minutes had passed since Bulkeley had made the decision to attack alone.

"Fire one," Bulkeley quickly shouted. Chandler immediately hit the firing key after hearing the command to initiate the launching of the forward port-side torpedo. A second torpedo was soon unleashed. Each firing key set off a black powder impulse charge at the rear of the torpedo tube. The force of the small blast shot the torpedo out of the tube. "The sound of the forward starboard torpedo coming out of the tube and hitting the water made a 'hrooosing' plunk," Richardson remembered. The underwater missile quickly disappeared into the night as it raced towards the enemy.

Bulkeley knew the boat was now in a precarious position. There was no time to linger around to assess the results of the attack or to launch additional torpedoes. He yelled for a hard right and full speed. "I spun the wheel to the hard right and advanced the throttles to their maximum limit," Richardson recalled. The Packard engines then took over, allowing *PT-34* to dash off into the night. Looking back, crewmen glimpsed an explosion near the target's waterline followed by a brilliant fireball mushrooming up into the night sky.

The boat escaped the immediate area untouched. "*PT-34* cleared the bay at top speed; at 1:55 am a fire was seen in Port Binanga and then two large flashes," Bulkeley wrote. The sailors speculated the secondary explosions were magazines erupting on the target. The 34 boat, though, was not yet out of trouble.

Only one of the torpedoes unleashed towards the enemy actually left the boat. "Port torpedo didn't fire, sir," an unknown voice suddenly shouted out. "She's making a hot run."[8]

From his position in the conn Richardson knew right away that something was wrong. "There was a terrific whine to the left of the cockpit," he recalled. "I looked over to find the number one torpedo sticking out of the end of the torpedo tube and making a high shrill screaming whine. It was stuck in the tube with its engines and propellers turning at an amazing velocity due to the lack of water resistance." The roar of the boat's engines was partially drowning out the sound of the torpedo.

It was a situation all PT sailors dreaded. When the small blast of the impulse charge failed to eject the torpedo out of the tube, usually due to a malfunction, the weapon stayed in place with its motor running, continuing to build up speed and heat as a result of there being no water available to slow down the propellers. At some point the casings around the motor would become white hot. Full disintegration could follow, with deadly shrapnel flying in all directions.[9]

An additional, more serious, threat came from the possibility of the warhead exploding. Every time the bow of the speeding boat dipped in a wave a splash of water came across the deck, turning the impeller on the tip of the warhead. The weapon would become fully armed after a certain number of revolutions. A blow to the warhead, such as the forceful slap of a wave, could detonate it, causing a large explosion.[10] The PT boat—and crew—would be blown out of the water.

Every man aboard *PT-34* knew the seriousness of the situation. The only way to defuse the crisis was to stop the torpedo's propeller—and quickly. All engines aboard the boat were cut, allowing the 34 to slowly drift to a stop. "Complete silence," Richardson remembered of what happened next. "All engines had stopped simultaneously and this new silence was far more nerve-racking." He noticed many of the crewmen were congregating on the starboard side of the boat to be as far away as possible from the problem torpedo.

Torpedoman's Mate First Class John Martino, however, jumped into action. He ran below to the crew's head for a handful of toilet paper before rushing to the torpedo. Straddling the hissing torpedo, while partially hanging over the water, he carefully stuffed wads of toilet paper into the vanes of the propeller.

It was the equivalent of a life and death operation. Finally, after Martino's calm work under tremendous pressure, the propeller blades stopped turning. Only then was everyone aboard able to breathe a sigh of relief. The immediate crisis had passed, but the torpedo was still hanging more than halfway out of the tube.

The 34 boat could not linger any longer. Gunfire was again coming from the direction of Binanga Bay, but was not yet close to the boat. The Japanese were on full alert and likely searching for the intruder who torpedoed their ship. "We proceeded out about 3 miles from the entrance to await developments," Richardson recalled. It was possible the damaged vessel could get under way in an attempt to leave the bay, or another ship might present itself as a target. "In either of these possibilities we had two more torpedoes which were anxious to do their part in sinking an enemy ship." Looking back into Binanga Bay, the sailors could see the glow of a fierce fire burning. The rising moon seemed to slightly dim the brilliance of the blaze.

With no further targets, and the sailors eager to get out of the area, the PT set a course for the designated meeting point near Corregidor. The boat would not be able to pass through the defensive minefields until daylight, however, lest it be mistaken for an enemy vessel in the darkness. The squadron commander hoped to find *PT-31*, as she had not been heard from since the start of the mission.

Bulkeley and Chandler went below deck to catch some sleep, leaving Richardson to man the conn. Crewmen topside continued trying to free the stuck torpedo. "All attempts failed to get this damaged torpedo out until 6:00 am, when it broke off into the sea," Bulkeley wrote. The weapon slightly hit the deck on its way overboard. "The thump brought Lieutenant Bulkeley and Chandler on deck, but there was no damage done by the falling torpedo so they retired back below," Richardson remembered.

The 34 boat arrived off the Corregidor minefields well in advance of the 7:00 am meeting time. Morning light, however, revealed she was alone. There was no sign of *PT-31*.

Bulkeley reported the results of the mission to Admiral Rockwell later in the morning. He brought the good news of hitting the enemy ship—the first real enemy blood to be drawn by the torpedo boats during the campaign—and the bad news of the missing *PT-31*.

Rockwell shared that army observers positioned on top of Mariveles Mountain with powerful binoculars saw the ship sink. The soldiers reported her to be a 5,000-ton armed merchantman equipped with 5½-inch guns.[11] The vessel had been shelling army positions on the west side of Bataan. The description roughly matches what eventually became known as armed merchant cruisers—auxiliary ships of various sizes fitted with guns for support duties.

Bulkeley returned to Sisiman Cove with the satisfaction of knowing the first attack mission undertaken by his boats was a qualified success. The missing 31 boat, however, brought spirits down among his sailors. All the squadron commander could do was hope for the best for his lost men as he wrote his report of the action. "It is presumed that she ran aground near Mayagao Point or was beached near there after being taken under fire," he wrote. "It is felt that with as capable officer as [Lieutenant] (jg) E. G. DeLong that the officers and crew stand a good chance of return along the beach."

Little did Bulkeley know, at the very time of his writing, that Delong and his men were still alive and struggling for survival. The majority of the 31 boat's crew would make it back alive. Their fate, though, would not be known for a couple of days.

It did not take long for Bulkeley's exploits to go public. At noon (Eastern Standard Time) on January 20, 1942, the Navy Department released a communiqué about the battle in Binanga Bay. It was the 31st press release made public since the start of the war. "A motor torpedo boat under Admiral Hart's Far Eastern Command entered Binanga Bay, inside the entrance to Subic Bay, Philippine Islands, and torpedoed an unidentified enemy vessel of 5,000 tons in a night attack," the communiqué began. "This small boat carried out its difficult task while under fire of machine guns and 3-inch shore batteries. Lt John D. Bulkeley has been commended for executing his mission successfully."[12] No mention was made of the missing *PT-31*.

The news media across the country immediately ran with the information. There was at last something positive coming out of the Pacific after an endless stream of bad news. It was not much, but it was something for the eager public—weary of hearing about setbacks and defeats—to grab hold of. It quickly became national news.

On the same day of the navy communiqué, and more than 10,000 miles from the Philippines in Long Island City, New York, an unsuspecting Alice Bulkeley was getting ready to retire for the evening. It was 6:59 pm. She had already put her young daughter to bed when she was startled by the sudden pounding on the front door of her apartment. When she opened the door, a throng of reporters flowed into the living room. Flashbulbs started bursting as reporters were shouting questions about her husband.

Only when the scene slightly settled down did Alice learn of her husband's actions in the Philippines. "I'm very pleased," was all she could tell reporters.[13] Alice had not seen him since his departure for the Philippines the previous August. John's last letter home had come from the Cavite Navy Yard about a week before the attack on Pearl Harbor. She was suddenly no longer just married to a naval officer, but to a genuine American war hero.

Citizens across the United States found out about the action by picking up newspapers on the morning of January 21 or by hearing flash news reports on the radio. "U.S. Hammers Jap Vessels," appeared in bold print across the front page of the *New York Daily News*. "Navy Hero in Daring Blow at Japs," was the headline in the *San Antonio Light*.[14]

The *New York Times* ran the story on page five, proudly reporting Bulkeley as a native New Yorker. The article provided biographical information on the squadron commander and details about PT boats—a weapon largely unknown to the general public. The paper extolled the virtues of the boats, and even exclaimed that the craft "have speed up to 79 miles per hour and carry enough explosives to sink a battleship."[15] It seemed almost everyone knew about the little torpedo boats and their famous commander in the course of a few short days.

The daring raid in Binanga Bay drew public attention to PT boats—and John Bulkeley—for the first time. A postwar review of Japanese records, however, fails to support the sinking claim. It does not diminish in the least the heroic attack made by the men aboard *PT-34*. Their torpedo very likely did hit something.

A close look at the records finds the 3,028-ton cargo vessel *Aso Maru* and the auxiliary minesweeper *Banshu Maru 52* were both reported damaged in Subic Bay on January 20. Japanese sources attribute the harm to mines.[16] Both ships were believed to have survived the damage, with *Aso Maru* credited as being sunk by the American submarine *Redfin* in 1944.[17] The fate of *Banshu Maru 52* is unclear, but it is unlikely she outlived the war. Although it may never be known for certain, it is possible one of these vessels was the victim of Bulkeley's torpedo a day earlier.

CHAPTER 19

The trouble for Edward DeLong's *PT-31* began shortly after arriving at the entrance of Subic Bay. The last hour of January 18, 1942 found the boat idling on one engine off the Bataan coast about a mile southwest of Ilinin Point. Only the center engine was operational, providing a speed of seven knots. Both outboard engines had stopped running. "The same old trouble," DeLong complained of the problem, "wax in the carburetors."[1] Engineers labored below deck, working in cramped, dimly lit conditions, cleaning strainers and jets in an effort to get to the motors working. "At this time I was about to turn south past Mayagao Point and return to Ilinin Point at 1:00 am for rendezvous with *PT-34*," DeLong continued.[2]

The crew was abruptly faced with a new problem when the fresh water cooling system unexpectedly shut down, rendering the center engine inoperable. Sailors worked with buckets and hoses to refill the system with fresh water from the galley while the 34 drifted powerless in the night. Work was nearly completed when scraping and crunching—menacing sounds to any PT sailor—suddenly radiated from the bottom of the hull. The noise was coming from the center propeller hitting a coral reef—*PT-31* had run aground. It is unclear how far off the Bataan coast the boat was located.

All three engines were eventually fired up immediately after the engineers' restoration work was completed. "As soon as the engines were started a gun (about 3 inches) in the vicinity of Ilinin Point commenced firing in our direction," DeLong reported. The Japanese had either seen—or more likely heard—the boat. Shell splashes gradually edged closer to the stranded craft, but none hit the PT. The next three hours were spent trying to free the boat from the reef.

Gunner's Mate First Class James Culp remembered the frantic work. "We swam out anchors and tried to pull off without success. The sharp coral had cut into the wooden hull and held us fast," he recalled. "The tide was going out, and we were in a progressively desperate state."[3] The sailors heard a distant rumble of an engine and attributed it to *PT-34*.

DeLong raced the engines in a determined attempt to back off the reef, but nothing seemed to work. The reverse gears eventually burned out. He then made the momentous decision to abandon ship when it was clear that all efforts to free the boat had been exhausted. He was pretty sure the closest land was probably held by the Japanese.

The boat captain now had to deal with two issues—destroying *PT-31* to keep her from falling into Japanese hands and finding a way to lead his men safely out of enemy territory. The best chance for the latter was to get to land before daylight. A total of 13 sailors, including the skipper, were aboard the 31 boat. Ensign William Plant was serving as the executive officer.

The sailors used ingenuity in preparing to leave the ship. "The engine room canopy was cast loose and mattresses lashed to it for use as a life raft," DeLong wrote. "At 3:00 am the raft shoved off with all 12 men on board, Ensign Plant in charge, and proceeded out to the edge of the reef to wait while I destroyed the *PT-31*." The distance to the end of the coral was thought to be about 100 yards.[4]

The men under Plant's control encountered problems shortly after departing the PT. The raft proved unwieldy and difficult to maneuver. It soon started to drift away, moving into ever-deeper water.

At the same time, DeLong was not having an easy time back aboard the boat. "I had some difficulty in getting *PT-31* to burn," he wrote. "Finally after chopping holes in the gasoline tanks and blowing holes in the boat with hand grenades, the boat was burning sufficiently and I

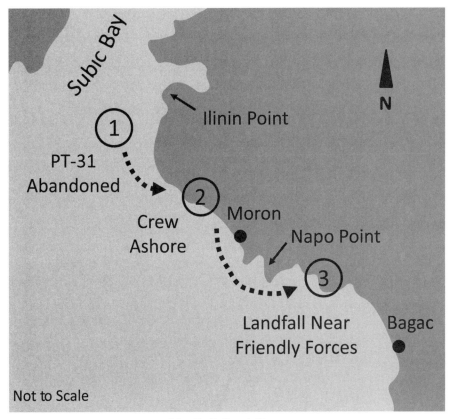

Map 7: DeLong's Escape

took to the water at 3:40 am." The boat captain, however, was unable to find the rest of his men. The makeshift raft had drifted beyond voice range.

The sailors on the raft feared their skipper had not made it off the burning boat when DeLong failed to readily appear after she started burning. Daylight was coming soon and getting to land was imperative. Death or capture would certainly result if the men were caught fully exposed and nearly defenseless on the raft in the open sea. The majority of the group decided it was time to swim for shore, as the land would at least provide some cover. It was about 5:00 am.

Not everyone, though, was able to make the swim. Machinist's Mate First Class Rudolph Ballough and Quartermaster Third Class William Dean were non-swimmers. Plant decided to stay with them on the raft while the others struck out for land. The trio would attempt to guide the raft ashore together and then link up with the larger group. The plan did not work. Plant, Ballough, and Dean were never reunited with their shipmates.

DeLong kept probing hopelessly for his men. "I searched for the raft until approximately 5:00 am when I made my way to the beach at a point about one half mile south of the boat and remained there until dawn," he wrote. While DeLong swam for shore, the fire on the boat reached the torpedoes, exploding the warheads in a fury of flames.

James Culp was the senior enlisted man among the nine swimmers. The group made it to land without incident, but knew they were behind the front lines on the Japanese side. It would likely be too dangerous to move around during the daylight hours. The men decided to hide during the day and move south at night in an attempt to pass through the lines to the American side. Culp led the men into a clump of trees and underbrush on the edge of the beach.

Unlike his men, DeLong started moving with the morning light. "At dawn I proceeded down the beach about half a mile where I picked up the tracks of nine men," he continued. "I followed and found them in a clump of bushes below Mayagao Point."

Culp's men saw a distant figure walking towards them at about 8:00 am. They were ecstatic to find it was DeLong. The arrival of the boat captain rounded the group off at an even ten men. He quickly learned of their experience getting ashore and of the three missing men. There had been no sign of them since the group split apart nearly three hours ago.

The sailors were thought to be positioned about 2 or 3 miles south of the entrance to Binanga Bay. The main American–Filipino defensive line was still 3 or 4 miles further south and there was fighting nearby. "The Japanese forces were at this time conducting an offensive operation in the vicinity of the village of Moron and there was considerable action between Mayagao and Moron," Delong reported. A large amount of artillery and small-arms fire could be heard further inland. Enemy planes were also sighted in the immediate area.

There was no way for the sailors to know which side was advancing or retreating. DeLong's pressing concern was to avoid capture. "I immediately posted a watch in our clump covering all quadrants to observe enemy movements and our own artillery fire," he wrote. It included posting a lookout in a tree.

The sailors were careful not to be spotted from above. "Japanese planes were in the air almost constantly, with the greater concentration immediately after dawn and just before dark," DeLong continued. "During midday practically no planes were in the air." The aircraft were operating from a field somewhere to the north or northeast, but not far away given the low altitudes. "As soon as one observation plane landed, another would take off within five minutes."

The stranded sailors were in a precarious position, wedged between the ocean and the fighting further inland. The combat appeared to be edging closer. "The infantry action in the early morning seemed rather heavy, with our forces using rifles and Lewis guns and enemy forces using smaller-caliber rifles only," DeLong recorded. The latter was concluded based on rifle casings the men found in the immediate area. "The greatest firing was about 1 mile from us in the vicinity of the mouth of the Batalan River." Artillery fire subsequently picked up a short time later, with the shells bursting near the infantry battle. DeLong thought it was coming from 75-millimeter guns.

The artillery fire moved further away to the northwest as the day progressed. DeLong concluded the Japanese were retreating. "If this continued I was determined to make a run for our own lines around the beach at about 3:00 pm, believing that our chances would be better during daylight." It was not DeLong's only plan. "In the meantime I had planned as an alternate method obtaining two or three bancas and making our way by night around into Bagac Bay to beach at dawn." The bay was an indentation located at about the midpoint of the west coast of Bataan. The adjacent land area was behind the front lines and known to be friendly positions.

The native dugout canoes, often featuring outriggers, were used by Filipinos throughout the islands. "From our vantage point I had already spotted one large banca about half a mile toward Moron," DeLong wrote. "We had obtained canvas for use as a sail and had stripped barbed wire entanglements for rigging."

DeLong had to be extremely careful in every decision he made, since his men were lightly armed. The group only had six pistols and one rife—it was not enough firepower to win a shootout with heavily armed Japanese soldiers. "I had ordered that unless we were rushed by superior numbers we were to allow any scouts to come in to the clump and then club them with the butt of a pistol or rifle," he wrote.

The boat captain "abandoned any hope of making it around the beach" when American artillery sounded like it was pulling back at about 3:00 pm. There were no more Japanese planes in the air. DeLong's next move was to send two of his men to investigate the bancas.

He and Culp then went to scavenge for food. They only found some used coffee grounds in an abandoned shack. It was enough for each of them to enjoy a cup of coffee after starting a small fire. "At this time Japanese soldiers could be heard to the eastward and could be seen occasionally to the northward and along the beach in the vicinity of the mouth of the stream north of us." The shipwrecked sailors could not stay in the area for too long without being spotted.

"At about 5:00 pm the two men returned and reported that the two bancas appeared to be in good condition, but required out-rigging," DeLong recorded. "At about this time we sighted from our tree lookout what appeared to be two light armored cars or light tanks about 1 mile north heading down the trail toward the stream north of us. The bridge over this stream was partially broken down as I had been up there earlier in the afternoon looking unsuccessfully for water."

The sailors would have to move out that night. They now had two bancas, one large and one small, for their escape. The group left their hideout at twilight to move towards their getaway boats.

Culp covered the sailors as they began to move the final stretch towards the water. "I was the rear guard with the only rifle," he recalled. "As the first of the crew topped some sand dunes they were silhouetted against the setting sun." It was unclear if the group had been spotted by the enemy.

Culp eventually took up a position behind the last dune as the others prepared the boats. He could hear voices in the distance. DeLong organized the men and the meager equipment. "We had found two paddles, one board and two shovels for paddling, plus the gear for rigging a sail if the wind was favorable," DeLong recalled. "I also obtained a [tow] line to tow the small banca." They rigged the craft before moving to the water while dragging the boats behind them.

The plan was for DeLong to take charge of the large banca with a total of six men aboard. Culp was to lead the four men in the smaller canoe as it was towed behind. "When we shoved off I wished to get well clear of the beach before attempting sailing," DeLong wrote.

Both boats, however, capsized shortly after the men boarded. Everyone ended up in the water and some of the equipment was lost. The spill damaged the rudder and outrigger of the larger banca. Culp's smaller canoe would now have to provide the power to tow the larger one. "After righting the bancas we had two bailers and two paddles left between the two bancas," DeLong recalled. "With this we managed to become more or less seaworthy." Darkness fully blanketed the area to cover their departure as the sailors shoved off for good at about 10:00 pm. By that time it was clear that enemy troops were within 200 yards of the beach.

The canoes headed southeast in the direction of Napo Point. Conditions aboard were tight, with little room for the men to move around other than paddling. "The four of us paddled until about midnight," Culp recalled. "I stopped and sent the three men with me, one at a time, back to the large boat to be replaced."

"At about 1:30 am I made the first attempt to round Napo Point but hit a very strong head wind," DeLong wrote. "We continued to head around until about 3:00 am when my men were exhausted and we were barely holding our own, so I decided to chance a landing at dark." The boat captain picked a point to go ashore, unsure if the area was held by friend or foe.

The bancas made land at about 3:30 am somewhere in the vicinity of Napo Point, possibly just to the south of it. Moving inland, the sailors crossed a barbed wire entanglement only to find themselves facing a steep cliff. "The spot I picked for a landing was such that at high tide it was impossible to move along the beach and there was only one trail leading up over the cliff," DeLong wrote.

The boat captain could not be certain what was on the other side of the cliff and did not want to find out in the darkness. He kept the men in place until dawn, when they were spotted by Filipino troops. The sailors were fortunately able to identify themselves as friendly before any shooting. It was a stroke of good luck that the area was not occupied by the Japanese.

The shipwrecked sailors were taken to American Army Captain George Cockburn at a nearby field headquarters tent. The soldiers must have certainly been surprised to see the band of weary sailors. DeLong recalled the army officer "gave us food and water and arranged for transportation for us back to Mariveles." The PT men arrived at their destination at about 5:30 pm on January 20.[5]

Boat captain DeLong was proud of his sailors. "I wish to heartily commend my men for their fine spirit and courage during some very adverse and trying conditions," he wrote. "All hands conducted themselves in such a manner as to make any commanding officer indeed proud."

The squadron members were ecstatic when the surviving sailors from *PT-31* arrived back at the base. "We'd never really expected to see them again," Robert Kelly recalled after hearing the news while still in the hospital.[6] Iliff Richardson recalled DeLong and his men were "very much fatigued."[7] He eagerly listened as the former boat captain explained the nearly two-day ordeal. Bulkeley's squadron was now down to four boats.

The three other sailors from *PT-31* did not fare as well as the larger group. Plant, Ballough, and Dean were captured shortly after their raft made landfall. Information as to their fates is sketchy, but none survived the war.

According to James Culp, who later crossed paths with Plant as a POW, the three made it safely to shore and promptly fell asleep near the beach in the edge of the jungle. The sailors awoke to find themselves surrounded by three Japanese soldiers. Plant was apparently shot in the leg after lunging towards one of the troops. All were taken prisoner, roughed up, and interrogated. Ballough and Dean were thought to have been executed a short time later.

It is known that Plant stayed in the Philippines as a POW until late 1944. He was among the hundreds of sick and starving prisoners loaded aboard *Enoura Maru* at the Manila docks for a voyage to Japan. The transport was one of many "hell ships," where Allied POWs endured horrific conditions. The men were crammed into a hold previously used to transport horses, but never cleaned. Sickness and disease spread quickly owing to the filthy conditions.[8] The Japanese vessels transporting POWs were often unmarked, meaning that Allied airmen and submariners had no way of knowing the vessels were carrying prisoners.

The voyage only went as far as Takao, Formosa, where *Enoura Maru* was sunk by aircraft from the American aircraft carrier *Hornet* on January 9, 1945. Plant was among the many prisoners who did not survive the sinking.[9] It was a sad final chapter to close out the story of the men from *PT-31*.

CHAPTER 20

The action in Binanga Bay during the night of January 18–19, 1942 was not the only PT boat operation of the day. Admiral Rockwell's war diary records a second mission taking place that same evening. "Sent *PT-41* to reconnoiter south shore [of] Manila Bay in the vicinity of Ternate where Japanese were reported to be placing heavy guns."[1]

It all began earlier in the day when a gaunt and weary-looking American army officer arrived unexpectedly at the PT squadron operations shack in Sisiman Cove. He asked for John Bulkeley's help in trying to find the exact position of Japanese artillery in the hopes it could be destroyed by their own guns. The squadron commander agreed to lend some assistance.

Ternate stood directly across from Corregidor on the southeast shore of Manila Bay. Japanese commanders sought to occupy the area with two purposes, one strategic and the other tactical. They saw strategic value in occupying Ternate to help sever the lines of communication between American positions around Manila and southern Luzon prior to the retreat into Bataan. The tactical value of the location was largely limited to a place for heavy artillery to bombard Corregidor.

George Cox was at the helm as the 41 boat ventured out into the night. Although the boat prowled quietly along the coast, her sailors were unable to find any enemy gun positions. A Japanese artillery unit had already been dispatched to the area, but had not yet arrived when *PT-41* conducted her reconnaissance mission.[2]

The voyage, however, was not uneventful. Cox ordered his machine guns into action after spotting several clusters of Japanese troops on a beach about 2 miles from Ternate. Army officials later reported eight Japanese soldiers were killed and an additional 14 were wounded during the attack.[3]

The PT patrols off Bataan continued in the days following the action in Subic and Manila Bay. The limited number of available boats often dictated that many patrols would be carried out by single PTs. Bulkeley was now certain he needed his second in command back in action.

Robert Kelly was still confined to the hospital on Corregidor as a patient. His infected finger was not yet fully healed. Kelly's attempts—almost daily—to gains his doctor's approval for release had thus far been unsuccessful.

Bulkeley went to Corregidor after returning from his jaunt to Binanga Bay. The squadron commander ventured into a different world when he descended into the Malinta Tunnel. The facility operated 24 hours a day, with people coming and going at all hours.

The lateral passageways off the main tunnel were crammed with people, often working in tight company. Sanitary conditions were deteriorating as toilet and washing facilities became overcrowded. Obstacles placed near the main entrances to keep out Japanese bombs, coupled with damage to the power plant, interfered with the air flow, making for unbearably hot temperatures.

The hospital was perhaps the most crowded area of all. It had recently experienced a large influx of sick and wounded soldiers since the defenders abandoned Manila and withdrew to Bataan. Patients were lying in every available space, including passageways. The smell of sweat and death hung heavy in the air.

Bulkeley gave his executive officer a first-hand account of the action in Binanga Bay. The squadron commander was then able to help convince the doctor to release Kelly. The hospital stay had taken a physical toll on the sailor. He had lost over 30 pounds and was pale. "I had to promise them faithfully I would show up every other day for treatment, but the point of it was I got out of that place," Kelly recalled.[4]

The executive officer rejoined the squadron just in time to experience a stretch of action encompassing the last part of January and continuing into February. Kelly kept his promise to the doctor by making regular trips over to Corregidor—both for treatments and to see his favorite nurse.

The early morning hours of January 21 found *PT-32* cruising near the entrance to Subic Bay. Although not in top operating shape, the boat was back in the patrol rotation after undergoing repairs to the damage caused by the recent engine explosion. The voyage was uneventful until a large vessel was suddenly sighted leaving the bay. Thought to be either a tanker or cargo ship, she looked to be about 6,000 tons.

The 32 closed for an attack, unleashing two torpedoes at close range. "There were no reassuring explosions at the time the torpedoes were due to strike the target," the boat's executive officer Henry Brantingham recalled. "Perhaps they hit but did not explode, or maybe they ran too deep, under the target."[5] Rockwell's war diary simply noted both torpedoes passed ahead of the vessel.

PTs 34 and 41 encountered an unidentified submarine on the very next night. No action was taken, as it was unclear if the underwater craft was friend or foe. The submarine did not surface and the PTs lacked depth charges to attack.

Robert Kelly was back in Sisiman Cove on January 22. He would soon resume command of *PT-34*, but first needed to get back up to speed as to what was happening with the boats. He wasted no time in putting to sea. *PT-34* was up for the evening patrol off the west coast of Bataan, with Barron Chandler still serving as boat captain. Both Bulkeley and Kelly were aboard for the voyage. Iliff Richardson was still serving as the boat's executive officer. He remembered it was "an ordinary patrol which covered the Bagac Bay area north of Mariveles."[6] It was a clear moonless night.

At about 2:00 am Bulkeley and Kelly took over control of the boat, allowing the other two officers to go below deck for some sleep. Chandler and Richardson were still asleep when two small lights were sighted off the starboard bow. "Course was changed to the right, speed was increased and general quarters was held," Bulkeley wrote. "Closer investigation disclosed a small launch on a parallel and opposite course approximately 2 miles offshore headed down the coast."[7]

Richardson remembered battle stations were quietly manned so as to not attract unwarranted attention. He and Chandler were not wakened. The slow movement of the object raised the possibility it could be the raft used by the three missing men from *PT-31*. It could have drifted out to open sea. Although a remote chance, it certainly was possible.

Bulkeley decided to challenge the boat. He moved up to the bow of the PT while gunners carefully trained their weapons on the target. The lights on the other craft went out as the 34 slowly inched closer, eventually closing to about 50 yards' distance. Bulkeley yelled out "Boat ahoy" in a loud voice. Only silence followed. Some bullets whizzed past the squadron commander's head after he shouted out a second time. The machine guns on *PT-34* then opened fire as if perfectly timed, setting off a rapid sequence of events. It was just after 4:40 am.

The action brought Chandler and Richardson scrambling topside from below. "I was [awakened] at this time by our violent machine-gun firing, and ran to the cockpit, followed by Chandler close behind," Richardson wrote of the action. "The burst firing of our machine guns was punctuated by bullets hitting the 34 and whining all around the cockpit. Very soon I could see this long low boat and the yellow purple flashes coming from it between the times when it was being hidden almost from view by orange streams of tracers coming from the 34's starboard turret."

The PT circled the enemy craft while keeping it under constant fire. In addition to the 34's four machine guns—two twin 50-calibers and two smaller single Lewis guns—additional firepower came from small arms, with Bulkeley firing away with a Thompson submachine gun and at least one man from the engine room shooting a rifle.

A sailor in the conn area fell during the height of the gunfight. Kelly turned around after hearing someone yell, "I've been hit." Bulkeley was putting another clip into his gun when he saw Chandler slump over in pain. He was bleeding from his feet. A bullet had gone through both of his ankles. Bulkeley and Kelly pulled him out of the conn onto the engine room canopy. A shot of morphine was quickly administered as the fighting continued unabated.[8]

The darkness initially made exact identification of the target difficult, but it was later determined to be some type of landing craft. Bulkeley thought the enemy boat was heading straight towards Bagac Bay. Kelly saw it was full of troops and protected by armored plating at the bow and stern. He thought the craft was cleverly maneuvering, trying to keep the armor facing the PT at all times. The two discussed the possibility of ramming the enemy vessel, but decided against it.

The 34 boat circled the target a total of three times. The landing craft seemed to be getting lower and lower in the water as the running gun battle continued. "At 4:58 am the enemy's fire was silenced and the launch rapidly sank," Bulkeley wrote. "Due to the darkness it was impossible to rescue survivors." Crewmen aboard the PT could now turn their full attention to helping the wounded Chandler.

Seaman First Class Willard Reynolds served as both the boat's cook and medic. The wounded boat captain was taken below for further attention. Chandler remembered Reynolds "tried to do the best he could. He poured almost an entire bottle of iodine on my wounds, and I almost went through the overhead."[9] Tourniquets were put on both legs to help stop the bleeding.

The patient was made as comfortable as possible and left to rest. Chandler remembered Bulkeley occasionally coming below to check on his condition. "I wasn't doing so well, but I didn't tell him that."

Bulkeley was unable to immediately take the 34 boat to Corregidor, so that Chandler could be delivered directly to the hospital. He had to wait until full daylight. Traversing the protective minefields was simply too dangerous to attempt in anything less. The boat would have to remain at sea for several more hours.

The specific details of the type of craft sunk and number of enemy casualties was unknown to the sailors. Chandler was the only one injured aboard *PT-34*—somewhat miraculously, given the number of bullets exchanged. Bulkeley counted "14 bullet holes though port and starboard staterooms and topside conning station."

The boat initially remained on patrol in the immediate area of the gunfight. Kelly thought it was odd that a landing craft would be operating alone. He wondered if the boat had companions. "After sinking the enemy launch a search was made of the area for approximately 1½ hour[s]," Bulkeley recorded. After finding nothing, and attracting the unwarranted attention of friendly shore batteries, it was time to set a course for home.

The PT had barely started her return trip when lookouts sighted something about 3 miles off the shore of Bataan near Luzon Point. The location was less than ten miles up the coast from Mariveles. It soon became clearer in the increasing brightness of the morning light. The craft was another launch, though definitely smaller than the first one.

With a wounded man and plenty of action behind them, Bulkeley asked the crew if they wanted to go after the new target. A resounding yes came back, with even Chandler weighing in on the issue. The 34 closed to attack, cutting off the enemy vessel while opening fire. "A continuous deadly stream of machine-gun bullets raked the landing boat from stem to stern, in bursts of 30 or 40 shots each," Richardson remembered. The gunfire seemed to be bouncing off armor plating, as the Japanese craft showed no signs of slowing. The return fire, though, was light and sporadic.

American gunners kept up the fire even as *PT-34* closed to within 50 feet of the target. A bullet then hit the fuel tank, sending up a mushroom of smoke and flames. The Japanese vessel lost all power before slowly drifting to a stop. The craft was damaged and taking on water. Bulkeley ordered the 34 to pull up alongside the stricken craft so he could board her. After tossing in two hand grenades to silence any additional resistance, the squadron commander jumped aboard with gun in hand. He found the launch was filled with a watery mix of blood and oil nearly a foot deep, with more seawater flowing in through the damaged hull.

It soon became clear why the return fire was light—the craft was manned by only three Japanese. Bulkeley pointed his gun in the direction of an officer. The individual immediately dropped to his knees calling out "Me surrender! Me surrender!"[10] Sailors then threw a rope over the side. "Two wounded Japanese (including one officer) were taken prisoner after surrendering on their knees and were hoisted aboard the *PT-34* as prisoners of war," Bulkeley reported. "A third Japanese already dead was left in the launch."

The squadron commander grabbed anything he could find of importance, tossing items up onto the deck of the PT boat. The bounty included several briefcases, papers, and knapsacks—anything that seemed to be of potential intelligence value. It was soon clear the craft would not be afloat much longer. Kelly helped pull Bulkeley back aboard just as it sank from under him.

A sailor armed with a pistol stood over the Japanese as *PT-34* raced towards Corregidor. The officer was kneeling with his eyes closed, undoubtedly expecting to be shot at any moment. Bulkeley instead gently wiped away oil from his eyes and examined his head wound. The Japanese enlisted man was gravely wounded. He feebly asked for a cigarette, prompting one of the sailors to light one up and bend over to put it in his mouth.

Kelly judged the soldier to be about 18 years old and no more than 5 feet tall. The officer was older, but not much larger. He marveled at how these two little men, who just a short time ago had put up such a fierce fight, were now harmless as they sat on deck. "What a crazy world," he exclaimed to Bulkeley.[11] The squadron commander simply nodded in agreement.

Help was waiting when *PT-34* pulled up to the North Dock at Corregidor. "I helped to carry Chandler across the oily and bloody decks to a waiting army car and then to the hospital in the main tunnel where he was given immediate treatment," Richardson wrote. "The two Japanese were given first-aid treatment during this absence, and returned to the 34 to be taken to Mariveles for transfer to a Bataan hospital."

The prisoners were eventually put ashore on Bataan. The ambulance doctor gave them a quick look over before pulling away. He thought the officer would make it, but had doubts about the enlisted man. The young soldier died on the way to the field hospital.

Bullet holes on *PT-34* clearly revealed she had been in a fierce fight. "As a sign of victory, the crew of the 34 wired a Japanese bayonet and a helmet to the top of the mainmast," Richardson recalled. A silver chevron was also painted on each side of the pilot house.

Unknown to the sailors at the time, the men aboard *PT-34* had actually stumbled into the middle of a secret Japanese operation to land troops behind the front lines on the west coast of Bataan. The maneuver was part of the larger effort to wrest control of the peninsula from the American and Filipino defenders. The plan had been conceived about a week earlier while forces were locked in heavy fighting along the main battle line. It was based on similar operations used with great success against the British in Malaya.

A battalion of Japanese soldiers packed aboard landing boats had departed from Moron on the night of January 22. Their destination was Caibobo Point, a location well behind the front lines in MacArthur's Service Command Area. A host of problems soon beset the seaborne invaders.

The invasion force was moving south just as *PT-34* was venturing north for patrol, putting the two on a collision course. The first landing craft sunk by the 34 was fully loaded with troops. Other craft in the immediate vicinity somehow evaded detection by Bulkeley's men before escaping south. Rough seas were soon encountered, causing even greater confusion among the Japanese boat crews. Poor preparations resulted in the leader of the operation using a large-scale map. It was found to be wholly inadequate for attempting to find a small point of land at night in an unfamiliar area.

The disoriented invasion flotilla was not only lost, but became separated into two smaller groups. Neither was able to make it to the designated landing zone. The first group landed about 4 miles south of the objective. The remaining part of the battalion went even further south, coming ashore at Longoskawayan Point, close to Mariveles.[12] The second, smaller craft engaged by *PT-34* certainly must have been a straggler making the return trip north after the landing.

The fighting on land started on the morning of January 23 after lookouts spotted a group of about 300 Japanese soldiers moving inland from Longoskawayan Point. The men stationed in the area were a group of irregulars largely comprising American airmen, sailors, marines, and Filipino Constabulary members. Most had little training as infantry, but attacked the invaders with unparalleled bravery. The defenders were able to push back the Japanese, but could not defeat them.

Over the next three weeks, the opposing forces clashed in was became known as the Battle of the Points. The name was derived from the many small points of land jutting out into the sea along the southwest coast of Bataan. The terrain favored the defenders, with sharp cliffs along parts of the coast and thick forests inland.

Both sides called for reinforcements after the initial skirmish. American artillery and heavy mortars began shelling the enemy as regular Filipino soldiers were dispatched to the area. Japanese commanders committed additional soldiers to the fight, with landings taking place on the nights of January 26–27 and February 1–2.[13]

The Americans and Filipinos, however, were slowly gaining the upper hand. Wainwright fully understood the seriousness of the threat. He soon committed additional ground forces, including elements of the Philippine Scouts and tanks.

The minesweeper *Quail* provided naval support during part of the fighting. One of Bulkeley's PT boats would also help out in the later stages of the fight. Additional seaborne help came from the ever-resourceful sailors aboard the tender *Canopus*. Three of her 40-foot motor launches were converted into "Mickey Mouse battleships," with boiler plates used for armor. Each was equipped with a light field cannon and an assortment of machine guns for firepower.[14] The boats were put to good use, firing on Japanese troops holed up in caves and for a makeshift amphibious operation. The few remaining P-40 fighters still able to fly also helped in the effort. A Japanese attempt to extricate the beleaguered forces met with disastrous results. Only 34 soldiers were safely evacuated.[15] The Battle for the Points was over by the second week of February. The Japanese plan to create havoc behind the front lines ended in defeat.

CHAPTER 21

There was no letup in the action at sea for the PT boats while the Battle of the Points raged along the southwest coast of Bataan. Nightly patrols during the time were typically conducted by two boats, or a single PT accompanied by a vessel of the inshore patrol group. A trio of boats—PTs 41, 32 and 35—encountered the enemy while on patrol in late January and early February.

Dwindling fuel supplies allowed for only a single boat to venture out during the evening hours of January 24, 1942. It was *PT-41* under the command of George Cox. Also aboard were John Bulkeley and Edward DeLong, fresh from his dramatic escape from enemy territory after the sinking of the 31 boat.

The 41 had patrolled the previous night in company of the armed yacht *Maryanne*. The pair traveled north along the Bataan coast to the entrance of Subic Bay, but found no sign of the enemy.[1] The PT was now alone as she ventured into the same territory.

The boat went down to one engine as she approached Subic Bay just before 10:00 pm. She was slowly inching forward at idling speed in near silence when Bulkeley sighted the shadowy outline of a vessel west of Sampaloc Point along the southwest coast of Subic Bay. The transport was about a half-mile from shore in a small cove.

Bulkeley initially decided on a cautious approach. The PT remained on one engine as she moved in for an attack, while the men quietly manned their battle stations. The boat then shot forward after going to full speed when reaching a point about 2,500 yards from the target.

Cox manned the wheel while DeLong took position on the torpedo director. "At 800 yards the starboard aft torpedo was fired," Bulkeley explained. "This torpedo ran hot, straight and normal and struck the transport amidships and exploded." DeLong was able to follow the weapons path right up to the point of detonation.

The terrific explosion momentarily lit up the immediate area. The light allowed Bulkeley to see the target was "a 4,000–6,000-ton transport, which appeared to be of new construction, in that it was streamlined and had comparatively small stack," he wrote. "She appeared to be heavy laden and low in the water, and lying to."[2] The blast sent small pieces of wreckage showering the water all around the PT boat.

The transport opened fire just as the first torpedo was launched, but the 41 was not hit. A small disturbance in the water off the transport's stern indicated she was trying to get under way. "At 500 yards a second torpedo was fired," Bulkeley continued. "Its tail struck the deck of *PT-41* on leaving the tube." The second shot had no chance of hitting the target owing to the fouled aim. Cox was beginning to think it was about time to leave the area when Bulkeley yelled "Let's get the hell out of here!"[3]

The 41 made a hard left turn to begin her getaway, raking the transport with machine-gun fire as she briefly passed parallel. Shore batteries suddenly opened fire at about the same time. Flashes on land revealed that four to six guns were firing from a distance of nearly 10,000 yards. Bulkeley noted, "splashes of the shells were observed on both sides of the boat, close aboard and astern and ahead of the boat. Due to zig zagging of the boat, no shells struck."

Lookouts spotted some type of netting stretched across the entrance of the cove as the PT sped away from the action. Bulkeley described it as a "motor torpedo boat obstruction net." He thought it was a trap, as the netting seemed just large enough to be able to foul the boat's propellers, leaving her dead in the water and a sitting duck for Japanese gunners. "This net was cleared by about 20 yards on the starboard bow," he reported.

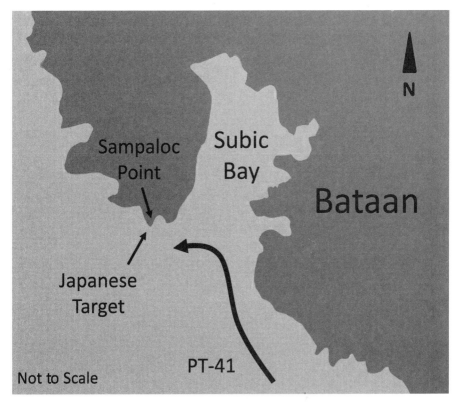

Map 8: PT-41 Subic Bay Action

The 41 was soon in the safety of open waters. Crewmen later attached a broom to the top of the boat's mast. Sailors in Sisiman Cove immediately knew it was a successful patrol when the 41 entered the cove with the broom proudly flying high. Bulkeley simply described the action as "a classic torpedo attack delivered at full throttle in the face of enemy fire."[4]

A Navy Department communiqué released on January 26 announced a 5,000-ton enemy vessel was sunk by a PT boat in Subic Bay. Bulkeley, Cox and DeLong were all mentioned by name. Navy officials noted the "motor torpedo boat penetrated the water adjacent to its objective despite net and boom defenses laid down by the enemy."[5] The American public eagerly read about the new war heroes—John Bulkeley and his PT men.

The squadron commander was not at sea when the next action took place on the night of February 1. It was time for *PT-32* to patrol as part of the normal rotation, even though she remained less than fully functional due to the engine explosion in January. Her assignment was to reconnoiter the west coast of Bataan.

The 32 could make a top speed of just 22 knots, and parts of her hull were held together by a jury rig of wire and braces.[6] She had only the two forward torpedo tubes still mounted to her deck. Vincent Schumacher was the boat captain, but Edward DeLong was aboard for the voyage as officer in tactical command.

The PT pulled away from the dock in Sisiman Cove at 6:45 pm accompanied by *Maryanne*. The voyage, however, did not get very far. The armed yacht developed engine trouble, requiring both boats to stop near LaMonja Island. The tiny isle was directly west of Corregidor and south of Mariveles. The patrol resumed after nearly an hour's delay, with the pair sailing west at a speed of 10 knots before turning north to parallel the Bataan coast. It was a clear moonless night.

"At about 8:45 pm gun bursts were visible in the vicinity of Bagac, indicating either bursts from our own artillery or gun fire from some ship off Bagac," Schumacher reported. "The distance was such that it was impossible to determine which at the time." The area was near the front lines of the land fighting. No action was taken as the PT cruised past.

DeLong and Schumacher had no idea that they were about to become entangled in the ongoing Battle of the Points. Less than a week ago, General Homma had directed his subordinates to reinforce the beleaguered Japanese forces trapped in pockets along the southwest coast of Bataan. He wanted the units to push inland in the direction of Mariveles. The plan required additional missions, even more risky than the previous ones, to land troops at night.

The plan was compromised when a Filipino foot patrol on the opposite side of Bataan found a copy of the orders on a dead Japanese officer.

The document was quickly translated, revealing the enemy's intentions. American commanders took immediate action by alerting lookouts on the west coast, moving a tank battalion to the threatened area, and readying the few remaining planes for action.[7]

The Japanese were on the move while *PT-32* was quietly patrolling off Bataan. Nearly a battalion of enemy soldiers, crammed into 12 or more

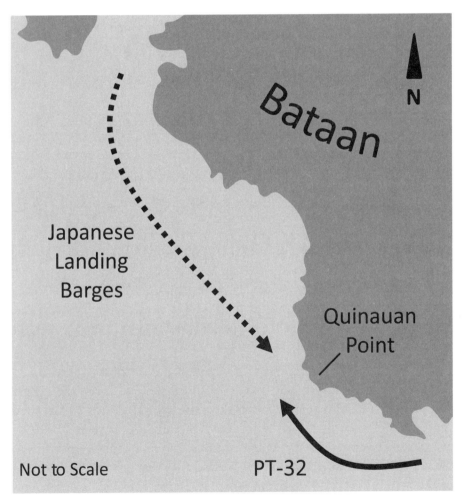

Map 9: PT-32 Action off The Points

landing barges, were sailing south from Subic Bay. Their destination was Quinauan Point northwest of Mariveles. American lookouts spotted the small flotilla and sent a flash message to General MacArthur's headquarters. The resulting counterattack encompassed American and Filipino forces on land, at sea, and in the air.

Four P-40 fighters loaded with 100lb bombs rose from the small airstrip on the southeast corner of Bataan. The planes represented the last remnants of MacArthur's once-powerful air force. The pilots had no trouble finding the enemy fleet after clearing the Mariveles Mountains. The small air armada swooped down to attack the Japanese barges with bombs before circling to make a strafing run.

Troops moved into positions near the coast to ensure the enemy met a fierce reception from land. It began when American heavy artillery guns opened fire, sending volleys of shells hurling towards the barges. Filipino soldiers later joined in with machine guns and small arms as the craft moved closer to the shore.

There is no information to suggest that DeLong and Schumacher had any specific knowledge about the larger operation going on in their patrol area. The 32 boat was traveling north at 9:16 pm when a ship was sighted dead ahead about 5,000 yards away. The PT took a course almost straight north to close for a torpedo attack. Schumacher reported the course was used "in order to put the bright moon more in position to silhouette the ship and to eliminate the possibility of being illuminated by searchlights from the beach in the vicinity of Luzon Point."[8] Having no heavy weapons, *Maryanne* continued on patrol. She played no role in the attack.

The two working engines quickly pulled the 32 boat's speed up to her maximum 22 knots, but it seemed insufficient to catch the target. "As soon as *PT-32* increased speed the ship sighted turned and headed approximately north toward Subic Bay," Schumacher wrote. "By 9:45 pm it was evident that the enemy ship was making more speed than the *PT-32* as she drew away and was almost lost against the background of the beach." By 10:00 pm the target was hardly visible, even though course had been adjusted in an attempt to close the gap.

Above left: John D. Bulkeley served in a variety of positions as a young naval officer before assuming command of Motor Torpedo Boat Squadron 3 in 1941. He arrived in the Philippines just before the start of the Pacific War and returned home a national hero less than a year later. *(US Navy/National Archives)* Above right: Robert Kelly served with distinction while in the Philippines as Torpedo Boat Squadron 3's executive officer and as boat captain of *PT-34*. A hospital stay kept him out of some of the unit's early actions, but he returned in time to participate in the evacuation of Douglas MacArthur. *(US Navy/ National Archives)*

Iliff D. Richardson joined the Navy in 1940 after traveling the world. He was sent to the Philippines after completing officer training in Chicago. Richardson's first assignment in the Philippines was duty aboard the old minesweeper *Bittern*. A chance encounter in late 1941 led him to transfer to John Bulkeley's PT boat squadron. *(US Navy/National Archives)*

PT boats under construction at the ELCO factory in Bayonne, New Jersey. The small craft were made of wood and carried no armor plating to protect the crew. Often referred to as plywood boats, the hulls of PT's were actually made of mahogany planks. *(US Navy/National Archives)*

Above: The navy tanker *Guadalupe* transported the boats and personnel of Torpedo Boat Squadron 3 from the Brooklyn Navy Yard in New York to Manila, Philippines in the fall of 1941. The lengthy voyage included stops in California and Hawaii. *(US Navy/National Archives)*
Below: The PT boats were placed on the deck of *Guadalupe* for the long voyage across the Pacific. Seen on the right of the photo, *PT-41* served as John Bulkeley's squadron flagship. *(Courtesy of WW II PT Boats Museum and Archives, Germantown, TN)*

Above: A rare photo shows PT boats operating near the Manila docks prior to the start of the war. The boats were initially based in Manila after arriving in the Philippines, but were later transferred to the nearby Cavite Navy Yard. *(Courtesy of WW II PT Boats Museum and Archives, Germantown, TN)* Below: *PT-32* was one of six small wooden torpedo boats under John Bulkeley's command. The craft were so new that formal tactics and doctrine had not yet been developed at the start of World War II. *(Courtesy of WW II PT Boats Museum and Archives, Germantown, TN)*

Above: Manila Bay was long known as one of the best deep-water harbors in the Far East when the United States took control of the Philippines after the Spanish-American War. Decades later in World War II the American defense of the Philippines centered on holding key points around the bay. *(US Navy/National Archives)*

Below: Located at the end of a small finger of land jutting out into Manila Bay, Stanley Point was the center of operations for the U.S. Asiatic Fleet based in the Philippines. The narrow peninsula contained the Cavite Navy Yard, a large radio tower, ammunition dump, naval hospital, and fuel storage tanks. This aerial view of the Cavite Navy Yard shows the six PT boats of John Bulkeley's squadron moored to a small dock. The photo was taken in late 1941, just before the start of the Pacific War. *(US Navy/National Archives)*

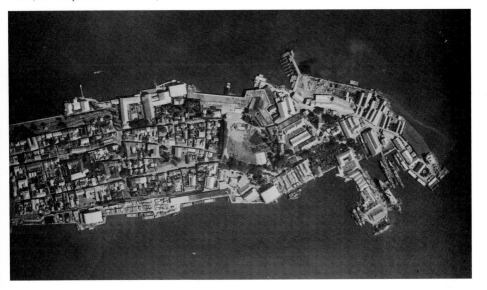

Rear Admiral Francis Rockwell was appointed commander of the Sixteenth Naval District in 1941. He oversaw a number of naval bases in the Philippines and some local defense forces, including John Bulkeley's PT boats. *(US Navy/National Archives)*

Positioned off the west coast of Bataan, Subic Bay was the scene of some of Torpedo Boat Squadron 3's early attacks against Japanese shipping. The daring operations made headlines back in the United States, often as the only good news coming out of the otherwise bleak Pacific front. *(US Navy/National Archives)*

Japanese bombers attacked the Cavite Navy Yard just days after the start of the war. The largest American naval facility west of Pearl Harbor was demolished in a single stroke along with most of Torpedo Boat Squadron 3's spare parts and supplies. *(US Navy/National Archives)*

Left: Sailors work to load a torpedo aboard a PT boat. The American versions of the underwater weapon packed a powerful punch, but were plagued by a variety of problems during the early part of the war. *(US Navy/ National Archives)*

Below: The evacuation of General Douglas MacArthur from the embattled island of Corregidor in March 1942 was the most famous undertaking by the torpedo boats in the Philippines. The general (left) is seen here aboard *PT-525* on October 24, 1944 during his triumphant return to the Philippines. *(US Navy/National Archives)*

Above: Much of John Bulkeley's short stay in the United States after returning from the Philippines was spent promoting the burgeoning PT boat service. It included attending the launching of *PT-103* at the Elco factory on May 16, 1942. *(US Navy/National Archives)*

Below: Robert Kelly returned to the front lines of the South Pacific in command of his own PT boat squadron. He is seen here aboard *PT-153* near the island of Rendova on June 30, 1943. *(US Navy/ National Archives)*

Schumacher and DeLong thought the target was a cruiser. The vessel, however, was actually the minelayer *Yaeyama*. She made for an inviting target, spanning 280 feet in length and displacing just over 1,300 tonnes. Her armament consisted of two 4½-inch cannons and some machine guns.[9] *Yaeyama* had been lurking near Quinauan Point, shelling shore positions in support of the landing operation.

Sailors aboard the PT thought the enemy boat was moving north to get under the protection of shore batteries in Subic Bay. "At about this time the ship either slowed or stopped and turned toward the eastward," Schumacher reported. "We closed rapidly to about 5,000 yards at which time (10:10 pm) we were illuminated by a large searchlight from the ship." The PT continued to move toward the target, even though the brightness of the beam temporarily blocked it from view.

PT sailors would soon learn there was nothing more terrifying than being caught in a Japanese searchlight. It was usually a sure sign that a hail of gunfire would soon be on the way. "The first salvo was fired from the ship in a very few seconds after illuminating and landed about 500 yards ahead of the *PT-32*," Schumacher reported. The second salvo fell about 200 yards in front of the PT. The men could see that each salvo contained two shells.

The starboard torpedo was fired using an estimate of the last known angle and speed of the target before she disappeared behind the glare of the searchlight. The Japanese ship was about 4,000 yards away. The port torpedo was fired minutes later after the range had closed to between 3,000 and 3,500 yards, just as the third salvo of gunfire splashed in the water about 200 yards behind the 32 boat.

The PT then turned due south to get out of the immediate area running at a speed of 25 knots, the extra power becoming available when the weight of the torpedoes left the boat. The sailors aboard the PT made an unsuccessful attempt to shoot out the searchlight at about the same time. "For about two minutes there was no evidence of increasing range and gunfire continued from the enemy ship with two gun salvos, apparently four guns firing," Schumacher continued.

An explosion suddenly detonated on the target somewhere below the searchlight. Schumacher recalled it was "definitely not gunfire and debris came up into searchlight beam. There was a pause in firing, although the searchlight continued on and the ship apparently slowed as the range started opening." Both Schumacher and DeLong believed the second torpedo hit the target, causing her to slow.

The PT boat finally started to pull away from the minelayer. The gunfire, however, resumed and the torpedo boat did not escape the grasp of the searchlight until about 10:30 pm when the 32 made a sharp right turn. "After losing the *PT-32* in the beam, there were about three salvoes fired into the knuckle of the turn, after which the searchlight went out," Schumacher reported. "It came on and made several sweeps thereafter, but did not pick up the *PT-32* although it passed over two or three times."

The 32 boat rendezvoused with *Maryanne* after slipping away from the Japanese minelayer. The pair was ordered to stay in the vicinity of LaMonja Island until dawn when Schumacher's boat returned to Sisiman Cove. The *Yaeyama* reported only slight damage attributed to gunfire from shore.[10] The real cause could have been the torpedo from *PT-32*.

CHAPTER 22

It was becoming more difficult for the PT sailors to keep their boats in fighting condition as each day of February passed. The standard practice was to change out the Packard engines after 600 hours of operations. Lack of parts and equipment, however, made it difficult to do. Six of the squadron's nine spare engines were already lost—one during the aerial attack on Cavite Navy Yard, three when Manila fell to the enemy, and two more on Corregidor from bombing. John Bulkeley's boats had logged about four times the recommended hours, and speed began to suffer as a direct result.[1]

The boats had been rotating time in the floating dry dock *Dewey* for repairs and maintenance ever since *PT-35* began a three-day stint on January 27. The 41, 34 and 32 followed in succession, with all of the boats having their bottoms cleaned and repainted. The latter, though, underwent additional hull and engine repairs using crude parts manufactured aboard *Canopus*.[2]

Maintenance issues, however, were only part of the problem. The squadron's gasoline supply was getting dangerously low and all of the spare torpedoes were gone. The only available underwater weapons were the torpedoes still on the boats.

Chief Machinist's Mate Carl Richardson tried to keep the sailors' spirits up by constantly developing elaborate wagers on the outcome of the war. Most were based on when, not if, the Americans would win. The odds seemed to shift almost daily based on various unrelated topics, including the disposition of *PT-41*'s mascot—a monkey named

Admiral Tojo.[3] The predictions provided a humorous if only momentary diversion.

Gasoline and ammunition were not the only supplies running low. "The food situation was getting tough," Robert Kelly recalled. Fresh food such as meat, fruit, and vegetables were long gone. The sailors, however, were eating substantially better than the soldiers on Bataan. Breakfast often consisted of pancakes made without eggs or butter. A mixture of sugar and water provided the syrup. "Then for dinner, it was always canned salmon and rice, and you don't know how tired you can get of canned salmon until you eat it regularly for a few months," Kelly added.[4] The men had earlier stumbled across a cache of the canned fish. The food soon became a staple.

The executive officer was able to get ahold of some fresh meat during one of his visits to Corregidor. It came aboard one of the few blockade runners to make successful passage from the south. The supply was enough for the men on the boats to have two meals.

Another change in the menu came when a sailor with good aim killed a tomcat with his pistol. The cat had been roaming the area around Sisiman Cove for some time. It was boiled the same day and served for dinner. Bulkeley thought it tasted great, remarking how similar it was to roast duck. The other sailors did not agree.

The only true delicacy came in the form of ice cream supplied by *Canopus*. The tender had barrels of ice cream mix, a freezer, and a very generous commanding officer. He served the ice cream to any sailor who came aboard as long as the supply lasted. Bulkeley was known to be a regular customer.

The final action in the Bataan area for the PT boats took place on the night of February 17–18. It again centered on Subic Bay. The Japanese were rumored to have ringed the bay with gun emplacements, making any PT boat operations in the area extremely dangerous, if not suicidal. Reports of Japanese destroyers lurking in the bay, however, were enough to spur Bulkeley to action.

He ventured north with two boats—PTs 35 and 41. Anthony Akers commanded the 35 boat, with Bulkeley aboard. George Cox was the boat

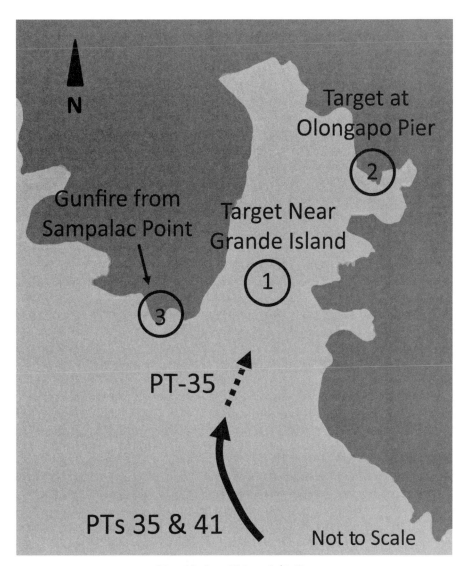

Map 10: Last Visit to Subic Bay

captain of *PT-41*. Rather than have his boats become trapped in Subic Bay, the squadron commander planned to lure the Japanese into a trap of his own. The PTs would proceed together to the entrance of the bay under the cover of darkness. Bulkeley would take the 35 boat into Subic in the hopes of attracting the attention of a destroyer. The PT was then to lead her out of the bay for the waiting 41 boat to attack with torpedoes, assuming the destroyer gave chase. It was a risky, but workable, plan.

At 10:45 pm the 35 boat cautiously moved into the entrance of Subic Bay. Grande Island stood dead ahead in the distance. The small land mass was positioned in the middle of the narrowest point of the bay's entrance.

Lookouts quickly sighted a small patrol vessel. She appeared to be "a diesel-driven fishing trawler of about 200 to 400 tons." Although not the destroyer Bulkeley hoped to find, it was a target nonetheless. He ordered a high-speed attack. "At this point the vessel was entering east side of the channel by Grande Island," Bulkeley recorded. "The range was about 1,000 yards."[5] The 35 unleashed a single torpedo. Although the underwater missile appeared to run normally, it was thought to have passed under the shallow hull of the target without exploding.

A second, larger vessel was then sighted in the distance. The new target, possibly a tanker, was behind the patrol trawler to the east of Grande Island. She appeared to be near the Olongapo Pier on the east side of the bay. A single torpedo was fired. *PT-35* was now dangerously far into Subic Bay, prompting Bulkeley to order an immediate retirement.

No enemy vessels were in chase as the two PTs met outside of the bay. The boats passed Sampaloc Point long enough to spray suspected shore batteries with machine-gun fire before turning south. "A fire was seen in Olongapo after retirement," Bulkeley reported. The source, however, was unknown, as no explosions were seen or heard from either torpedo. Although the army later reported a large tanker sank next to the pier in Olongapo after burning through the night, the squadron commander claimed no hits for the evening.[6]

The rest of the patrol was uneventful. "Patrol was instituted 50 miles due west of Subic to abeam Corregidor until dawn," Bulkeley reported. "Nothing was sighted."

While the high-profile action was taking place off Bataan and Subic Bay, the boats were also assigned the less glamorous duty of what Iliff

Richardson remembered as "special missions." The work included a variety of operations, including escorting the occasional inter-island steamers and submarines who ran the Japanese blockade to bring supplies to Corregidor.

The steamers typically came north from Cebu, doing most of the traveling at night to avoid detection. One or two PT boats sailed down to the Verde Island Passage to meet the blockade runners for the final leg of the journey. The duty included guiding the arriving vessel through the minefields around Corregidor. The trip required the PTs to go past Fortune Island, a small speck of land south of the entrance to Manila Bay. The island, occupied by the Japanese early in the Luzon campaign, was used as a navigation point for their own warships. The sailors assumed it was also an enemy lookout point and integral part of the blockade, making the voyages south extremely dangerous.

Richardson remembered *PTs 34* and *41* were assigned such a mission on a bright moonlit night. "As we approached the rendezvous at Verde Island Passage, the lookout suddenly pointed to the shore on the starboard beam," he wrote. "There could be seen clearly against the background of the mountains the wakes of three ships; probably destroyers in formation."[7] Robert Kelly ordered general quarters as the 34 speeded up to attack. *PT-41* had already moved ahead to meet the blockade runner. The tension was high, for a single PT challenging three destroyers was a risky—if not outright suicidal—operation.

No ships, however, could be clearly seen as the boat drew closer to the targets. "Finally the binoculars revealed a series of tiny coves more or less evenly spaced against the background and the wakes were nothing but waves breaking on the rocky beach," Richardson recalled. "We all laughed at the folly, [Lieutenant] Kelly as much as the rest of us." He added "the attack was not revealed to any of the other boats for fear of ridicule."

The rest of the mission was uneventful, with the small vessel *Legaspi* safely escorted to Corregidor. The steamer made two successful runs to Corregidor, but her luck ran out on the third attempt. She was sunk by a Japanese gunboat on March 1.[8]

When a steamer or submarine departed Corregidor, the boats were often called upon to create a diversion. Many Americans believed a Japanese submarine was stationed off the entrance of Manila Bay at all times to intercept any departing ships. *PT-34* was one of the first boats asked to perform the task. "We got under way as we would on an ordinary patrol and then proceeded out to sea at a reasonably high speed, presuming that the whine of our high speed propellers would be heard by the enemy submarine," Richardson recalled. "For one hour we proceeded this way and then reversed course." While the 34 boat created the noise, *PT-41* escorted a departing submarine safely though the minefield. "Our very valuable submarine proceeded safely out to sea."

While the special missions were not making any headlines, the work was helping a trickle of supplies to reach the beleaguered defenders. Richardson and his crewmates had no idea that the PT activity around Bataan was about to come to an abrupt end.

Bulkeley was now a well-known figure in the Philippines, due to his daring forays into enemy-held waters. Gone, though, was the clean-cut naval officer look that he possessed at the start of the war. Lieutenant Malcolm Champlin, who served on Admiral Rockwell's staff, remembered the PT boat leader taking on the persona of a modern-day pirate. "He wore a long, unruly beard and carried two ominous looking pistols at his side," Champlin recalled. "His eyes were bloodshot and red-rimmed from constant night patrols and lack of sleep."[9] He also remembered Bulkeley's "nervous energy was tremendous and never seemed to give out."

The squadron commander knew his days on Bataan were numbered. The Japanese advance was stopped at the rear battle position, but disease, exhaustion, malnutrition, and dwindling supplies were all taking a heavy toll on the defenders. Everyone from high-ranking officers down to lowly foot soldiers recognized it was only a matter of time before the fighting was over.

Bulkeley needed to find a way to escape before the declining supply of gasoline gave out for good, dooming his men to become prisoners when the peninsula fell to the enemy. His plan was to stage a daring escape to China.

Little information is available about the plan to go to China. The idea seems to have originated sometime in December with the intended destination of Hong Kong. The endpoint was changed to China after the British colony surrendered to the Japanese in late 1941.

Bulkeley's prewar experience in China may have played a role in the decision. By February 1942 the plan was under serious discussion among Bulkeley and a few select officers.

It was for the most part a closely guarded secret. Reporter Clark Lee was one of the few outsiders told of the idea. He spoke regularly with Bulkeley, and had even spent time aboard a PT for a few night patrols. Iliff Richardson recalled Lee spending time aboard several boats, but not seeing any action. "He always went out one day too soon or one day too late," Richardson remembered.[10]

Bulkeley explained the situation in terms of fuel. "We've got only about enough gasoline for one good operation and we have only a few torpedoes left," Lee reported the squadron commander told him. "Then we'll be tied up here."[11]

The squadron commander wanted to travel across the South China Sea to make a landing between Hong Kong and Swatow, China. The area was thought to be thinly held by the Japanese. The sailors would then move inland to Chungking, the provisional capital of China, where American planes could fly them out. The plan, of course, required the appropriate arrangements with friendly Chinese to be worked out in advance. The treacherous voyage across about 675 miles of open water would require every drop of available gasoline.

Reporter Lee, who was also looking for a way to escape, wanted to help. "I have made friends with a Chinese officer, Lieutenant Colonel Chi-Wang, who is stationed at headquarters of the Philippine Army in Bataan," he told Bulkeley. "I'll bring him down here and introduce you two and ask him to send a message to Chungking getting approval for your landing." The individual was serving as a liaison officer to American forces and was now trapped like everyone else on Bataan.

Lee later wrote that the plan was not only approved by officials in Chungking, but by Admiral Rockwell as well. The admiral must have considered the boats capable of getting out of the Philippines and completing the long voyage under their own power.[12] Bulkeley planned to take the entire squadron—about 78 men—in his four boats. Lee, fellow reporter Nat Floyd of the *New York Times*, and officer Chi-Wang were also going to make the journey. Preparations for the voyage were under way, but then suddenly came to an abrupt halt. Bulkeley and his PT boats were about to be called upon to undertake a dangerous mission that would forever cement their place as heroes in American history.

PART III

EVACUATION

CHAPTER 23

Thousands of miles away in Washington, DC it was clear to top American leaders that the situation on Bataan was hopeless. No large-scale reinforcements were able to get to the embattled troops and the weary defenders probably could not hold out much longer. The remnants of General MacArthur's Luzon army would be sequestered on Corregidor once Bataan fell. The fortress island would not be able to withstand the Japanese onslaught for an extended amount of time.

The idea of evacuating Philippine President Manuel Quezon was first discussed in Washington in late December. MacArthur, however, pushed back, fearing a collapse of Filipino morale if their leader departed. By early February, with the battlefield situation much worse, the general relented. President Roosevelt and his military advisors approved a plan for Quezon and other key staff members to be removed from Corregidor as needed. The timing was left up to MacArthur.

Events then took a surprising turn when Quezon, embittered over the lack of visible American help and reinforcements, sent Roosevelt a desperate proposal asking for the United States to immediately grant the Philippines full independence. The Philippine leader wanted to declare his country neutral, hoping both American and Japanese forces would then depart. A message from MacArthur followed that reflected the strain of the overall situation. "You must be prepared at any time to figure on the complete destruction of this command," the general wrote. He also warned of an "almost violent resentment" of Filipinos against the United States.[1]

MacArthur may have become even further stressed after hearing of the fall of Singapore on February 15. The loss of the prized possession would go down in history as one of the greatest defeats ever suffered by the British Empire. It was another success in an unbroken string of Japanese victories across the Pacific. The triumph likely meant additional Japanese troops were available to be thrown into the Philippine battle.

Roosevelt issued a sharp response refuting the unlikely scenario of Philippine neutrality and alluding to the ultimate defeat of the Japanese. "Whatever happens to the present American garrison we shall not relax our efforts until the forces which are we are now marshalling outside the Philippine Islands return to the Philippines and drive the last remnant of the invaders from your soil."[2] Roosevelt sent a separate message only to MacArthur. He gave him permission to surrender Filipino troops, if deemed necessary, but not American forces.

Other people of importance began leaving Corregidor, while the messages went back and forth between MacArthur and Washington. High Commissioner Sayre departed on a submarine bound for Australia. Manuel Quezon, his neutrality idea negated, left aboard the submarine *Swordfish* on February 20 along with his family and key staff members.[3] Before departing, the tearful president took off a ring and slipped it on MacArthur's finger. "When they find your body, I want them to know you fought for my country."[4] Quezon's party disembarked on the central Philippine island of Panay two days later.

Quezon completed an important business transaction before departing Corregidor. He arranged to pay MacArthur $500,000 for his work in building up the defenses of the Philippines. The general accepted the payment in what later became one of the most controversial episodes of his long career. Roosevelt allowed the transaction, but it was kept secret for decades until uncovered by a researcher in the late 1970s.[5]

Discussions in Washington soon turned to the possibility of evacuating MacArthur. The general was enormously popular on the home front, even ascending to hero status, as the only Allied commander holding back the Japanese onslaught in the Pacific. The general's rise was in part due to his subtle, but very effective, public relations campaign.

Most of what the American public read about the ongoing battle in the Philippines came from press releases originating from MacArthur's headquarters. Of 142 press releases issued between December 1941 and March 1942, 109 mention only the general. The reports were often peppered with key phrases, such as "MacArthur's men," giving the impression of the general personally leading his soldiers in battle.[6] Frequently left out were the names of combat units and the officers on the front lines who were actually doing the fighting.

MacArthur's status on the home front was definitely not shared by all of the weary, sick, and hungry soldiers on the front lines of Bataan. Many resented "Dugout Doug" for managing the battle from the safety of his tunnel on Corregidor. Some soldiers, however, held out to the bitter end, believing MacArthur would somehow pull off a rescue of the beleaguered forces.

With the Philippines defense doomed to eventual defeat, the loss of the popular American general to a certain death or to become a Japanese prisoner would be a substantial propaganda victory for the enemy. Roosevelt and other key leaders realized MacArthur could be of greater benefit in the total war effort.

Less clear, however, was whether the general would be willing to leave his men in the field. The move was tantamount to abandoning the Philippine nation. An old friend of MacArthur had already warned officials the general would not leave unless it was done in a way that "his honor and his record as a soldier" were not lessened.[7]

Roosevelt met with a small group of top advisors on February 22. In conference with Army chief Marshall, Admiral Ernest King, and key advisor Harry Hopkins, he decided to extricate MacArthur from the Philippines. The president issued orders, in his name, for the general to proceed to Australia via the southern Philippine island of Mindanao. He was to assume command of all American forces in Australia.

A radiogram of the presidential order was quickly sent to Corregidor with a decoded copy handed to MacArthur at 12:30 pm on February 23.[8] The general at first thought about resisting the order. He even considered resigning his commission and staying to fight with his men as a volunteer soldier. His staff helped to convince him the order must be followed. Most assumed men and materials were already massed in Australia waiting for MacArthur to lead an immediate counterattack.

MacArthur sent a reply to Marshall agreeing in principle to the request to leave. However, he asked to delay the timing of his departure. "Please be guided by me in this matter," he urged. "I know the situation here in the Philippines and unless the right moment is chosen, for this delicate operation, a sudden collapse might occur. These people are depending on me now."[9]

MacArthur needed to ensure the situation on Bataan had sufficiently stabilized after the stretch of recent fighting. Marshall took the request to the president. Roosevelt agreed to let the general determine the timing of his escape. MacArthur expected his departure to take place on or about March 15.

Work began immediately to make the appropriate arrangements for the operation. Japanese naval activity was increasing around the Philippines, making any type of escape operation risky. Japanese radio propagandist Tokyo Rose recently announced with cheer that MacArthur would be hanged on the Imperial Plaza in Tokyo if captured.[10] The submarine *Permit* was to be made available for transporting the general to Mindanao. She was expected to be at Corregidor by March 14.[11] Planes would fly up from Australia for the remainder of the trip south.

It clearly was MacArthur's decision to use PT boats for the first part of the escape mission. The historical record around the timing and details of the decision, though, is somewhat hazy. Various accounts have MacArthur planning to use the submarine, with PTs only as a back-up alternative, and only deciding to use boats at the last minute. Other versions, however, indicate he was planning to use the PTs all along.[12] The amount of planning involved for the PT operation seems to support the latter.

The general began working on a short list of key staff members to depart with him. A larger issue, though, was who would succeed him in command of the Philippines. MacArthur eventually chose General Wainwright. The leader of the Luzon forces had capably led the rearguard action allowing the American and Filipino troops to escape into Bataan.

The situation south and west of the Philippines continued to deteriorate as arrangements progressed for MacArthur's departure. The Japanese had already captured Malaya, Singapore, and Borneo. Imperial forces were now poised to take control of the Dutch East Indies. Allied commanders hoped to slow the advance as the enemy approached the island of Java, the seat of the colonial Dutch government.

Allied naval power in the region suffered a series of devastating defeats during the last days of February. A combined force of American, British, Dutch, and Australia warships was dealt heavy losses in the battle of Java Sea beginning on February 27. The Asiatic Fleet's flagship *Houston* and the Australian light cruiser *Perth* were sunk a few days later in the battle of Sunda Strait. There was no stopping the Japanese invasion forces.

Enemy ground troops captured the Dutch capital of Batavia on March 1. Dutch authorities surrendered about a week later.[13] The south Asian colonial empires of Britain, France, the Netherlands, and United States were now largely under Japanese rule. Only scattered pockets of resistance remained in the Pacific. The largest was the Philippines, but the American and Filipino defenders were now almost completely surrounded. If MacArthur was going to leave Corregidor, he had better do it soon.

The first hint that a secret operation was in the works came on February 18, when an unlikely visitor arrived at Sisiman Cove to see John Bulkeley. It was Lieutenant Colonel Sidney Huff, an aide to General MacArthur. The army officer came with a question. "Do you think that your boats could take a party on a sea run of a few hundred miles, say down to Puerto Princess on Palawan?" Bulkeley thought for a moment before replying. "No question about it. You have something specific in mind?" Huff then became somewhat evasive. "Maybe. I'll be able to tell you more about it later in the month."[14]

The brief discussion continued with Huff asking if the PT boats required any special materials or equipment for such a mission. "No, nothing special," Bulkeley replied. The squadron commander was aware of many potential needs—clean gasoline, torpedoes, and spare parts—but knew full well none were available.

Less than two weeks after Huff's visit came another surprise—Bulkeley was notified that MacArthur wanted to take a ride in one of the boats. The squadron commander left Sisiman Cove for the short trip to the North Dock on Corregidor on March 1. MacArthur, his wife Jean, and some officers boarded *PT-41*. Four P-40 fighter planes flew overhead while the 41 boat spent about half an hour cruising nearby waters. Bulkeley showed the general various features of the boat during the short voyage.

MacArthur had a surprise after the PT returned to the North Dock. He announced that Bulkeley was being awarded the Distinguished Service Cross for his actions in defense of the Philippines. The real reason for the trip was for MacArthur to find out if his wife could handle the rough ride of a PT boat. Jean said she could manage it.

MacArthur invited Bulkeley to go with him to Topside, an area on Corregidor where he maintained a small office in a damaged building. The two walked together into a nearby field. The area was littered with bomb craters from the pounding air and artillery attacks. Bulkeley thought the general looked gaunt.

The visit to Corregidor concluded with some more private meetings. MacArthur started talking when it was clear no one else was around. He was going to Australia. "I have been peremptorily ordered to leave by the president," he disclosed with unbridled dismay.[15] He told Bulkeley he wanted to use PT boats—not a plane or submarine, as the Japanese might be expecting—for the first leg of the journey to Mindanao. The remainder of the trip would be done with airplanes. MacArthur asked if he could pull it off. Bulkeley promptly responded "General, it'll be a piece of cake!"[16]

Huff was surprised when the general first mentioned the use of PT boats to him and several others. Most of MacArthur's advisors assumed the departure would be accomplished by submarine, based on the information from Washington and the precedents set by those who had already left. "That's what I expected too," Sidney Huff later wrote. "In fact, it hadn't entered my mind that we would go any other way."

"I had a talk with Lieutenant Bulkeley," MacArthur told Huff. "He tells me we have a chance to get through the blockage in PT boats. It won't be easy."[17] The general added the boats could put up a good fight if an enemy warship was encountered. MacArthur was known to have a dislike for confined spaces. He would rather take his chances on PT boats than in the claustrophobic environment aboard a submarine.[18] Huff later wrote that most of the other evacuees would have preferred the underwater option.

Huff reports that he, Bulkeley, and Harold Ray began putting together an operational plan based on the four available PT boats. The work was done in secret, as very few people were aware MacArthur had been ordered to leave. Other preparations were made simultaneously, such as scrounging up enough food to take for the voyage.

The evacuation order only authorized MacArthur, his family, and Richard Sutherland to depart Corregidor. The general, however, wanted the list expanded to include key staffers who could serve at his new headquarters in Australia. In the end it was Sutherland, not MacArthur, who drew up the final list of passengers.[19]

The ending list reached a total of 21 individuals, including army and navy officers as well as one enlisted man. In addition to MacArthur's wife and young son Arthur, a Chinese nurse was to join the group. She had been with Arthur since his birth and the general feared she would be killed if left behind due to her association with his family. Admiral Rockwell was selected to make the trip, along with Ray, as the sole navy representatives.

There was plenty of work to do on Bulkeley's end. He needed to both keep the departure plan secret from his men until the appropriate time and prepare his PTs for the grueling voyage as best as possible. The journey to Mindanao required the weary boats to travel over 500 miles. The distance was not much shorter than the proposed run to China.

The preparation work included scraping the boat bottoms, checking compasses, and trying to overhaul the engines. The latter was a tremendous undertaking, given the meager facilities and no spare parts. Gasoline was collected and combined. The length of the voyage necessitated extra fuel be stored in drums topside. Decks were reinforced with wooden planks to withstand the extra weight.

Every boat was reconditioned. "The *PT-34* was given a complete cleaning and repainting of the decks [and] canopy topsides," Iliff Richardson recalled. "The color was a dark green used in camouflaging the boats in wartime." Word quickly spread among the sailors that each boat would undergo a "captain's inspection"—the first since the war began. "The inspection was held as scheduled and the 34 was found to be in good practical condition."[20] Assorted vessels from the inshore patrol groups took over many of the nightly PT patrols during the time.

Richardson recalled "it was obvious to everyone that there would be a change" for the squadron. It was based on activity beyond the work on the boats, such as "the issuance of regulation army high-topped shoes, tropical fatigue hats and complete army packs, canteens and rifles for every man in the squadron. Special racks for the rifles were installed in the pilot house where the rifles were immediately accessible, and the rest of the new equipment was stowed in convenient places." He recalled that none of the squadron leaders were talking about what was in the works.

The officers also created a diversion by continuing to build up the facilities at Sisiman Cove as if the unit was planning to stay for a while. Among the improvements were fixing up the galley and mess hall. The latter was cleaned and screened in for the comfort of the men.

Robert Kelly remembered the boat crews becoming inquisitive about the various preparations. They eventually had to be told something. Bulkeley intimated they were getting ready to travel to Cebu in the southern part of the islands. He described it as a glamorous place with a plentiful supply of food, torpedoes, and gasoline, not to mention beautiful girls. It seemed to work, but the squadron commander knew the supply situation in the south was just as desperate.

Next was what to do about the two war correspondents and Chinese officer expecting to make the run to the China coast. Bulkeley told them the plan to go to China was still in place, but it likely would not happen for a long time. He recommended they take advantage of any other opportunity to leave the area, should one come about.

The squadron commander had been visiting MacArthur's headquarters on a regular basis since being let in on the escape plan. The missing piece of information he needed most was the departure date. MacArthur summoned Bulkeley on March 9. He called the sailor the "buckaroo with the cold green eyes."[21] The general told him the plan was to leave on March 15. The date was also communicated to Washington. It gave Bulkeley sufficient time to make the final preparations.

The press back in the United States was clamoring to know when MacArthur was going to leave Corregidor, even though there had been no official announcement that such would take place. It was a regular topic on radio broadcasts and in newspapers. Reporters even brought it up at one of President Roosevelt's press conferences.[22]

The Japanese may have been listening, as the second week of March brought a sharp increase in enemy naval activity around Luzon. Minelayers were spotted in Subic Bay and surface patrols were thought to be roaming off Corregidor. Most concerning, however, was a report of a Japanese destroyer division moving north from the southern Philippines.[23]

The enemy movements were likely nothing more than a coincidence. However, it did not seem so to those planning the general's escape. "It was all too apparent that the Japanese Navy not only expected General MacArthur to leave Corregidor, but would do everything it could to intercept him," Bulkeley later recalled.[24]

The squadron commander initially only told his executive officer of the escape plan. Kelly was struck hard by the realization that the mission was the beginning of the end for the unit. "Of course, to us this meant that the China trip—our last hope of seeing America and escaping death or a Japanese prison—was gone forever," he later said. "Now the MTBs were like the rest here in the islands—the expendables who fight on without hope to the end."[25] He assumed the boats would stay in the southern islands after the voyage.

Space constraints meant Bulkeley could not take all of his men south, as he had hoped to do during the escape to China. Sailors of the base force, extra boat crews, and even some officers had to be left behind. The list included Barron Chandler—he was still hospitalized on Corregidor.

Edward DeLong would also not be making the trip south. Without a boat since the loss of *PT-31*, the officer took command of *Trabajador* in late February. The old harbor tug had been pressed into service as a tender for the PT boats. Richardson remembered the old vessel as a "requisitioned salvage tug boat that was acting as a motor torpedo boat tender; assisting in loading torpedoes and unloading torpedoes and in repair and upkeep of PT engines." Five members of the lost 31 boat went with their former boat captain.[26] All became prisoners when the Philippines fell to the Japanese.

Robert Kelly was among the PT officers who were envious of DeLong. *Trabajador* had a cabin, wardroom, and a real galley along with a mess attendant to prepare meals. Bulkeley and Kelly were known to visit to the tug for an occasional bite to eat.

MacArthur was also making his final plans for the impending departure. He decided to appoint General Wainwright to lead all forces on Luzon—essentially Bataan and Corregidor—but intended to retain overall command of the Philippines from his new post in Australia. It was part of a larger plan to split the Philippines into four smaller command zones.

Wainwright received a call from General Sutherland on the evening to March 9 to come to Corregidor the next morning for a meeting with MacArthur. The chief of staff pulled him aside upon his arrival at the Malinta Tunnel. Sutherland quickly told him of MacArthur's imminent departure and about the reorganization plan before taking him to see the general.

MacArthur and Wainwright met at the small Topside cottage about a quarter of a mile away from the tunnel. An occasional rumble of cannon fire permeated across the water from Bataan. "He was tired, but he grinned and shook hands with me," Wainwright recalled of the encounter. MacArthur repeated much of what Sutherland had already said, making sure it was known that he was leaving under protest after repeated orders from the president.

The conversation then turned to Bataan. "We're alone, Jonathan," MacArthur started. "You know that as well as I. If I get through to Australia you know I'll come back as soon as I can with as much as I can. In the meantime you've got to hold."[27] Wainwright promised to do all he could, but knew it was a hopeless cause. "You'll get through," he assured him.

The talk continued for a short time about Bataan before MacArthur drifted into an explanation of why some officers were being evacuated, while others left behind. MacArthur gave him a box of cigars and two large jars of shaving cream as the meeting neared an end. "Good-bye, Jonathan. When I get back, if you're still on Bataan I'll make you a lieutenant general," MacArthur said in closing. "I'll be on Bataan if I'm alive," Wainwright replied. The promise to hold Bataan weighed heavily on Wainwright's mind as he slowly made his way to the North Dock.

MacArthur's plan to retain control of the Philippines was counter-manded by officials in Washington shortly after his departure. Wainwright was given command of the entire Philippines and was promptly promoted to a three-star general. He moved his headquarters to Corregidor on March 21.[28] In the coming weeks, the general would do his best to keep his promise to MacArthur about holding Bataan. He was faced with a desperate situation, meager resources, and no hope for reinforcements.

Bulkeley was called to MacArthur's office on the morning of March 11. It was four days before the planned departure date. The general informed him of a change of plans, perhaps made for security reasons. He was told "to have your boats ready for us to board at [7:30 pm] today."

The escape mission was about to get started.

CHAPTER 24

John Bulkeley had no time to lose in making the final preparations for the most important assignment of his naval career to date. He returned to Sisiman Cove from the meeting with General MacArthur at about noon on March 11. It was finally time to let his other boat captains in on the secret evacuation plan. Bulkeley called an impromptu meeting with Robert Kelly, Anthony Akers, George Cox, and Vincent Schumacher.

The squadron commander outlined the operation, revealing Admiral Rockwell's secret operation orders, dated March 10, along with some charts he had created for the mission. All four PTs would make the 560-mile trip to the southern Philippines. Bulkeley stressed the need for the boats to stay together during the long voyage. A total of 21 passengers were to be divided among the boats.

The PTs were to depart from various locations around the tip of Bataan and Corregidor so as not to draw any unwarranted attention from roaming Japanese scout planes. The group would proceed south under the cover of darkness after gathering near the entrance of Manila Bay. Philippine patrol boats planned to stage a diversionary action during the evening hours off Subic Bay as an added safeguard.[1] The distance to Mindanao was too great to be covered in a single night and it was too dangerous for the boats to be operating in the open seas during the daytime in plain sight of patrolling Japanese planes and warships. The plan therefore called for a stopover at the approximate midpoint of the journey.

The boats were to arrive at Tagauayan Island at about 7:30 am on March 12. The small island, in the Cuyo group off the western

Philippines, was an ideal location to hide out during the daylight hours. A late-day departure for the last leg of the journey would put the boats at their final destination, Cagayan on the northern coast of Mindanao, at 7:00 am on March 13. A group of B-17 bombers at the Del Monte airfield was to then complete the final leg of the evacuation by taking the general's party to Australia.

Admiral Rockwell ominously warned "enemy air and surface activity is to be expected along the route."[2] The orders contained a series of explicit instructions of what to do in various circumstances, beginning with mechanical problems—a likely scenario given the boats' worn-out engines and impure gasoline. "If any boat breaks down, she will transfer passengers and proceed independently or transfer all personnel and scuttle ship if necessary—last boat in the column is designated to go alongside disabled boat."

Bulkeley was under orders to use evasive tactics to avoid contact with the enemy. If, however, the PTs were discovered and attacked by warships, the lead boat, carrying MacArthur, was to turn away while the remaining boats closed to attack the enemy. A host of alternative plans were included in Rockwell's orders to provide Bulkeley guidance in a wide range of possible scenarios involving delays or enemy activity.

Although originally scheduled to take MacArthur's party out of Corregidor, the submarine *Permit* now played an important back-up role in the operation. She was directed to rendezvous with the boats at the Tagauayan Island stopover. The undersea boat could take aboard all passengers in case the PTs encountered serious problems or could otherwise not make Mindanao.

One of the final sections of Rockwell's operational document provided the most up-to-date picture of enemy activity in the general area of the mission. It was filled with reports of Japanese surface vessels sighted close to islands on Bulkeley's path south, including Mindoro, Panay, and Negroes. Increasing naval activity around Subic Bay was noted, including movements in the area of vessels up to cruiser size.

The report also warned of Japanese planes on the prowl. "Considerable air activity has been reported in the Visayan area. Apparently ferry flights are being made from Formosa to Manila, thence to Davao," Rockwell

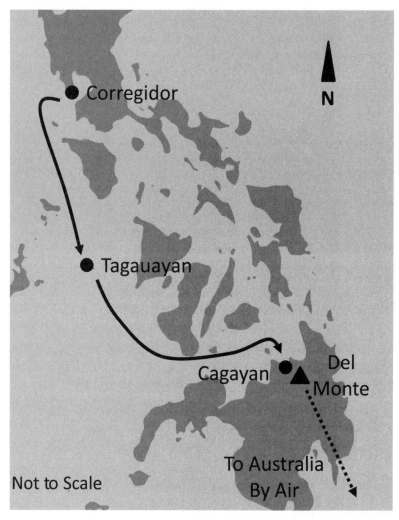

Map 11: MacArthur's Escape Route

noted. "En route these planes search the interior waters of the archipelago."[3] An inter-island steamer had been recently strafed and the city of Cagayan—MacArthur's disembarking point—was bombed.

Bulkeley's evacuation mission ended at Mindanao. The PTs were to "proceed as instructed under separate orders" after all the passengers were safely delivered to Cagayan. The separate orders, however, had not yet been provided.

The officers' meeting ended with Bulkeley announcing they were departing that very night. It led to a last-minute flurry of activity to get the PTs ready. The crew's gear was moved back into the galley to make space available for the passengers. Any available extra parts were loaded aboard. Landing equipment previously gathered for the trip to China was taken off. The same process was going on simultaneously aboard all four boats.

Twenty steel 55-gallon drums of gasoline were lashed to the deck of each boat to allow the PTs to make the complete journey. The fuel had been combined from various sources around Bataan and Corregidor. It represented the last of the diminishing supply.

Sidney Huff and Jean MacArthur were working behind the scenes on Corregidor to ensure there was enough food for the voyage. He later recalled "quietly transferring canned goods to the general's quarters in the tunnel, where we had four duffel bags, one for each boat. For more than a week we collected food in small quantities and Jean carefully divided it among the four duffel bags."[4] The bags were distributed one per boat just prior to departure.

Reporter Nat Floyd showed up at Sisiman Cove while the final preparations were being completed. The timing could not have been worse. The *New York Times* newsman had contact with the PT men on previous occasions. He seemed suspicious about all of the activity. Bulkeley made it known that he had no objections if Floyd somehow became a stowaway on one of the boats and was not found until the voyage was already under way. Clark Lee later wrote that Floyd was hiding below deck in the lazarette of *PT-41* when she departed later in the evening.[5] The small compartment at the rear of the boat was an ideal place for a stowaway.

Robert Kelly knew the departure marked the end of seeing Nurse Peggy. He wanted to be able to say a final goodbye. There was no phone at her hospital, but she was due to call him later that same night after her shift ended to discuss a date they had set for March 15. Kelly knew he could no longer keep the date and her call was probably going to be too late as he would have already departed.

Kelly decided to pen a letter, intending to drop it off at Corregidor during the departure. He had no sooner completed his writing when he

was paged for a call on the signal corps phone. It was Peggy. Her shift
had changed, allowing her to call early. Kelly broke the bad news about
his impending departure, although he could not reveal where he was
going. Their conversation abruptly ended when the phone connection
was broken. "It seemed a couple of generals wanted to talk to each
other," Kelly later quipped.[6] They were unable to get back in touch
before Kelly left for the voyage south.

The fading daylight of March 11 found both the PT sailors and passengers ready to start the evacuation mission. MacArthur stepped onto the
porch of his Topside cottage at 7:15 pm. "Jean, it is time to go," he told
his wife.[7] The general, his wife, son Arthur, and Cantonese amah, Ah
Cheu, were soon on their way to the Malinta Tunnel. Once there they
met up with other evacuees. Some cars were on hand for the short trip
to the North Dock. A few soldiers stopped to watch in the dim light
as the vehicles were loaded with passengers and luggage. A few of those
departing quietly said farewell to friends.

"It was a tense and unhappy and uncomfortable few minutes," Huff
remembered of the departure from the tunnel. "Nobody said much."
MacArthur had one last request just prior to leaving. He ordered the
four-star license plates be taken off his car and added to the luggage for
use in Australia.

A PT boat was already waiting dockside for the passengers. *PT-41* had
earlier slipped out of Sisiman Cove bound for Corregidor to be ready
for the 7:30 pm pickup. Bulkeley commanded the boat in concert with
George Cox. The PT was softly idling as her crew patiently waited.
The sailors could plainly see the dock area showed the scars of war from
weeks of bombing and shelling.

The cars pulled up to the wide concrete pier, allowing the passengers
to begin a slow walk toward the PT. Each person was carrying a bag
or suitcase. Bulkeley limited each passenger to one suitcase weighing
no more than 35 pounds. Jean's suitcase had a label attached from the
New Grand Hotel in Yokohama, Japan. The couple had briefly stayed at

the hotel on their honeymoon. Ah Cheu's few belongings were wrapped in a handkerchief. MacArthur brought his cane, but no luggage. He was out of uniform, wearing civilian wingtip shoes.

Some of the passengers shook hands with a few spectators. Bulkeley greeted the MacArthurs as they approached his boat. He hauled aboard their two suitcases. Huff helped Jean and Ah Cheu aboard, stumbling a bit in the process on some charred timbers. Young Arthur needed little help hopping onto the boat. He was clutching his stuffed animal, affectionately named Old Friend. Also coming aboard were Richard Sutherland, Huff, Navy Captain Herbert Ray, and Army Major Charles Morhouse. The latter was a doctor who MacArthur had selected to be the attending physician for the voyage.

MacArthur briefly stopped to talk with General George Moore, who commanded the harbor defenses. He had been previously instructed to destroy all armaments if Corregidor fell to ensure the weapons could not be used by the enemy when the Americans returned. "George, keep the flag flying," MacArthur now told him. "I'm coming back."[8]

MacArthur overheard a short snippet of conversation between two nearby enlisted soldiers as he moved towards the boat. They were talking about his odds of making a successful escape. "What's his chance, Sarge, of getting through?" Another replied "Dunno. He's lucky. Maybe one in five."[9] Bulkeley could read the fear and abandonment on the faces of those about to be left behind standing on the pier. "It would have taken an axe to cut the thick emotional atmosphere on the dock," he later recalled.[10]

An officer on the dock gave MacArthur a hand as he stepped aboard *PT-41*. The general briefly looked back at the once-beautiful Corregidor. "My eyes roamed that warped and twisted face of scorched rock," he later recalled of the moment. "Gone was the vivid green foliage, with its trees, shrubs, and flowers. Gone were the buildings, the sheds, every growing thing."

All of the passengers were now aboard. MacArthur turned to Bulkeley. "You may cast off, Buck, when you are ready."[11] The general raised his gold braided cap in a farewell salute to the crowd standing on the pier as *PT-41* slowly started moving away from the dock. American artillery abruptly rumbled, with a barrage of diversionary gunfire filling the air with a stench of gunpowder. Bulkeley's PT boat then disappeared into the growing darkness of the night.

A second group of passengers departed from Bataan. Master Sergeant Paul Rogers boarded an admiral's barge at the North Dock on Corregidor. He was the only enlisted man among those chosen to evacuate. "I was the last man aboard," he later wrote. "Before I had sat down, the navy chief cast off the line and the coxswain turned the launch out across the channel, toward Bataan." It was a short voyage. "Mariveles Mountain loomed in the foreground, and we approached a small dock at Sisiman Cove where two torpedo boats were lined up on either side. We walked onto the dock and broke into groups."[12]

Rogers was among four men to board *PT-35*. Ensign Bond Murray was aboard assisting boat captain Akers. Others went to *PT-34*.

Iliff Richardson remembered the last hours before *PT-34*'s departure. "At 5:00 pm the officers and crew of the 34 ate for the first time at the mess hall at the base ashore," he later wrote. "It was also the last time, because the base was abandoned that same night." Henry Brantingham was now serving aboard the boat. "After everyone had taken a bath, Lieutenant Kelly told Brantingham and myself that he was moving out of his stateroom and suggested that we do the same and sleep forward in the crews compartment—if we slept," Richardson continued.[13]

Kelly saluted as Admiral Rockwell came aboard *PT-34*. He was joined by a trio of army officers—General Richard Marshall, Colonel Charles P. Stivers, and Captain Joseph McMicking. "These officers carried only a limited amount of luggage which the crew of the 34 carried to the staterooms below," Richardson later wrote. "The barge cast off and proceeded back to Corregidor." The torpedo boat departed immediately.

Schumacher took *PT-32* to the Quarantine Dock at Mariveles for a 7:15 pm pick up. Ensign Cone Johnson served as the boat's executive officer. Five army officers—four of whom were generals—came aboard for the voyage.

All four of the boats were soon on the move. The PTs rendezvoused on schedule at 8:00 pm near the turning buoy just inside of the mine channel. The boats slowly crept through the channel in a single file with Kelly's *PT-34* in the lead. "The interval between the boats was 30 yards and the formation proceeded at idling speed, through the minefields out to the open sea," Richardson remembered.

Bulkeley was perched in the conn area of *PT-41*. "I had virtually memorized the minefield positions, and I mentally ticked them off—four, five, six," he later recalled.[14] He then flashed a signal for the boat captains to pour on speed by opening their throttles. The 41 boat took the lead position with *PT-34* last in the column. The PTs disappeared into the safety of the moonless darkness, leaving Bataan, Corregidor—and hopelessness—behind.

The boats traveled west after leaving Manila Bay moving as much as 5 miles out to sea to be away from any large land masses. The group was now traveling in a diamond formation. The flagship *PT-41*, in the lead position, set the pace for the other boats. The route west required the PTs to pass some small islands before turning south to parallel the larger island of Mindoro.

Bulkeley hoped to escape the immediate area unnoticed. However, lights were suddenly spotted on tiny Cabra Island about 50 miles southwest of Corregidor. Bulkeley took it to be signal fire—they had been seen! It was a time-honored signal used throughout maritime history calling attention to a blockade runner on the move. Enemy lookouts—or Philippine traitors—might be trying to warn Japanese authorities of their escape. If the signal was seen on one of the large islands, such as Luzon or Mindoro, Japanese activity was sure to follow as soon as daylight allowed, possibly in the form of bombers at dawn or ships later in the day.

The squadron commander had reason for concern, based on a report he received just prior to departure. A last-minute reconnaissance flight by one of the few remaining P-40 fighter planes sighted two Japanese warships—a destroyer and cruiser—operating in the vicinity of Mindoro. The destroyer was seen in Apo Pass East just west of island. The cruiser was off the southwest coast. Both were near the path of the escape route.[15]

Bulkeley gave Cabra Island a wide berth as the boats passed. The small flotilla then turned southeast, heading towards the Mindoro Strait. The body of water, measuring a little more than 50 miles wide at the narrowest point, separated Mindoro from some small islands to the southwest. The position of Apo Reef, sometimes referred to as Apo Island, divides the strait into an east and west passageway.

Bulkeley set a course for Apo Pass West to keep far away from the reported destroyer. It was only 3 miles wide, due to shoals on the west side. It was unlikely any Japanese warship would be operating in the narrow confines of the pass. The situation, though, was about to get much worse, as the area was experiencing some bad weather.

Sailors aboard *PT-41* were able to make out the faint outline of Apo Island at about 11:00 pm. Bulkeley used it as a checkpoint for navigation, having only a compass and basic chart for the voyage. He thought MacArthur and Sutherland were pleased with the progress of the mission thus far.

The initial part of the trip found the PTs moving through moderate seas with waves up to 2 feet. It made for a rough ride due to the speed and hulls of the small boats—especially for army personnel not used to traveling on the open sea. The weather conditions quickly grew worse.

A strong easterly wind churned up large waves, with swells topping off at 15 to 20 feet. The boats were violently tossed around while going through the peaks and troughs. Each PT was shaking as if the wooden hulls were about to come apart. Torrents of water crashed onto the decks, thoroughly drenching anyone topside.

The rough ride created a new problem for the crewmen. The movements threatened to jar loose the drums of gas lashed onto the deck of each boat. Serious damage to both people and equipment could result if the heavy objects came free. Two boats were forced to slow down, as a precaution, while sailors worked to better secure the drums.

The winds made the temperature feel much colder than normal. The PT sailors had trouble keeping control of the boats. Binoculars could not be kept dry. The men were soaking wet, cold, and hanging on for dear life as the torrents of water pelted them in the face. It was the travelers, though, who were in the worst shape.

Most of the passengers aboard *PT-41* became seasick soon after the rough seas started. MacArthur began the trip on deck, but retreated below after becoming soaking wet and seasick. The general lay down on a mattress Huff had arranged to have hauled aboard for the voyage. His face was ashen and eyes were ringed with dark circles. He later likened it to "a trip through a concrete mixer." Jean stayed at her husband's side, providing what little comfort she could. She seemed to be doing reasonably well. Young Arthur and Ah Cheu, both seasick, were in the officers' bunks. Arthur was running a fever.

Bulkeley was not able to offer any help to his guests. As the commander of the operation and skipper of the lead boat, he had to keep the voyage on course. The squadron commander remained in the conn with George Cox. At about 20-minute intervals he turned over the wheel to Cox and took a compass reading before going below deck, where he had the only detailed chart of the area among the four boats. Bulkeley used the information to plot the estimated course. It was a guess, but the best that could be done under the difficult circumstances.

It became increasingly difficult for the four boats to stay together as the night grew older. Visibility was near zero due to the foul weather and no moon. None of the boats were in perfect operating condition due to the continuous operations and lack of spare parts. Engine problems or fuel straining issues slowed some of the PTs during the evening. Shortly after midnight the boat captains were struggling to keep track of each other.[16]

CHAPTER 25

Robert Kelly hoped his *PT-34* had the power to keep up with the other boats, but soon found out she did not. His craft gradually fell back until he was nearly 200 yards behind *PT-41*. Admiral Rockwell was not pleased, but mostly remained patiently quiet, as his concern continued to build.

Kelly tried to explain the situation to the admiral. The boat was the only one not fully overhauled and the engines were filled with carbon. A good speed could not be obtained until it burned off. Rockwell would have none of it. His concern finally boiled over. "Damn it. Let's close up," he ordered.

The executive officer knew he had to do something—and quick. "I sent a whispered message to the engine room, ordering them to disconnect the throttle, and to push the carburetors up with their hands as far up as they would go," he later said. "We now had on every possible ounce of power, but the admiral still wasn't satisfied."[1]

The 34 boat started to close on the flagship, although she appeared to be slow going. At about the same time, John Bulkeley gave the order to slow his boat. Before Kelly could do much of anything, his boat shot past *PT-41*, much to Rockwell's dismay. The admiral was equally astonished a short time later to find out the boat did not have a pelorus for navigation. When the admiral questioned how they navigated on the PTs, Kelly responded "By guess and by God, sir." The startled Rockwell openly wondered if they would reach their destination.

The four PTs lost contact with each other by 3:30 am.[2] Weather and breakdowns doomed the plan to stay together. Bulkeley tried to find the other boats over the next three hours, but was unsuccessful. Each boat captain now had to find the rendezvous on their own.

The engines on *PT-34* abruptly stopped about half an hour later. It was the old nemesis that had been plaguing the squadron for months—clogged fuel strainers. Kelly reluctantly explained to Rockwell the cleaning process would take about half an hour as crewmen frantically began work to fix the problem. The PT drifted to a stop as the other boats quickly disappeared over the horizon.

Kelly's boat was not the only PT having trouble. Vincent Schumacher's *PT-32* was at a disadvantage from the start, having only two working engines. "The previously patched deck over the engine room was cracked and leaking badly from damage caused by a deck load of one thousand gallons of fuel in drums," her boat captain explained. "The bolts holding the center shaft tail strut were sheared off, rendering the shaft out of commission and causing a leak into the after compartment."[3]

The seawater grounded out the ignition system on two of the engines. The boat idled along on one engine after unsuccessful repairs. The 32 eventually stopped to clean fuel strainers. She fell behind and became separated from the others.

The onset of dawn marked the end of a sleepless night for Schumacher. The boat captain thought he was miles from the other PTs. He was exhausted, cold, and soaking wet as he stood topside with two army generals—Spencer Akin and Hugh Casey. The PT was rolling in the bumpy seas while a fierce wind hit the faces of the men.

An unidentified vessel was suddenly sighted approaching the boat from the stern. The morning light was not yet fully developed, allowing for only a pale image in the distance. Schumacher quickly took it to be a Japanese destroyer. "She has 5-inch guns," he exclaimed. "If we resist it means the lives of all the men in the boat."[4]

Schumacher conferred with the two generals about the possibility of opening fire on the vessel. "We're damn well going to resist," Casey bluntly said. The pair agreed he should make the appropriate preparations for action, with Akin suggesting to wait until the target was in range before taking any additional steps.

The boat captain yelled orders to his crew to get prepared for action—man the guns and get ready to fire torpedoes. At about the same time he thought about trying to outrun the ship. The generals agreed it was a good idea. Akin was getting ready to drop a bag filled with confidential coding devices over the side. Schumacher decided to dump the drums of gasoline in an effort to lighten up the PT for speed. One by one the containers of precious fuel fell into the ocean after the ropes were cut. There was now no possibility of the boat making Mindanao—if she survived the encounter with the approaching warship.

The PT boat was only able to gain a few knots of speed, but it had no effect—the enemy warship was still closing the distance.[5] Schumacher assumed he would have to fight it out with the larger adversary. He took another look through the binoculars, and with the benefit of better light and a closer image, determined it was not a Japanese destroyer, but another PT boat. Casey came to the same conclusion. "That's one of our boats," he shouted.

The approaching boat was *PT-41*. Passenger Herbert Ray first spotted the approaching craft. He shouted to Bulkeley the PT "has uncovered its 50 calibers and swung out the torpedo tubes. Looks like she is attacking!" The squadron commander then saw the fuel drums toppling over the side as the boat gained speed.

Nearly everyone aboard the 41 yelled and waved, but it seemed to have no effect. Bulkeley started to turn his boat to present a more familiar silhouette. "I started to try gunning us out of his path when I saw 32's wake subside and its bow slip rather shamefacedly into the sea," he later recalled.[6] The flagship was soon pulling up alongside *PT-32*.

General MacArthur quickly came into clear view to the sailors aboard the 32 boat. He was wearing his gold braided cap and field jacket. The general was soaking wet.

Schumacher later commented on the misidentification. He cited two lookouts who were standing on each side of the flagship's small bridge area. "Those high lookouts added a 'superstructure' that was uncharacteristic of the low, smooth silhouettes of the early PT boats," he said. "I mistook two men for substantial parts of the ship's superstructure."[7]

The distance of the initial sighting, condition of the sea, and dim light also played important roles in the error.

Bulkeley was bristling with anger at Schumacher's poor judgment. It could have jeopardized the entire rescue operation and risked MacArthur's life. "Everybody was hoarse by then," he later said. "Everybody but me, and when I got through telling off the 32's crew I was hoarse, too." Bulkeley wanted the boat captain to recover the gasoline drums. The slow and cumbersome process, though, was soon abandoned as too risky in the open waters. Bulkeley ordered his gunners to sink the remaining drums.

The lost time during the evening voyage meant the boats were not close to the meeting point at Tagauayan Island. Bulkeley knew the two PTs could not stay in the open waters—especially during the morning hours when the risk of Japanese air attacks was highest. He decided to seek shelter in the cove of a little island.

The small land mass, somewhere among the Cuyo Islands, was not much more than a quarter of a mile wide. The area did, however, offer a cove with an abundance of shallow water. Enough, Bulkeley thought, to keep away any prowling Japanese warships.

The squadron commander likened the tropical island to something right out of a movie set, complete with lush palm trees and a white sand beach. The small cove featured crystal-clear water and a coral bottom. There were some deserted huts, but no people. The only local inhabitant was a skinny dog.

Bulkeley deemed it unsafe for the passengers to leave the boat. Everyone stayed aboard except for a lone sailor who ventured to the opposite side of the island to take position as a lookout. The squadron commander knew it was a risk as the boats would have to get under way in a hurry if spotted by planes—even the lookout might have to be left behind. The initial plan was not to depart the safety of the cove until darkness.

The MacArthurs came topside to enjoy the bright sunshine after the night's harrowing voyage. Jean, Arthur, and Ah Cheu sat in wicker chairs on deck. Arthur later played with the cook's pet monkey. General MacArthur was becoming restless and concerned about meeting the other boats at Tagauayan. He sometimes paced the deck as the day slowly passed. The general conferred at various times with Casey, Sutherland, Ray, and Bulkeley about what to do next.

There was no easy answer to the current predicament. A daylight departure put the boats at risk of being sighted by enemy warships. Staying in the cove provided good protection from seaborne threats, but not from the air. "I figured the morning would be the dangerous time for bombers, if they knew we had slipped out, so by [2:00 pm] I felt it was safe to get under way, and we threaded down through the little shoaled channels between the islands, which would defy a destroyer or cruiser to follow, approaching the last one, which was our general rendezvous," Bulkeley later said. The timing of the departure would give the boats enough time to make the meeting point well before the scheduled departure for the final run to Mindanao.

The PTs again encountered some rough seas, making the short voyage difficult for many of the passengers. The MacArthurs mostly stayed below deck, while some of the other passengers lay sprawled out topside. "That's the wettest bunch of generals I have ever seen," Bulkeley jokingly commented to Ray. *PT-34* was already there waiting by the time Bulkeley and Schumacher arrived at the designated Tagauayan meeting spot at separate times close about 4:00 pm. Kelly's boat made it through a host of problems to make the meeting point. Anthony Aker's *PT-35* was the only boat whose location was unknown.

Dawn was almost at hand when the engines on *PT-34* began running again. Cleaning the fuel strainers took about 35 minutes, only slightly longer than Kelly previously estimated to an impatient Admiral Rockwell. The boat was alone, with a scan of the horizon revealing no sign of the other PTs. It was a dangerous time of day for a single boat to be sailing in Japanese-controlled waters and all the sailors aboard knew it.

Kelly pointed the boat towards the Cuyo Islands. He realized there was no possibility of making the 7:30 am rendezvous on time. The executive officer had never been to this part of the Philippines before and only Bulkeley's flagship had a detailed chart of the area. Kelly studied it prior to the start of the mission to get a general layout of the region. His lone map, a large-scale diagram of the Philippines, showed the island group as a set of small dots.

Rockwell wondered how they would be able to find the meeting spot out of the dozens of small islands. Kelly had made a pencil sketch of Tagauayan from Bulkeley's chart in case the boats became separated—a brilliant decision in retrospect. The admiral was skeptical, but had no alternative but to go along with it.

Iliff Richardson recalled the sight of the Cuyo Island group. "Hundreds of small islands dotted the sea, some high and rugged and almost bare of vegetation; others, low and palm fringed with a cream colored margin of sandy beach," he wrote. "Most of the islands had small bays that would be suitable to anchor PT boats in, with the further protection of hills obscuring three quarters of the horizon, and enemy ships as well."[8]

Kelly and Rockwell eventually found an island thought to be Tagauayan. Both agreed, after a careful study of the terrain, it closely matched the pencil drawing. The 34 boat cautiously entered the cove on the west side of the island, but found it to be empty. "We circled the island—no sign of the other three boats," Kelly later recalled.[9] He speculated the flagship may have ducked into one of the small islands for shelter after it became apparent they could not make the rendezvous on time. Rockwell was not so optimistic.

There was nothing more the men could do but wait. *PT-34* dropped anchor in the cove just after 8:30 am. A low cliff overlooked the small inlet. The surrounding land was covered with tropical green foliage. A nearby hill, the only large one on the island, looked to be about 500 feet high.

Kelly allowed only two sailors to go ashore. Radioman First Class David Goodman and Quartermaster First Class Albert Ross were rowed to the beach in a small boat, commonly called a punt, carried on the PT's forecastle. "Their orders were to climb to the top of the highest hill on the island and remain there for the rest of the day," Richardson recalled. "They were to send news of any and all vessels or airplanes sighted, by using the semaphore signal flags."

Refueling started as soon as the small boat returned to the PT. It was a necessary step for allowing the boat to make the final leg of the journey. The laboriously slow process took most of the morning.

"The drums were unlashed and rolled up to the gas tank openings and then emptied one at a time," Richardson explained. "After the refueling was completed, the empty drums were thrown into the water and two men in the punt held the small openings in the drums underwater until the drums sank." The sailors were careful to ensure no sign of their visit to the cove remained. "Floating drums seen by an airplane or submarine might conceivably bring about an investigation which could prove disastrous."

Henry Brantingham remembered it took good swimmers to be able to hold down each drum until it filled with water. "Noise of gunfire was not desired," he later wrote. He recalled a feeling of great relief when the refueling process was finally completed. "We felt much better with the trip halfway over and with the heavy and hazardous deck load of gasoline no longer aboard."[10]

The temperatures climbed as the day went on, culminating with sweltering conditions during the afternoon hours. The three army passengers seemed to enjoy the sunlight nonetheless after enduring a terrible bout of sea sickness the night before. They began to inquire about breakfast—a good sign the illness had passed. The meal was planned, but it had to be postponed until noon. All of the electricity on the boat was turned off during the refueling as a precaution to mitigate the risk of an explosion.

Later in the day the lookouts signaled that a group of natives lived on the other side of the hill. Some had come by to see the Americans. They reported observing a large ship—type unknown—going south the day before. The natives seemed uneasy about having visitors on their small island. The two sailors were about to head back down to the boat when they suddenly sighted an approaching ship. Kelly picked up his binoculars to find PT-32 approaching. Bulkeley's flagship arrived a short time later. Three of the boats—and General MacArthur—had made it through the first leg of the perilous journey.

CHAPTER 26

The submarine *Permit* appeared on the ocean's surface shortly after 6:30 pm on March 12 just southwest of Mindoro Island. She had been at sea since departing Surabaya, Java on February 22 for her fourth war patrol.[1] Lieutenant Commander Wreford G. Chapple was under orders to proceed south for a rendezvous off Tagauayan Island with the four PT boats transporting General MacArthur to the southern Philippines.

The Tagauayan stopover, representing the approximate halfway point between Corregidor and Mindanao, was a critical juncture in the evacuation mission. The submarine played an important backup role in the operation by giving MacArthur the option of continuing the journey under the sea. Chapple's boat was an insurance policy in case of mechanical problems with the PTs, enemy activity, or any other type of unanticipated event.

A host of critical decisions lay ahead for the sailors and soldiers aboard the three PT boats as the craft lay anchored in the small cove. Foremost was how to proceed for the final run to Mindanao. A second question centered on what to do about *PT-32*. A final choice was what, if anything, should be done regarding the missing *PT-35*.

MacArthur had the final say on how to continue to Mindanao. Sidney Huff thought the general was considering abandoning the PT boats after the rough ride. "He wasn't enough of a sailor to enjoy this kind of travel," Huff later wrote.[2] MacArthur called generals Casey and Akin over to *PT-41* shortly after the flagship arrived. Richard

Sutherland, Admiral Rockwell, and John Bulkeley joined the small conference. The choice was limited to the two available options—proceed as planned in the PT boats, or transfer aboard the submarine *Permit*, expected to arrive at dawn the next morning, to complete the journey underwater.

Akin was concerned the Japanese were aware of MacArthur's departure and possibly actively looking for him. Casey wanted to continue with the PTs, noting the most difficult part of the escape had already been accomplished.[3] Bulkeley knew the passengers had a rough voyage thus far. He warned the seas would again be turbulent once they set sail, possibly even worse than the night before.

Rockwell seemed nervous about staying in the cove and was anxious to get going. He mentioned the *Permit* might never arrive. "I think we should get the hell out of here—now!"[4] The admiral wanted to stay on the PT boats. Sutherland agreed it was the best option.

MacArthur was undecided, but Rockwell assured him of good weather and calm seas. The general then agreed to proceed on the PTs as originally planned. He did, however, give Sutherland a warning. "Dick, I can't do anything to Rockwell. But if it's rough tonight, I'll boil you in oil."[5] It was decided the boats were to leave at 6:00 pm while it was still light to assure an on time arrival at Mindanao. The timing of the departure was not to Bulkeley's liking, due to the risk of traveling during the daylight, but he was over-ruled by MacArthur.

Next was the question of what to do about *PT-32*. The boat could not continue after having lost her deck load of extra gasoline. The army passengers were divided among the 34 and 41 boats for the last leg of the journey. Iliff Richardson remembered *PT-34* adding four additional army officers.

Bulkeley took exception when one of the generals suggested the crews on the two departing boats be reduced to better accommodate the increased number of passengers. Any sailors left behind would be stranded on the small island. The squadron commander was able to win the argument and no changes were made.[6]

Bulkeley directed Vincent Schumacher to stay behind with his *PT-32* to rendezvous with *Permit* the next morning. He was to tell her

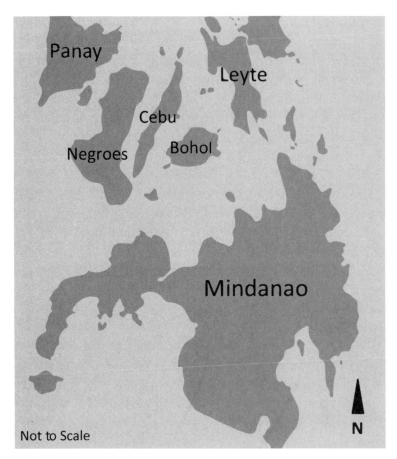

Map 12: Southern Philippines

captain that the two other boats left for Mindanao with the passengers as planned. Schumacher was then to proceed to Iloilo on the island of Panay, a distance of about 125 miles, for fuel and repairs before traveling down to join the other boats at Cagayan. Schumacher later had a different version of the instructions. He recalled Bulkeley's verbal orders were simply to "make out as best you can" after the *Permit* meeting.[7]

The whereabouts of Anthony Aker's *PT-35* was unknown. The boat was carrying four army passengers. She had not been seen since becoming separated from the group in the rough seas the night before. There was nothing Bulkeley and Kelly could do about the missing boat. No modifications were made to the departure plans.

The two PT boats pulled out of the cove at about 6:00 pm, heading southeast towards Mindanao. Kelly's boat took the lead, with *PT-41* trailing after. The idea was to have the 34 boat bear the brunt of the heavy seas, while the 41 followed behind in the smoother wake to provide a more comfortable ride for the MacArthur party.

"As the rendezvous island disappeared behind us, everyone was keeping a close look out," Richardson wrote. "There was still about half an hour before the sun sank."[8] Darkness came fast in the tropics, with only a short period of twilight. It could not, though, come quickly enough for the PT men as events in the early evening unfolded.

The sailors were confronted with a crisis less than an hour after departure. A lookout on *PT-34* suddenly yelled out "Sally-ho! Looks like a Jap cruiser!"[9] Kelly quickly grabbed his binoculars and trained them on a point off the port bow. The hull was low in the heavy seas but he could clearly make out the warship's mast and superstructure in the fading daylight.

The enemy vessel was on the southern horizon traveling in an easterly direction. She appeared to be about 5 miles away. The PTs were on course to pass directly across the bow of the enemy. Bulkeley took immediate action, ordering the boats to turn west, into the glow of the setting sun, at maximum speed. The top speed, however, was only about 20 knots because the boats were overloaded with extra passengers.

Kelly knew Japanese cruisers could go much faster than 20 knots when fully powered up. The chances of the small boats outrunning the warship did not seem good. The best hope was for the PTs to avoid detection just long enough for the area to be overcome with darkness. The sailors would know almost immediately if the enemy spotted them, as the cruiser would abruptly change course to head in their direction and pick up speed. Gunfire was sure to follow—maybe inaccurate at first until the Japanese gunners found the range.

MacArthur was below deck lying on the mattress aboard *PT-41*. He was seasick. Jean was at his side providing what little comfort she could.

Both heard the rush of activity above, along with the sailors' conversation about sighting an enemy warship, but neither said or did anything. The subsequent dreadful moments of tension passed slowly for everyone aboard the boats. Robert Kelly waited on *PT-34* for the sun to slowly set to usher in the darkness. He later recalled the process seeming to take weeks. Fortunately there were no clouds to block the glow of the sunset. The tension was equally thick on *PT-41*. "She's holding her course. She can't have spotted us," a lookout said to reassure those around him.[10] The sailor was right. The Japanese cruiser continued on her course, showing no sign of having spotting the PTs.

By 7:00 pm the danger had passed, with the boats amazingly escaping detection. Bulkeley attributed it to the increasingly rough waves hiding the PTs' low profiles. Perhaps the glow of the sunset helped to mask the small craft from sight. It was likely a little bit of both. Darkness quickly overtook the Philippine waters, allowing the small boats to disappear into the safety of the blackness.

The boats resumed their southeast heading towards Mindanao as the seas continued to turn wicked. The bad weather made navigation a difficult undertaking. The compass on *PT-34* spun wildly as the small boat was tossed about in the rough waters. The sailors could only estimate a course—there was no way to stay on an exact heading. Rockwell later called the navigation "pretty sketchy."[11]

The worst weather conditions were encountered from 1:00 am to dawn, when the boats faced heavy waves up to 15 feet high and periodic blinding rain squalls. "Speed was reduced to 18 knots about 1:00 am and even then so much water drenched the cockpit that the helmsman had difficulty in steering his course," Richardson wrote. "The helmsman was sent into the pilot house after a short while on the new speed, to steer from the secondary steering station." Rockwell, Kelly, Henry Brantingham, and Richardson remained on the bridge exposed to the elements. The sailors donned raincoats, commonly known as oilskins, in an attempt to keep their clothing dry.

The tired sailors had had little or no sleep for more than two days. It was a struggle to stay awake due to exhaustion and the tremendous monotony of the night. "Rhythms, consisting of smack (as the bow hit the wave), then the heavy salt spray hitting the face and hands and throbbing against the oilskins; the salt water got into the eyes and nose and dribbled into the mouth and into the collars of the oilskins, drenching the dry clothing underneath," Richardson wrote of the night. "The knees were still bent for the next jolt and sagged a little as it hit the boat. This rhythm of events continued minute after minute with unvarying monotony."

He wanted to go to sleep—and did so for the briefest of moments. "It may have been for one second or five seconds or more, but I awoke, looking straight ahead into the gloom and bracing myself against the jolts," Richardson continued. "By auto-flagellation, I immediately became awake and looking at Lieutenant Kelly, I saw that he was also fighting off sleep."

The situation was the same on *PT-41*. More than one sailor dozed off while manning the flagship's wheel. Bulkeley was worried about the boats making it through the night. He wondered "if we'd hear the splintering sound of cracking wood that would signal the end."[12]

The passengers aboard the 41 were left on their own, mostly below deck, as crewmen focused on the ordeal topside. Sidney Huff settled into a small area on the steps in the lower compartment. "I could see MacArthur sitting below me on the mattress," he later wrote. "Jean seemed to be asleep." Huff had just drifted off to sleep when he suddenly heard the general's voice.

MacArthur could not sleep and wanted to talk. "What had happened, I soon realized, was that he had had time to think back over our defeat in the Philippines and he was now trying to analyze it and get it all straight in his mind," Huff recalled. "And to do that, he wanted to think out loud." It was the start of a bizarre monologue that was to last almost two hours.

All Huff could do was listen, even though he was barely able to hear the general's slow and methodical speech over the loud drone of the engines. MacArthur talked as if rewinding the events in the Philippines over the last five years. Among the many topics recounted were his plans to build up the nation's military, struggles to get enough funding, and disagreements with officials in Washington. He choked up when talking about his departure from Corregidor. Huff could see the events were weighing heavily on the general, but also knew that MacArthur was determined to go forward.

"Sid, if we ever get to Australia, the first thing I'm going to do is to make you and Diller full colonels. Good night," MacArthur said in closing. "Thank you, general. Good night," Huff replied, before trying to fall back asleep. MacArthur kept his promise.

Most of the passengers on *PT-34* retreated below deck with the onset of seasickness. An exception was a terribly ill general who was draped over one of the torpedo tubes. He waved off a sailor offering to help get him below, telling the young man to "let me die here!"[13]

Rockwell was shivering cold as he stood in the small bridge area, but he would not leave his topside post. "The general's going to give me hell for this in the morning," he bemoaned, thinking of his advice to MacArthur for continuing with the PT boats.[14] Kelly eventually went below to find the admiral a sweater, inadvertently stepping on two seasick generals sprawled out on the deck in the darkness. He noticed an air officer sleeping comfortably in a bunk, apparently immune to seasickness because of the many bouncy plane rides he had endured.

Richardson soon ventured below to get a cup of coffee. "As I turned the galley light on, I saw and heard the most seasick general in the United States Army," he recalled. "Later, by his own testimony, he would have signed away the remainder of his life's salary to be put ashore." Richardson heard the general faintly calling for a bucket. "I set the coffee jug down and reached for the bucket." The plea was repeated in a louder voice. "The bucket arrived too late," he remembered. There was nothing he could do to help.

Kelly posted a lookout at the stern of the boat to keep a careful watch on *PT-41*. Neither boat captain wanted to become separated as had happened on the first leg of the journey. It was a difficult task, as the PTs often disappeared during the crest and swelling of waves.

The boats were heading in the right direction in spite of the bad weather. Neither PT ran aground among the numerous reefs in the general area—a miraculous stroke of good fortune. The pair slipped through the sea traffic lane between the islands of Tagauayan and Panay.

The sailors hoped to get a smoother ride by moving close to the coast of Negros. A Japanese searchlight suddenly switched on while the boats were passing close to the big island, sending a single beam of white light panning across the sky. Lookouts must have mistaken the rumbling of the Packard engines for airplanes. The PTs continued past unnoticed.

Only the Mindanao Sea stood between the boats and Cagayan once the PTs made it safely past Negros. The sailors were able to find Silino Island, a tiny land mass situated between Mindanao and Negros, at about 2:00 am.[15] It allowed them to then set a firm course for Cagayan, a distance of less than 100 miles.

Dawn ushered in some calmer seas. The daylight revealed land dead ahead. Kelly thought it was the peninsula jutting out just west of Cagayan. Rockwell agreed with the assessment, shaking his head with satisfaction. "Good navigation, Kelly," the admiral said. "I wouldn't have believed it possible."[16]

Passengers aboard the 34 started rustling and were soon coming topside to get ready for making port. Among those visiting the bridge was the army air officer. He had previously flown over Cagayan and was sure Kelly was 60 miles off the mark. Any doubts were quickly put to rest when the Cagayan light came into view.

Kelly slowed his boat to let *PT-41* pull forward. The move allowed Bulkeley to use his detailed charts to lead the boats into port. Huff remembered the last tense moments leading up to the arrival. "Everybody was alert and craning his neck as we rounded the last bend," he later recalled. "The harbor without a Japanese flag looked mighty good."

The MacArthur family came topside for the final approach. The general stood near the bow of the PT with his gold braided cap glistening in the sunlight. He was unshaven and his eyes were bloodshot, but seemed to have recovered well from the previous night's ordeal.

The PTs pulled up to the dock at 7:00 am on March 13. "As we approached the dock, no one could be seen to even handle our lines in mooring," Richardson remembered. "Suddenly several U.S.

Army officers were seen but there were no civilians present." The mooring marked the official end of the long sea excursion.

MacArthur called together the sailors from both boats. "It was done in true naval style," he told the group. "It gives me great pleasure and honor to award the boats' crews the Silver Star for gallantry and fortitude in the face of heavy odds."[17]

The general helped his wife step off the boat before turning to Bulkeley to issue a personal thank you. "You've taken me out of the jaws of death, and I won't forget it." Bulkeley was temporarily at a loss for words. "Well, thank you, sir," he responded.[18] MacArthur vowed to try to get Bulkeley and some of his key men out to Australia.[19]

The sailor and general embraced in a warm handshake as MacArthur began leaving the boat. Bulkeley queried the general, just as he was about to depart, as to his orders. MacArthur thought for a brief moment. He told him to conduct offensive operations in the area and wished him good luck.

General William Sharp was among the officers waiting for MacArthur ashore. A party of soldiers accompanied the commander of the Mindanao land forces. Curious Filipinos began to appear to watch the proceedings.

The passengers also departed *PT-34*. "An improvised gangway was placed between the dock and the boats and before the officers disembarked they shook hands with Kelly, Brantingham, and myself," Richardson wrote. He remembered the guests could not be happier to get off the boat. "It was readily seen that all of the army officers were the most happy to have arrived. The moment their feet touched solid ground, sea sickness vanished and exuberance took its place."

The passengers piled into half a dozen waiting cars. They were soon traveling 5 miles inland to the Del Monte airfield for the final leg of the journey to Australia. A guest lodge and clubhouse had been made ready for the general.

The portion of the evacuation mission spearheaded by Bulkeley and Kelly was now over. The arduous trip of 560 miles was made through Japanese-patrolled waters on worn-out PT boats. The exhausted sailors had braved bad weather and contended with limited navigational instruments to safely deliver the general to his destination. "For one not versed in the ways of the seas who had not made this voyage, it would be difficult to visualize the rigors of that night or odds against success of the mission," Kelly later wrote of the undertaking. "The fact that the destination was reached on time was the result of damn fine seaman's intuition."[20] It would be remembered as one of the most perilous missions undertaken during the early days of World War II in the Pacific.

CHAPTER 27

The evacuated passengers were already inland when the third PT boat arrived at Cagayan. Anthony Akers guided *PT-35* into port during the midday hours of March 13. He safely delivered four army passengers, including intelligence officer Colonel Charles A. Willoughby.

Radioman Third Class William Konko was aboard the 35 for the voyage. Konko enlisted in the Navy at Cleveland, Ohio in April 1939. He joined Motor Torpedo Boat Squadron 3 on August 12, 1941—the very day of the unit's commissioning.[1] He served as the radio operator aboard the boat.

John Bulkeley had not seen the 35 boat since the first night of the voyage south. "That evening we started out together," Konko recalled. "The following morning we were by ourselves."[2] The PT may have passed dangerously close to Mindoro Island during the darkness. She experienced engine troubles, same as the other boats, most likely related to the bad gasoline.

Akers opted to spend the daylight hours hiding along a small uninhabited island when it was clear *PT-35* was not able to make the Tagauayan Island rendezvous at the appointed time. He thought it was only several miles away from the meeting spot. The crew cooked breakfast for the passengers as everyone prepared to spend the day in the hot sun.

Army passenger Paul Rogers remembered they eventually had company. "During the long afternoon a fishing boat appeared from around the island, creating uncertainty and excitement," he later wrote.

"We were afraid that the crew were Japanese or would radio the Japanese of our whereabouts. They may not have been sure of our status and intent, since we were running without any identification."[3] It was a great sense of relief when the Filipino fishermen aboard the boat revealed an American flag before pulling alongside. "I suppose they also had Japanese flags so they would be prepared for any eventuality," Roger later quipped.

Akers decided to cautiously proceed to Tagauayan late in the day. "When we arrived at the rendezvous spot we found the 32 boat there and in turn they informed us that the other two boats had already shoved off," Konko recalled. Akers soon set out for Cagayan.

Konko remembered the PT approaching an unknown island, most likely on the second day of the voyage while the boat was en route to Mindanao. "We decided to go near the beach, this mainland and try to get information of our whereabouts," he explained. "We approached within 100 yards of the beach when we noticed civilians running up and down the beach. Finally, a Filipino soldier came out with signal flags, more or less warning us not to approach the mainland." The same individual soon ventured out in a banca to confer with the army passengers. Konko did not know what was discussed, but *PT-35* moved out soon afterwards.

The passengers were worried about making the final destination, but the boat eventually reached Cagayan. "The army authorities met us and had transportation for the passengers," Konko explained. "Later on we tied up with the other boats." Bulkeley was pleased to be up to three boats.

The squadron commander knew the voyage south to Mindanao would be a one-way trip for his boats. There was no going back to Bataan. He was provided with a new set of operating orders, penned by Richard Sutherland on behalf of General MacArthur. It formalized the brief conversation that took place and expanded on the verbal instructions MacArthur gave the squadron commander while departing *PT-41*.

The document was to cover PT boat operations beginning on March 16. "His mission is to attack hostile shipping, operating primarily in Visayan waters, but at times in the waters north of Mindanao," Sutherland wrote. Local army commanders were directed to provide Bulkeley with "all available information with reference to enemy movements and shipping." Additionally, the soldiers were to offer "supplies, equipment, and rations for his personnel and aviation gasoline and lubricants for his torpedo boats and such repair facilities as may be required and available." Bulkeley was to report his presence to the local army commanders in whatever area he might be operating. Sutherland clearly foresaw a limited timeframe. "Upon completion of the offensive mission, due to destruction of material or lack of essential supplies, Lieutenant Bulkeley will proceed to Mindanao, reporting upon arrival to the Commanding General, Mindanao Force."[4] The remaining PT boats were now on their own to fight until the end.

The offensive operations, however, did not start immediately. Bulkeley was directed to hide his boats until MacArthur left Mindanao.[5] There was no need to draw any unwanted attention to the area while the general was still hiding out at Del Monte.

Bulkeley's trip south marked the first time any of his PT boats had ventured into the region. All of the time had previously been spent north in the waters around Luzon. The sailors had to quickly learn the geography and war situation in the area.

The squadron commander probably already knew that Mindanao dominated the southern Philippines in size and importance. It represented the second largest island in the archipelago with more than 35,000 square miles. The island featured a jagged coastline with an abundance of small bays and inlets—ideal for PT boat operations. The interior was mountainous with limited hard-surface roads, making land movements difficult almost anywhere away from the coast. The main city of Davao was positioned in a small bay on the southeast coast.

A quick study of a map showed the PT sailors that Mindanao was separated from Luzon by the Visayan Islands. The group represented the middle section of the archipelago. It includes an assortment of medium-sized islands, including Panay, Negroes, Cebu, and Leyte.

The defenders of the southern islands were almost all Filipino. They faced many of the same problems plaguing the soldiers in the north—scarcity of basic supplies, outdated weaponry, little training, and a shortage of ammunition. The soldiers, however, also suffered from an almost total lack of firepower, with no tanks or antitank cannons of any type. Artillery was limited to a small number of antiquated mountain guns sent down from Manila in December.[6] When MacArthur ordered the withdrawal to Bataan, he notified his commanders in the south to expect no further help from the army on Luzon. He ordered the majority of forces in the southern area to be moved to Mindanao in defense of the important airfield at Del Monte.

MacArthur's leadership restructuring, put in place just prior to his departure from Corregidor, split the southern region into two separate command areas. General Bradford Chynoweth was put in charge of a group of small garrisons in the Visayan Islands. General Sharpe retained control of the larger force on Mindanao.

The war situation in the Southern Philippines was markedly different than on Luzon. The Japanese invasion plan focused on capturing Manila. It was later modified to battle the defenders on Bataan and Corregidor. General Homma did not have enough forces at his disposal to invade the southern islands at the same time.

The Japanese did strike in the south during the month of December. The operations, however, were small in scale and primarily done to secure positions in support of the conquest of Borneo. A contingent of Japanese troops landed near Davao on December 20. The Filipino defenders were only able to offer token resistance before withdrawing. The enemy soldiers quickly established a foothold around the city, but went no further. Naval units quickly moved into the bay to establish a small seaplane base.

The second landing took place four days later on the island of Jolo, southwest of Mindanao near Borneo. Further operations in the area were subsequently limited to air and naval reconnaissance.[7] Homma was focused on the battle for Luzon.

The fate of the southern islands was not necessarily tied to Luzon. American planners thought soldiers in the region could continue to fight the enemy even if Bataan and Corregidor were lost. Perhaps the area could be held and used as a jumping-off point for a counterattack when reinforcements eventually arrived, or even become a base of operation for guerillas.

Bulkeley's immediate concern, during his first days at Mindanao, was the whereabouts of Vincent Schumacher's *PT-32*. He had not been heard from since the boat was left behind at Tagauayan. The squadron commander hoped the PT could obtain fuel at Iloilo on the island of Panay, as he directed, and then join the others in Mindanao.

Bulkeley did all he could to try to locate the missing boat. He boarded a small army plane to fly over the coasts of Tagauayan, Panay, Negroes, and neighboring islands. The effort, however, revealed no sign of her. It would be another month before Bulkeley learned the true fate of the boat. He had no idea the 32 was already sunk.

The submarine *Permit* began circling Tagauayan Island at about 2:00 am on March 13 looking for signals at the rendezvous point. She sighted *PT-32* moving towards her about three hours later. The vessels met about one mile southwest of Tagauayan. Schumacher notified Lieutenant Commander Chapple of MacArthur's departure and that the submarine was to "remain in vicinity of Tagauayan Island for 48 hours."[8] The undersea boat was the backup in case the evacuees were unable to depart Mindanao via airplane.

Schumacher reviewed the state of his boat after the others departed for Cagayan. He noted "two engines were out of commission and the third unreliable due to seawater leakage into the engine room." He recorded the PT was down to 1,000 gallons of fuel.

The boat captain concluded *PT-32* would not be able to make the voyage for fuel, as Bulkeley had directed, or anywhere else. "Because of the unsafe condition of the vessel, the prevailing easterly wind, and the rough sea, and the probability of the third engine being flooded and put out of commission, the possibility of making a safe landing on the island of Panay was considered remote," he wrote. Schumacher decided to scuttle to boat "in order to safeguard the lives of the crew."[9]

During the morning hours, all the crewmen of *PT-32*—15 men in total—moved to the submarine. Food, some navigational equipment, and all classified documents were also transferred. *Permit's* 3-inch deck gun opened fire just a few minutes later, with the shells ripping apart the PTs wooden hull. It took 11 rounds of ammunition to sink the 32 boat.

The submarine then dove to be out of sight. It was too risky to remain on the surface during the daylight hours. Chapple shortly received new orders directing him to proceed to Corregidor. *Permit* arrived in Manila Bay late in the day on March 15, mooring next to a tug off Mariveles. She delivered a small cargo of ammunition for the Bataan defenders. Eight members of *PT-32's* crew departed early next morning for Corregidor. Schumacher, Ensign Cone Johnson, the boat's executive officer, and five other PT sailors remained on board. They were joined by 40 new passengers. The submarine pulled out with 111 total people aboard—more than double her normal complement.[10]

A long voyage south to Australia followed. The submarine attacked three Japanese destroyers shortly after leaving Corregidor. A harsh depth charging followed, undoubtedly making for an uncomfortable ride for the passengers unaccustomed to such conditions.

Bulkeley was furious when he found out what happened to *PT-32* many weeks later. He deplored Schumacher's unilateral decision to scuttle his boat and wondered why no attempt was made to salvage badly needed parts to be used as spares and ordnance. The squadron commander's report of the loss, dated April 23, 1942, contradicted Schumacher's version of events in several key details.

The squadron commander felt the condition of the boat was "good" when he last saw her on March 12. He thought patchwork repairs could have been made to the leaking center strut. "This condition should have been remedied at the time, as replacement struts and shallow water diving equipment were available on *PT-32*," he wrote. "Even if repairs were not effected, this boat was able to make 20 knots when it parted company."[11]

Bulkeley also disputed the amount of gasoline on the boat. "The *PT-32* had about 1,900 gallons of gas aboard, enough for 300 miles at 20 knots, and the nearest island (Panay) was approximately 60 miles distance, where gas could be obtained." He saw no problem with the boat proceeding further to Iloilo. "He had sufficient gas to accomplish this mission."

The divergent accounts were never rectified. The war continued on, with many more pressing matters needing the attention of navy men. For the short term, though, the squadron had lost one more boat.

As Bulkeley fretted about *PT-32*, the remaining sailors looked forward to some down time. "We took the boats out, anchored them off the beach a little ways and took a much-needed rest," recalled DeWitt Glover after all the passengers disembarked.[12] Henry Brantingham remembered the boats later moved to a small pier across the inlet from Cagayan. "A few hours later, we were more tangibly rewarded when a truck arrived from Del Monte and delivered at least a half ton of fresh pineapples, compliments of General MacArthur," he later wrote. "You can imagine how we appreciated the first fresh fruit we had seen in over three months."[13]

The food situation was not perfect going forward, but was far better than when the boats were at Bataan. Glover remembered they were dependent on the army for the food supply. "Sometimes their deliveries were not on time," he later said. "We did all our cooking on the shore, the cooks using their initiative for making the stoves, and bringing the food aboard the boats hot."

The PTs eventually moved to be close to a small beach somewhere to the east. The 34 boat dropped anchor about 70 yards from a coral reef. The anchor line seemed secure and tight. Iliff Richardson remembered "a holiday routine went into effect so that everyone 'could take in the slack,' and get a little sleep."[14] The sailors were invited to eat a meal ashore with members of an Army Air Force squadron. Buses provided the transportation inland. The crew of the 34 divided into two sections for the event.

It was about this time the boat was struck by great misfortune. It was already dark when Richardson returned from the dinner. He arrived aboard just in time to hear someone shout "We're dragging anchor." The boat was slowly moving with the tide—towards the coral reef.

Robert Kelly ordered the engine be started immediately, but there was a crunching sound before the PT could move. The boat was aground on the reef. The sound quickly changed to thumping and a rapid vibrating noise. At least one propeller hit bottom and the engines soon sputtered out.

Richardson knew the situation was bad. "Each succeeding wave of a flooding tide threw us higher on the reef," he wrote. "All hands were immediately in the water to try and push the 34 off, but all these efforts were to no avail. An examination of the anchor line showed that the anchor had held, but the connecting shackle pin had been broken or fallen out." The item was sadly just another victim of constant use and a lack of spare parts—the same issue that had been plaguing the PT sailors for months.

The 41 boat was not far away, but Bulkeley was not on board. Kelly called over to get a tow. A valiant attempt was made, but it was unsuccessful. The PT was firmly stuck. Kelly went to bed disgusted when he was sure nothing else could be done in the darkness to free the boat.

CHAPTER 28

General MacArthur arrived at the Del Monte airfield expecting to see four B-17 bombers ready to whisk his party to Australia. He instead found only one. Four army planes had taken off from airfields in Australia for the mission, but two turned back after developing engine problems and the third crashed in bad weather approaching Mindanao. It was clear his party would not be able to depart immediately as had been planned, but instead had to wait.

MacArthur received some troubling information about his former superior shortly after arriving at Del Monte. Philippine President Quezon had left Corregidor with his family and close staff aboard the submarine *Swordfish* in late February. The group transferred to the small motor ship *Don Esteban* off Panay. The passengers were put ashore on the southern end of the island, but subsequently moved to neighboring Negroes. Quezon's health was declining, a victim of tuberculosis, but he was at least temporarily safe from advancing Japanese forces. He was reluctant to leave the Philippines, not wanting to be seen as abandoning his people.

The feisty Filipino had long been an ardent supporter of the United States. Quezon, however, grew bitter as the campaign continued over the lack of help from America. His support was now thought to be wavering after Japanese leaders promised to grant the Philippines independence in a propaganda radio broadcast.

A report reached MacArthur the day after he arrived at Del Monte of seven Japanese destroyers maneuvering off the coast of Negroes.[1] The warships could be moving in to capture the president. Or might Quezon be planning to board the vessels voluntarily? MacArthur decided it was best for the Filipino president to depart the Philippines. He again called on the PT boats to complete the mission.

The general dispatched an aide to find John Bulkeley. The squadron commander was still with his boat at Cagayan. He was exhausted from a lack of sleep, but nonetheless grabbed a submachine gun and jumped into the jeep for the ride to Del Monte.

Bulkeley met with MacArthur on the veranda of an old clubhouse. The general's scruffy appearance, bloodshot eyes, and wrinkled uniform make it clear he was still suffering from the effects of the voyage. He seemed agitated and his face was flushed. The general explained he had a special mission for the PT boats. He directed Bulkeley to find Quezon on Negroes and bring his entire party back to Mindanao. "We're sending Quezon to Australia to form a Philippine government-in-exile—whether he likes it or not!"

Bulkeley was then introduced to Don Andres Soriano, an aide to Quezon. The Filipino was to serve as a guide for the mission. The meeting ended with MacArthur shaking the hands of both men. The general told the squadron commander to use "whatever means necessary" to get Quezon back.[2]

All of the heavy bombers in Australia under army control were in poor condition owing to extensive action around Java, round trip flights to the Philippines, and the lack of available spare parts. The four planes assigned to pick up MacArthur were the best available. The Navy did have some newer B-17s in the region. The service, however, was unwilling to have any of its planes used in the operation. The use of the army planes was the end result of some behind-the-scenes heated inter-service bickering.

MacArthur was appalled at the decrepit condition of the lone B-17 to arrive at Del Monte. The plane was spattered with oil and had malfunctioning brakes. Worse yet, the superchargers needed to obtain maximum speed at high altitude were no longer working. The plane was rated for flight only under emergency conditions.[3]

MacArthur considered the craft unworthy of flying and the pilot too inexperienced for such an important mission. He immediately sent scathing messages to Australia and Washington requesting that the "best three planes in the United States or Hawaii should be made available with completely adequate and experienced crews."[4] Anything less, the general suggested, would condemn his entire group to death.

Some additional inter-service bickering followed, but three new B-17s were soon made available from the Navy command in Australia— perhaps under orders from officials in Washington.[5] The planes were scheduled to arrive at Del Monte late in the evening of March 16. MacArthur's group assembled at the airfield at about 8:00 pm. Two B-17s eventually arrived and made a perilous night landing on a runway marked by flares. The third plane turned back early in the flight with mechanical problems.

Two planes might be able to fit all of the passengers, if they crowded in tightly, but it was unclear if there would be enough space for luggage. "It was decided that if all the baggage were left behind the two planes could carry the entire party," Admiral Rockwell later wrote. "This was done, and we took off shortly after midnight with both planes heavily overloaded, two hours behind schedule, and with the passengers laid in head to foot like so many sardines in a can."[6]

The planes headed east to clear the Mindanao coast before turning south for Darwin, an isolated city on the northern coast of Australia. The passengers with access to a window were treated to a spectacular sunrise as the aircraft traveled over the Dutch East Indies. The B-17s were directed to Bachelor Field, about 45 miles south of Darwin, after the pilots learned the city was under attack by Japanese planes.

MacArthur's plane touched down at about 9:00 am on March 17. The general turned to Richard Sutherland upon landing. "It was close, but that's the way it is in war," MacArthur said of the escape. "You win or lose, live or die—and the difference is just an eyelash."[7]

MacArthur shook hands with every crewmember from the two planes shortly after landing. Each was awarded a Silver Star. He then inspected a small, somewhat ragtag, honor guard of American troops from a nearby antiaircraft battalion.

A small group of reporters later pressed MacArthur for a statement. "The President of the United States ordered me to break through the Japanese lines and proceed from Corregidor to Australia for the purpose, as I understand it, of organizing the American offensive against Japan, a primary objective of which is the relief of the Philippines," MacArthur said. "I came through and I shall return."[8] The last phrase, so casually stated, became the general's famous rallying cry as the war progressed.

MacArthur assumed he would take command of a powerful army assembling for an immediate counterattack on the Philippines. He asked an officer where the U.S. Army in Australia was located. "So far as I know, sir, there are very few troops here," he replied. MacArthur was astonished in disbelief. "Surely he is wrong," he turned to Sutherland.

The officer was correct. There were actually more troops on Bataan than in all of Australia. "God have mercy on us," MacArthur muttered under his breath. He later wrote it was his "greatest shock and surprise of the whole war."[9]

There was no army waiting for MacArthur to command. There were neither tanks nor artillery and no troops ready to deploy to the Philippines. It was a bitter pill for the general to swallow.

MacArthur traveled south to his new headquarters in Melbourne. He was soon appointed Supreme Commander of Allied Forces in the Southwest Pacific area. The general would not be able to help his beleaguered men still trapped in the Philippines, but would eventually liberate the islands while leading a portion of the counterattack against the Japanese Empire.

The initial efforts to free the grounded *PT-34* were unsuccessful in spite of the dedicated effort of her crew. Robert Kelly awoke early the next morning to find the boat high and dry, bow first resting on the reef, with only 6 inches of water around her stern. A crowd of natives stood nearby gazing at the stranded craft.

Kelly knew his men could not free the boat without help. He flagged down an army sergeant in charge of a small diesel tug and asked for a tow. The soldier readily agreed. The craft went by the name *Misamis*, a region on the island of Mindanao. "The tug, however, was a tug in name only, being so diminutive that we all had doubts in the beginning," Iliff Richardson recalled. The vessel may have been closer to a motor launch then an actual tugboat.

The operation was timed to coincide with the morning high tide. "The tug captain first tried a steady pull. The 34 wouldn't budge," Richardson continued. "Then by getting a short run, with some slack in the towing cable, the captain tried to jerk the 34 off."[10] The PT boat still would not move. The towing post on the tug then broke off completely, effectively ending the operation.

The dawn of March 15 brought a renewed effort to get *PT-34* off the reef. John Bulkeley came by early, and did not think the prospects of the saving the boat were good. "I'm afraid we'll have to blow her up if the enemy comes," he told Kelly. "She's certainly done her part, but this may be the end."[11] He departed, leaving it up to the executive officer to decide how to proceed.

Kelly was determined it would not be the end of the boat. The crew met in the forward compartment, where the skipper gave a passionate speech about the PT. Everyone agreed to try to save her. "Our 'never say die' skipper would not admit defeat, and set in motion a marathon effort to free the boat," Henry Brantingham recalled as the outcome of the meeting.[12]

Richardson was sent ashore to get help. "In all cases the army was more than considerate," he recalled. He returned with a party of laborers. Equally importantly, however, he also brought an assortment of tools and some dynamite.

The sailors pooled their money together—meager amounts since they had not been paid since the start of the war—to hire native workers to help in the effort. "All hands took turns over the side, excavating coral from beneath the boat, piece by piece, using a small crowbar, fire axes, screwdrivers, and bare hands," Brantingham wrote. It was dangerous work, as the coral was razor sharp. The men also used the time to clean off some of the marine growth that had accumulated on the hull below the waterline.

The PT needed to move about 25 yards to get off the reef and into deep water. "As near as possible, we tried to clear a channel in the coral," Richardson wrote. Big pieces of coral were loosened using quarter or half sticks of dynamite. The strenuous work continued with about 30 laborers participating. The effort eventually yielded some results as nightfall approached.

A second tugboat, about a third larger than the *Misamis*, happened on the scene in the early evening. Kelly felt enough progress had been made, along with the approaching high tide scheduled for 9:00 pm, to warrant another attempt to pull the PT off. It involved both tugs.

With the tow post of the *Misamis* gone, sailors wrapped a cable around her wheelhouse. A line was then sent over to the second craft. There was a delay when it was determined the engineer was not aboard the second tug. Machinist's mates Paul Eichelberger and George Shepard, both engineers on the 34 boat, climbed over to the tug in order to help out with the diesel engines.

The initial pull, conducted about 15 minutes before the peak of high tide, yielded no results. "At maximum high tide, there was a sudden huffing and puffing and a shower of sparks from the smoke stacks and the towing bridle became taut," Richardson wrote of the second attempt. "This time a steady strain was applied. After about 5 minutes of steady pulling, the 34 moved 6 inches to seaward." It was substantial progress.

At about this time, a group of three army officers arrived on the scene in a small native boat to see if they could be of any help. The 34 pulled free of the coral reef just before they came aboard. She was now back in deep water.

The PT sustained serious damage below the waterline. The propellers, struts, and rudders were all badly mangled—and there were no spare parts to use as replacements. The hull, fortunately, had not been pierced, so there was no danger of the boat sinking. The larger tug towed the 34 boat to a dock at Bugo on the east side of the inlet opposite of Cagayan. Arrangements had been made to use the dock as a refueling station for the boats. The 34 arrived in the middle of the night and moored adjacent to *PT-35.*

Now that *PT-34* was freed from the coral reef, the next issue for Kelly to overcome was how to get her back into working order without the benefit of repair facilities or spare parts. Bulkeley heard of a small machine shop up the coast near the village of Anacan. He thought they might have some tools to fix up the boat. He passed the information on to Kelly and recommended he give it a try.

The executive officer again enlisted the help of *Misamis* the next day. The 34 was soon under tow, slowly moving northeast along the Mindanao coastline towards Gingoog Bay. Richardson remembered it was "the slowest sustained speed the 34 ever traveled and she was humbled but indomitable." He remembered the journey continuing through the night and a small tug appearing the next morning from the Anacan Lumber Company. "Mr Walters, the manager of the company, was on board, hailing the 34 and then told us that he would take the tow line and take us to our buoy and explain later," Richardson continued.

When Kelly decided to fire up the PT's engines as a test, worried crewmen on the tug scanned the sky for approaching Japanese planes. The 34 was taken to a more secluded area rather than the main pier. The sailors were told Japanese planes regularly flew over the pier, making it too dangerous, for all involved, for the PT to dock there in plain sight.

Work began the next day to get the boat back in working order. "The 34 was moored to a buoy at the bow and to pilings astern; in this way the stern was always in shallow water so that the native divers could do their underwater work under less difficulty," Richardson wrote. Additional projects were also undertaken, including repairing an auxiliary generator used to operate the stove and performing some routine maintenance on the torpedoes.

The natives held their breath diving underwater to remove parts. The sailors pounded the mangled propellers back into shape as best they could. The proprietor of the mill took other parts to the small machine shop for work. The locals seemed fearful the boat might attract unwanted attention from Japanese planes, but the concerns proved unfounded.

Brantingham remembered the area featured a small native village, with a pipeline made of bamboo bringing fresh water from a spring somewhere up in the hills and a tree near the beach that seemed to constantly attract fireflies. Some type of small living organisms created luminosity in the seawater. "We were able to inspect them in daytime simply by dipping a bucket of water from the sea and bringing it aboard," he later wrote. "Any moving object in the water, at night, always left a visible trail."

Richardson wrote of enjoying a more relaxed atmosphere after enduring months of rigorous patrols off Bataan. "Most of the days were spent in doing routine ship's work, which in most cases could be finished in the forenoon," he later wrote. Sailors would go ashore in groups during the afternoon. The PT officers were known to occasionally join a poker game with their army counterparts.

The casual environment extended to the sailors' clothing, although the PT men were never ones for formal uniforms during wartime conditions. "During daylight hours almost everyone aboard would don undershorts for a sun bath, the length of which depended solely on inclination and resistance," Richardson wrote. It led to a humorous incident involving the boat captain.

A small launch came out to the PT twice a day to deliver food, water, and workers. Kelly was below deck one afternoon when the launch arrived with Mr Walters. He came topside, clad only in his underpants and slippers, to welcome the visitors.

The first person to come aboard was the wife of one of the American civilian workers. "However, without the slightest bit of embarrassment, Mr Kelly shook her proferred hand and welcomed her aboard," Richardson recalled. "Mr Walters then introduced about four more male visitors, who Mr Kelly acknowledged as they came aboard. After this was done he made a brief excuse and went below to get some more clothes."[13]

It would have been an embarrassing situation for most naval officers. "This is probably the only case on record of a boat captain on an American naval vessel, receiving a lady aboard, dressed in shorts—period," Richardson continued. "The lady in question was genuinely gracious and made light of the matter."

The slow repair process continued for the better part of two weeks. Enough progress was eventually made to put *PT-34* back together. Kelly fired up the engines for a test run. The 34 could make 12 knots, with strong vibrations radiating from the back end. It was the best repair possible under the primitive conditions.

The squadron commander paid Kelly a visit about this time. Bulkeley had quite a story to tell about the mission to rescue President Quezon. However, this time the evacuation operation seemed more like a kidnapping.

PART IV

SCATTERED

CHAPTER 29

The directive from General MacArthur was clear—get President Quezon back to Mindanao by whatever means necessary. John Bulkeley was uneasy about Don Andres Soriano, the individual the general assigned to be his guide. He was unsure of his true loyalty. It was nothing more than a gut reaction. Bulkeley made a mental note that if he did not come back due to Soriano's duplicity, then the Filipino would not survive the mission either.[1]

Bulkeley was down to only two operational boats. He would command the overall operation riding with George Cox in *PT-41*. Anthony Akers accompanied the flagship in *PT-35*. The boats were ready to go late in the day on March 18.

Quezon was hiding on the southern tip of Negroes, a distance of slightly more than 100 miles from Cagayan. The squadron commander was expecting a dangerous voyage. "Aerial reconnaissance showed seven enemy destroyers off Negroes Island from Dumaguette to Saiton," Bulkeley wrote.[2] It was the same report that alarmed MacArthur, spurring him to action about Quezon. The warships were thought to be arrayed across the southern approaches to Negroes, possibly to prevent the president's escape.

The two PT boats slipped out of Cagayan at 7:00 pm on March 18. The pair quickly disappeared in the darkness while traveling northwest across the Mindanao Sea. The pick-up was to take place at the small city of Zamboanquita on the southeast tip of Negroes. Bulkeley did not have a detailed chart of the island and was not familiar with the area. Soriano would be waiting on shore to help facilitate the mission. The PT boats sighted a Japanese destroyer during the voyage, but were able to avoid the warship without being seen.

The boats separated near Apo Island, a small land mass about 4 miles off the coast from Zamboanquita. Akers kept *PT-35* on patrol about 2 miles out to sea to prevent any surprises from the enemy destroyers roaming in the area, while Bulkeley proceeded in for the pick-up. The squadron commander cautiously approached the small harbor in total darkness. The entire town was blacked out.

There was no sign of Quezon's party as *PT-41* pulled up to the dock. Bulkeley waited for about an hour, but still no one showed up. Soriano then arrived alone. He explained that Quezon had received a telegram from General Wainwright advising him it was too dangerous to leave because of the Japanese destroyers.[3] The president had decided not to go, but had no way to contact Bulkeley as the PTs were already on route as these events transpired.

Soriano suggested they visit Quezon in person. Perhaps he might change his mind knowing the rescue boats had already made the voyage from Mindanao. It required the PTs to proceed about 15 miles northeast up the coast to Dumaguete. Only the 41 boat, though, made the trip.

PT-35 was patrolling near Apo Island when the boat was suddenly rocked by a thud immediately followed by a splintering sound. Akers quickly realized it was some sort of collision. "Unfortunately we hit a submerged fish trap, puncturing [a rather] large hole in the bottom of the boat," William Konko later recalled.[4]

The damage was confined to an area near the bow of the boat. The collision ripped a 20-foot strip of wood from the bow, allowing water to pour into the forward compartments. Crewmen scrambled to contain the flooding using a pump and buckets. The boat captain decided to continue with the patrol while Bulkeley ventured north in search of the president. The squadron commander was notified of the accident by radio.

The engines were muffled as *PT-41* quietly edged close to Dumaguete. Bulkeley decided to disembark when the water became very shallow—there was no need to risk running the 41 aground. He grabbed a Thompson submachine gun before jumping over the side to wade into shore. Bulkeley was joined by Soriano and two heavily-armed crewmen. The squadron commander had quietly told his escorts to shoot the Filipino if it looked as though they were going into a trap. His instructions were clear. "Any monkey business and Soriano goes down first."[5]

They did not find Quezon after arriving ashore, but instead encountered a constable who told them the president had already left the area. The Filipino added he had been instructed to give a message to any Americans who came by—the president was not going to leave the island. The constable would not reveal any additional information. However, he changed his mind at gunpoint, telling the sailors Quezon had gone to the town of Bais.

Bulkeley, his armed escorts, and Soriano traveled north in a borrowed pair of old cars. Bais was about a 25-mile drive. Once there, a local directed the group to the house where Quezon was staying. Repeated calls by Soriano eventually brought the president to the front door. The small figure, dressed in night clothes, was suddenly staring at someone who looked like anything but an American naval officer.

Bulkeley's appearance made him look more like a sinister pirate. He wore old oilskins instead of a uniform, and muddy boots. The squadron commander's black beard complemented his long hair and bandana. He was armed with a submachine gun, two pistols, and a knife.

Quezon, his hands shaking, produced the copy of Wainwright's telegram and repeated his intention of not leaving. It was about 2:30 am. Bulkeley knew there was no more time to waste. He forcefully told the president, in no uncertain terms, that he and his party were going back to Mindanao and then on to Australia under direct orders from MacArthur. "I am ready to go," Quezon finally admitted in a soft voice.[6]

The family and other members of the presidential party were quickly rousted out of bed and loaded into the cars for a speeding drive through the countryside back to Dumaguete. They found the 41 boat docked at a decrepit pier. The process of loading passengers and luggage aboard began immediately, but did not start out smoothly. "The party consisted of his

Excellency, Manual Quezon, wife, two daughters, the Vice-President Osmena, Major General J. Valdes and nine members of the presidential cabinet," Bulkeley wrote.

It was a chaotic scene at the dock. Some of the Filipino passengers were hotly debating the best place to sit and there seemed to be more luggage than available space. Bulkeley quickly put an end to it. "That's it, folks," he exclaimed. "Everyone get aboard and forget the damn suitcases!"[7] The squadron commander also squelched some last-minute hesitations on the part of Quezon. By 3:22 am the PT was on the way back to Mindanao.

The presidential party were not the only passengers on the crowded boat. Crewmen aboard *PT-35* were unable to stop the inflow of water after she hit a submerged object. Akers became increasingly concerned about the ability of the boat to stay afloat after the two forward compartments were flooded. He decided to abandon ship, transferring the crew to *PT-41*. The 35 boat was allowed to beach herself by slowly drifting to shore.

Konko remembered the uneasy Quezon asking about the number of PTs available for protection during the voyage. "We had informed him we had six boats, actually we had one," Konko wrote. "That was to keep him up in spirits."

The 41 ran into foul weather less than an hour into the return voyage. A large wave crashed against the boat, jarring two torpedo tubes. "Sir, two of our torpedoes are loose," an excited crewman reported to Bulkeley. "The retaining pin[s] have broken."[8] The weapons were pushed part way out of the tubes, starting hot runs. The hissing of compressed air and racket of spinning propellers created a horrifying sound for those not familiar with the weapons.

A frightened Quezon recalled seeing a flame shoot out from one of the torpedoes. "This seemed to us to be our end," he later wrote. Alarmed passengers, scrambling to get away from the tubes, rushed to the opposite side of the boat. Bulkeley and Soriano attempted to restore calm while Quezon tried to figure out what was happening. "I sought to explain to myself what was going on and in my ignorance I could only think that a fire, however innocent its cause, was not the proper surroundings for an instrument as deadly as a torpedo."[9]

The president was correct in his assumption. The spinning motors on the torpedoes first turned pink and then red hot with no water to act as a coolant. Since both weapons were armed, the force of a heavy wave could be just enough to set off the warheads in a fiery explosion.

Chief Torpedoman's Mate James Light and Torpedoman's Mate First Class John Houlihan joined Bulkeley in taking action. The men worked fanatically to jettison the torpedoes while at the same time keep from falling overboard in the rough seas. The dangerous situation was finally diffused when both torpedoes fell into the water. Konko remembered "the torpedomen put extra charges in and fired them off. That made everybody happy."

The remainder of the voyage was uneventful. The trip came to an end at 6:00 am on March 19 when *PT-41* arrived in Oroquieta, a city on the northern coast on Mindanao about 60 miles west of Cagayan. Bulkeley had radioed ahead to alert authorities of his arrival. American soldiers were on hand to greet the presidential party.

The Filipino president put a red bandana over part of his face in an unsuccessful attempt to slip past a crowd on the wharf unnoticed. He was quickly recognized by cheering locals. "We went directly to the church, where we gave thanks to God in our gratitude," he later wrote. The grateful president later awarded the Distinguished Conduct Star of the Philippines to Bulkeley, Cox, Light, and Houlihan.

Quezon flew to Australia and later traveled to the United States. Bulkeley's initial hunch about Soriano proved to be unfounded. In the end, he was dedicated to seeing the mission through to a successful conclusion.

Konko remembered Quezon shaking hands with every sailor and leaving some money for the crew. Bulkeley made preparations for *PT-41* to head back to Cagayan. "In the meantime we went ashore, bought up liquor, bread, candy and all of the stuff we had missed before," Konko recalled.

Three unidentified vessels were spotted in the distance a short time after the 41 boat left Oroquieta. Crewmen prepared for evasive action, thinking it could be some Japanese destroyers heading out from Cagayan Bay. "We turned about and started for the beach," Konko continued. "In case they were Jap destroyers we'd make off on the land. However, it was soon found out to be three large sailboats, so we proceeded on our course." The short voyage was uneventful until the very end. "As we entered Cagayan Bay we tied up to a sunken vessel," Konko related. "Just as we had secured our boat ten Zero planes were overhead: whether they were searching for us we do not know, but that was the first time we all took off for fox holes on the beach." The PT boat was not attacked.

With his second successful evacuation mission completed in less than two weeks, Bulkeley was now free to focus on his desire to begin offensive operations in the southern waters. He needed more PTs to do such work, and the effort to increase the number of working boats would take up the rest of March. Only one—*PT-41*—of the three remaining boats in the squadron was fully operational. Kelly's *PT-34* could only hobble along at slow speed after emergency repairs to her mangled struts and propellers.

The exact whereabouts of *PT-35* was unknown. She was presumed to have drifted ashore on Negroes. The uncertain future of the 35 led Bulkeley to transfer her crew to land duty. Anthony Akers, Ensign Bond Murray, and a group of enlisted men were detached from the boat shortly after the 41 returned from the Quezon mission. Konko remembered the men first lived in native huts near the beach before moving inland to work on various tasks with the army at Lake Lanao. "Some were at motor pools, some were building bases for PBYs if they would ever come in," he recalled of the duties.

The large inland lake, formed when water filled a crater from an extinct volcano, was located slightly west of the center of Mindanao. It stood at an elevation of 2,300 feet above sea level. The lake was the second-largest body of fresh water in the Philippines.[10]

American commanders were concerned about the possibility of Japanese seaplanes landing on the lake. Some of Akers' men were given the mission of setting up a small flotilla of gunboats for defense. They were eventually able to round up an assortment of six small vessels to arm with machine guns for lake patrols. Bulkeley later referred to the group as the Lake Lanao Navy.[11]

The best hope for increasing the number of operational PT boats lay with the Opan Shipbuilding and Slipway Corporation near the Cebu City. The company's facilities did not include a dry dock, but had a modern machine shop and a marine railway. The latter was a railway with tracks going down to the beach and into the sea. Small boats could be loaded onto a train car and then pulled ashore by a winch.

Bulkeley conferred with Kelly about getting *PT-34* over to Cebu for more complete repairs. The executive officer thought his boat was seaworthy enough to make the trip. The pair set out, with Kelly's slow boat setting the pace for the voyage. Hopefully no Japanese would be encountered.

"It was a bright moonlight night with calm tropical weather," Iliff Richardson recalled of the voyage. The boats left Mindanao heading northwest. "At a certain point course was changed to north northeast as we passed through the channel between Bohol and Cebu. Due to the very dangerous shoal water and the lack of navigational lights, it was necessary to lay to until daybreak before entering the channel to Cebu (City)."

All hope for restoring *PT-35* to a workable condition was not lost. Although damaged and partially flooded, the PT did not sink. She also eventually arrived at Cebu City for repairs. Bulkeley had enlisted the Army's help in locating the boat in the aftermath of the Quezon mission.

Richardson remembered that two American civilians working for the Quartermaster Corps out of Dumaguete found her close to the shore of Negroes near the edge of a reef. "Their first step was to anchor the 35 to the reef, to prevent her from being washed in further towards the shore with every high tide," he wrote. "Work was then commenced on the holes in the forward compartment bilges, still full of water."[12]

The tugboat *Bacolod* arrived from Cebu City a day later. She carried a small American work party, comprising of both navy and army personnel, along with her Filipino crew. "The first move was to take every removable piece of equipment off the 35 and stow it ashore, and this took the rest of the day to accomplish," Richardson continued. "It was also necessary to set two anchors out to seaward to keep the bow of the 35 into the sea in case of rough weather at high tide. This would keep her from dragging further into the shore."

The three propellers were taken off as a precaution to prevent possible damage. A patch was put over the hole in the forward hull. Work was temporarily interrupted when the sailors received a report of 11 unidentified submarines approaching the area. "Upon receiving this information, the machine guns on the 35 were taken to the beach and placed on a slight promontory nearby to prevent possible seizure of the 35," Richards wrote. No sign of the submarines was ever seen.

The PT boat was deemed ready to move shortly after the completion of the on-site work. She was slowly towed up the coast the Cebu City. The various loose parts taken from the boat were loaded on the tug for the voyage. A navy officer was stationed aboard the 35 to man the pumps, if necessary, and scuttle the boat if the Japanese were encountered.

The only danger came when the PT and tug became targets of some sporadic gunfire from land as the pair slowly passed close to the shore. Army officials later received a report from Filipino locals that two Japanese destroyers had come close to land. *PT-35* was safely delivered to Opan Shipbuilding. She was pulled out of the water by the marine railway for permanent hull repairs.

March slowly faded into April while the boats were at Cebu City. Bulkeley hoped the repair facilities at the shipbuilding company would soon have his three PTs back in working order. At the same time, further north on Luzon, the battle for Bataan was nearing an end.

CHAPTER 30

The situation on Bataan continued to deteriorate for the Americans after the PT boats moved south on the MacArthur evacuation mission. Japanese troops pierced the first defensive line in early 1942, forcing the defenders to retreat south to a secondary line, but they could not advance further. General Homma was compelled to stop and request reinforcements. The exhausted American and Filipino soldiers were in no position to counterattack. The result was a temporary stalemate.

The frontline now stretched east–west across the center of the Bataan Peninsula. To the north were 50,000 Japanese troops. Nearly 80,000 American and Filipino soldiers were south of the line.[1] General Wainwright had not received any reinforcements, and only a trickle of food supplies made it to Bataan from an occasional blockade runner or submarine. Most of the defenders were worn out, sick, and close to starving.

Homma was ready to attack by the end of March after his army was bolstered by 15,000 fresh troops and additional fire support. The morning of April 3 opened with a thunderous barrage from 150 heavy artillery guns and mortars. A torrent of shells rained down on the defenders in what was undoubtedly the most devastating bombardment of the campaign to date.[2] Japanese airplanes quickly joined the attack, with heavy bombers unloading strings of bombs on selected targets and fighter planes flying low to strafe at will.

The result of the onslaught was devastating. Defensive positions were demolished, communication lines cut, and field artillery knocked out. A growing pall of smoke hung over central Bataan from burning sugar cane fields and bamboo thickets set aflame by the ordinance.

The ground attack then began in earnest, with the Japanese focusing on the area around Mount Samat—the center and weakest point of the defensive line. The Filipino defenders were routed in a series of fierce battles. Additional attacks followed, with Japanese troops advancing under heavy gunfire support. Defensive positions all along the front line started to crumble in a matter of only a few days, with the worst enemy penetrations occurring on the center and eastern sides of the line.

American and Filipino soldiers were soon in full retreat, moving south across many parts of the peninsula. It was clear the Bataan defenders would not be able to hold out much longer unless the front was quickly stabilized. The situation facing Wainwright and his subordinate generals was grim.

All three of John Bulkeley's remaining PT boats were undergoing repairs at the Opan Shipbuilding and Slipway Corporation in Cebu City while the Bataan defenders struggled to stop the Japanese advance further north. The city and shipbuilding company became the squadron's new operating base when the boats lost the services of the tender *Canopus* and floating dry dock *Dewey* after leaving the Manila Bay area.

The sailors took careful precautions to keep the PTs hidden from Japanese planes. "Assisted by the shipyard, each boat made a framework of timber over the bow," Iliff Richardson wrote. "It was constructed in such a manner that when covered with palm leaves, the pointed bow was converted into a square bow; if seen from the air, the boats would look more like barges. The rest of the decks, torpedo tubes, and canopy were covered with palm leaves and gunny sacks which completed the camouflaging."[3] The ingenious disguise took a mere 5 minutes to either add or remove once the initial construction work was completed.

The machine shop at Opan Shipbuilding was run by Morrison "Dad" Cleland. The 71-year-old American was originally from Minnesota.

He had been in the Philippines since 1914. Robert Kelly described him as a "typical hulking frontiersman. Didn't look a day over 50 and was a kind of patriarch in those parts."[4]

Bulkeley and Kelly soon found Cleland to be a welcoming host. He invited the pair out to dinner for what turned out to be nothing short of a grand feast. The meal included crab meat cocktail, lobster Newburg, roast duck, and bottled beer to wash everything down. It was the best meal the officers had eaten in months.

The shipyard workers were able to repair the damaged hull of *PT-35*. Barnacles were scraped off her bottom and a new coat of paint applied. It appeared the boat once thought to be lost was now ready to return to action. Her skipper and crew, however, had already been transferred ashore on Mindanao.

Bulkeley appointed Henry Brantingham to be the new boat captain of the 35. A composite crew was assembled from the sailors aboard *PT-34* and *PT-41*. The arrangement left *PT-34* with a complement of two officers and eight enlisted men.

Plenty of work was also done to Robert Kelly's boat. *PT-34* was hauled out of the water for repairs to her damaged propellers and struts. Her bottom side was cleaned for the first time in five months.

Some of the PT sailors enjoyed liberty ashore and a short respite from the war while their boats were under repair. Cebu City was the second-largest city in the Philippines. Although it had been attacked by air a couple of times and even once shelled from the sea, the city had thus far escaped the large-scale destruction wrought by the Japanese in areas further north. Richardson remembered "one motion picture theater was still operating, as were a few stores and cafes."

All of the sailors were paid while in Cebu City for the first time since the war began. The payments started a sort of frenzied celebration. Kelly recalled the men on his boat alone dropped about $2,000 over the course of three days going from bar to bar.[5] Poker games with army soldiers sprang up overnight.

It was not all fun, however, as the sailors were soon put to work. The area had become the way station for submarines running supplies north to Corregidor. When an undersea blockade runner paid a visit, it was usually done under a cloak of secrecy.

Richardson remembered one night when no liberty was granted. "That night a skeleton crew was left aboard each PT boat, and everyone else proceeded on board the *PT-41* to Shell Island, which is about 600 yards from the pier area of Cebu City," he wrote. "All hands were cautioned to say absolutely nothing of what they had seen or done on that night." The general public was kept away from the area. The sailors were about to have a rendezvous with an American submarine.

The submarine *Seadragon* departed Australia on March 18 for her second war patrol. She was originally assigned to ply the waters off the coast of French Indochina, but was later diverted to Cebu City. Her mission was twofold: deliver torpedoes to Bulkeley's PT boats and load supplies for a run up to Corregidor.

She arrived at Cebu City during the evening hours of April 3. Richardson was among a group of sailors who were waiting. He remembered "the throb of large diesel engines was heard and soon after the long black form of a United States submarine was seen. By some very expert ship handling, in a strong current, this submarine was finally moored alongside."[6]

Seadragon unloaded two torpedoes for the PT boats and took aboard supplies for the trip north. Her crew, the PT sailors, and other local American servicemen worked together in the endeavor. She was unable, however, to complete her stay by dawn and had to move out to sea. It was too risky for the submarine to stay surfaced in the plain sight of Japanese air patrols.

The timing created a problem. A second submarine was due to arrive on April 4. *Snapper* was already off shore, waiting to come into Shell Island. Richardson was chosen to venture out in a pilot boat to notify *Snapper* that her visit had to be postponed until *Seadragon* completed her work.

The task was not an easy undertaking. "With no charts, compass or navigational equipment, it was only after considerable delay caused by groundings on the treacherous shoals that I finally saw the submarine," he recalled. "The moon had just risen and there was light enough to see that all the machine guns on the ship were trained on our pilot boat." It was an uneasy feeling, but he thought it was "a commendable action for safeguarding the sub."

Richardson passed word to *Snapper*'s captain to delay his visit by one day. "I returned to Shell Island to help load the *Seadragon* and to go into the wardroom and drink coffee with the officers, who also had much news of the war outside of the Philippines," he wrote. The submarine also offloaded two additional torpedoes for the PT boats. *Seadragon* pulled out of Shell Island, loaded with 34 tons of supplies, just before 3:00 am on April 5 bound for Corregidor. She passed the waiting *Snapper* on her way out to sea.[7]

The second submarine pulled into port towards nightfall on the same day. The purpose of the visit was the same. She offloaded four torpedoes for the PTs while supplies were hauled aboard for the trip north. Four of the newly acquired torpedoes went to *PT-35*, with the remaining two going to *PT-41*. The submarine used compressed air to charge up all of the torpedoes for the PT men. *Snapper* left for Corregidor during the early morning hours of April 6 loaded full with 46 tons of supplies.[8]

The sailors spent a total of three days doing arduous work aboard the submarines. The food and supplies were loaded anywhere possible, including the empty torpedo tubes. Kelly's back and arms were aching from the heavy lifting, but he could not help but think of Nurse Peggy as he loaded the undersea boats. Perhaps some of the very food he was touching would make it to her.

"The rewards for our labors on loading these subs were not only torpedoes and the satisfaction of helping in a small measure those still fighting on Bataan, but also the news and American magazines, only two months old, of which both submarines were divested by mutual consent," Richardson reflected. It was not long before his PT was back in the water and ready for action.

The critical repairs to *PT-34* and *PT-35* were essentially completed by April 8. The 34 went back into the water the next day and moored alongside a dock. She was to undergo a 24-hour soaking period before returning to action. Liberty was granted to half of her crew to go ashore.

The 35 boat was not as fortunate. She did not stay in the water for very long. "The *PT-35* was found to be leaking and it was necessary for her to be hauled out again on the 8th to repair the leak still in her forward compartment bilge," Richardson recalled.

None of the sailors knew the PT squadron was about to be called into action against Japanese warships that very night. The return to battle was made possible by the dedicated work of the yardmen at Opan Shipbuilding. "Dad" Cleland was more than happy to help and refused to accept payment for his work, telling Bulkeley "You fight'em and I'll fix'em."[9] Cleland stayed in Philippines after the Japanese took over and survived the war. He passed away in 1948.[10]

The timing of getting at least one of the PTs back in action was good. The city was awash with rumors that the long-dreamed-of American offensive to relieve the Philippines was finally on its way north from Australia. It proved to be untrue—it was the Japanese who were on the move.

CHAPTER 31

John Bulkeley received a report of Japanese warships in the area during the late afternoon of April 8. The information was specific—something for which he could take immediate action. Army airplanes spotted two enemy vessels traveling south off the west coast of Cebu at 5:20 pm. Cebu was a narrow land mass spanning almost 140 miles from north to south. The reconnaissance report placed the ships at about the midpoint of the island. "The estimated enemy speed was 5 knots," Bulkeley recorded. "It was believed that the enemy would arrive at the strait between Cebu and Negroes Island's south point at midnight."[1]

It was unknown why the Japanese vessels were in the confined waterway, but Bulkeley later speculated the pair may have been searching for inter-island steamers. The squadron commander studied the charts and knew it was a perfect set up for an ambush. The long body of water, known as Tanon Strait, between Cebu and Negroes was not very wide anywhere, but it closed to a channel of less than 4 miles at the southern tip where the two islands came together.

Tanon Point was the southernmost tip of Cebu. Once the warships reached the point, the enemy would be able to control ship movements around Negroes, Cebu, and other neighboring islands, as well as threaten the approaches to the Mindanao Sea.

Bulkeley sent word for the boats to be prepared to depart by 7:00 pm. With *PT-35* back out of the water, only the 41 and 34 boats were available for the action. *PT-34* would have to forgo the soaking period for her newly repaired hull recommended by the yard workers.

Not all of the men ashore on liberty could be located in the city on such short notice. Two sailors from *PT-35* were pressed into service aboard the 34. The boat was soon ready to go. "I hope this isn't another wild goose chase," Kelly commented.[2] It would not be.

The PTs departed at dusk, with the flagship, manned by Bulkeley and George Cox, serving as the lead boat. Kelly and Richardson followed in *PT-34*. Henry Brantingham stayed behind in Cebu City with the 35 boat.

The boats traveled south along the east coast of Cebu. "A light offshore breeze was blowing from the northwest as we proceeded south; but the sea was calm, being protected by the islands of Bohol and Cebu on either side," Richardson wrote. "The night was clear and the outlines of the island peaks and valleys could be seen in silhouette against the starlit sky." Kelly sent Richardson below for some rest. "As I went below, I was particularly pleased with the sound of the grinding whine of the engines and vibration-less shafts and propellers." The young officer instantly fell asleep.

Bulkeley wanted to take the Japanese by surprise. He planned to have the PTs in position about 3,000–4,000 yards southeast of Tanon Point by 11:30 pm. The island of Cebu would partially obscure their location, allowing the boats to idle until the enemy was spotted.

"The plan of attack, if there were only one target, was for the *PT-41* to lead the attack from the target's port beam," Kelly recalled of the squadron commander's instructions. "The *PT-34* was to follow, attacking from the port bow. If two targets were seen to emerge from Tanon Strait, then each boat would attack separate targets, with the *PT-41* leading the attack."[3] Strict radio silence was to be maintained throughout the operation. The sailors wanted to prevent tipping off the Japanese as to their presence.

The PTs arrived in position as planned during the last hour of April 8. "Weather conditions were ideal," Kelly wrote. "It was [a] dark night with no wind and calm seas. Moonrise was about 2:00 am." The pending action was to take place in a narrow body of water between Cebu, Negroes, and Siquijor Island. The latter was a small island surrounded by coral reefs about 16 miles southeast of the bottom tip of Cebu.

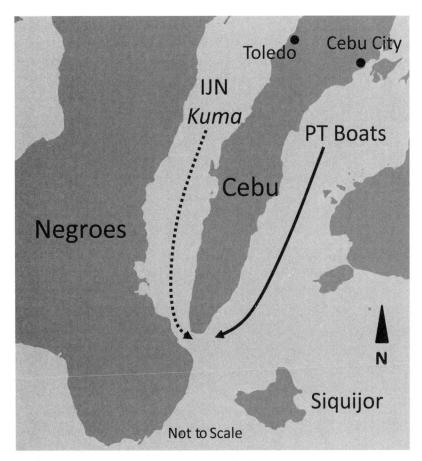

Map 13: Sea Battle off Cebu

Lookouts on each boat carefully scanned the horizon for any sign of movement. DeWitt Glover aboard *PT-41* spotted the enemy and alerted the others. "There she is!" A moment later he added "Jumping Jesus! There she is!"[4] Emerging from the darkness was not a destroyer, but a Japanese cruiser.

The situation played out almost exactly as Bulkeley had hoped. He recorded the warship was "heading on course east directly south of Cebu Island, distance 2 miles, speed about 5 knots." He identified her as a *Kuma*-class light cruiser.

Kelly thought the enemy light cruiser was a smaller *Tenryu*-type vessel. Bulkeley's identification, however, proved correct. The target was *Kuma* herself—the most powerful warship the PT men had tangled with to date. She weighed 5,870 tons with an overall length of 535 feet. The vessel was armed with seven 5½-inch main battery cannons and an assortment of smaller guns. Her top speed was about 31 knots.[5]

Japanese sources report *Kuma* departed Subic Bay for the southern islands on April 4. The torpedo boat *Kiji* was operating with her on the evening of April 8.[6] The torpedo boat was not the equivalent of the speedy American PT boats, but rather a much larger vessel. *Kiji* was almost 300 feet in length and could only make 30 knots at full speed, but packed a powerful punch. She was armed with three 4.7-inch guns and one smaller antiaircraft cannon.[7]

The PT men initially only sighted the light cruiser. "No other vessels could be seen at the time, although her escorts must have either been obscured by the Negroes coastline or been following some distance astern," Kelly wrote. The boat captain called the crew to general quarters.

Richardson awoke from sleep and raced to his battle station—the boat's wheel. He arrived just as the PT had slowed to idling speed. "The cruiser loomed bigger and bigger in the semidarkness as we continued on," he wrote.

PT-41 moved to be able to attack the target from her port side. She closed to about 500 yards at idling speed before Cox gave the order to fire two torpedoes. Both ran erratically, missing the cruiser at the bow and stern.

The PT increased speed while circling to the right in preparation for firing her two remaining torpedoes. "*PT-41* then fired two single shots which passed under the cruiser at her bow and beneath per bridge," Bulkeley wrote. Both the squadron commander and Cox saw the torpedoes run true, but no explosions were observed.

The 34 boat moved into attack position, approaching broad on the cruiser's bow, while *PT-41* was making her torpedo run. Kelly made sure all of the machine guns were ready for action on a moment's notice. Chief Machinist's Mate Velt Hunter and Quartermaster First Class Albert

Ross manned the two single-mount 30-caliber guns on the forward deck. Chief Commissary Steward Willard Reynolds was stationed on the port side dual 50-caliber machine gun, while Torpedoman's Mate Second Class David Harris manned the same weapon on the starboard side. A sailor was positioned below deck with extra boxes of 50-caliber bullets ready pass to the gunners as needed.

Kelly carefully watched the target through the torpedo director from his perch in the conn area. Richardson was manning the wheel nearby. "Steering was easy, and my job was simply to line up the forward radio antenna mast with the metal brace supporting the windshield and alter course as necessary to keep these lined up with the cruisers mid-section," he later wrote. "All was silent aboard, except the noise of the exhaust and an occasional terse command from Mr Kelly."

The target loomed closer and closer. Kelly finally unleashed two torpedoes at a distance of 500 yards. The weapons were set to run at a depth of 6 feet. "The cruiser appeared to come to life at about that same instant and was seen to be increasing its speed rapidly," Kelly wrote.

A searchlight near the back of *Kuma* suddenly snapped on and briefly flashed skyward before panning across the ocean surface. Richardson remembered it looked "like a lighthouse beacon, dazzlingly brilliant on eyes already accustomed to the darkness." He thought it was more powerful than looking directly at the sun. The beam of light momentarily touched *PT-41* before settling on *PT-34*. "Apparently the engines of the PTs (there were no mufflers on PTs at that time), plus the powder flash from the torpedo impulse charges, had aroused the cruiser," Kelly reported. "The two torpedoes of the *PT-34* passed considerably astern due to the cruiser's unexpected increase in speed."

The sailors on the 34 knew what was coming next. The cruiser opened fire with her main battery guns and an assortment of smaller automatic weapons. "The white orange flash of the 5-inch gun from the cruiser was accompanied by the scream of the shell and then two explosions," Richardson recounted. "One from the gun and the other from the exploding shell as it hit the water several hundred yards astern of the 34."

Kelly ordered Reynolds to open fire at the searchlight. "Streams of our own orange tracers poured in the direction of the cruiser as I came right so that the port gun would bear on the target," Richardson wrote. "Bursts from the twin 50-caliber machine guns cut paths in the darkness and sometimes ricocheted from the water high into the air." The searchlight was not hit in spite of the torrent of bullets sent her way.

The boat captain gave a continuous stream of commands as he attempted to dodge the enemy fire. Richardson carefully repeated each as he turned the wheel in one direction or another. He glanced up to momentarily see a geyser of water spout up several hundred yards behind the boat. Japanese machine guns could also be heard rattling in the background, mixed amongst the booms of the big guns.

Richardson then heard "a new and very un-nerving blub-blub-blub-blub-blub—at about 1½-second intervals." He took it to be some type of antiaircraft gun. Suddenly an explosion occurred almost directly overhead, knocking him to his knees and sending a chilling fear through his body. He did not seem to be hurt and the boat was still in one piece. Richardson leapt back up to the wheel and continued following Kelly's commands.

At about the same time the 41 made an abrupt U-turn, causing Kelly to lose sight of her. "Thereafter the movements of the *PT-41* were unobserved by the *PT-34*, due to being almost constantly blinded by enemy searchlights for the next 10–15 minutes," he wrote.

Bulkeley was able to see *PT-34* was in trouble. He was out of torpedoes, but could help with machine guns. The 41 raced past the starboard side of *Kuma*, raking her with machine-gun fire to draw attention away from Kelly's boat. The squadron commander also wanted to "give the illusion that there were many torpedo boats in the vicinity."

Kelly decided to make another attack run on the enemy, in spite of the heavy gunfire falling all around the 34. The PT dropped back about 2,500 yards to turn around and then approached the *Kuma* from almost dead astern. "It was estimated that the cruiser was making 20–25 knots," he recalled. "The *PT-34*'s speed was now about 32 knots. Pursuit was maintained for about 5 or 10 minutes, by which time the *PT-34* was within 300 yards of the cruiser, whose searchlight beam was depressed almost to the vertical in order to keep the *PT-34* illuminated."

It was too dangerous for the 34 to approach any closer. The boat was under intense fire. Kelly ordered his machine guns to open fire on the searchlight. A voice from behind the conn suddenly yelled "Reynolds is hit."[8] The gunner fell with grave wounds to his throat and shoulder.

Kelly now had to make a critical decision. The position of the PT was a bad set up for a torpedo shot—almost from dead astern—but waiting any longer might result in the boat being blown out of the water. He gave the order to fire his last two torpedoes. The weapons lashed out towards the target's starboard quarter.

It was now time for the PT to get away—and fast. The 34 boat made a sharp turn to the right and increased to maximum speed in an attempt to retire to the south. A Japanese destroyer—possibly the torpedo boat *Kiji*—suddenly appeared about 2,000 yards away. The warship opened fire on *PT-34*, which was still under illumination and fire from the cruiser.

"Hard right," Kelly screamed out. "Rudder is hard right," Richardson repeated as he turned the wheel. "As we turned sharply to the right, the white wake produced in line with our previous course momentarily fooled the cruiser's searchlight operator and we were out of its beam. I eased the rudder, as we had almost reversed course, and the searchlight picked us up again."

The events continued to unfold at a furious pace. "The cruiser turned, apparently to follow us and prevent our escaping the destroyer closing us to port," Kelly wrote. The boat captain thought he was trapped. "Just then two spouts of water some 20 feet high and 30 feet apart were seen by me through the binoculars to appear amidships at the cruiser's waterline at 5-second intervals. My first reaction was that the cruiser had been hit by two rounds from the destroyer firing on me to starboard."

Chief Torpedoman's Mate John Martino was also keeping a close eye on the target. He reported to Kelly that the cruiser was hit by the torpedoes. She had apparently turned directly into the path of the underwater missiles. "All this had occurred in less than a minute after firing," Kelly wrote. "The cruiser's searchlight immediately began to fade as though there had been a power failure aboard. All its guns stopped firing and that was the last I ever saw of it."[9]

With the cruiser seemingly out of action, Kelly could focus on slipping away from the enemy on his starboard side, a vessel he believed was a destroyer. The 34 was now caught in the warship's searchlight and was taking heavy fire. "As a result of having expended its torpedoes and being light on fuel, the PT-34 could now make a maximum speed of about 38 knots," Kelly wrote. He was able to get away from the second warship after about 10 minutes of running at high speed, zigzagging, and making a series of sharp turns.

The getaway could not have come soon enough. "Moments were like years," Richardson recalled. "The increased speed of the Mighty 34 seemed a snail pace."

Without torpedoes, there was little more PT-34 could do to fight the enemy. Kelly decided it was best to get out of the area before more Japanese warships showed up. He set a course for Cebu City.

Bulkeley's diversionary tactics did not seem to attract the attention of Kuma except for some scattered small-caliber fire. He saw PT-34 attack the cruiser. The squadron commander later noticed "the enemy ship was observed to be totally enveloped in a heavy brown yellowish cloud of smoke. Her searchlight beam was growing weaker by the moment," he wrote. "PT-34 appeared to have hit her."

Lookouts on PT-41 suddenly spotted a second Japanese warship approaching fast. She snapped on a searchlight and briefly shone it on the cruiser. Bulkeley thought he saw her sinking by the stern. The second enemy vessel was the same one chasing after the 34 boat. "PT-41 attempted to create an illusion again of many torpedo boats in the vicinity by firing bursts of tracers of a 50-caliber machine gun at different positions, but this did not deter the second enemy vessel from attacking PT-34," Bulkeley recorded.

Bulkeley decided to turn back to get a better look at the sinking cruiser. Just then a third Japanese warship, not previously seen, abruptly appeared off the PT boat's stern. "PT-41 had only one engine running at this time for the sake of quietness," he added. The enemy caught the 41 in a searchlight beam and opened fire, but stopped after only five salvoes.

The plan to return to the cruiser was quickly abandoned, with the 41 instead departing at high speed. The squadron commander left the area certain the enemy cruiser was going under. Based on his previous observations he believed "that she could not possibly have stayed afloat."

Japanese destroyers suddenly seemed to be everywhere. Two more enemy ships were sighted as *PT-41* was approaching Siquijor Island. The path north to Cebu City looked like it was blocked with enemy activity. Bulkeley concluded the only safe way out was to go south towards Mindanao. He set a course for Misamis Bay on the north coast of the island. The area was known to have shallow water. It was a safe place that enemy warships would not follow.

Both PT boats were now leaving the scene of the battle. The break in action allowed Kelly to take stock of the condition of his boat. The boat captain directed Harris and Ross to take Reynolds below deck to the forward compartment "and find out how badly he's hurt."[10] He was given first aid in an attempt to slow the bleeding and allowed to have a smoke.

The 34 avoided any large-caliber shells hits, which would have been devastating, but was riddled with many small bullet holes. The main mast was shot away, rendering the radio useless. Such a precise hit required the shell to have passed less than 10 inches over Richardson's head—most likely the exact moment he was knocked down. One matter of note was that the boat's souvenir—a mounted Japanese bayonet—was shot away. "Our victory emblem had been shot down," Richardson lamented.

The lull in action did not last very long. Kelly was confronted by a Japanese destroyer a short time after starting his voyage north. "Only by swerving to the left was a collision avoided, and we passed down their starboard side close aboard without their firing a shot," he wrote of the encounter. "They immediately turned and commenced pursuit, illuminating us with their searchlight and taking us under fire with their main battery."

The chase lasted until about 1:30 am, when speed allowed *PT-34* to pull 5 or 6 miles away from the enemy warship. The sailors were able to see searchlights far to the south until about 2:00 am. "After the danger was past, all hands were secured from general quarters and the regular watch was set," Richardson recalled. Looking off in the distance, he saw "the moon came up in full splendor over the hills of Bohol, lighting the whole coast with a lunar brilliance rivaling the sun." Most of the crew, except for the injured Reynolds, later gathered near the conn to rehash the battle.

The sea battle off Cebu was now over. The calendar showed the date had passed to April 9. The sailors had no way of knowing the day would also mark the end of the gallant defense of Bataan.

CHAPTER 32

The fate of the Bataan defenders was largely decided on April 6, when exhausted American and Filipino troops made a desperate effort to push back the Japanese to regain control of the front line. The counterattack was done under the direction of General Edward King, who was serving as General Wainwright's commander of the Bataan garrison. The plan was well conceived, but largely hopeless given the poor condition of the troops and lack of heavy weapons. The soldiers nonetheless carried out the strike with grim determination, knowing there was no alternative.[1] A renewed Japanese attack, however, began almost simultaneously with the American counterattack. The results were decisive, with Japanese forces routing the approaching defenders in a series of fierce battles.[2] American and Filipino forces were unable to stop the advancing enemy and were forced once again to retreat.

Japanese units advanced south down the eastern side of Bataan and in the center part of the peninsula past Mount Samat and Mariveles Mountain. American and Filipino coastal defense units and reserves, many once allocated for beach defense, were now on the front lines. American soldiers, Philippine Scouts, and Philippine Regular Army men streamed south via every route possible, including rugged terrain, main roads, and jungle trails. "All hell's broken loose," an American sergeant yelled to some soldiers guarding a bridge. "The lines have broken just down the road! Get out!"[3]

Reports began reaching General Homma on April 8 of defenders retreating to Mariveles and small boats moving into positions all along the southern tip of Bataan.[4] It was clear the Americans were planning to move as many men as possible over to Corregidor. The general rushed into motion a series of new attacks to cut off the retreat at Mariveles.

A scene of chaos quickly gripped the southern tip of Bataan as some defenders struggled to form a last stand line of defense, while others made ready to escape to Corregidor. Hospitals were flooded with new streams of wounded soldiers from the front. Conditions were already overcrowded due to the mass of sick patients undergoing treatment. The medical facilities now stood in the direct path of the approaching Japanese forces.

Wainwright ordered another counterattack during the late hours of April 8. King, however, had already concluded the situation was hopeless and the only viable alternative was surrender. He called his staff together for a midnight meeting. He was aware of General MacArthur's standing order against surrendering. King did not ask for any advice or opinions, but made clear the "ignominious decision" to capitulate was his alone. "I have not communicated with General Wainwright," he told his men, "because I do not want him to be compelled to assume any part of the responsibility." He concluded additional fighting would simply be a waste of life. "We have no further organized means of resistance."

King dispatched a white-flagged officer to the front lines to arrange terms of surrender with the Japanese. It was not long before word of the action reach Corregidor. Down in the tunnel, the duty officer told Wainwright of what was happening. "Go back and tell [him] not to do it," the general shouted. It was too late. He woefully passed the news onto MacArthur. King surrendered unconditionally at about 12:30 pm on April 9, 1942.[5] A deepening silence soon settled over Bataan. Wainwright held no grudge against King for his actions. "Let me say here that I have no criticism of General King for accepting the situation and surrendering," Wainwright later wrote. "It was a decision which required great courage and mental fortitude."[6]

News of the fall of Bataan cast an ugly gloom over MacArthur's headquarters in Melbourne, Australia. The general canceled all of his appointments and spent most of the day alone in his office. It was a tremendous blow to an individual with such a long association with the Philippines Commonwealth.

An aide entered the MacArthur's office late in the day to find him grim faced with tear streaks running down his cheeks.[7] "I knew it was coming, but actual word of the surrender came to me as a shock," MacArthur later wrote.[8] The bitter memories of the ordeal never left him. Corregidor now stood alone against the Japanese assault on Luzon.

The sea battle off Cebu was the fiercest encounter the PT men had with the Imperial Japanese Navy to date. The results, however, are somewhat less than clear. Sailors on both boats described seeing the light cruiser *Kuma* sustain what was thought to be serious damage as a result of the final two torpedoes fired by *PT-34*. John Bulkeley reported to have "left her in sinking condition."[9] Several American army and civilian personnel stationed in the region, who were in a position to see the results of the action, reported the warship had been sunk.

Japanese sources, however, do not corroborate the sinking claim. Postwar records confirm *Kuma* battled the PT boats on the night and location in question, but report she was only hit near the bow with a single torpedo that did not explode.[10] No additional information is available on the extent of the damage. The light cruiser survived the encounter and was sunk by a British submarine near Penang off the west coast of Malaysia on January 11, 1944.[11]

There were certainly more enemy warships in the area on the night in question than just *Kuma* and *Kiji*. Japanese sources indicate four destroyers and an assortment of smaller vessels were involved in operations near Cebu during the same timeframe. None beyond the light cruiser and torpedo boat, however, reported battling PT boats.[12]

The lack of sinking does not in any way diminish the heroic effort made by the sailors. It was a daring attack against a powerful enemy. In his battle report, Bulkeley noted Robert Kelly "is particularly commended for the execution of his attack under most difficult and hazardous conditions in a most efficient and courageous manner." The squadron commander hoped to have his executive officer receive the Medal of Honor.

A U.S. Navy Department communiqué issued late in the day on April 21 announced the action. It reported the PT boats battled a light cruiser protected by four destroyers. "Enemy counteraction finally forced the retirement of the attacking PT boats after they had seriously damaged one enemy light cruiser and left it in sinking condition," the release stated.[13] The communiqué identified the boats as PTs 34 and 41, but neither Bulkeley nor Kelly was mentioned.

Bulkeley's plan to slip away from Japanese warships to hide out in the shallow water of Misamis Bay on the north coast of Mindanao had worked perfectly. His *PT-41* arrived in the area at about dawn on the morning of April 9. No enemy ships followed him south from the previous night's sea battle.

The squadron commander knew it was too dangerous for the PT to be out on open waters in the daylight. The crew spent much of the day resting after a long night of action. Bulkeley had no knowledge of the whereabouts or condition of *PT-34* and her crew. He last saw the boat trying to get away from Japanese warships after staging the daring torpedo strike against the enemy cruiser.

The squadron commander was keeping a secret as his remaining boats operated in the southern waters—his wife was pregnant with their first boy and the expected due date was drawing near. The baby was born on April 5. However, Alice had no way of notifying her husband of the event. She named the boy John Bulkeley, Jr. in honor of his father, whom she and several close relatives did not think would survive the war.[14]

Bulkeley may not have had much time to celebrate even if he had learned the news. The dizzying series of events would continue to unfold at a frantic pace. Like Kelly further north on Cebu, he would soon be trying to get out of the way of the advancing Japanese.

CHAPTER 33

The early morning hours of April 9 found *PT-34* moving towards Cebu City. The day marked Iliff Richardson's 24th birthday. As events were to develop, however, there would be little time or reason to celebrate.

The boat was carrying wounded gunner Willard Reynolds, who had been shot in two places during the night's action. "He was given first aid and in view of his injuries it was decided to try to enter Cebu Harbor that night rather than waiting for day break since there was no pharmacist's mate or medical officer aboard the *PT-34*," Kelly wrote. The boat captain only had a general map of the region without much detail. "None others had been available in Cebu."[1]

The challenge was to get to the boat safely into the port. The waterway approaching the city was narrow. "Although it was a bright moonlight night, navigation was still difficult," Richardson recalled. "The entrance to Cebu City has a particular distinction of being boarded by shoals, with Mactan Island on one side and Cebu on the other. Navigation is further restricted by indistinct mountain ranges and indistinct foregrounds, with few recognizable points to be used for fixes."[2]

The 34 was inching forward on soundings at idling speed. Kelly took over the wheel to guide the boat during the final approach. Something did not seem right to Richardson. "There was a gentle grating and we were aground," he wrote of what happened next. Crewmen looking over the side with a flashlight could see the water was about 20 feet deep—plenty of room for a PT boat—but pinnacles of coral were spiraling upwards to within 5 feet of the surface. Kelly thought it looked like a petrified forest.[3]

It was 4:30 am. Dawn was coming soon and a stranded torpedo boat would certainly make an inviting target for any Japanese planes prowling in the area. Crewmen quickly shed clothing before going over the side in an attempt to rock the boat loose. The initial round of shaking was not able to free her.

In the meantime, Kelly remembered a small gift Nurse Peggy gave him back on Bataan. It consisted of some codeine tablets and a sedative. She had said to use it in case he was ever wounded in battle. The boat captain pulled it out of his locker and gave it to the wounded Reynolds. He was now topside and doing somewhat better.

It did not look like *PT-34* was going anywhere soon. The boat was stuck short of the channel leading into Cebu City. Kelly decided to send Richardson ashore in a rowboat to find an army doctor and make arrangements for a tugboat to come out to help free the PT.

"As I was getting dressed, the punt was lowered into the water," Richardson recalled. "I strapped my service .45 automatic pistol to my waist and put on my cap (which was never worn under way because of the wind) and boarded the punt." Two sailors rowed him close to the shore, a distance estimated to be about 200 yards. He jumped out and gave the small boat a push back towards the PT before wading through the shallow water to land. "After stumbling in the rough sand filled with crab holes, I arrived at a fisherman's hut and yelled." The owner eventually appeared and made arrangements to get the sailor to a train station a little more than a mile away.

The railroad was in the village of Minglanilia, about 9 miles south of Cebu City. Richardson was able to phone the local army headquarters. "I requested the officer on duty to send a tug to Minglanilia and to have an ambulance at Pier I in Cebu at 5:00 am to pick up a wounded man; also to have everything ready [to] place four more torpedoes aboard the 34 and the same for the 41," he wrote. "This last statement made the officer at the other end of the line curious, so I told him we had had an engagement with the Japanese cruiser."

Unbeknownst to Richardson, *PT-34* was able to break free of the coral on her own while he was making these arrangements ashore. It was the result of an hour-long dedicated effort of rocking and wobbling the boat, backing her engines, and crewmen helping in the water. The center propeller and strut were bent, but the 34 had otherwise avoided more serious underwater damage. It was nothing that "Dad" Cleland would not be able to easily fix—if they could get the boat back to his shop.

Kelly now faced a critical decision. Morning light was starting to arrive, but it revealed the area was blanketed with a thick low fog. Trying to find the channel to Cebu City would be no easier than in the darkness. The boat captain decided to wait until better light.

It took until about 7:30 am for the sun to burn off enough of the fog for the boat to safely proceed towards the channel. "Under ordinary conditions it would have been considered suicidal to have been operating in this area after daylight," Kelly wrote. "However, the army authorities had assured us of air cover and given us the assigned radio frequencies of the planes. These planes were scheduled to arrive that morning from Australia to form an escort for coastal steamers due to leave Cebu the next day carrying food for Corregidor."

Kelly had no way to confirm these arrangements since his radio was out. He instead had "every confidence that the planes would be there, having seen a copy of the dispatch concerning them the night before." The only planes, however, he would see during that morning would be Japanese.

Richardson returned to the beach after talking with the army officer by phone to find no sign of his boat. "After a fruitless native boat trip around the bay, it could be seen that the 34 had gotten off the coral by herself and left," he wrote. He then traveled directly to the army headquarters with the help of a car and driver from the local Philippine Constabulary.

"I canceled the order for the tug which was formerly needed for the 34, and told one of the staff officers of the engagement." Richardson learned an ambulance was already waiting at the pier just as requested.

He decided to go there to await the arrival of his boat. The morning fog had burned off, allowing Richardson to see that there was some kind of action taking place in the distance to the south. Planes were diving at a steep angle towards a boat in the water. He could also see the tracers of machine-gun bullets streaming skyward. He suddenly realized the vessel under fire was *PT-34*!

The attack started when the 34 was suddenly rocked by a bomb exploding in the water just off her port bow. It was shortly after 8:00 am. The blast blew a hole in the crew's washroom, knocked the port side 30-caliber machine gun off its mounting, and blew in the windshield in front of the conn area. It also showered the topside of the boat with mud and water.

Kelly initially thought the attackers were American planes mistaking him for an enemy vessel. He looked up, however, in time to catch a glimpse of the red Japanese emblem on the second plane diving towards the boat. The men aboard the 34 boat had been taken by complete surprise. "We had not heard any planes due to the noise of our engines," Kelly recalled. "Four Japanese floatplanes were seen to be diving on us out of the sun, the first already having dropped its bomb."

Japanese sources indicate the aircraft were most likely Mitsubishi F1M Pete floatplanes from the seaplane tender *Sanuki Maru*. The vessel had been supporting the invasion of the Philippines and surrounding areas since the start of the war.[4] Each Pete biplane was armed with three machine guns and could carry two 132lb bombs.[5]

The two 50-caliber machine guns on the 34 were already manned and opened fire immediately, sending a spray of tracer bullets towards the attackers. The pair was soon joined by the starboard 30-caliber gun. Crewmen quickly broke out extra ammunition to feed the guns.

The 34 was under constant attack for at least the next 15 minutes. "The planes dove from about 500 feet altitude strafing as they came out of the sun," Kelly wrote. A total of eight bombs were sent hurling towards the boat. "All were near misses (under 25 yards)." The boat captain had limited options for getting the PT out of harm's way. "Since the *PT-34* was in a narrow channel and only had two engines, maneuvering was extremely difficult," Kelly reported. Their best chance for survival rested with the gunners.

The first strafing pass killed David Harris at the starboard 50-caliber mount. The torpedoman slumped over with a grievous bullet hole in his throat before falling down to the deck. John Martino rushed to take over the station, but found the gun had also been hit and was out of action. The next two planes hit the port 50-caliber gun.

Albert Ross was able to extract a small amount of revenge when a string of bullets from his 30-caliber gun hit one of the attackers. A trail of smoke quickly sprouted behind the floatplane as it sped past. "It was presumed to have crashed (although it was not seen to hit the water) since it was not seen during any subsequent attack," Kelly noted. Bullets from an ensuing plane knocked the 30-caliber gun off its mount and onto the deck, ripping open Ross's thigh in the process.

All of the guns were now out of action, various crewmen had been injured, and the boat was peppered with bullet holes—in addition to the many received during the night battle. Aside from Harris killed and Ross wounded, Velt Hunter had been shot in the arm and Willard Reynolds was hit again.

"Chief Torpedoman Martino, who was acting as executive officer, rendered first aid to the crew and kept me informed of our damage," Kelly wrote. "When I received word that the engine room was flooded with about 3 feet of water and the engines could not last much longer, it was decided to beach the boat since we could no longer fight." The boat was run aground just off Kawit Island, a small land area just south of Cebu City, at about 8:20 am.

The beaching did not end the attack. The Japanese planes kept strafing, wanting to ensure their prey was destroyed for good. All the sailors could do was to get the wounded men off the boat to a hiding place ashore.

Only four members of the crew—Kelly, Martino, Radioman First Class David Goodman, and Machinist's Mate First Class George Shepard—were unhurt. "These men assisted me in removing the dead and wounded to a place of safety ashore despite the continued strafing of the remaining three float planes, which remained in the area until about 9:30 am," Kelly wrote. They worked as fast as they could under the difficult circumstances. The boat captain went below deck into the engine room and found Hunter. His arm had practically been blown off.

Kelly next came across Reynolds. He went below to lie in a bunk during the attack since he was unable to help in the defense of the boat. A bullet came through the side, hitting him in the midsection. "I'm done for, sir," he told his skipper. "I'll be all right here. You get out the others."[6] Kelly would not accept it. He and Martino carried him ashore.

The boat was sitting in shallow water on a shelf of uneven coral reefs. Kelly estimated it was over 1,000 yards to the beach. Some of the sailors made the mistake of taking off their shoes. They paid dearly by enduring painful cuts on their feet from the razor-sharp coral as they worked to get the wounded ashore.

Richardson did not sit idle as he helplessly watched his boat under attack from the pier in Cebu City. He found a native doctor before commandeering a canoe in an attempt to reach the beached boat. He climbed aboard *PT-34* from the stern after arriving when most of the injured were already ashore. Richardson immediately noticed the starboard engine was still running and went down into the engine room to turn it off before moving into the next compartment forward.

"I observed, in passing the tank room, that at least 200 bullet holes had drilled every part of the ship from decks and fixtures to tubes and canopy," Richardson recalled. "Blood and empty cartridge cases littered the bullet riddled deck." He then came across Harris. "He was still warm but I could feel no pulse." Moving into the forward compartment revealed it to be in a shambles, though empty of people. Harris was later carried off to land. Kelly wanted to make sure he received a proper burial.

Once ashore, Kelly found a group of native soldiers in the area, who were able to obtain some stretchers to carry the wounded to the side of the island facing Cebu. From there they could be loaded into a launch to be taken to the mainland for transportation to a hospital. He left Shepard in charge to ensure it happened without any problems.

Kelly took the canoe over to Cebu. He needed to report the previous night's actions to the American authorities. There was no communication from Bulkeley, possibly due to the 34 boat not having an operational radio. Kelly had last seen *PT-41* during the frantic night battle and wanted to know the whereabouts of the squadron commander—if he was still alive.

Working on behalf of his boat captain, Richardson also left the beached PT and went to see the local navy authorities. There was still hope *PT-34* could get fixed up and rearmed to return to battle. He met with the acting senior officer present, Commander Ryland Tisdale.

"I requested that arrangements be made to pull the 34 off at high tide and to get her to Opan as soon as possible," Richardson wrote. "Commander Tisdale invited me to breakfast and then asked how much damage had been done and if I thought it could be repaired. I answered that considerable damage had been done but that even if she could not be repaired, the 34 had valuable guns and parts still on board." The commander expressed concern that the remaining Japanese planes would come back to complete the destruction of the boat. However, he agreed to make the arrangements nonetheless.

Two pilot boats set out to help *PT-34* a short time later. Richardson was aboard one of the small craft accompanied by three American naval officers and some Filipino soldiers. Work was under way on sweeping up the empty cartridges, clearing debris, and examining the condition of the machine guns, when two or three Japanese floatplanes suddenly appeared, diving out of the sun for another surprise attack.

Neither pilot boat fared well during the ensuing encounter. One ran aground after unsuccessfully trying to escape. The other was virtually sliced in half by machine-gun fire. Richardson remembered that two Filipino soldiers were killed during the ordeal.

The planes now focused their attention on *PT-34*, making a series of bombing and strafing runs. None of the bombs found the target, but the boat burst into flames after being hit by bullets. Richardson thought the fire started in the forward compartment. It was about 12:30 pm.

A couple of men from the pilot boats attempted to go back aboard the PT. They abandoned the idea after it became clear nothing could be done to put out the flames. "Almost as soon as they reached the beach of Kawit Island, the gasoline tanks caught on fire and dense clouds of pungent black smoke and cherry orange flame signaled the end of U.S.S. *PT-34*," Richardson wrote of watching his boat go up in flames like a funeral pyre.

The gallant PT had fought her last battle. Richardson and the other surviving sailors from the 34 would soon discover they had little time to lament the loss of their boat. The Japanese were about to invade Cebu.

General Homma initially believed that all American and Filipino forces capitulated when General King gave up the fight on Bataan. He was dismayed to find the surrender, however, was only for the soldiers under King's command on the peninsula. It did not include the forces on Corregidor or in the southern islands. The end of the fighting on Bataan and the arrival of fresh reinforcements from Malaya now put Homma into a position to strike south.

Little action had taken place in the southern part of the Philippines since a small contingent of Japanese troops had landed on December 20, 1941 on the southeastern coast of Mindanao near Davao. Homma's plan was to first take control of the three of the largest islands in the south before dealing with the large number of smaller islands. He wanted to capture Cebu and Panay, striking in that order, before turning his attention to Mindanao.

General Bradford Chynoweth oversaw the defense of the Visayan Islands from his headquarters in Cebu City. The garrison on Cebu totaled about 6,500 men, most of whom were Filipino. An assortment of American Army officers and a small number of navy personnel were part of the force. Some defensive fortifications had been constructed in recent months, but trying to defend the island with poorly equipped soldiers against a mobile foe would prove to be a nearly impossible task.[7]

Chynoweth had no illusions about trying to repel a Japanese invasion. As a result, much of the defensive effort had thus far been focused on developing Camp X. The position was located in a small valley between two mountain ranges in the interior of the island. American officers planned to use the strongpoint as the center of military operations after the Japanese arrived on Cebu and possibly as a base for future guerilla actions. "Camp X was made the hub around which the island defenses were built," recalled one American officer.[8] The area was also rumored to hold a cache of ten million pesos from the Philippine government.[9]

The American command on Cebu was notified of an approaching Japanese convoy during the afternoon of April 9.[10] The invasion force of three cruisers and 11 transports was coming from the south. The ships split into two groups during the late evening hours. The larger cluster headed for Cebu City, while the second moved up the west coast of the island.

Japanese warships were plainly visibly off Cebu City at dawn on the morning of April 10. Troops started to come ashore a short time later and quickly began approaching the city. A second amphibious landing took place simultaneously near the city of Toledo on the opposite side of Cebu.

The only American help to stem the invasion came in the form of 13 bombers, including ten of the new twin-engine B-25s sent up to Del Monte from Australia on April 11. The aircraft flew offensive missions across the region for several days, including B-25 attacks on enemy positions around Cebu. Various Americans on the ground, including Kelly and Richardson, reported seeing the planes over Cebu City.[11]

The Cebu Military Police Regiment of about 1,100 Filipinos under the command of an American officer was responsible for defending Cebu City. The fight for control of the city, however, lasted for only a day. The outgunned defenders fell back in an orderly manner, buying critical time to demolish key bridges on their way out as Japanese troops entered the city.

The enemy landing on the west coast near Toledo was equally successful, with enemy forces seizing control of the immediate area before moving inland. Defenders were unable to keep control of a critical road traversing the island from east to west. The loss led to the end of the organized defense on the island, including the abandonment of Camp X. General Chynoweth fled north into the hills on April 12 to organize a guerilla movement.[12]

CHAPTER 34

The remaining American servicemen on Cebu were soon scrambling to get out before the Japanese took control of the whole island. Robert Kelly, Iliff Richardson, and Henry Brantingham were part of the exodus. Their stories of escape occurred simultaneously in a frenzied "every man for themselves" atmosphere.

Richardson helped get the wounded sailors from the beached *PT-34* to medical help. He left the boat for good after she was set afire during the second attack by Japanese planes. Crewman David Harris was already dead, but there was still hope for some of the other injured sailors, including Willard Reynolds. The latter made it to the hospital, but did not survive the operating table, succumbing to the grievous wounds suffered in the sea battle and air attack. Richardson remembered his dying words as "I'm going to be pretty sick, ain't I."[1] He no sooner made the statement than he took his last breath.

"I went into the morgue of the Southern Island Hospital in Cebu and cut off one of the dog tags on Harris and [one] from Reynolds," Richardson recalled. The executive officer of the 34 now set out to make funeral arrangements. He met soldier Tom Jurika in the process.

Jurika was born and raised in the Philippines by American parents who had business interests in the Commonwealth. He knew the southern islands well.[2] Jurika had access to an apartment in a well-known building in Cebu City and arranged to have Richardson spend the night.

It was a place for the weary sailor to get some food and rest. Richardson learned of the Bataan surrender while listening to an American radio station broadcasting from Corregidor. He was too tired to think much about it. He fell asleep with his wet, muddy, and blood-stained boots still on his feet.

The sound of rumbling explosions ended Richardson's slumber in the early morning hours. He stayed in bed for a time, wondering about the sounds, until a large blast shook the entire building. He arose to find Jurika was already gone and the apartment empty. It looked like the whole city was burning, with a pall of smoke hanging in the air.

Richardson headed outside into the eerie smoke-filled streets. He soon found Jurika, who told him the Japanese were coming. "I was stupid from all the feeling of excitement I had and looked past him out into the harbor," Richardson wrote, searching for a sign of the enemy.[3] "No," Jurika exclaimed while pointing, "they're landing about 10 kilometers down."

The army was burning anything of value in the city to keep it from falling into Japanese hands. Richardson and Jurika jumped into action to help. "All I did was to help burn the warehouse down with gasoline," Richardson later recalled.[4] The men quickly began spreading around four tins of gasoline they found in the army building. The accelerant was set off with some matches to create an instant inferno.

Richardson remembered the demolition was an all-inclusive undertaking. "In the scorched-earth policy we were able to blow up about 16 ships, all the torpedoes, and the docks and the dry docks and burn all of the quartermaster warehouses, including all of the downtown area, and they hit everything, it was a very good job," he later said.

The pair knew it was time to get out of town—and fast. They went back to the apartment to get some canned food. Richardson could plainly see the Japanese troops coming ashore unopposed in the distance through his binoculars. It looked to him like the enemy soldiers were conducting a routine drill.

The two then set out on foot, thinking it was safer than driving. The pair used their pistols to shoot the engines of some abandoned cars on

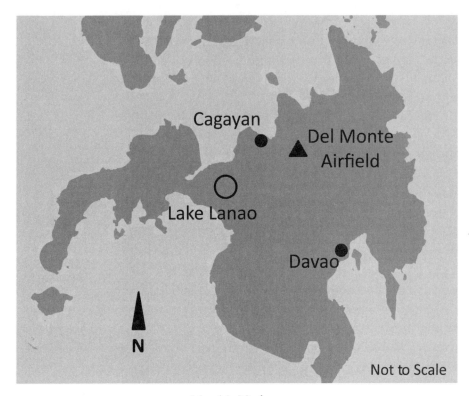

Map 14: Mindanao

their way out. They even rolled Jurika's car over a cliff, operating under the theory that the less left for the Japanese the better.

The scene of chaos in Cebu City was now apparent in the full daylight. Buildings were on fire everywhere, sending billows of smoke spiraling skyward. Japanese planes could be occasionally seen above.

The pair went to the home of Americans Cecil John (CJ) and Charlotte Martin outside of town. CJ was the port captain for Cebu City and a local businessman. Charlotte did volunteer work for the army.[5] Richardson first became acquainted with her at the local hospital. The location of the house provided a good viewing point to the activities in Cebu City. Richardson saw enemy soldiers moving through the city. Some Japanese ships came into the harbor a short time later, pulling up to the docks unopposed.

The Martins prepared a fine meal for the guests, complete with champagne. The food and drink was comforting, but only provided a short respite from the war for the servicemen. Richardson and Jurika decided to stay the night. The heat from the burning city could easily be felt, even though the house was more than 6 miles away from the nearest flames. A reminder of the burning fires, in the form of a flickering red light dancing around the walls of the house, stayed throughout the night.

The guests left the Martin house the next morning after it had been strafed by Japanese planes. The pair had to keep moving to remain one step ahead of the enemy. They were heading into the interior of the island, away from the known Japanese positions near the coast, in an effort to link up with the army.

Richardson was already exhausted from his time aboard the PT boat, but soon discovered he was now in for a lot of walking. Moving inland put the men in an area of rolling hills and rugged mountains. They mixed among the streams of local civilians and soldiers who were also trying to get away from the Japanese. Many of the people did not seem to know where they were going.

The pair eventually came across Colonel John D. Cook near the village of Adlaon in the hills north of the city. The American army officer was attached to the large Army Quartermasters' depot in Cebu City.[6] Jurika decided to continue on in an attempt to find the American headquarters. Richardson volunteered to stay with Cook, even though he did not have a high opinion of him.[7]

The sailor was put in charge of a motor pool of about 20 vehicles. The men under him were mostly Filipino, largely workers with few weapons of any type. Their mission was to move vital supplies away from the approaching enemy. It was arduous work, starting early in the morning and continuing into the late evening hours.

Richardson's position was fast becoming precarious as the Japanese started advancing inland from Cebu City. Enemy planes were now making regular attacks in the area. One bomb hit a moving truck, but the remainder mostly missed the motor pool.

The situation became much worse when the Japanese seized the village of Busay on the road leading directly to the location of the motor pool. Richardson phoned Cook's command post seeking permission to burn the trucks. The excited colonel said he would get back to him. The pool of men began to shrink as some were killed or wounded in the air attacks. Those assigned to evacuate the injured did not return. Most of the others fled when the Japanese moved even closer, bringing the sound of gunfire.

"I kept sitting by the telephone," Richardson later recalled. "I had my cans of gasoline set up in a line along the line of trucks, waiting for the orders to scorch the earth. I was afraid to do it without orders."

The orders never came. Richardson and the last remaining Filipino took off, running in different directions, when a hail of bullets signaled the arrival of the enemy. The Filipino fell lifeless to the ground after being shot, but Richardson kept running. He escaped the immediate area, going directly to Cook's outpost. He angrily told the colonel the motor pool was overrun by the Japanese, who now had the remaining trucks. Cook immediately ordered the command post abandoned and departed without giving Richardson any orders.

The sailor decided not to follow the soldiers, but took off on his own. He eventually hid in a cave for a couple of days with two American civilians before finding a group of American soldiers. The Japanese were now thought to be closing in from both the east and west. Richardson joined a small group who decided to leave the area on foot. They arrived at Danao, northeast of Cebu City, after what seemed like an endless period of walking. Richardson was now thoroughly exhausted and not sure he could walk much farther.

The group escaped Cebu by going east and eventually arrived at Tacloban on the larger island of Leyte. It was the headquarters of American Colonel Theodore Cornell, whose force of about 2,500 men held Leyte and the adjacent island of Samar. The Japanese had not yet arrived on these islands. Richardson had the satisfaction of making it out of Cebu alive. His journey was over for the moment, but he still wanted to go down to Mindanao in the hopes of getting a flight to Australia.

Henry Brantingham was still with *PT-35* at the Opan shipyard when the Japanese began their landing on Cebu. The repairs on the boat were not yet complete. He was ordered to burn the boat to keep her from falling into Japanese hands. "While preparing the boat for demolition some 15 minutes after the initial notice had been given, heavy explosions occurred in the oil compounds, throwing debris, oil, and heavy smoke over the shipyard," he wrote.[8] Brantingham took the name plate off the boat before starting the fire.

"Remembering my experience with *PT-33*, I used the same method, but with more caution," he explained. "I used a long wick to start the fire and explosion."[9] One of the last two PT boats left in the squadron was quickly shrouded in a sudden onrush of flames. The boat captain and crew then took a launch over to Cebu City.

Brantingham briefly stopped to send an international wire to his lady friend (and future wife) back in Queens. It was nothing more than an Easter greeting. "A little careless with geography, she though Cebu was somewhere in Hawaii, and was not greatly worried," he later wrote.

The officer and his sailors, however, had plenty to be worried about. Their plan was to head into the hills in the hope of somehow getting to Mindanao and eventually Australia. The party consisted of the boat captain, ten other sailors, and a lone civilian.[10] The group started their journey carrying heavy packs, but eventually discarded the large items deemed too cumbersome as the trails became increasingly difficult to navigate. Brantingham only kept his pistol, some ammunition, and his wallet full of paper pesos. He was fortunate to have kept his money out of the bank. Many of his men had lost most of their funds after the Manila Bank was taken over by the Japanese.

Brantingham briefly encountered Richardson about four days into the cross-island journey. The Japanese were thought to be about 10 miles away. He tried to convince the officer to join his group, but was unsuccessful. Brantingham recalled that Richardson was "personally directing the withdrawal of vital food and medical supplies from what were then untenable positions, and Ensign Richardson insisted on continuing this work in spite of constantly being bombed and strafed by Japanese airplanes, refusing to evacuate from Adlaon and join my party, believing his services were required here."[11]

The Brantingham group continued to head west, passing near native villages and sleeping in Nipa huts. They encountered a hillside farmer, who provided them a fine meal of boiled cornmeal and chicken. The man refused payment. Aside from the special meal, the sailors' main diet throughout the journey was green coconuts and bananas.

The group eventually arrived at a small village on the west coast of Cebu. The stay was short, however, as the men quickly departed back into the hills after locals warned them that the town was held by the Japanese. Their sudden disappearance was noticed by the enemy authorities.

The sailors were followed at a distance by a small group of Japanese soldiers, thought to be no more than three or four men. Brantingham felt they had enough weapons—an assortment of rifles, pistols and shotguns—among the group to be able to stage an effective ambush. They found a good location, set up, and then waited, but the enemy never came. The soldiers must have become suspicious as they returned to the village.

Brantingham knew the men could not stay in the jungle. He also knew the village, even though it was occupied, held the key to their escape. They passed through the town under the cover of darkness to find three canoes, one with a sail, along the beach. The sailors took to the sea. "The sailboat took the lead, and towed the other two boats in tandem," Brantingham later wrote. "Helping along with paddles, we reached the east coast of Negroes the following day, and landed without incident."[12]

The new island was free of Japanese—at least for the moment. The men used a Texaco map to follow the main road to Dumaguete on the southeastern part of the island. They were able to find two local fishing boats willing to take them to Mindanao for a fee. The departure was delayed when four Japanese warships passed through the area going south. The trip was eventually made under the cover of darkness. Brantingham's group arrived on the west coast of Mindanao after a nearly two-week-long journey.

Robert Kelly wanted to know if John Bulkeley was still alive after the night sea battle. He went directly to the local U.S. Army headquarters after going ashore near Cebu City on April 9. A colonel told him there had been no word from the PT commander, but that he would send out a radio message in an effort to get more information. The officer suggested Kelly should provide a report of the action to the American general in charge of the area and accompanied him to the bar of the American Club.

The general had evidently just concluded a meeting at the establishment and was now having drinks with some officers and civilians. The PT man wanted to provide details of the night action so the information could be radioed up the chain of command. Kelly was wound up after having gone through the battle, beaching *PT-34* during the air attack, and seeing some of his crewmen wounded and dying. He also wanted to know why the rumored American offensive and air cover had never materialized.

The general was apparently too busy to see him. The angry boat captain hung around for a while at the bar having a Coke with the colonel before finally giving up. He went to "Dad" Cleland's place at the shipyard and found Henry Brantingham still there waiting for the repairs on *PT-35* to be completed.

At about this time, Richardson telephoned with the news that Reynolds had died. Arrangements had been made for Reynolds and Harris to be buried in an American cemetery with an honor guard and a clergyman officiating. The tentative plan was for the services to take place at 4:00 pm the same day. Kelly made plans to meet Richardson back at the American Club so they could go to the funeral together.

Kelly waited at the club as the appointed time came and passed, but his executive officer did not show up. A truck eventually arrived with a Filipino soldier bearing a message that the funeral had been postponed until the next morning. Kelly was now on his own, alone and with no boat, in a city where he knew almost no one. He was befriended by an American civilian who was one of the managers at the club.

The friendly stranger invited Kelly to his home outside of town for a meal with his family and some rest. It was an offer the weary sailor could not refuse. Kelly first located the remaining unwounded men from his boat and gave them some money to go out on the town.

The American's home was on a small hill overlooking Cebu City and the harbor area. Kelly ate a good meal before retiring early for the night. Turning on a bedside radio revealed the awful news of the Bataan surrender. Kelly's thoughts must have gone in many directions, and certainly may have included thinking about Nurse Peggy, now trapped on Corregidor. He was, however, very exhausted and eventually fell sleep.

The rest ended abruptly with the sound of a loud crash. "It was a hell of an explosion which woke me up in the darkness, and for a minute I didn't know where I was," Kelly recalled. "Through my window which overlooked the town and harbor beyond, I could see fire rising on the outskirts."[13] A glance at his watch revealed the time was 4:25 am.

Kelly was now wide awake. His host was gathering information on the telephone—the Japanese invasion had started and the Americans were demolishing key points in the city. One of the large explosions was at the oil refinery. The boat captain rushed to get back into the city to find his three enlisted sailors, but was stopped short by army sentries. No one was allowed back into town, everyone must get out. He was never reunited with the three sailors from his boat.

The city was burning up before his very eyes, but Kelly was able to pick up a large number of small bits of information as the morning progressed. It was almost like pieces of a puzzle—Japanese troops coming ashore at two locations, Bulkeley was not dead, but rather made it safely to Mindanao, Richardson was helping with the demolition, Brantingham was set to scuttle *PT-35* at the shipyard, and his beloved 34 boat was not able to be saved.

A key decision faced the sailor that had to be made soon—where should he go? Some soldiers were telling him to go to Camp X. They said it had enough food and supplies to be able to hold out for a long time. The roads and bridges leading to the hideout were going to be demolished by retreated forces to prevent the Japanese from moving inland. Kelly was not sure, so he went back to the American's house outside of town. He watched as troops entered the city. There was some sporadic fighting, but the Japanese were clearly winning the battle with ease.

Enemy planes were also in control of the sky. Some were dropping leaflets, while others went about strafing cars trying to leave town. By 2:30 pm it was time to go.

The only available map of the island was the large-scale one he had pulled out of the PT boat. Some soldiers had previously pointed out the location of Camp X. A report then arrived of a Japanese landing on the west coast of Cebu. Kelly just simply did not believe that the enemy would not be able to find and overrun the stronghold. He decided against going to Camp X.

He started off alone on foot, heading west on hilly trails with the hope of somehow making an escape off the island. Kelly eventually joined up with some American civilians going in the same direction. They owned plantations on the island and could speak the local dialect.

The small group slept in huts among farm animals and swarms of flies. They paid locals whenever possible to prepare meals of rice, corn, and sometimes roasted chicken. Banana leaves were used for plates with pieces of bark serving as eating utensils. Sometime later in the journey, the men encountered a group of American soldiers who told them Camp X was taken by the Japanese. Kelly was glad he had followed his hunch.

The travelers eventually made it to a town on the west coast of Cebu. Kelly estimated the journey encompassed 42 miles. It included some steep hikes and crossing five mountain ranges.[14]

There were no boats available in the area, as most had already been used for evacuations. The men continued down the coast to a smaller village where they found a very young Filipino officer, who Kelly thought was nothing more than a kid, in command of about 20 soldiers. He told them the Japanese were about 10 miles away. An enemy tank had previously ventured up the one paved road in their direction only to stop short and turn around. The troops were planning to blend into the civilian population when the Japanese returned.

The soldiers helped Kelly's group find enough bancas to carry everyone. The men sailed to a neighboring island, arriving soaking wet. They were met on the beach by native guards—thankfully not Japanese soldiers. Kelly then parted ways with the American civilians. It took some time, along with an assortment of car rides and voyages in small boats between islands, but he eventually made it to Mindanao.

CHAPTER 35

The Japanese attack on the southern part of the Philippines did not stop with the capture of Cebu. A total of three amphibious landings took place on Panay, starting on the morning of April 16, 1942. The largest was near the main city of Iloilo. None of the invasions was opposed. The battle for control of Panay was essentially over by April 20, when Japanese forces were in control of all the key points on the island.[1] Some of the defenders refused to give up the fight, and instead faded into the jungle to begin guerilla warfare. The rapid seizure of Cebu and Panay put the Japanese in firm control of the region.

General Homma was now free to turn his attention to Mindanao—the largest of the southern islands. The land mass featured a rugged mountainous terrain with an interior of jungle rainforests. General William Sharp had begun planning for the defense of the island shortly after his arrival in January. He started a crash training program for the mostly Filipino soldiers under his command and focused on building up defensive positions. The general faced a host of problems, including having few heavy weapons, an abundance of antiquated rifles, and scarce amounts of ammunition. Most of his troops had only the most basic amount of training when the enemy arrived.

Mindanao became the target of a three-pronged assault starting on April 29, when Japanese forces came ashore unopposed midway up the coast on the western side of the island just south of Lake Lanao. The invasion force comprised nearly 5,000 men.[2] The troops split into two groups after securing the beachhead. One began moving north towards Lake Lanao, the other south in the direction of Davao. Filipino soldiers defending the route to the lake staged a fighting retreat, but could not stop the advancing enemy. The enemy moved into the area around Lake Lanao during the first days of May.

Japanese units on the southern part of Mindanao were also on the move in an operation designed to coincide with the amphibious invasion. Soldiers stationed around Davao Gulf, who had recently relieved those in the area holding the beachhead since December, began moving north to link up with the new invaders. The forces met inland about halfway between the two starting points. In less than a week, the enemy controlled all of the western and southern regions of the island.

The final prong of the Mindanao attack began on May 3, just as the enemy was overrunning the lake region, when Japanese forces landed at two locations along the northern coast in the vicinity of Cagayan. The battle for the critical region would decide the fate of the island. Sharpe defended the area with local forces and his reserve units. Filipino infantry units initially put up a stiff defense near the beachhead, but the Japanese were able to break through to begin their advance towards Del Monte. The airfield was currently the last American lifeline with Australia.

The defenders withdrew to organize a last-stand line in the vicinity of Mangima Canyon. The formidable natural barrier was near the airfield and a strategic intersection of two roads. The key location could not be held after several days of hard fighting. An organized withdrawal turned into a full rout.

General Sharp radioed the bad news to MacArthur. "North front in full retreat," he reported. It was soon followed by the more terse "May sign off any time now."[3] The area was in enemy hands by May 9.

The fight for Mindanao was largely over after the fall of Del Monte and the defense line around the canyon, with the Japanese in control of nearly all of the important points on the island. Only scattered pockets of defenders remained, with some planning to head into the hills to organize with locals as guerillas.

It was during the chaotic final weeks of April on Mindanao that some of the torpedo squadron's senior officers were able to escape to Australia. All of them were keenly aware of MacArthur's pledge to give the PT men priority for evacuation. Getting to the actual evacuation points alive and securing a spot on a plane proved to be a challenging undertaking.

John Bulkeley now had the last remaining PT boat of his squadron. He wanted to get *PT-41* fueled up, rearmed and back into action. The squadron commander, however, had one last piece of unfinished business from General MacArthur. He had been asked by the general to look over the Cotabato River basin on the southwest coast of Mindanao. MacArthur made the request before departing for Australia, perhaps under the belief that there was an army waiting for him down south for an immediate return to the Philippines.

Bulkeley was not familiar with the area, but quickly organized some locals to complete the task. The natives paddled around the area in bancas, disguised as fishermen, measuring the water depth using strings laden with rocks. The findings were charted on rudimentary maps. Bulkeley sent the combined information to Australia. He included a concise note summarizing his feelings on the matter: "Cotabato River beaches no good for large-scale landings."[4]

The squadron commander next traveled to Cagayan in order to report to Sharp, the local army commander, as directed in his previous orders. He reported "that one enemy ship had been believed to have been sunk and that information was requested as to the possibility of proceeding to Cebu City the next night."[5] Sharp broke the bad news to Bulkeley that it was too late. The Japanese were already landing on Cebu. The torpedoes were gone and no more fuel was to be issued to PT boats. The remaining aviation gasoline was needed for planes arriving from Australia for evacuation runs.

It was the end of the line for the 41. "General Wainwright then directed that *PT-41* be removed to Lake Lanao," Bulkeley continued. She was to join the small fleet of improvised gunboats to help prevent Japanese seaplanes from landing on the inland lake.

Next came some disturbing news about *PT-34* from some aviators who left Cebu just ahead of the Japanese. The airmen told Bulkeley that Robert Kelly along with three enlisted men had been killed and all of the other crewmen were wounded. Kelly and the deceased sailors were supposedly buried on Cebu. "The crew were in a hospital in Cebu City," Bulkeley noted. "It is assumed that they are prisoners of war by now. But this is not official information whatsoever." Although unconfirmed, the report was unsettling nonetheless.

Bulkeley was now a squadron commander with no more boats to command. He reported to Sharp for duty as directed in the final set of orders provided to him prior to MacArthur's departure for Australia, but did not stay on the island for very long. The general notified him on April 13 that he was to depart for Australia on orders from MacArthur. The plane was leaving that very night.

The squadron commander initially felt bad about departing. Thoughts crossed his mind of how it would be viewed by his men. He was departing for safety, while they were abandoned to a dismal fate. Bulkeley then saw the matter from a different angle, believing if he could get to Australia himself, then maybe he could convince MacArthur to evacuate all of his men.[6] The general certainly had shown plenty of appreciation to the PT sailors who took him out of the desperate situation on Corregidor. Bulkeley passed word of the plan to his subordinates. He left George Cox in command of the squadron, operating under the belief Kelly was dead.

Bulkeley climbed on board a B-17 at Del Monte Field during the evening of April 13. It was loaded with passengers eager to make a safe passage out of the Philippines. Japanese planes attacked the base just as the bomber was getting ready to take off. The plane was hit, causing one engine to sputter to a stop. The passengers may have thought it was the end of the flight, but the pilot was determined to get the bomber airborne—and did. The aircraft flew all the way to Australia on three engines.

Bulkeley made it out of the Philippines alive. He survived to fight another day. His former flagship, however, had reached the end of her fighting days.

The 41 was about to undergo her final journey to become a gunboat on Lake Lanao. DeWitt Glover was one of the *PT-41* crewmembers helping to get the boat ready. He recalled, "we spent about a week in the job of dismantling her, taking the engines out, the torpedo tubes off, everything that was moveable or that would come off was removed from the boat to lighten her. On the seventh day I think, I forgot the date, we took the *PT-41* over to the entrance of the Agus River, crossed the sandbar at the mouth of the river and tied her up to the bridge where she was to be taken out of the water," he continued. The mouth of the river was on the northern coast of Mindanao directly above Lake Lanao.

It was the last stop before going overland to the lake—a trip of about 15 miles.[7] The transportation was the responsibility of the army. The PT sailors had one last thing to attend to before turning over the boat to landlubbers. "There we took everything off the 41 that we wanted as souvenirs—the commission pennant, the flags, the clocks—and officially took her out of commission," Glover later said.[8] He remembered hearing of plans to recommission her once on the lake.

Army personnel made a gallant effort to haul *PT-41* inland. Her engines actually made it to the lake by truck, but the boat did not. One story said it was simply a matter of running out of time with the enemy closing in on the area around the lake. Another had her making most of the journey before arriving at a trestle bridge that the boat was too large to cross.[9] In either case, the end result was that the venerable 41 boat, veteran of many sea battles in the defense of the Philippines, was burned to prevent capture by the Japanese.

The last leg of Kelly's long journey to Mindanao was facilitated by a Chinese smuggler. The individual was in the business of moving luxury goods among various southern islands in the Philippines. He delivered the PT man to a small village on the northern coast of Mindanao in exchange for a hefty payment in pesos.

Kelly found the village to be entirely abandoned, except for one old man. The senior was able to communicate that a PT boat had briefly stopped there about a week ago and was able to draw a rudimentary picture of her skipper. The drawing closely resembled Bulkeley. It was enough information to convince Kelly his superior was alive. He hitched a ride in a truck east to the coastal town of Iligan, where he found *PT-41* moored dockside.

A startled George Cox was the first to see the executive officer. A parade of astonished crewmen then appeared one after another. DeWitt Glover was among the dumbfounded sailors to see the executive officer. "It had been reported to us that he was dead, so we thought we were seeing a ghost," he later recalled. "He had quite a few stories to tell us about the men that had been left in Cebu. He said he himself was going to try to get out by plane."[10]

Kelly assured them all that he was very much alive. Cox told the story of an aviator who arrived in the area from Cebu—apparently the same one who spoke with Bulkeley. The man said he talked with a Catholic priest who presided over a funeral service for Kelly and one other PT sailor. The executive officer was relieved. The story confirmed the two dead crewmen from the 34 boat had received a proper burial even in the chaos of the city falling into Japanese hands.

Cox then broke the news to Kelly that Bulkeley had already been evacuated to Australia. There was hope the other PT men would also be able to get out, but the situation was very fluid. The sailors were making the final preparations to turn *PT-41* over to the army for transportation to Lake Lanao before heading inland to see about getting a flight out.

Kelly decided to go to Del Monte to see General Sharp. He wanted to report the details of the night action and to see if someone could pass word to Australia that he was still alive. The general sent him to be near the airfield for possible evacuation, but issued a stern warning not to get his hopes up about being able to get out. The aviation gasoline supply was very low and it was unclear how many more planes were coming.

The army officer in charge of the area gave Kelly an equally gloomy assessment about the possibility of evacuation. He told the sailor his men were assembling a group of carabaos for a pack train to Lake Lanao. Kelly was assigned to lead the train once the preparations were completed.

All the PT man could do was to wait patiently. On the evening of April 23, he heard a radio news report of the sea battle of Cebu. It came from the navy news release a couple of days earlier. The announcer framed it as a great victory, but Kelly knew otherwise. Yes, he firmly believed they sank a Japanese cruiser, but it did nothing whatsoever to stop the enemy advance. He went to sleep with a sick feeling in his stomach.

Kelly was advised by the local army officer next morning of the progress on assembling the carabaos for the pack train. Most of the animals had been collected. The sailor was directed to look over the trail in advance of an expected departure. The trip would most likely start that very day. The phone rang when Kelly returned to his quarters to pack up his belongings. It was Sharp. He was to report to the airfield at once for evacuation.

"It was grim waiting at the airport," Kelly later recounted. Over 100 men were lingering around the immediate area with prioritized numbers and frayed nerves for an aircraft that could only carry a fraction of the people. It was unclear how many planes would come—maybe only one. Cox and Anthony Akers were also on the list, but had not yet arrived.

The droning sound of aircraft engines in the dark night sky finally announced an incoming plane—a single plane. It was about 10:30 pm. Thirty names were called off the list of waiting passengers in the order of priority numbers, including Kelly, Cox, and Akers, but only Kelly was present among the PT sailors to answer the call. Two army officers were getting ready to take the places of the missing navy men when Cox and Akers came running up just in time.

General Sharp was also at the airfield. He made a point to say goodbye to Kelly, telling him it was most likely going to be the last plane out. The general asked Kelly to pass along a message to MacArthur—send whatever help he could. Mindanao was likely going to fall in only a matter of days without additional troops and supplies. Sharp probably knew he was asking for the impossible and no help was forthcoming.

Sharp seemed resigned to his fate. He believed those chosen for evacuation would put their skills to good use in the war ahead. "The rest of us consider ourselves as being expendable, which is something that may come to any soldier," he said.[11] Kelly said a final goodbye and then boarded the plane.

The lumbering bomber took off to begin the long journey south. Perhaps the last six months were replaying in Kelly's mind—the long journey to Manila before the war, Cavite destroyed, sea battles, Nurse Peggy, MacArthur's evacuation, and the escape from Cebu—as the plane gained altitude slowly leaving the embattled Philippines behind. One thing was certain—Motor Torpedo Boat Squadron 3 was a squadron no more.

CHAPTER 36

The grim final chapter in the fall of the Philippines began to play out in the weeks after the surrender of Bataan. General Homma focused on preparing for the final assault on Corregidor. His artillery began a prolonged pounding of the fortress island. A prerequisite of the attack was the need to move American and Filipino prisoners, crammed in the southern area of Bataan, to prison camps under preparation further north on Luzon.

A host of factors combined to result in one of the most horrific episodes in the Pacific War—the Bataan Death March. It is important to note as a backdrop that surrender was strictly forbidden under Japanese military tradition, with prisoners often regarded as the lowest form of humanity. It was, however, no excuse for what was about to happen.

The Japanese were prepared to handle about 25,000 prisoners, but were suddenly faced with nearly three times that number.[1] Logistics quickly broke down. Most of the American and Filipino soldiers were already in poor health due to exhaustion, disease, and lack of food. Some could barely walk.

The majority of captives were forced to march, under the most brutal conditions, about 65 miles from Bataan to Camp O'Donnell in central Luzon. The men suffered a host of horrible atrocities along the way at the hands of Japanese soldiers. Most were withheld food and water. Prisoners were killed along the route by a variety of cruel means, including some who were beaten, bayoneted, shot, buried alive—and even run over by tanks. It is estimated that 600 Americans and between 5,000 and 10,000 Filipinos perished. About 60,000 survived the ordeal to face years of harsh captivity. Less than 60 percent of the Bataan prisoners survived the war.[2]

The ultimate blame for the ghastly event would eventually fall on Homma himself. He was tried as a war criminal in the Philippines after the end of the war. The general paid for the Bataan Death March with his life.

The final assault on Corregidor began on April 29 with an intensive preinvasion bombardment by artillery and aircraft. The more than 14,000 American and Filipinos crammed on the island endured a withering barrage that destroyed defensive positions, equipment, and killed people. Homma planned two amphibious landings, on opposite sides of the island, spaced apart by a day due to a shortage of landing boats. In the end, though, only one was needed to take Corregidor.

General Wainwright's position was nearly hopeless. While his beach defenders might be able to thwart the initial part of the assault, the enemy could throw waves of fresh troops into the battle. There would be no way to expel the Japanese once they were on the island.

The final step before the invasion was a thundering crescendo of the artillery barrage. More than 16,000 shells rained down on the island during May 4 alone.[3] The assault began the next day with the Japanese coming ashore on the northeastern part of the island. American Marines put up a fierce defense, hitting many of the landing boats with two artillery cannons that miraculously survived the preinvasion bombardment, but were unable to hold back the enemy from coming ashore.

Japanese troops, supported by several tanks, turned west from the beachhead to advance towards the entrance to the Malinta Tunnel. A counterattack by a mixed unit that comprised marines, sailors, and soldiers failed to slow the advance. The end of the battle seemed only days—if not hours—away.

Wainwright made the decision to surrender on the morning of May 6, after it became apparent there was no way to stop the Japanese from entering the Malinta Tunnel. His pledge to General MacArthur to hold the territory weighed heavily on his mind, but he feared a wholesale slaughter of the many defenseless servicemen in the underground hospital complex. The general had previously been released from the prior "no surrender" order by President Roosevelt, who gave him the full freedom and authority to make any decision necessary in the best interest of his troops.[4]

The southern Philippines had been discharged by Wainwright into a separate standalone command in a last-minute effort to only surrender the troops under his direct control on Corregidor. Homma would not accept it. He wanted all remaining forces in the Philippines to unconditionally capitulate. Wainwright reluctantly agreed, fearing retaliation against his men on Corregidor. The surrender document was drafted on Japanese terms. The beleaguered Wainwright traveled to Manila under Japanese escort on May 7 to broadcast the order over a public radio station. It was a humiliating duty for a defeated general.

All American and Filipino military units were directed to surrender within four days. Local commanders were to organize their troops, keeping all equipment and heavy weapons intact, and report to the closest Japanese officer. Wainwright closed his address by stating Japanese military units "will not cease their operations until they recognize faithfulness in executing the above-mentioned orders."[5] With the general's concluding statement, the American defense of the Philippines was over—at least officially.

John Bulkeley arrived in Australia with little more than the clothes on his back. Even his attire was incomplete, as he wore a jacket, but had no shirt underneath it. He was exhausted and did not have any money. A young lady from the Australian Women's Auxiliary Service was on hand when the plane landed. She took the exhausted sailor to her family's home, where he slept for 36 hours straight.

He revived from his slumber to find a big surprise. The family gave him a new uniform complete with socks, underwear, shoes, and $150 hidden in a pocket. Bulkeley could not have been more grateful. The family later refused his attempt to repay them.[6]

The squadron commander eventually traveled south, where he visited with MacArthur. The general had recently been appointed the Supreme Commander of Allied Forces in the Southwest Pacific area, a title that gave him control over an expansive area including Australia, the Philippines, New Guinea, and nearby islands—but little in the way of actual forces.[7] MacArthur was happy to see his rescuer. He invited Bulkeley to a luncheon honoring Manuel Quezon. The Philippine president was scheduled to depart shortly for the United States in order to set up a government in exile.

Bulkeley looked completely different than when the pair last met. Gone was the wild pirate look. The officer was now clean shaven, with shorter hair and a neat regulation uniform. Quezon was talkative during the event, relating the story of his rescue from the island of Negroes by an old "American sea wolf." He then turned to a puzzled Bulkeley to say "I want to express my sincere appreciation to your father, the sea wolf, and commend him on his great courage."[8] The room was soon awash with laughter, including that of Quezon once he realized his error. "If I had seen your face I would never have gone with you," the Philippine president later quipped to Bulkeley. Adding to reporters "He looked so young and fresh, I never would have trusted him."[9]

A short time later, the squadron commander was reunited with three of his officers—Kelly, Akers, and Cox. They briefly celebrated, but it was soon time to go home. All four received orders back to the United States for assignment to the newly formed PT training center in Rhode Island.

MacArthur asked to see Bulkeley before his departure. He instructed the officer to pass along a special message to the top brass in Washington. The first part of the message was to express disappointment over the lack of reinforcements sent to Bataan and stress the need to provide an army to retake the Philippines as soon as possible. The second portion was all about PT boats. "Motor torpedo boats should be the basis of a separate branch of the service for specialists, and who must have confidence in their boats," MacArthur expressed.[10] He spoke of how the boats could be effectively used in the Pacific, requesting 200 be sent to his command. The conversation lasted almost an hour.

The four PT men departed Australia for the long journey east. The trip took them to Canton Island, where they crossed paths with some marines heading east to New Zealand. The soldiers would subsequently endure heavy fighting on Guadalcanal in the South Pacific. They were fascinated with the first-hand account of the MacArthur escape mission.

"We stayed in adjoining rooms in what had been the old Pan Am guest house," Marine officer Merrill Twining later wrote. "Far into the night the PT boat commanders regaled us with the story of their breakout and perilous journey. They spoke warmly of MacArthur, but were more than a little critical of some of the staff officers who accompanied him and who tried to force Bulkeley to abandon the crew of one of the two PT boats when it became disabled."[11] Twining fought in World War II and the Korean War before retiring as a general.

The journey continued with a stop in Hawaii. The men then proceeded on to San Francisco, landing on May 7. The stopover included a short press conference—the first one conducted by PT sailors. The officers provided a riveting account of their action off Bataan, Cebu, and the MacArthur rescue mission. "When our usefulness was at an end and our mission was completed, we were flown out of the islands on orders from General MacArthur," Bulkeley told the reporters.[12] The men dined on hamburgers before boarding a commercial airliner for an overnight flight to New York City. "Sure beats the hell out of boiled tomcat," Bulkeley told Kelly.[13]

Reporters rushed to file their stories. Excerpts of the press conference appeared in newspapers around the country. The public was eager to hear from the hero sailors in person, as they had previously only been subjects of navy press releases.

Alice Bulkeley was waiting with the couple's newborn son when the plane rolled to a stop at New York's La Guardia Airport the next morning. The couple's 19-month-old daughter Joan was at home. Alice had previously received a cable from her husband telling her that he was all right. She immediately noticed he had lost some weight during the time in the Philippines.

A crowd of reporters was also waiting. Bulkeley briefly spoke of his time in the Philippines, offering the opinion "that with a couple of hundred torpedo boats we could sweep the Japs from the sea." He described the enemy as "very brave and courageous, and very pugnacious fighters who will fight until they are wounded or dead. But we can still lick them."[14]

It was time for the family to go home. "A little rest, a little home life, and plenty of mom's home cooking," Bulkeley told the reporters of his immediate plans before departing with his wife and son.[15] He was prepared to enjoy a short leave granted by the Navy. The time off, however, would prove to be anything but restful.

The departure of the senior squadron officers left the remaining PT sailors scattered and disorganized during the final weeks of the Philippines defense. A contingent of the former boat crews were on Mindanao hoping to get a flight out even as Bulkeley returned home and the siege of Corregidor played out to the dreadful conclusion. Most were still on the southern island when the Japanese invaders arrived. Their stories close the tale of Motor Torpedo Boat Squadron 3's short, but eventful, life in the Philippines.

CHAPTER 37

The frantic last days and weeks before Mindanao fell into Japanese hands found an assortment of PT sailors mixed together with local defenders on the western portion of the island. Most were in the vicinity of Dansalan on the northern side of Lake Lanao. Many were still hoping to get out to Australia, either by air from Del Monte or through some other means. In the interim, they were helping out in whatever way they could while biding their time in the hopes of escape.

Henry Brantingham, William Konko, and DeWitt Glover arrived in the area not as a group, but at different times and under varying circumstances. Although the three were in the same general area, they were not necessarily in close contact. Their paths, however, briefly crossed during an evacuation mission conducted by two PBY seaplanes.

Konko arrived in the lake region with other crew members of *PT-35* when the boat faced an uncertain future after striking a submerged object off Cebu. "We had been carrying on with various duties, we were evacuating American missionaries, some were running trucks, some were idle," Konko recalled.[1] Glover was ordered to help work on the setting up of the Lake Lanao Navy after turning over *PT-41* to the army.

The flotilla of small boats was given the mission of protecting the lake from any airborne invaders. "They also built what we called 'speed bancas,' the bancas being the name for the native craft, but the speed meaning that we put an outboard motor on them, mounted a 30-caliber Browning amidships and put ammunition on it, and they were to be used against any seaplanes and troops that might come in," Glover later said.[2]

Glover was soon given a different assignment—to work on preparing an area to accept incoming PBY seaplanes. He was one of only a few sailors working with airmen from the Fourteenth Bomb Squadron. "I spent approximately nine days there, nine nights, without any sleep and lots of running around trying to get things ready—the only man who had any idea what a PBY was like and what to do with them when they came in," he later said.

At about this time, the PT men heard the news of their squadron commander departing Mindanao for Australia. Anthony Akers then assigned Konko also to help out with the PBY preparations. It was one of the last orders the officer gave before departing for Australia. "He said that they were expecting two planes to come in on the lake and that I was to go down and work in conjunction with the army and act as a signalman. He said it would only take a few days and we would get back to our outfit."

The mood among the sailors became somber when word arrived of Robert Kelly, Akers, and George Cox all leaving for Australia from Del Monte. "Well, we felt rather low upon hearing this," Konko later said. "We had one officer left—that was Ensign [Bond] Murray who was executive officer." Konko likely had no idea there was another PT officer in the area.

Henry Brantingham arrived on the west end of Mindanao by boat with some sailors from *PT-35* after staging a long and perilous escape from Cebu. The group traveled to Del Monte in a rickety bus in hopes of getting a flight out. Their names were added to a long list of would-be evacuates. It was unclear if they would be given any special priority as members of the PT squadron—much to their disappointment.

The prospects of getting out any time soon did not look promising. Brantingham decided to go back west, ending up at a hotel in Dansalan on the lake. Along the way he encountered *PT-41* making her overland journey—perhaps providing him the first evidence of the flagship surviving the sea battle off Cebu. He and his men reported for duty to a local navy officer shortly after their arrival. It happened to be Commander Ryland Tisdale.

Brantingham was one of many PT sailors to come in contact with Tisdale while in the lake region. The 47-year-old officer had retired from the Navy in 1936 after serving for 25 years, but returned to active duty about four years later. Tisdale arrived in the Philippines in January 1941.[3] He spent time on Luzon and Cebu before ending up on Mindanao.

Thousands of miles to the south in Darwin, Australia, two American PBY seaplanes were completing the final preparations for takeoff. The pair was airborne and traveling north by the late afternoon hours of April 27.[4] Their destination was Lake Lanao. The planes were the wings behind a special mission codenamed Flight Gridiron—a daring flight to the embattled island of Corregidor.

The aircraft were packed full with a cargo of medical supplies, fuses for antiaircraft shells, and radio parts.[5] The return trip was to evacuate a small group of select personnel. The lake was to be a refueling stopover point both coming and going. It would be the last opportunity for Brantingham, Glover, and Konko to leave Mindanao.

The seaplanes arrived at Lake Lanao as planned under the cover of darkness during the early morning hours. "The first plane came in and dropped down, refusing to answer any recognition signal at all," Glover recalled. "The other plane dropped too far away from us for us to go near him. We went over to the first plane that came in, still no recognition signal of any sort."

Glover was the skipper of a small speed banca with a native operating the motor at the rear of the craft and an army airman manning the machine gun amidships. "I told him to load his gun and wait," Glover later said. "I had a small searchlight. I turned it on trying to find some insignia on this plane. For about half a minute I looked and could not find any insignia and was ready to tell him to open fire when way up on the bow of the plane was a small star about 4 inches across." Glover considered himself to be very lucky after learning one of the 50-caliber machine guns on the plane was pointing directly at his small boat.

The seaplanes quickly refueled before immediately taking off for Corregidor. Not a minute of time could be wasted due to the tight schedule. "None of us thought they would [ever] come back," Konko remembered.

The planes landed under a blanket of darkness on the south side of Corregidor, away from the Japanese guns pounding the island from Bataan. General Wainwright arranged for small boats in the area to race their engines to help conceal the arrival of the aircraft.[6] It was just days before the final Japanese amphibious assault on Corregidor.

The seaplanes returned to the lake the next day loaded full of passengers, including 20 nurses. The guests disembarked to spend the day ashore while the planes were camouflaged. Departure was planned for the evening hours under the cover of darkness.

Among the evacuees was Edward DeLong. The young PT officer stayed behind on Bataan in command of the tugboat *Trabajador* after losing his boat near Subic Bay. The Navy later reported the tugboat was most likely was sunk by Japanese artillery shells off Corregidor.[7]

Konko was surprised to see his old squadron mate. "I told him about what happened to the rest—taking off for the south," he said about some of the senior officers departing. "He told me about [how] their ship had been bombed and they were sent to Corregidor, the men were in the fox holes with machine guns having [a] rather hard time." Konko also spoke with some of the nurses. "Incidentally this one nurse who knew Lieutenant Kelly inquired of him and the rest of the officers," Konko continued. "We told him that they took off for [the] south." It was not Nurse Peggy, as she was not among the passengers.

The PBYs were ready to depart for the final run to Australia by nightfall. "Ensign Murray was along with the passengers," Konko recalled. "He said he did not want to leave us behind but that he had orders and had no alternative." The two had past conversations about heading into the jungle hills together one day, but it was not to be. "Prior to take off he gave me his pistol and a few packs of cigarettes, the same with Lieutenant DeLong."

Sailors cast off the lines after the engines of the planes were sufficiently warmed up, allowing the PBYs to move out from the small beach area into the lake in preparation for departure. The first plane took flight after some difficulty owing to strong winds and choppy water. The second PBY struggled to taxi into takeoff position with strong turbulence pushing the craft back towards shore.[8] Everyone aboard suddenly heard a crushing sound when the plane hit a submerged rock, punching several holes in the fuselage.

A frantic effort ensued to keep the craft afloat. A blanket was stuffed into one of the holes as the pilot pointed the plane back to shore where it was eventually beached. It came to a rest with a portion of the craft partially submerged. "The passengers got out immediately," Konko said. "All of us used the empty drums, worked like hell trying to keep the plane from sinking."

The plane was thought to be too damaged to fly again. All removable equipment was offloaded. A soldier took the passengers to a safer place to wait for another rescue plane to be sent from Australia.

A small cadre of sailors and airmen worked frantically, trying to find materials to repair the plane as rumors of a Japanese landing on Mindanao began circulated. The effort lasted more than a day. The largest hole was eventually repaired and the pilot was confident he could get the plane airborne. The original group of evacuees, however, could not be found.

One individual who did find the plane, however, was Henry Brantingham. Ryland Tisdale happened to be taking the newly arrived officer on a tour of the area around the lake. He was pointing out various locations along the route, discussing how the sites could be used to help defend the area. Five other PT men from the 35 boat followed at a distance in a different vehicle.

The tour stopped at the small beachfront area used as the makeshift base for the PBYs. The group found the two seaplanes in the process of refueling for the trip to Australia. Brantingham knew nothing about the Flight Gridiron mission. However, he presumed the planes came from

Corregidor as most of the passengers were nurses and civilians. His five men later assisted in the repairs of the damaged plane and ended up staying aboard. Tisdale directed Brantingham to board as well, saying that he preferred to stay behind. The PT men were going to Australia.

The former boat captain gave Tisdale a parting gift before getting aboard the aircraft. "He had been eyeing my nickel-plated six gun, and pointedly told me that I wouldn't be needing it in Australia," Brantingham later wrote. "Of course, I gave it to him then and there, with holster, belt, and remaining cartridges."[9]

The sailor then climbed into the plane for the escape south. Tisdale remained on Mindanao helping to defend the area around Lake Lanao until the very end. He was killed by local natives who were collaborating with the Japanese on May 23, 1942.[10]

Konko remembered the word spreading around the area "that the pilot intended to take out all PT personnel." Glover heard the same from an Ensign Hoffman who had been working on repairing the plane. Hoffman told him "to get all the PT men I could find, send them out to the plane." Glover was only able to round up a few before he was stopped by an officer.

By this time it was no longer a rumor that the Japanese were coming. The enemy was approaching Lake Lanao via road after making an amphibious landing on the west coast of the island. The officer wanted to slow their advance. "His idea was to mount 50 calibers on trucks and run them down the road: even if the tanks stopped the trucks, the trucks would be in the way and we might stop them with 50 calibers," Glover recalled. The idea was later abandoned as foolish. The delay was just long enough for Glover to miss the PBY flight out.

Konko also missed the flight, but it was due to very different circumstances. "When I got down to the beach, I noticed several other fellows were down there also, but we were unfortunate not to get any transportation out to the plane as there had been no bancas or the launch as a few army personnel had taken use of them in hopes of getting out," he later explained. "We could see the plane off the island, warming up his engines."

An expanse of water stood between the PT men and the PBY ready to take them away. The sailors, though, were unable to get to it. Japanese planes were seen flying overhead as reports reached the men of enemy troops approaching the area, backed by tanks and meeting little opposition. "We stood on the beach and the plane was taking off," Konko recalled. His last best hope for escape was soon airborne, winging south towards Australia and freedom. "When some of the army personnel returned, they were disgusted because they were refused the opportunity to go down because they were in the army."

Time had expired for the remaining PT men, as Japanese troops poured into the area. Glover was at a small army camp near the lake. "We had orders to wait for Commander Tisdale until [7:00 am] that morning when he would be around to give us orders," he later said. "Commander Tisdale, nor anybody else, ever appeared that morning. The only people that appeared were the Jap planes followed by their tanks and infantry."

A ringing bell in the base suddenly signaled some type of urgent emergency. It was almost immediately followed by a hoard of soldiers running wildly through the camp. They were not Japanese, but Filipinos. Glover could see the men were "heading backwards, anywheres [sic] backwards just to get away from the advancing Japanese. We watched them come through the camp and go, looked around and found that the only people remaining were the 12 of us."

The group of Americans quickly decided it was time for them to leave. A nearby road looked like the best way to escape. "We went down the road; four of the boys struck out on their own, but eight of us stayed together," Glover continued. "We decided to get off the road as the road was filled with these Philippine soldiers in their blue uniforms—looked like an aviator's holiday for strafing."

The men ran off the road away from the Filipinos. "We took off across the country, had no idea where we were going except to get into the jungle and out of the way of the Japs," he recalled. "We would have a better chance there." The group traveled inland for five or six hours before coming across an army medical team with a small camp area. They stayed overnight and ate some boiled rice. "Nothing with it, just plain boiled rice," Glover recalled. "Kind of hard to take but at a time like that it tasted pretty good."

Glover left the medical camp, continuing his journey inland. He was no longer moving with a group. He eventually met a man named Jacob Deisher. The American was an old Philippine hand who owned two sawmills and five mines on Mindanao. He was heading to a jungle hideout with his family. Deisher had gathered enough provisions to last for two years and needed help moving some of his supplies.[11] Glover decided that going with the American was his best option. "So that night we started our evacuation."

Konko was not with any of the other navy men when the enemy finally arrived. "Well, I was with a few army personnel there," he later said. The men were discussing their options and decided it was best to head for Del Monte. They went to a nearby army barracks only to find the place in shambles. "Some men had taken off in different directions," Konko continued. His small group went into town, finding a prominent local Filipino resident. He offered to take the servicemen out to his farm, away from the approaching enemy, and did so by car. The group now numbered five men.

The stay proved to be a short one. The Filipinos at the farm were anxious to have the men leave. They did not want to be caught helping Americans when the Japanese arrived. "And we felt the same," Konko related. "We didn't want any harm to come to them. They told us to go off into the interior a little ways with some friendly natives, which we did."

Word soon arrived of the American surrender. "The Filipinos told us," Konko recalled. "We didn't believe that. And we knew our attempt to reach Del Monte Field was blocked also because the Japs were up the highway leading up to the airfield." He was aware of the reported Japanese atrocities in China and did not like the prospects of becoming a prisoner. He decided not to surrender. Konko would instead take his chances going into the hills to become a guerilla.

There was one PT officer still trying to get to Mindanao while the drama of the last evacuation planes was playing out. "At this time I wanted to get down to Mindanao because General MacArthur had promised all the PT officers that we had first priority to get out by plane at such time as the boats would be lost," Iliff Richardson remembered. His plan, however, was thwarted when Japanese troops overran the airfield at Del Monte. "I went via Leyte down to Mindanao just in time to be two days late to catch the last planes."[12]

The situation on the island was precarious—there were no more evacuation planes coming up from Australia and the defense was on the verge of full collapse. Then the surrender order suddenly came from General Wainwright. "And the army told me that if I didn't get off the island that I'd have to surrender, but that I was navy, that I was not attached there," Richardson continued. "I could get off the island, so I went back to Leyte."

Army officials essentially told him the same back on Leyte—surrender or get off the island. Richardson was determined not to surrender, but rather decided to try to make it to Australia by small boat. He was not alone. Eleven airmen, who had escaped from Del Monte, volunteered to go with him. Richardson later recalled, however, that there was also one PT sailor among the group.[13]

He was able to procure a small sailboat using army funds. The craft featured a dug-out hull with built up sides and a double outrigger for stability. "It had a single mast with quite a large sail, it was approximately 35 to 38 feet long," Richardson later said. It took several days to collect supplies and provisions for the trip.

Richardson boarded a small Filipino vessel docked in the area looking for maps. The captain had some local charts of the Philippines, but nothing for Australia. He did have a geography book containing a map of the entire Pacific on one page. The captain ripped out the page and gave it to Richardson. Something was better than nothing.

The other men gathered anything they could find to equip the boat for the long journey. "I believe I had about four tons of equipment, or of supplies on the boat, including eight sacks of rice, about 200 gallons of water and dried fish, dried peas and some milk and some jam, and 2,300 cigars to keep the boys in smoking and six quarts of liquor, which we were going to use when we crossed the equator." Other supplies included a compass from a crashed P-35 fighter plane, a watch, and some life jackets.

The craft departed Tacloban with a small contingent of army soldiers on hand for the sendoff. A loud cheer erupted on land as the boat pulled away. Richardson had to contend with the fact that most of the men of the craft were not sailors. "They knew just about as much how to run a sailboat as I knew how to fly a plane, and all we had to make the 1,500-mile trip to Australia was a school map of the Southwest Pacific, but at least we were off," he later said.

It was a dangerous—if not outright suicidal—undertaking. The boat was dubbed *Leyte Luck* before departing Tacloban. The men would need every bit of available luck to make it safely all the way to Australia.

The boat traveled south along the east coast of Leyte. It took several days at sea for the men to fully figure out the nuances of running the craft, but once they did the small vessel was able to gain some speed. "I've never gone so fast outside of a PT boat as I did on this," Richardson later recalled. A few small rain squalls were encountered along the way, but nothing to cause serious problems.

The craft passed through the Hinatuan Passage off the northern part of Mindanao. Richardson later found out that the narrow waterway, situated between Mindanao and some smaller adjacent islands, was only traversed at certain times and with great caution by local natives. The area had a strong current with a few whirlpools. The boat made it into open waters after clearing the passage.

Richardson would have to navigate through a maze of small islands representing the far eastern end of the Dutch East Indies once south of the Philippines, yet still remain west of the large island of New Guinea. Of immediate concern, though, was getting past Mindanao, after which the chances of being spotted by the Japanese would hopefully begin to diminish. "We had no sextant and navigational equipment of any kind," Richardson said. "I made a pair of parallel rulers out of a piece of bamboo."

The voyage came to an abrupt end on the seventh day at sea, a date Richardson later recalled as being May 18.[14] "After sailing about

100 miles, we capsized during a storm off the east coast of Mindanao," he later explained.[15] Richardson thought they were about 8 miles from land when the boat overturned.

There were few good options for the stranded men. Staying at sea risked being spotted by a Japanese plane or warship. Swimming to shore would be extremely difficult, but offered the best chance of survival. "Eight of us elected to swim in, four remained on the overturned banka [sic] with the mast sticking straight down, very near the Mindanao Deep." The area off the Mindanao coast was known to be among the deepest parts of the Pacific Ocean. The swim was a grueling ordeal. "I was in the water 13 hours before reaching shore and one soldier who was in the water died after reaching land," Richardson continued. The entire complement from *Leyte Luck* made it to shore either by swimming or later pick up from a native boat.

The servicemen were cared for by local natives. "We managed to get recuperated in about two or three weeks," Richardson later said. "But the Japs had put out an order that unless soldiers surrendered by the twentieth of May they would be considered as outlaws or bandits; well at that time we were recuperating flat in bed and so we said, okay, we'll be bandits!" Richardson's career as a PT sailor was effectively over. The coming years would be spent in the jungles of the Philippines.

The fall of Corregidor, the Japanese taking control of Mindanao, and Wainwright's surrender order all took place in a short span of time. The battle for the Philippines was essentially over by the middle of May. The surrender order, however, was slow to gain traction across the southern region of the commonwealth. Local commanders on various islands, whose situations were not nearly as dire as Corregidor, were preparing to move to well-stocked jungle hideouts to begin a guerilla campaign, knowing full well it would be difficult for the Japanese to flush them out.

General Sharp faced a critical decision. While he had been militarily defeated on Mindanao, his command extended across the region. Many islands in the south contained no Japanese soldiers. Although the general was no longer under Wainwright's direct authority, he came to understand the difficult situation facing his counterpart to the north. Sharp decided to give up, telling his commanders on May 10 the surrender order was "imperative and must be carried out in order to save further bloodshed."[16]

Many defenders laid down their arms as commanded. Some American servicemen, however, did not, and went into the hills to continue the struggle as guerillas. Organized resistance in the Philippines ended by June 9, 1942. The battle had lasted almost exactly six months.[17]

CHAPTER 38

John Bulkeley was one of the first heroes of the Pacific War to return to the United States. The exploits of his squadron in the Philippines had been widely reported, making him a well-known figure on the home front. The days following his arrival in New York were filled with a packed schedule of events. Fellow New Yorkers Robert Kelly and Anthony Akers joined him for some of the appearances.

On May 11, 1942—Mother's Day—the officer and his wife attended mass at a Catholic Church in Brooklyn. Neither was Catholic, but Bulkeley told reporters he was attending in honor of a priest he encountered in the Philippines who helped out sailors and soldiers alike. Crowds of well-wishers applauded him outside the church. Later in the day he joined his mother to lead a parade. The event was attended by a horde of cheering people.

A few days later, Bulkeley, Kelly, and Akers participated in a parade through Manhattan kicking off a week-long drive to raise $3,000,000 for the Army and Navy Emergency Relief Fund. It was attended by a record number of people, with many showering confetti from high-rise windows. The event included a welcome by New York Mayor Fiorello LaGuardia, who praised the officers as heroes. "I cannot begin to tell you how overwhelmed I am, and Lieutenant Kelly and Ensign Akers are, to receive a welcome in our home town," Bulkeley said. "This is something that every boy in New York in his childhood has looked forward to."[1]

The program also included performances by musician Jimmy Dorsey, singer Danny Kaye, and other stars.

The three officers were on hand for the May 16 launching of a new PT boat at the Electric Boat Company factory in Bayonne, NY. It represented an updated design more powerful than the type used in the Philippines. Alice was given the honor of christening the new boat. Bulkeley turned the event into a pep rally, telling stories of his squadron's exploits in the Philippines and asking the nearly 2,000 workers in attendance, "Are you going to give us the boats?" The answer, of course, was a resounding yes.[2] The factory was soon turning out PT boats by the dozen, with many bound for the Pacific.

Bulkeley's homecoming even made the pages of *Time* Magazine. A May 18 article entitled "Welcome Home" told of the hero's return to New York. It was even more press for the popular sailor.

Bulkeley reported for duty as experimental officer at the new Motor Torpedo Boat Squadron Training Center in Rhode Island at the conclusion of his short leave. He remained attached to the center through September.[3] During the stay he was promoted one rank to lieutenant commander. Bulkeley, along with Kelly, Akers, George Cox and later Henry Brantingham, drew upon their real combat experience while teaching sailors preparing to serve aboard PT boats.

The famous torpedo boat sailor was now the name and face of the burgeoning PT service. No one knew better the type of individual needed to man the small craft. Bulkeley frequently traveled around the country recruiting sailors. "We've got to get the best men," he remarked during a visit to a naval officer training school in Chicago. "Their job will be very dangerous and will require as much initiative, daring, and resourcefulness as any assignment in the Navy."[4] There was no shortage of eager men wanting to serve aboard the boats. Among those who volunteered was a young man from Massachusetts named John F. Kennedy.

August 4, 1942 was a special day for Bulkeley. He and Alice were in Washington, D.C. for a private audience with President Roosevelt. The officer was to receive the nation's highest decoration for valor—the Medal of Honor. General MacArthur initially nominated Bulkeley for the award shortly after he arrived in Australia. Admiral Ernest King, however, would have none of it. The chief of naval operations made sure the official request came from him—a navy man.[5]

Bulkeley approached the White House gate with no invitation or other type of written confirmation as to the purpose of his visit. He wore a khaki navy uniform. The suspicious guard called the president's office. Two staffers soon appeared to take Bulkeley—and only him—inside. Alice accompanied him for the event, but had to remain outside.

The officer was escorted directly to the Oval Office. He remembered a couple of nervous aides lingering outside the door. It seemed they did not want him to upset the president by telling him too many details about how bad things really were in the Philippines.

Roosevelt was seated at a desk. He gave his guest a warm greeting with an inviting smile before reading the citation. Bulkeley leaned over, allowing the president to put the Medal of Honor around his neck. "Thank you, sir," Bulkeley modestly said.[6] A photographer snapped a picture of the two shaking hands. It appeared in newspapers across the country the very next day. At the end of the gathering, Roosevelt whispered into Bulkeley's ear for him to "come back later this evening and have a chat."[7]

The award was not issued solely for the evacuation of MacArthur, but covered Bulkeley's entire time in the Philippines. The citation noted the difficult circumstances faced by the PT men. "The remarkable achievement of Lieutenant Bulkeley's command in damaging or destroying a notable number of Japanese enemy planes, surface combatant and merchant ships, and in dispersing landing parties and land-based enemy forces during the four months and eight days of operations without benefit of repair, overhaul or maintenance facilities for his squadron, is believed to be without precedent in this type of warfare."[8]

The officer returned to the White House in the evening as directed. He found Roosevelt in the Oval Office along with some top staff members. Bulkeley was not intimidated in the least by the setting. He passed along MacArthur's message, just as the general had instructed back in Australia, for reinforcements and spoke candidly about what happened in the Philippines. It was exactly what the staff members did not want the president to hear. Bulkeley departed past somber advisors after Roosevelt gave him a sincere thank you.

The Medal of Honor was one of many accolades Bulkeley received for his action in the Philippines. Other awards included the Navy Cross, Silver Star, and the Distinguished Service Cross (Army) with Oak Leaf Cluster. The Navy Cross was for his actions in Binanga Bay while aboard *PT-34*.

It soon became time for the sailor to bid farewell to his family and return to sea duty in the Pacific. Bulkeley assumed command of Motor Torpedo Boat Squadron 7 in October 1942. The unit operated around New Guinea in support of advancing American forces under the command of Bulkeley's old friend MacArthur. Much of the action was not fighting large enemy warships as in the Philippines, but against small Japanese barges.

The next assignment took the PT commander halfway around the world to the European theater of the war. The Allies were preparing to invade France when Bulkeley commissioned Motor Torpedo Boat Squadron 2 (the second unit to bear the name). The unit arrived in England on April 24, 1944. The boats served as part of the screening force during the invasion of Normandy on June 6, 1944. The assignment was one of protection, including guarding against German E-Boats (torpedo boats) and sinking floating flares dropped by the enemy. Bulkeley was awarded the Legion of Merit for his actions.

The need for PT boats along the Atlantic coast of France rapidly diminished once the Allied forces advanced inland from Normandy. Bulkeley assumed command of the destroyer *Endicott* on July 18, 1944, his first command of a warship larger than a PT boat. In subsequent months he operated in the Mediterranean in preparation for the Allied invasion of southern France.

On August 17, in advance of the amphibious assault, the *Endicott* and 22 PT boats staged a successful diversion, helping to mislead the enemy as to the actual location of the landing. A running gun battle later ensued with two German warships. Both enemy vessels were sunk and over 200 enemy sailors were captured, including both captains.

The final wartime assignment brought the battle-hardened officer back to the United States. Bulkeley, now holding the rank of full commander, reported to the Bethlehem Steel Company's plant on Staten Island, New York in August 1945. He assisted in the final completion of the new destroyer *Stribling*. Bulkeley put the warship into commission on September 29, 1945.[9] By this time the war in the Pacific was over.

Postwar assignments took Bulkeley around the world. He was again thrust into the public spotlight in the early 1960s while commanding the American naval base at Guantanamo Bay, Cuba during a time of heightened tensions with the communist nation. The sailor initially retired from active duty in 1967, but was later recalled to head the Naval Board of Inspection and Survey. He retired for good, holding an admiral's rank, in 1988 after an amazing 55 years of service.

The admiral reflected on his hero status in a 1987 television interview. "I don't know what a hero is," he said. "This business of the captain taking all the credit, ordering someone else and so forth—that's not it. The men who do the actual fighting, man the guns, they're the guys that really win the war."[10] John Bulkeley died at the age of 84 on April 6, 1996 at his home in Silver Spring, Maryland. He is buried in Arlington National Cemetery.[11]

Robert Kelly received numerous citations for his action in the Philippines. The highest award, the Navy Cross, was for his daring torpedo attack against the Japanese light cruiser during the April sea battle of Cebu and ensuing effort to save his crew when *PT-34* was destroyed by aircraft.

He reported to the training center in Rhode Island on May 21, 1942. His duty there, however, was short, as he subsequently spent nearly three months at the Naval Hospital in Chelsea, Massachusetts convalescing from wounds received in the Philippines.[12] He was promoted to lieutenant commander during the stay. Kelly put Motor Torpedo Boat Squadron 9 into commission on November 10, 1942. The unit was assigned to the South Pacific, arriving in the Solomon Islands in May 1943. It was not the Pacific front that Kelly previously knew. The United States had turned the tide of the war and was now pushing back the Japanese.

The squadron advanced alongside American amphibious forces moving up the island chain, eventually operating from a new forward PT base at Rendova Island. The boats made regular patrols to protect the flank of army units put ashore on the adjacent island of New Georgia. Kelly was at sea with three boats on the night of July 3–4 when he encountered an approaching force of Japanese destroyers, presumably on a mission to attack the new American beachhead.

The squadron commander had not received updated information on the movements of friendly vessels in the area, forcing the torpedo boats to move in close to make a visual identification. The destroyers quickly surrounded the PTs, resulting in a close-range battle lasting about ten minutes. The boats used sharp turns and smoke screens to survive, but the enemy warships were moving too fast to be hit by torpedoes. "However, despite this it is considered that it was an extremely successful engagement in that the enemy was forced to retire without ever having approached within range of our beachhead," Kelly wrote of the encounter. "Had the PTs not intercepted them, the damage they might have inflicted would have been considerable."[13]

The boats under Kelly's command later faced a formidable foe in armored Japanese barges. He was actively involved in helping to develop effective countermeasures and finding ways to increase the firepower of PT boats. The unit continued to advance as friendly forces island-hopped across the South Pacific. Kelly joined the staff of the area PT boat command in February 1944, assuming the rank of full commander less than a month later. He remained in the South Pacific until May of the same year when he was ordered back to the United States.

Marriage was the first order of business for the sailor once back on the home front. Kelly married Hazel Mae Babcock at a May 28 ceremony held in Dedham, Massachusetts.[14] He was briefly assigned duty in Rhode Island before transferring south to a naval base in Miami, Florida.

Like his former squadron commander, Kelly moved up to a bigger warship during the waning days of the conflict. He assumed command of the destroyer *Irwin* on May 3, 1945, staying aboard her for the remainder of the Pacific War. Under Kelly's command, the vessel provided fire support during the battle for Okinawa, helped rescue survivors of the sunken destroyer *Twiggs*, and escorted occupation troops to Japan at the end of hostilities.[15] He was awarded the Bronze Star for his actions.

Postwar assignments included teaching at the Naval Academy, command of an icebreaker, leading a destroyer division in the Mediterranean, and serving in the Navy's Caribbean Command. He retired from the Navy in 1961 with the rank of captain, taking up residence in Maryland. His career after the service included working for defense contractor Martin Marietta and the State of Maryland. Robert Kelly died on January 23, 1989 at the age of 75.[16]

Most of the other PT officers who were evacuated from the Philippines saw some additional service with the boats during the war. Akers, Cox, and Brantingham all spent time at the training center in Rhode Island helping teach the legions of new PT sailors getting ready to head out to war. All eventually returned to sea duty. Cox commissioned Motor Torpedo Boat Squadron 40 in April 1945. The unit was sent to the Pacific, but saw no action. Akers commanded a squadron of boats stationed in Hawaii during 1943.

Brantingham returned to the Pacific front in 1943 as the executive officer of Kelly's Squadron 9. The duty put him in the New Georgia area during the month of August, allowing him to participate in the rescue of Lieutenant (jg) John F. Kennedy and surviving crewmen from the sunken *PT-109*. He assumed command of Squadron 5 on January 24, 1944. The boats were still fighting the Japanese in the Solomons when he transferred to other duties in August of the same year.[17] Brantingham later served aboard destroyers in the Mediterranean and Pacific.

Cone Johnson and Vincent Schumacher were the other two officers who escaped to Australia. Schumacher was reprimanded for poor judgment in the loss of *PT-32* during the MacArthur evacuation mission. He later transferred to submarine service.[18] Many other PT sailors never made it out of the Philippines.

CHAPTER 39

The majority of the 83 members of the PT squadron were unable to escape before the Japanese took control of the Philippines. They endured the final descent and bitter end along with the other airmen and soldiers, both Filipino and American. Five men were known to have been killed in action aboard PTs 31 and 34. The others were widely scattered among various islands, including Luzon, Cebu, and Mindanao, at the time of the surrender.

Some sailors had been stationed at Mariveles when Bataan surrendered and were presumed to have become prisoners at that time. It is unclear if any were part of the Bataan Death March. More fell into Japanese hands with the fall of Corregidor, where two officers and 29 enlisted men were thought to have helped man the beach defenses.[1]

Postwar records indicate a total of 38 PT sailors were known for certain to have been prisoners of the Japanese. Many were moved from the Philippines to prison camps in Japan or Manchuria in 1944. Nine died en route or at the new camps. Twenty-nine were liberated at the end of the war. The squadron's total dead or missing, from all causes, is listed as 18—three officers and 15 enlisted men.[2]

Among the dead were Ensign Bond Murray and Edward DeLong. Both were aboard the ill-fated PBY that struck a submerged rock trying to take off from Lake Lanao. Neither was aboard when the plane finally escaped after the frantic repair work was completed. The two officers became prisoners and died in captivity.

A handful of the PT men did not surrender at all, but blended into the jungle to join the Philippine guerilla movement. It was an especially popular choice among sailors in the southern islands, where the freedom of movement was less restricted than in the north. The region was also the last area to lay down arms in the surrender, allowing more time for individuals to make decisions.

William Konko, Francis Napolillo, DeWitt Glover, and John Tuggle joined Machinist's Mate First Class John Lewis and Chief Machinist's Mate Paul Owen working for Colonel Wendell Fertig on Mindanao. The American Army engineer was the commander of all of the guerillas on Mindanao. Some of these men were evacuated in 1943.[3]

Konko was not among them. He recovered from a bout of malaria, with the help of locals, before becoming active in Fertig's group working in the area of communications. "I was in charge of one of the radio stations that was established," he later said. "I remained on the island until January 1945, at which time I was evacuated and brought back home."[4]

Konko called his mother in Cleveland, Ohio after leaving the Philippines. "I'm okay, and I'll tell you what happened to me when I see you soon," he told her in an early morning call.[5] The sailor had been listed as missing for the last three years. He was soon at home visiting his mother in person. "It was the first time I'd been home, or in any other decent house, in four years. Why, I couldn't remember a thing about the old place, not even how the rooms were laid out."[6] There was one officer among the guerilla group who ended up not on Mindanao, but further north on Leyte.

When Iliff Richardson's daring attempt to escape all the way to Australia in a small boat failed, it marked the beginning of a jungle odyssey that would last over two years. "The next year we spent on the east coast of Mindanao without money, medicine or clothes," he later recalled.[7] Richardson was kept hidden by locals. He used the time to complete a manuscript about his PT boat duty.[8] It provided a brilliant first-hand account of his time with Bulkeley's squadron from his transfer to the torpedo boats through the sinking of *PT-34* off Cebu. He eventually returned to Leyte to become an active member of the guerilla forces.

The Philippine guerilla movement began in late 1942 as a confusing mix of unorganized groups scattered around many regions. From its chaotic beginnings, the movement eventually grew into a force of nearly 250,000 spread amongst various islands of the archipelago.[9] They were united in their undying belief that the Americans—and MacArthur—would return as promised. The general helped organize and support the guerillas by sending agents and equipment by submarine.

The guerilla forces in the Leyte area were led by Colonel Ruperto Kangleon. The capable Filipino solider, who served in the American Army during the defense of the commonwealth, escaped Japanese captivity before assuming his important role in the underground movement.[10] Kangleon united various bands of guerillas on Leyte and established the framework of a rudimentary civilian government. By October of 1943 he commanded an army of about 3,200 well-trained men.[11] Richardson played an important role in Kangleon's command, serving for a time as the colonel's chief of staff.[12] He eventually rose to the rank of a major in the guerilla army.

The former PT sailor accomplished duties in a variety of areas, both civil and military. "I was able to help Colonel Kangleon in the establishment of his civil government in making several new departments in his army, including the mint, which was a civilian government function run by the army because we could commandeer supplies, paper, notebook paper, typewriting paper, to print the money with," he later recalled. Richardson also helped organize all of the available medical supplies. "You could have kept the whole works in two ordinary doctor's bags, all the medicine thrown in. There was very little of anything."[13]

The official whereabouts of Richardson was a mystery to the outside world as he began his work with the guerillas. Bulkeley listed Cebu as his last known location in his May 21, 1942 report.[14] The Navy classified him as missing in action, notifying his mother of the situation. Almost a year later on June 6, 1943, a letter from the Navy Department offered her little additional information, noting "the list of prisoners submitted by the Japanese through the medium of the International Red Cross has so far failed to include the name of your son."[15]

It was soon learned, however, that Richardson was alive and well with the guerillas. His mother eventually received some hand-written letters from her son forwarded to her by the army intelligence service. "They gave me no idea of what he was doing or what island he was on," she later said. "I only knew he was somewhere in the Philippines."[16] Richardson's naval rank was advanced to lieutenant during his time on Leyte.

Planners on MacArthur's staff were in dire need of information as their forces advanced across the Pacific towards the Philippines. The guerillas provided a stream of accurate intelligence on Japanese strengths and movements as well as the mood of the people. Richardson helped in the endeavor by setting up radios and reporting ship movements. It was a dangerous undertaking, as the Japanese attempted to find the radios by tracking the signals. "So, I built the most mobile [radio] station in the Orient," he later said in an interview. "We moved every three days."[17]

Richardson had no advanced notice of the American return, but knew it was getting close when friendly planes started appearing over the area. "We cheered ourselves hoarse," he recalled of the first time the American aircraft came in force. "The Filipinos pointed up to the sky and asked 'American?' and I nodded yes. I was proud that day."[18]

The American return to the Philippines came on October 20, 1944, when forces under MacArthur's command landed on the east coast of Leyte. Richardson was picked up a few days later by an American destroyer. He was subsequently summoned to the light cruiser *Nashville*, then serving as the leader's flagship. "I then talked to General MacArthur for about ten minutes," he later said.[19]

Orders dated October 28, 1944 detached the sailor-turned-guerilla from duty in the Philippines. He made a long journey back to the United States. Naval records indicate he reported for duty in Washington, D.C. on November 18. Richardson remained stateside for the remainder of the war. He was assigned to the Navy's Industrial Incentive Division, an area that helped to keep up the morale of workers on the home front. Richardson, however, also spent time with the Branch Magazine and Book Division, an offshoot of the Navy's Office of Public Relations.

The sailor met Pulitzer Prize-winning war correspondent Ira Wolfert sometime after the landing of American forces in the Philippines. The author already had two successful books on the Pacific War. Wolfert and Richardson collaborated on a book project about the sailor's experiences as a guerilla. The result was the 1945 book *American Guerilla in the Philippines*, published by Simon and Schuster. It mostly focuses on the gripping account of Richardson's post-PT boat career as a guerilla.

Although Wolfert is listed as the book's author, the story is told with Richardson as the central character—largely in his own words. Reviewers noted the book as "a swift-paced adventure story, easily absorbed and absorbing, with a credible and likeable hero" and that Richardson's "story is an engrossing thriller."[20] It was the basis of the 1950 movie of the same name starring Tyrone Power.

Richardson was awarded the Silver Star and an Oak Leaf Cluster for the Silver Star for his time with the PT boats. After leaving active duty he went to Houston, Texas to marry Coma, the young lady he met before the war in Chicago. He stayed in the area working as a life insurance salesman, business executive, and consultant. Late in his life, he donated a copy of the manuscript written in the Philippines about his time aboard the PT boats to the National Museum of the Pacific War in Fredericksburg, Texas. Iliff Richardson passed away on October 10, 2001 at the age of 83.[21]

Various other individuals from the Philippines campaign who in some way touched Torpedo Squadron 3 followed many paths through the war. Admiral Francis Rockwell held positions in both the Atlantic and Pacific Fleets as the conflict progressed. He was actively involved in planning the recapture of the Aleutian Islands in Alaska from the Japanese during 1943.[22]

General Douglas MacArthur was instrumental in the counterattack against the Japanese Empire in his role as the supreme commander of Allied forces in the Southwest Pacific. Forces under his command advanced across New Guinea and various islands, leading up to his famous return to the Philippines. "I have returned," he said while wading ashore on Leyte. "By the grace of Almighty God, our forces stand again on Philippine soil."[23]

By early 1945, American forces were again in control of many parts of the Philippines, including the area around Manila Bay. MacArthur returned to Corregidor on March 2. The fortress island had recently been recaptured after a fierce 12-day fight. His transportation was *PT-373*. It was a symbolic journey since he had departed almost exactly three years earlier on *PT-41*. The general commented, "we went back to the Rock the same way we had left it."[24]

Sidestepping criticism over his handling of the Philippine defense, MacArthur became massively popular with the American public. Behind the public persona, however, he regularly squabbled with naval commanders in the Pacific and leaders in Washington. The general was a magnet for controversy and publicity, with an intriguing mix of brilliance and arrogance. MacArthur was later given command of all American Army forces in the Pacific. He accepted the Japanese surrender aboard the battleship *Missouri* in Tokyo Bay on September 2, 1945.

General Jonathan Wainwright spent over three brutal years in Japanese captivity, with much of it spent in China. He was repatriated in time to attend the surrender ceremony in Tokyo Bay. He was a skeleton of his former self when he was reunited with MacArthur at the same event. His name would long be associated with the fall of the Philippines—a symbol of both American heroism and defeat.

EPILOGUE

The story of Motor Torpedo Boat Squadron 3 received a substantial and lasting boost from one individual—William L. White. He grew up as a reporter in Emporia, Kansas where his famous father published the *Emporia Gazette* newspaper. White was a respected journalist by the start of World War II, who had previously spent time with the *Washington Post* and *Fortune*. During the conflict he became a war correspondent for a consortium of 40 American newspapers and the Columbia Broadcasting System.[1]

White had the good fortune of crossing paths with John Bulkeley, Robert Kelly, Anthony Akers, and George Cox. He conducted extensive interviews with the four officers at the Torpedo Boat Training Center in Rhode Island. The reporter immediately went to work turning the interviews into a full manuscript entitled *They Were Expendable*. The book became a national bestseller after publication in late 1942, with excerpts printed in *Readers' Digest* and *Life* magazine. Four of the seven book reviewers for the *Chicago Tribune* ranked the work as among the best nonfiction works of the year.[2]

The story begins at the start of the war and follows most of the subsequent activities undertaken by the squadron, including the interactions between Robert Kelly and Nurse Peggy. The narrative is told largely in the words of the four officers, from their point of view, and concludes with their escape to Australia. Inaccuracy surrounds much of the factual information pertaining to the sea battles and fall of the Philippines—as was commonly the case with most wartime books. Neither the author nor the PT officers had any way of verifying the various battle outcomes. The story provided the American public, eager for information about the war, with a gripping firsthand account taken directly from the front lines of the Pacific. It bolstered the already strong PT lore established by news reports and Bulkeley's stateside appearances.

Nurse Peggy from the book was publicly identified at Lieutenant Beulah "Peggy" Greenwalt of the Army Nurse Corps in early 1943.[3] She was unable to escape to Australia prior to the fall of Corregidor and was among a group of nurses captured by the Japanese. Beulah spent 33 months as a prisoner in the Philippines before liberation by American soldiers in 1945.

The idea of adapting the book into a movie was first devised by film company Metro-Goldwyn-Mayer (MGM) and the Navy in 1942 for use as wartime propaganda.[4] However, delays prevented the production from release while the war was still ongoing. Filming began on February 1, 1945 in Key Biscayne, Florida and the Florida Keys. The area provided similar scenery to the Philippines. The Navy supported the venture by lending real PT boats for use in the production and supplying airplanes from nearby bases.

The director was the legendary John Ford, who himself experienced war first-hand as a navy cinematographer. Robert Montgomery and John Wayne were tapped to play the fictionalized versions of Bulkeley (John Brickley) and Kelly (Rusty Ryan), respectively. Donna Reed played army nurse Sandy Davyss, a representation of Nurse Peggy.

The movie benefitted from having a host of individuals with navy experience (including Montgomery, who was an actual PT boat skipper during the war), realistic action scenes, and crisp photography. The plot loosely follows the storyline of the book, focusing on the sailors of the squadron and their actions, including the evacuation of General MacArthur. The film is noted for its authenticity and realism.[5]

They Were Expendable was released in December 1945. It occurred several months after conflict was over and public interest in war-related movies was starting to subside. As a result, the picture was not as big a hit as originally expected. A *New York Times* critic smartly noted "if this film had been released last year—or the year before—it would have been a ringing smash."[6]

Two additional setbacks occurred when the movie became entangled in a pair of lawsuits—both centering on the romance between the characters of Ryan and Davyss (Kelly and Nurse Peggy). Robert Kelly was awarded $3,000 for the libelous portrayal of him by John Wayne.[7] The second lawsuit came from Beulah Greenwalt. She claimed her portrayal as Davyss was "a humiliating invasion of privacy" and "cheapened her character."[8] She was awarded $290,000 in 1948, a large sum for the time. "It's a good story, but it's not me at all," she later said.[9]

The view of *They Were Expendable* gradually changed as decades passed. New generations of viewers, many with no direct connection to the war, were introduced to the film. Today many regard the picture as one of the better movies of the World War II era, with some considering it a high point in the careers of several key participants.[10]

The Squadron 3 PT sailors stepped into the forefront of action at sea during the darkest days of World War II in the Pacific, when no other significant American naval forces were available to hinder the Japanese advance in the Philippines. In addition to fighting a much stronger enemy, the sailors had to contend with the destruction of their main operating base, lack of spare parts, meager repair facilities, bad gasoline, the terror and uncertainty that accompanies war, and a high command that did not fully understand the capabilities of the new torpedo boat weapons. Yet, in true American naval tradition, they persevered.

A thorough examination of Japanese postwar records does not support any of the sinking claims made by the squadron. It does not, however, lessen to any extent the heroic courage displayed by the young sailors in the face of almost insurmountable odds. Poor torpedoes (as was to be well documented later in the war), inexperience, over-eagerness, or just plain bad luck may have all conspired to thwart the best efforts of the PT men. The torpedo boats did succeed in harassing enemy movements, in a small way contributing to helping the beleaguered defenders hold out much longer than expected. In the process, the squadron gave the American public a tiny glimmer of hope from the otherwise bleak Pacific front.

The PT boat service was greatly expanded as the war progressed, just as General MacArthur requested. A total of 768 boats were built during the conflict, including those sent to various allies.[11] Throngs of young American sailors answered the recruiting call to serve on the PTs, with many eager to follow in the footsteps of Bulkeley and Kelly.

The craft operated in almost all theaters of the war, battling warships, barges, and aircraft, while also participating in rescues and a wide variety of special operations. The boats are perhaps best remembered for the actions in the Philippines and Solomon Islands in the South Pacific. The PT sailors fought with bravery and determination. Two PT sailors were awarded the Medal of Honor (John Bulkeley was one), with a litany of individual awards going to a long list of others.[12]

Today, few Americans know of the exploits of Torpedo Boat Squadron 3 in the Philippines. The number of people with firsthand memories of World War II is rapidly fading away. Bataan and Corregidor no longer evoke painful feelings of desperation and defeat. The names John Bulkeley, Robert Kelly, and Iliff Richardson are largely unknown. A modern U.S. Navy warship bears Bulkeley's name, serving as a small reminder of the brave officer who led a group of sailors through desperate times at the start of World War II.

MACARTHUR'S EVACUATION MISSION

Passenger List

PT-41 (John Bulkeley)

General Douglas MacArthur
Mrs. Jean MacArthur – Wife
Arthur MacArthur – Son
Ah Cheu – Chinese Nurse
General Richard Sutherland
Captain Herbert G. Ray, USN
Lt. Col. Sidney L. Huff
Major C. H. Morehouse

PT-34 (Robert Kelly)

Rear Admiral Francis W. Rockwell, USN
Brigadier General Richard J. Marshall
Colonel Charles P. Stivers
Captain Joseph McMicking

PT-35 (Anthony Akers)

Colonel Charles A. Willoughby
Lieutenant Colonel LeGrande A. Diller
Lieutenant Colonel Francis H. Wilson
Master Sergeant Paul P. Rogers

PT-32 (Vincent Schumacher)
Brigadier General Spencer B. Akin
Brigadier General Hugh J. Casey
Brigadier General William F. Marquat
Brigadier General Harold H. George
Lieutenant Colonel Joe R. Sherr

Source: Lewis Morton. *U.S. Army in World War II: The War in the Pacific: The Fall of the Philippines.* (Washington, DC: Center of Military History, U.S. Army, 1989), 359

MOTOR TORPEDO BOATS SQUADRON THREE FINAL DISPOSITION OF BOATS

PT-31 Destroyed by her commanding officer on January 20, 1942 to prevent capture after grounding in enemy territory off Bataan

PT-32 Destroyed by her commanding officer on March 13, 1942 after running short of fuel during the MacArthur evacuation mission

PT-33 Lost on December 15, 1941 due to grounding while investigated unidentified lights off the Philippine coast thought to be an enemy submarine

PT-34 Destroyed by Japanese aircraft near Cebu City on April 9, 1942

PT-35 Set on fire by her commanding officer on April 12, 1942 while undergoing repairs in Cebu City to prevent capture by approaching Japanese forces

PT-41 Turned over to the army on April 15, 1942 for use as a lake gunboat on the island of Mindanao after all available gasoline and torpedoes were expended. She was later destroyed to prevent capture in advance of approaching Japanese ground forces

Source: CO MTBRON Three to CinC U.S. Fleet and Chief of Naval Operations. "Summary of Operations Motor Torpedo Boat Squadron Three from 7 December 1941 to 10 April 1942." May 21, 1942, 3.

NOTES

Prologue

1   William Breuer, *Devil Boats: The PT War against Japan* (New York: Jove Books, 1988), 10.
2   William Breuer, *Sea Wolf: The Daring Exploits of Navy Legend John D. Bulkeley* (Novato, CA: Presidio Press, 1998), 26.
3   Lewis Morton, *U.S. Army in World War II: The War in the Pacific: The Fall of the Philippines* (Washington, D.C.: Center of Military History, U.S. Army, 1989), 79.
4   John Costello, *Days of Infamy: MacArthur, Roosevelt, Churchill—The Shocking Truth Revealed: How Their Secret Deal and Strategic Blunders Caused Disaster at Pearl Harbor and the Philippines* (New York: Pocket Books, 1994), 16, and War Diary, Sixteenth Naval District, December 8, 1941.
5   William L. White, *They Were Expendable* (New York: Harcourt, Brace and Company, 1942), 8.
6   William Manchester, *American Caesar: Douglas MacArthur, 1880–1964* (Boston: Little, Brown & Company, 1978), 205.
7   Costello, *Days of Infamy*, 17.
8   Breuer, *Sea Wolf*, 27.
9   War Diary, Sixteenth Naval District, December 8, 1941.

Chapter 1

1   "Guadalupe" in Dictionary of American Fighting Ships, http://www.history.navy.mil/danfs/g9/guadalupe.htm (accessed November 14, 2013), 1.
2   "Ships Constructed at the Brooklyn Navy Yard." http://www.columbia.edu/~jrs9/BNY-Ships.html (accessed October 30, 2013), 1.
3   *Guadalupe* Deck Log, August 16, 1941.
4   *Guadalupe* Deck Log, August 17, 1941.

5 "Rear Admiral John Duncan Bulkeley, US Navy 1911–1996" in Naval History and Heritage Command Website. http://www.history.navy.mil/bios/bulkeley_johnd. htm (accessed May 30, 2013), 1. (Hereafter cited as "John Duncan Bulkeley.")
6 Bruce M. Bachman, *An Honorable Profession: The Life and Times of One of America's Most Able Seamen* (New York: Vantage Press, 1985), 6.
7 George W. Smith, *MacArthur's Escape: John "Wild Man" Bulkeley and the Rescue of an American Hero* (St. Paul, MN: Zenith Press, 2005), 29.
8 Breuer, *Sea Wolf*, 7.
9 Secretary of the Navy, *Register of the Commissioned and Warrant Officers of the Navy of the United States, Including Officers of the Marine Corps* (Washington, D.C.: Government Printing Office, 1941), 168–69.
10 "Sacramento" in Dictionary of American Fighting Ships, http://www.history.navy. mil/danfs/s2/sacramento-ii.htm (accessed November 25, 2013), 1. (Hereafter cited as "Sacramento.")
11 Breuer, *Sea Wolf*, 12.
12 Joan Bulkeley Stade, *Twelve Handkerchiefs: The Global Journey of Alice Wood Bulkeley through World War II and the Twentieth Century with an American Navy Hero* (Tuscan, AZ: Patrice Press, 2001), 46.
13 Ibid, 53–55.
14 Smith, *MacArthur's Escape*, 45, and "Sacramento," 1.
15 Bachman, *Honorable Profession*, 25.
16 Captain Robert J. Buckley, *At Close Quarters: PT Boats in the United States Navy* (Washington, D.C.: United States Government Printing Office, 1962), 483.
17 Henry Brantingham, *Fire and Ice* (San Diego, CA: ProMotion Publishing, 1995), 17.
18 "John Duncan Bulkeley," 1.
19 Breuer, *Sea Wolf*, 21.
20 Buckley, *Close Quarters*, 52.
21 Brantingham, *Fire and Ice*, 19.
22 Buckley, *Close Quarters*, 453.
23 John L. Tuggle Collection (AFC/2001/001/4840), Veterans History Project, American Folklife Center, Library of Congress, Washington, D.C.

Chapter 2

1 Gary Rottman, *US Patrol Torpedo Boats* (Oxford, UK: Osprey, 2008), 6.
2 Buckley, *Close Quarters*, 40.
3 Frank D. Johnson, *United States PT-Boats of World War II in Action* (Poole, England: Blandford Press, 1980), 15–17.
4 Richard B. Frank, *Guadalcanal* (New York: Penguin Books, 1990), 4..
5 Buckley, *Close Quarters*, 43.
6 Johnson, *PT-Boats*, 21.

7   Curtis L. Nelson, *Hunters in the Shallows: A History of the PT Boat* (Washington, D.C.: Brassey's, 1998), 85.
8   Buckley, *Close Quarters*, 44.
9   "An Administrative History of PT Boats in World War II," http://www.gdinc. com/AN_Admin_History_of_PTs-001.pdf (accessed November 13, 2013), 25. (Hereafter cited as "Administrative History of PT Boats.")
10   Buckley, *Close Quarters*, 44.
11   Johnson, *PT-Boats*, 14.
12   Smith, *MacArthur's Escape*, 47.
13   Buckley, *Close Quarters*, 47.
14   "Administrative History of PT Boats," 44–45.
15   "Packard V-12 Marine Engine," http://www.ptboats.org/20-01-05-ptboat-008. html (accessed November 26, 2013), 1.
16   David Doyle, *PT Boats in Action* (Carrollton, TX: Squadron Signal Publications, 2010), 8.
17   John Campbell, *Naval Weapons of World War II* (Annapolis, MD: Naval Institute Press, 1985), 157.
18   Howard F. West, *Iron Men Wooden Boats* (Westminster, MD: Heritage Books, 2005), xvi.
19   Rottman, *US Patrol Torpedo Boats*, 21.
20   Doyle, *PT Boats in Action*, 6, and Buckley, *Close Quarters*, 33.
21   Headquarters of the Commander in Chief, United States Fleet, "Motor Torpedo Boats: Tactical Orders and Doctrine" (Washington, D.C.: United States Government Printing Office, 1942), http://www.hnsa.org/doc/pt/doctrine/index.htm (July 20, 2010), ii.

Chapter 3

1   *Guadalupe* Deck Log, August 25, 1941.
2   Glen M. Williford, *Racing the Sunrise: The Reinforcement of America's Pacific Outposts, 1941–1942* (Annapolis, MD: Naval Institute Press, 2010), 4–5.
3   Ibid, 39.
4   Smith, *MacArthur's Escape*, 55–56.
5   *Guadalupe* Deck Log, September 25, 1941.
6   *Guadalupe* Deck Log, September 30, 1941.
7   "Captain Robert B. Kelly, U.S. Navy," in Robert B. Kelly Biographical Sketch and Service Record. United States Navy: History & Heritage Command. (Hereafter cited as "Kelly Biographical Sketch and Service Record.")
8   "Tennessee BB-43" in Dictionary of American Fighting Ships. http://www.history. navy.mil/research/histories/ship-histories/danfs/t/tennessee-bb-43-v.html (accessed July 7, 2015), 1.

9   "Armed Service Record—Chronologically" in Kelly Biographical Sketch and Service Record.
10 "George Cox Jr., Whose PT-Boat Evacuated MacArthur, is Dead." *New York Times*, January 11, 1972, 40.
11 "Anthony B. Akers, Ran for Congress." *New York Times*, April 2, 1976, 29.

Chapter 4

1   Bill Sloan, *Undefeated: America's Heroic Fight for Bataan and Corregidor* (New York: Simon & Schuster, 2012), 1–3.
2   John Hersey, *Men on Bataan* (New York: Alfred A. Knopf, 1942), 166.
3   Sloan, *Undefeated*, 3.
4   "The Spanish-American War, 1898," http://history.state.gov/milestones/1866-1898/spanish-american-war (accessed December 2, 2013), 1.
5   Ibid.
6   Morton, *Fall of the Philippines*, 3.
7   R. W. Robson, *The Pacific Islands Handbook* (New York: Macmillan Company, 1946), 350.
8   "Tydings–McDuffie Act," http://www.princeton.edu/~achaney/tmve/wiki100k/docs/Tydings-McDuffie_Act.html (accessed December 2, 2013), 1.
9   Robert Gorman, ed., *Great Events from History: The 20th Century, Volume I: 1941–1970* (Pasadena, CA: Salem Press, 2008), 3.
10 Spencer Tucker, ed., *The Encyclopedia of World War II: A Political, Social, and Military History, Volume II* (Santa Barbara, CA: ABC-CLIO, 2005), 782.
11 Gorman, *Great Events from History*, 1.
12 Samuel Eliot Morison, *History of United States Naval Operations in World War II Volume III: The Rising Sun in the Pacific* (Edison, NJ: Castle Books, 2001), 19.
13 Gorman, *Great Events from History*, 2.
14 Tucker, *Encyclopedia of World War II*, 784.
15 Ibid, 60.

Chapter 5

1   "Douglas MacArthur," http://www.history.army.mil/faq/mac_bio.htm (accessed December 3, 2013), 1.
2   Williford, *Racing the Sunrise*, 16.
3   Morton, *Fall of the Philippines*, 12.
4   Ronald H. Spector, *Eagle Against the Sun: The American War with Japan* (New York: Vintage Books, 1985), 73.
5   John Costello, *The Pacific War* (New York: Rawson, Wade Publishers, Inc., 1981), 29.
6   Morton, *Fall of the Philippines*, 19.

7   Spector, *Eagle Against the Sun*, 72.

8   Gerald Astor, *The Greatest War: Americans in Combat, 1941–1945* (Novato, CA: Presidio Press, 1999), 33.

9   Edward S. Miller, *War Plan Orange: The U.S. Strategy to Defeat Japan, 1897–1945* (Annapolis, MD: Naval Institute Press, 1991), 2.

10   Costello, *Pacific War*, 101.

11   Morton, *Fall of the Philippines*, 64.

12   Ibid, 31.

13   Morison, *Rising Sun*, 153.

14   John Gordon, *Fighting for MacArthur: The Navy and Marine Corps' Desperate Defense of the Philippines* (Annapolis, MD: Naval Institute Press, 2011), 21.

15   Dan Van Der Vat, *The Pacific Campaign* (New York: Simon & Schuster, 1991), 73–74.

16   Clayton Chun and Howard Gerrard, *The Fall of the Philippines 1941–42* (Oxford, UK: Osprey, 2012), 17.

17   Williford, *Racing the Sunrise*, 39, 52–53, 77.

18   Morton, *Fall of the Philippines*, 50.

19   Chun and Gerrard, *The Fall of the Philippines*, 19.

20   Spector, *Eagle Against the Sun*, 107, and Morton, *Fall of the Philippines*, 71.

21   Chun and Gerrard, *The Fall of the Philippines*, 23.

22   Morton, *Fall of the Philippines*, 21, 68, and Chun and Gerrard, *The Fall of the Philippines*, 23.

23   Morton, *Fall of the Philippines*, 42.

Chapter 6

1   Myrna Oliver, "Iliff D. Richardson, 83, War Hero," http://articles.latimes.com/2001/oct/23/local/me-60625 (accessed May 30, 2013), 1.

2   CO U.S.S. *Bittern* to Chief of the Bureau of Navigation, "Ensign Iliff D. Richardson, D-V (G), USNR; Data Concerning," August 25, 1941, 2, in "Iliff D. Richardson Service Record," National Personnel Records Center, St. Louis, MO. (Personnel Records are hereafter cited as "Richardson Service Record.")

3   "Interview with Iliff D. Richardson," Denton, TX: Admiral Nimitz Museum and University of North Texas Oral History Collection, 1997, 1–2. (Hereafter cited as "Interview with Iliff D. Richardson.")

4   V. R. Cardozier, *Colleges and Universities in World War II* (Westport, CT: Praeger Publishing, 1993), 12.

5   "Films: US Naval Reserve Midshipmen's School, WWII," http://www.library.northwestern.edu/node/2082 (accessed January 15, 2014), 1.

6   "Transcript of Naval Service of Lieutenant Iliff David Richardson, U.S. Naval Reserve," 1, in "Richardson Service Record." (Hereafter cited as ""Richardson Transcript of Naval Service."")

7 Chuck Hlava, "Rich Memories," undated newspaper article, http://www.cnac.org/emilscott/richardson01.html (accessed May 30, 2013), 7.

8 *Abbott Hall: USNR 1940—1945* (Chicago, IL: Abbott Hall Publications Committee, Nd), 8, 46.

9 "Coma Noel Richardson," http://www.legacy.com/obituaries/houstonchronicle/obituary.aspx?pid=154924215 (accessed January 22, 2014), 1.

10 Commander in Chief, U.S. Asiatic Fleet to Ensign Iliff D. Richardson, "Active duty—Modification of orders," February 1, 1941, 1, in "Richardson Service Record."

11 "Bittern," in Dictionary of American Fighting Ships, http://www.history.navy.mil/danfs/b6/bittern-i.htm (accessed January 10, 2014), 1.

12 Iliff David Richardson to CO U.S.S. *Bittern,* "Enclosure A and Statement Returned Herewith," 1, in "Richardson Service Record."

13 "Report on the Fitness of Officers for the Period from: April 1 to September 18, 1941," 2, in "Richardson Service Record."

14 Undated manuscript, Iliff Richardson Collection, Nimitz Education and Research Center, National Museum of the Pacific War, Fredericksburg, Texas, 1. (Hereafter cited as "Richardson Manuscript.")

15 Commander in Chief, U.S. Asiatic Fleet to Ensign Iliff D. Richardson, "Change of duty," October 22, 1941, 1, in "Richardson Service Record."

16 "Richardson Transcript of Naval Service."

17 Bachman, *Honorable Profession,* 162.

18 Ibid, 164.

19 Smith, *MacArthur's Escape,* 73.

20 "Richardson Interview," 5.

21 Breuer, *Sea Wolf,* 25.

Chapter 7

1 Morison, *Rising Sun,* 28.

2 Walter G. Winslow, *The Fleet The Gods Forgot: The U.S. Asiatic Fleet in World War II* (Annapolis, MD: Naval Institute Press, 1982), 3.

3 Morison, *Rising Sun,* 151.

4 Miller, *War Plan Orange,* 262–263.

5 Nelson, *Hunters in the Shallows,* 118–119.

6 Morton, *Fall of the Philippines,* 45–46, and Chun and Gerrard, *The Fall of the Philippines,* 23.

7 Gordon, *Fighting for MacArthur,* 323.

8 "Fifty Years of Naval District Development, 1903–1953," http://www.history.navy.mil/library/online/navy_dist.htm (accessed January 7, 2014), 1, 12.

9 Morton, *Fall of the Philippines,* 90.

10 Winslow, *The Fleet The Gods Forgot*, 5, and Morton, *Fall of the Philippines*, 46.
11 Winslow, *The Fleet The Gods Forgot*, 9.
12 Costello, *Pacific War*, 104.
13 Chun and Gerrard, *The Fall of the Philippines*, 14.
14 Morison, *Rising Sun*, 154.
15 Costello, *Pacific War*, 120.
16 Morton, *Fall of the Philippines*, 72.
17 Paul S. Dull, *A Battle History of the Imperial Japanese Navy* (Annapolis, MD: Naval Institute Press, 1978), 28.
18 Morison, *Rising Sun*, 166.
19 Chun and Gerrard, *The Fall of the Philippines*, 20–24.
20 Ibid, 28.

Chapter 8

1 Morton, *Fall of the Philippines*, 80.
2 Winslow, *The Fleet The Gods Forgot*, 49.
3 Van Der Vat, *Pacific Campaign*, 25.
4 Lewis H. Brereton, *The Brereton Diaries: The Air War in the Pacific, Middle East and Europe* (New York: William Morrow and Company, 1946), 34–35.
5 Wesley F. Craven and James L. Cate, *The Army Air Forces in World War II: Volume One—Plans and Early Operations, January 1939 to August 1942* (Chicago, IL: University of Chicago Press, 1948), 203.
6 Morton, *Fall of the Philippines*, 80.
7 Costello, *Days of Infamy*, 30.
8 Morton, *Fall of the Philippines*, 81.
9 Morison, *Rising Sun*, 169.
10 Brereton, *Brereton Diaries*, 40.
11 Sloan, *Undefeated*, 31.
12 Ibid, 32.
13 Craven and Cate, *Army Air Forces*, 210–11.
14 Edgar D. Whitcomb, *Escape from Corregidor* (Bloomington, IN: Author House, 2012), 17.
15 Sloan, *Undefeated*, 36.
16 Spector, *Eagle Against the Sun*, 108.
17 "MacArthur Denies Brereton Report," *New York Times*, September 28, 1946, 6.

Chapter 9

1 War Diary, Sixteenth Naval District, December 9, 1941.
2 Smith, *MacArthur's Escape*, 86.
3 "Richardson Manuscript," 7.

4 War Diary, Sixteenth Naval District, December 8, 1941.
5 Morton, *Fall of the Philippines*, 92.
6 Craven and Cate, *Army Air Forces*, 213–14.
7 Morton, *Fall of the Philippines*, 100.
8 Morison, *Rising Sun*, 176–77.
9 Morton, *Fall of the Philippines*, 107.

Chapter 10

1   Morison, *Rising Sun*, 171.
2   Ralph Emerson Hibbs, *Tell MacArthur to Wait* (New York: Carlton Press, 1988), 35.
3   Gordon, *Fighting for MacArthur*, 45.
4   War Diary, Sixteenth Naval District, December 10, 1941.
5   "Richardson Manuscript," 8.
6   Rockwell, Rear Admiral F. W. to CinC U.S. Fleet, "Narrative of Naval Activities in Luzon Area, December 1, 1941 to March 9, 1942," August 1, 1942, 3. (Hereafter cited as "Rockwell Narrative.")
7   Gordon, *Fighting for MacArthur*, 55.
8   "Seadragon" in Dictionary of American Fighting Ships, http://www.history.navy.mil/danfs/s8/seadragon-i.htm (accessed May 16, 2014), 1.
9   "Bittern" in Dictionary of American Fighting Ships, http://www.history.navy.mil/danfs/g9/guadalupe.htm (accessed May 16, 2014), 1.
10 Gordon, *Fighting for MacArthur*, 50.
11 H. Ford Wilkins, "Admiral at Cavite Narrowly Escapes Bomb; Filipino as His Side in Shelter Ditch is Killed," *New York Times*, December 15, 1941, 5.
12 Breuer, *Sea Wolf*, 31.
13 Sloan, *Undefeated*, 43.
14 White, *Expendable*, 19.
15 Francis B. Sayre, "War Days on Corregidor," *Life*, April 20, 1942, 96.
16 "CinCAF to OpNAV" in Rockwell, Rear Admiral F. W., "Supplement of Narrative for December 1, 1941 to March 9, 1942" (Volume One).
17 Smith, *MacArthur's Escape*, 92.
18 CO MTBRON Three to CinC U.S. Fleet and Chief of Naval Operations, "Summary of Operations Motor Torpedo Boat Squadron Three from 7 December 1941 to 10 April 1942," May 21, 1942, 4. (Hereafter cited as "Summary of Operations Motor Torpedo Boat Squadron Three.")

Chapter 11

1 Morison, *Rising Sun*, 184–86.
2 Craven and Cate, *Army Air Forces in World War II*, 218–219.
3 "Richardson Manuscript," 14.

4 Brantingham, *Fire and Ice*, 21.
5 "Summary of Operations Motor Torpedo Boat Squadron Three," 4.
6 Breuer, *Sea Wolf*, 34.
7 War Diary, Sixteenth Naval District, December 16, 1941.
8 "Summary of Operations Motor Torpedo Boat Squadron Three," 1.
9 Buckley, *Close Quarters*, 6.
10 "Richardson Manuscript," 16.
11 Ibid.
12 Gordon, *Fighting for MacArthur*, 74, and "Sinking of the SS Corregidor" in PT Boats, Inc., *Knights of the Sea* (Dallas, TX: Taylor Publishing Co., 1982), 112.
13 Breuer, *Sea Wolf*, 34.
14 "Richardson Manuscript," 18.
15 "Summary of Operations Motor Torpedo Boat Squadron Three," 2.
16 Buckley, *Close Quarters*, 9.

Chapter 12

1 "Rockwell Narrative," 6.
2 Morton, *Fall of the Philippines*, 110.
3 Chun and Gerrard, *The Fall of the Philippines*, 45–46.
4 Morton, *Fall of the Philippines*, 131.
5 Chun and Gerrard, *The Fall of the Philippines*, 48.
6 Morton, *Fall of the Philippines*, 163.
7 Chun and Gerrard, *The Fall of the Philippines*, 31.
8 Ibid, 161.
9 War Diary, Sixteenth Naval District, December 24, 1941.
10 Douglas MacArthur, *Reminiscences* (New York: McGraw-Hill, 1964), 136.
11 Spector, *Eagle Against the Sun*, 109.
12 Ibid, 111.
13 Morton, *Fall of the Philippines*, 179.

Chapter 13

1 "Richardson Manuscript," 32.
2 Brantingham, *Fire and Ice*, 22.
3 Ibid, 21.
4 "Rockwell Narrative," 6.
5 Morison, *Rising Sun*, 195.
6 War Diary, Sixteenth Naval District, December 26, 1941.
7 "Rockwell Narrative," 6.
8 Buckley, *Close Quarters*, 9.
9 Morison, *Rising Sun*, 198.

Chapter 14

1 CO PT-33 to CO MTBRON Three, "Report of Circumstances of Grounding on a Coral Reef off Luzon during Night Action," December 30, 1941, 1.
2 "Richardson Manuscript," 23.
3 Brantingham, *Fire and Ice*, 22.
4 "Narrative by Ensign D. L. Glover, Chief E. H. Offset & Chief F. J. Napolillo: Philippine Experiences," World War II Interviews (College Park, MD: National Archives), 1. (Hereafter cited as "Glover, Offset and Napolillo Narrative.")

Chapter 15

1 Chun and Gerrard, *The Fall of the Philippines*, 60.
2 Costello, *Pacific War*, 184.
3 MacArthur, *Reminiscences*, 136.
4 Clark Lee, *They Call it Pacific* (New York: Viking Press, 1943), 127.
5 White, *Expendable*, 52.
6 Ibid, 57.
7 Morton, *Fall of the Philippines*, 234.
8 Ibid, 164.
9 Elizabeth Norman, *We Band of Angels: The Untold Story of American Nurses Trapped on Bataan by the Japanese* (New York: Random House, 1999), 24.
10 Morton, *Fall of the Philippines*, 234.
11 Ibid, 236.
12 White, *Expendable*, 58.
13 "Rockwell Narrative," 9.
14 War Diary, Sixteenth Naval District, December 25, 1941.
15 War Diary, Sixteenth Naval District, December 31, 1941.

Chapter 16

1 "Pensacola" in Dictionary of American Fighting Ships, http://www.history.navy.mil/danfs/s8/seadragon-i.htm (May 27, 2014), 1.
2 Morton, *Fall of the Philippines*, 148.
3 "Message of Support to the Philippines," http://www.presidency.ucsb.edu/ws/?pid=16076 (accessed June 30, 2014), 1.
4 Spector, *Eagle Against the Sun*, 113.
5 Morton, *Fall of the Philippines*, 145.
6 Grace P. Hayes, *The History of the Joint Chiefs of Staff in World War II: The War Against Japan* (Annapolis, MD: Naval Institute Press, 1982), 33.
7 Costello, *Pacific War*, 186.
8 Breuer, *Sea Wolf*, 37.

9   Morton, *Fall of the Philippines*, 247.
10 MacArthur, *Reminiscences*, 136.
11 Costello, *Pacific War*, 183.
12 Chun and Gerrard, *The Fall of the Philippines*, 61.
13 Costello, *Pacific War*, 184.
14 Chun and Gerrard, *The Fall of the Philippines*, 53.
15 Morton, *Fall of the Philippines*, 271.
16 Sloan, *Undefeated*, 97.
17 Manuel L. Quezon, *The Good Fight* (New York: Appleton—Century Company, 1946), 53.

Chapter 17

1   "Canopus" in Dictionary of American Fighting Ships, http://www.history.navy. mil/danfs/s8/seadragon-i.htm (May 27, 2014), 1, and Morison, *Rising Sun*, 199.
2   "USS Dewey (YFD-1)" in NavSource Online: Service Ship Photo Archive, http://www.navsource.org/archives/14/0701.htm (accessed June 23, 2014), 1.
3   Nelson, *Hunter in the Shallows*, 134.
4   War Diary, Sixteenth Naval District, January 2 and 8, 1942.
5   CO PT-32 to CO MTBRON Three, "Narrative Report of Engagement with Enemy Aircraft while Moored at Sisiman, Luzon," n.d., 1.
6   ""Richardson Manuscript,"" 72.
7   CO MTBRON Three to Commandant, Sixteenth Naval District, "U.S.S. PT-35— Report of Condition of," January 13, 1941, 1.
8   Brantingham, *Fire and Ice*, 24.
9   War Diary, Sixteenth Naval District, January 11, 1942.
10 Chun and Gerrard, *The Fall of the Philippines*, 64.

Chapter 18

1   CO MTBRON Three to Commandant, Sixteenth Naval District, "Report of Attack on Enemy Vessels in Port Binanga, 19 January 1942," January 20, 1942, 3. (Hereafter cited as "Attack on Enemy Vessels in Port Binanga.")
2   White, *Expendable*, 67.
3   "Richardson Manuscript," 37.
4   Stewart H. Holbrook, *None More Courageous* (New York: MacMillan Co., 1942), 53.
5   "Attack on Enemy Vessels in Port Binanga," 1.
6   Smith, *MacArthur's Escape*, 133.
7   "Richardson Manuscript," 39.
8   Breuer, *Sea Wolf*, 42.
9   Buckley, *Close Quarters*, 10.

10 Breuer, *Devil Boats*, 26.
11 Buckley, *Close Quarters*, 10.
12 Office of Public Relations, U.S. Navy, *Navy Department Communiques 1–300 and Pertinent Press Releases* (Washington, D.C.: U.S. Government Printing Office, 1943), 22.
13 "Wife is Pleased," *Chicago Tribune*, January 21, 1942, 2.
14 Breuer, *Sea Wolf*, 45–46.
15 "New Yorker Leads Daring Raid on Foe," *New York Times*, January 21, 1942, 5.
16 Special Staff Military History Section, Fat East Command, *Imperial Japanese Navy in World War II: A Graphic Presentation of the Japanese Naval Organization and List of Combatant and Non-Combatant Vessels Lost or Damaged in the War, Part 2* (Washington, D.C.: U.S. Government Printing Office / BiblioGov, 2013), 172.
17 "Japanese Naval and Merchant Shipping Losses During World War II by All Causes—Appendix," in Naval History and Heritage Command Website, http://www.history.navy.mil/library/online/japaneseshiploss3.htm (accessed July 22, 2014), 34.

Chapter 19

1 Smith, *MacArthur's Escape*, 135.
2 CO PT-31, "Report of Circumstances of Loss of this Boat," January 23, 1942, 1. (Hereafter cited as "Loss of PT-31.")
3 Smith, *MacArthur's Escape*, 136.
4 Donald Young, *The Battle of Bataan: A Complete History* (Jefferson, NC: McFarland & Company, 2009), 51.
5 "Loss of PT-31," 3.
6 White, *Expendable*, 76.
7 "Richardson Manuscript," 44.
8 Michael Hurst, "The Story of the Bombing of the Enoura Maru," http://www.powtaiwan.org/archives_detail.php?THE-STORY-OF-THE-BOMBING-OF-THE-ENOURA-MARU-17 (accessed August 8, 2014), 1.
9 "World War II Prisoners of War Data File, 12/7/1941—11/19/1946" in National Archives Website, http://aad.archives.gov/aad/record-detail.jsp?dt=466&mtch=1&cat=WR26&tf=F&sc=11675,11660,11679,11667,11669,11676,11672,11673&bc=,sl,fd&txt_11660=William+Plant&op_11660=0&nfo_11660=V,24,1900&rpp=10&pg=1&rid=351155 (accessed August 11, 2014).

Chapter 20

1 War Diary, Sixteenth Naval District, January 18, 1942.
2 Morton, *Fall of the Philippines*, 264, 484.
3 Buckley, *Close Quarters*, 13.

4 White, *Expendable*, 76.

5 Brantingham, *Fire and Ice*, 26.

6 "Richardson Manuscript," 48.

7 CO MTBRON Three to Commandant, Sixteenth Naval District ""Report of Action of U.S.S. PT-34 on the Night of January 22–23, 1942," February 27, 1942, 1.

8 Breuer, *Devil Boats*, 30.

9 Breuer, *Sea Wolf*, 47.

10 White, *Expendable*, 81.

11 Breuer, *Devil Boats*, 31.

12 Chun and Gerrard, *The Fall of the Philippines*, 65.

13 Morton, *Fall of the Philippines*, 297.

14 Morison, *Rising Sun*, 201.

15 Morton, *Fall of the Philippines*, 324.

Chapter 21

1 War Diary, Sixteenth Naval District, January 24, 1942.

2 CO MTBRON Three to Commandant, Sixteenth Naval District, "Narrative Report of Operations of PT-41 Night of 24 January 1942, Obtained Hit on Merchant Ship Anchored West of Sampaloc Point, Philippines," January 26, 1942, 1.

3 Breuer, *Devil Boats*, 34.

4 Lee, *Pacific*, 200.

5 U.S. Navy, *Navy Department Communiqués*, 24.

6 Buckley, *Close Quarters*, 14.

7 Morton, *Fall of the Philippines*, 317–18.

8 CO MTBRON Three to Commandant, Sixteenth Naval District, "Report of Attack of PT-32 on Enemy Cruiser-Type Surface Ship off Subic Bay," February 3, 1942, 1.

9 Roger Chesneau, ed., *Conway's All the World's Fighting Ships: 1922–1946* (London: Conway Maritime Press, 1980), 208.

10 "IJN Minelayer Yaeyama: Tabular Record of Movement," in Imperial Japanese Navy Page, http://www.combinedfleet.com/Yaeyama_t.htm (accessed January 10, 2015) and Buckley, *Close Quarters*, 15.

Chapter 22

1 Howard F. West, *Iron Men Wooden Boats* (Westminster, MD: Heritage Books, 2005), 21.

2 War Diary, Sixteenth Naval District, January 27, 1942.

3 Holbrook, *None More Courageous*, 57.

4 White, *Expendable*, 92–93.

5 CO MTBRON Three to Commandant, Sixteenth Naval District, "Night Operations, PT-35 and 41 off Subic Bay, the Night of 17–18 February 1942," February 17, 1942, 1.
6 Winslow, *The Fleet the Gods Forgot*, 72.
7 "Richardson Manuscript," 58.
8 Morton, *Fall of the Philippines*, 396.
9 Breuer, *Sea Wolf*, 52.
10 "Richardson Manuscript," 79.
11 Lee, *Pacific*, 200.
12 Nelson, *Hunters in the Shallows*, 135.

Chapter 23

1 Hayes, *History of the Joint Chiefs of Staff*, 91.
2 Ibid, 92.
3 Buckley, *Close Quarters*, 19.
4 MacArthur, *Reminiscences*, 152.
5 Geoffrey Perret, *Old Soldiers Never Die: The Life of Douglas MacArthur* (New York: Random House, 1996), 271, and Van Der Vat, *Pacific Campaign*, 168.
6 Spector, *Eagle Against the Sun*, 118.
7 Morton, *Fall of the Philippines*, 353.
8 Richard Connaughton, *MacArthur and Defeat in the Philippines* (New York: Overlook Press, 2001), 281.
9 Morton, *Fall of the Philippines*, 357–58.
10 MacArthur, *Reminiscences*, 155.
11 Buckley, *Close Quarters*, 16.
12 Nelson, *Hunters in the Shallows*, 142–144.
13 Morison, *Rising Sun*, 379.
14 Breuer, *Sea Wolf*, 53.
15 Perret, *Old Soldiers Never Die*, 273.
16 Breuer, *Sea Wolf*, 54.
17 Sidney Huff, *My Fifteen Years with MacArthur* (New York: Lippincott, 1964), 51.
18 Perret, *Old Soldiers Never Die*, 273.
19 Connaughton, *MacArthur and Defeat in the Philippines*, 285.
20 "Richardson Manuscript," 86.
21 Breuer, *Devil Boats*, 36.
22 Breuer, *Sea Wolf*, 53.
23 Buckley, *Close Quarters*, 16.
24 Bachman, *Honorable Profession*, 34.
25 White, *Expendable*, 104.
26 "Summary of Operations Motor Torpedo Boat Squadron Three," 5.

27 Jonathan Wainwright, *General Wainwright's Story: The Account of Four Years of Humiliating Defeat, Surrender, and Captivity* (Garden City, NY: Doubleday & Company, 1946), 4.
28 Morton, *Fall of the Philippines*, 363.

Chapter 24

1 Buckley, *Close Quarters*, 17.
2 Commandant Sixteenth Naval District to CO MTNRON Three, "Operation Order," March 10, 1942, 1. (Hereafter cited as "Operation Order.")
3 "Annex D—Enemy Activity," in "Operation Order," 1.
4 Huff, *Fifteen Years with MacArthur*, 54.
5 Lee, *Pacific*, 202.
6 White, *Expendable*, 117.
7 MacArthur, *Reminiscences*, 154.
8 John Jacob Beck, *MacArthur and Wainwright: Sacrifice of the Philippines* (Albuquerque, NM: University of New Mexico Press, 1974), 144.
9 MacArthur, *Reminiscences*, 154.
10 Breuer, *Sea Wolf*, 57.
11 Manchester, *American Caesar*, 257.
12 Paul P. Rogers, *The Good Years: MacArthur and Sutherland* (New York: Praeger, 1990), 188.
13 "Richardson Manuscript," 87.
14 John Bulkeley and Jack Ryan, "MacArthur's Closest Call," *Family Weekly* (May 27, 1962), 4.
15 Buckley, *Close Quarters*, 17.
16 Smith, *MacArthur's Escape*, 190.

Chapter 25

1 White, *Expendable*, 121.
2 Beck, *MacArthur and Wainwright*, 145.
3 CO PT-32 to Secretary of the Navy, "U.S.S. PT-32—Report of Destruction of," March 15, 1942, 1. (Hereafter cited as "U.S.S. PT-32—Report of Destruction.")
4 John Toland, *But Not in Shame: The Six Months After Pearl Harbor* (New York: Random House, 1961), 271.
5 Buckley, *Close Quarters*, 18.
6 Bulkeley and Ryan, "MacArthur's Closest Call," 5.
7 Beck, *MacArthur and Wainwright*, 147.
8 "Richardson Manuscript," 89–90.

9   White, *Expendable*, 124.
10   Brantingham, *Fire and Ice*, 28.

Chapter 26

1   CO Permit to Commander, Submarines, U.S. Asiatic Fleet, "U.S.S. Permit (SS 178)—Report of Fourth War Patrol, Forwarding of," n.d., 4. (Hereafter cited as "U.S.S. Permit—Report of Fourth War Patrol.")
2   Huff, *Fifteen Years with MacArthur*, 61.
3   Beck, *MacArthur and Wainwright*, 148.
4   Breuer, *Sea Wolf*, 61.
5   Toland, *Not in Shame*, 272.
6   Smith, *MacArthur's Escape*, 197.
7   "U.S.S. PT-32—Report of Destruction," 1.
8   "Richardson Manuscript," 93.
9   Breuer, *Sea Wolf*, 62.
10   Bulkeley and Ryan, "MacArthur's Closest Call," 5.
11   Buckley, *Close Quarters*, 18.
12   Bulkeley and Ryan, "MacArthur's Closest Call," 5.
13   Breuer, *Sea Wolf*, 64.
14   Toland, *Not in Shame*, 273.
15   "Rockwell Narrative," 21.
16   White, *Expendable*, 141.
17   MacArthur, *Reminiscences*, 157.
18   Breuer, *Devil Boats*, 44.
19   White, *Expendable*, 143.
20   Beck, *MacArthur and Wainwright*, 267–68.

Chapter 27

1   Muster Roll, Motor Torpedo Boat Squadron Three, October 1941.
2   "Narrative by William F. Konko, Warrant Electrician, USN: Philippines Guerillas," World War II Interviews (College Park, MD: National Archives), 1. (Hereafter cited as "Konko Narrative.")
3   Rogers, *The Good Years*, 191.
4   "Summary of Operations Motor Torpedo Boat Squadron Three," 7.
5   Buckley, *Close Quarters*, 18.
6   Morton, *Fall of the Philippines*, 499.
7   Ibid, 498.
8   "U.S.S. Permit—Report of Fourth War Patrol," 5.

9   "U.S.S. PT-32—Report of Destruction," 1.

10 "U.S.S. Permit—Report of Fourth War Patrol," 5, and Smith, *MacArthur's Escape*, 211.

11 Bulkeley, Lieutenant J. D. to Commander Allied Naval Forces Southwest Pacific, "Announces Destruction of PT-32 at Tagauayan Island, P.I. 13 March 1942 and Request Investigation of Circumstances," April 23, 1942, 1.

12 "Glover, Offset and Napolillo Narrative," 2.

13 Brantingham, *Fire and Ice*, 28–29.

14 "Richardson Manuscript," 99.

Chapter 28

1   Breuer, *Devil Boats*, 46.

2   Breuer, *Sea Wolf*, 68–69.

3   Perret, *Old Soldiers Never Die*, 280.

4   Morton, *Fall of the Philippines*, 360.

5   Beck, *MacArthur and Wainwright*, 155.

6   "Rockwell Narrative," 22.

7   MacArthur, *Reminiscences*, 158.

8   Ibid.

9   Manchester, *American Caesar*, 270.

10 "Richardson Manuscript," 104.

11 White, *Expendable*, 124.

12 Brantingham, *Fire and Ice*, 29.

13 "Richardson Manuscript," 118.

Chapter 29

1   Breuer, *Devil Boats*, 49.

2   CO MTBRON Three to Commanding General U.S.I.P, "Report of Trip to Dumaguette and Lift of President Quezon and Party to Oroquita by PT-41," April 15, 1942, 1.

3   Buckley, *Close Quarters*, 20.

4   "Konko Narrative," 6.

5   Breuer, *Sea Wolf*, 69.

6   Breuer, *Devil Boats*, 49.

7   Bachman, *Honorable Profession*, 173.

8   Holbrook, *None More Courageous*, 59.

9   Quezon, *Good Fight*, 307–308.

10 Colonel Parker Hitt, "Amphibious Infantry: A Fleet on Lake Lanao," http://1-22infantry.org/history3/lanao.htm (accessed on January 24, 2015), 1.
11 Smith, *MacArthur's Escape*, 233.
12 "Richardson Manuscript," 112.

Chapter 30

1 Toland, *Not in Shame*, 281.
2 Morton, *Fall of the Philippines*, 421.
3 "Richardson Manuscript," 119.
4 White, *Expendable*, 156.
5 Ibid., 158
6 "Richardson Manuscript," 121.
7 CO U.S.S. Seadragon to Commander Submarines, U.S. Asiatic Fleet, "War Patrol Number 2—Report—Forwarding of," April 26, 1942, 4.
8 CO U.S.S. Snapper to Commander Submarines, U.S. Asiatic Fleet, "U.S.S. Snapper—Report of No 2 War Patrol. Period from 6 March 1942 to 25 April 194," April 25, 1942, 10.
9 Buckley, *Close Quarters*, 21.
10 Smith, *MacArthur's Escape*, 224.

Chapter 31

1 CO MTBRON Three to Commanding General U.S. Forces Far East, "Report of Night Action with Enemy Surface Ship off Cebu Island, By PTs 41 and 34," April 12, 1942, 1. (Hereafter cited as "Report of Night Action.")
2 "Richardson Manuscript," 126.
3 CO PT-34, "Report of Attack on Japanese Cruiser off Cebu Island and of Subsequent Loss of PT-34 to Japanese Air Attack while Attempting to Reach Cebu Harbor," n.d., 1. (Hereafter cited as "Report of Attack on Japanese Cruiser.")
4 Buckley, *Close Quarters*, 21.
5 Anthony J. Watts and Brian G. Gordon, *The Imperial Japanese Navy* (New York: Doubleday & Company, Inc. 1971), 73.
6 "IJN Kuma: Tabular Record of Movement," in Imperial Japanese Navy Page, http://www.combinedfleet.com/kuma_t.htm (accessed February 10, 2015), 2–3. (Hereafter cited as "IJN Kuma.")
7 Chesneau, ed., *Conway's All the World's Fighting Ships*, 197.
8 "Richardson Manuscript," 131.
9 "Report of Attack on Japanese Cruiser," 2.
10 "Richardson Manuscript," 131.

Chapter 32

1   Toland, *Not in Shame*, 285–86.
2   Morton, *Fall of the Philippines*, 437.
3   Toland, *Not in Shame*, 296.
4   Chun and Gerrard, *The Fall of the Philippines*, 77.
5   Morton, *Fall of the Philippines*, 466.
6   Wainwright, *General Wainwright's Story*, 82.
7   Major General Courtney Whitney, *MacArthur: His Rendezvous with History* (New York: Alfred A. Knopf, 1956), 58.
8   MacArthur, *Reminiscences*, 159.
9   CO MTBRON Three to CinC Allied Forces in the S.W. Pacific, "Report of Night Action off Cebu Island by PTs 41 and 34," April 21, 1942, 1. (Hereafter cited as "Report of Night Action off Cebu Island.")
10 "IJN Kum,." 2–3.
11 Buckley, *Close Quarters*, 24.
12 "Japanese Destroyers: Tabular Movement Records (TROMs)," in Imperial Japanese Navy Page. http://www.combinedfleet.com/lancers.htm (accessed February 17, 2015)
13 U.S. Navy, *Navy Department Communiqués*, 51.
14 Breuer, *Sea Wolf*, 86.

Chapter 33

1   "Report of Attack on Japanese Cruiser," 3.
2   "Richardson Manuscript," 139.
3   White, *Expendable*, 169.
4   "IJN Seaplane Tender Sanuki Maru: Tabular Record of Movement," in Imperial Japanese Navy Page. http://www.combinedfleet.com/kuma_t.htm (accessed February 10, 2015), 3–4.
5   Steve Cabral, "Floatplanes in Second World War at Sea," http://www.avalanche-press.com/floatplanes.php (accessed February 18, 2015), 3.
6   White, *Expendable*, 175.
7   Chun and Gerrard, *The Fall of the Philippines*, 81.
8   Lt Col William D. Miner, *Surrender on Cebu: A POW's Diary—WW II* (Paducah, KY: Turner Publishing Company, 2001), 167.
9   Col Hiram W. Tarkington. "There Were Others," unpublished manuscript, http://www.west-point.org/family/japanese-pow/ThereWereOthers/ManuscriptLinks.htm (accessed on March 7, 2015), 286.
10 Morton, *Fall of the Philippines*, 503.

11 Craven and Cate, *Army Air Forces*, 418.
12 Chun and Gerrard, *The Fall of the Philippines*, 81.

Chapter 34

1   "Richardson Manuscript," 152.
2   Louis Jurika, "A Philippine Odyssey," http://corregidor.org/crypto/intel_01/A%20 Philippine%20Odyssey%20-%20Louis%20Jurika.pdf (accessed February 25, 2015), 1.
3   Ira Wolfert, *American Guerrilla in the Philippines* (New York: Simon and Schuster, 1945), 20.
4   "Narrative by Lieutenant Iliff D. Richardson, USNR. Guerilla Experiences in the Philippine Islands," World War II Interviews (College Park, MD: National Archives), 3. (Hereafter cited as "Richardson Interview.")
5   "Inventory of the Charlotte Ellen Martin Papers," http://www.oac.cdlib.org/findaid/ ark:/13030/c8xw4mhj/entire_text/ (accessed February 27, 2015), 1.
6   Young, *Battle of Bataan*, 113.
7   Wolfert, *American Guerrilla*, 24.
8   Smith, *MacArthur's Escape*, 235.
9   Brantingham, *Fire and Ice*, 31.
10 Smith, *MacArthur's Escape*, 236.
11 "Brantingham Statement," in "Report of Night Action off Cebu Island," 1.
12 Brantingham, *Fire and Ice*, 32.
13 White, *Expendable*, 181.
14 Ibid., 186.

Chapter 35

1   Morton, *Fall of the Philippines*, 507.
2   Chun and Gerrard, *The Fall of the Philippines*, 84.
3   Morton, *Fall of the Philippines*, 519.
4   William Breuer, *MacArthur's Undercover War: Spies, Saboteurs, Guerrillas, and Secret Missions* (New York: J. Wiley and Sons, 1995), 25.
5   "Report of Night Action," 2.
6   White, *Expendable*, 194–95.
7   Buckley, *Close Quarters*, 26.
8   "Glover, Offset and Napolillo Narrative," 6.
9   H. J. Brantingham, "Notes on Conversation with Comdr. J. D. Bulkeley, USN, 27 December 1945," in "Report of Night Action off Cebu Island," 1.
10 "Glover, Offset and Napolillo Narrative," 7.
11 White, *Expendable*, 204.

Chapter 36

1 Costello, *Pacific War*, 228.
2 Ibid. and Spector, *Eagle Against the Sun*, 396.
3 Costello, *Pacific War*, 264.
4 Morton, *Fall of the Philippines*, 562–63.
5 Ibid., 572.
6 Breuer, *Sea Wolf*, 85.
7 Samuel Eliot Morison, *History of United States Naval Operations in World War II Volume IV: Coral Sea, Midway and Submarine Actions* (Edison, NJ: Castle Books, 2001), 249.
8 Breuer, *Devil Boats*, 62.
9 "Quezon Plans Trip in Latin America," *New York Times*, May 20, 1942, 3.
10 Buckley, *Close Quarters*, 27.
11 Merrill B. Twining and Neil G. Carey, *No Bended Knee: The Battle For Guadalcanal: The Memoir Of Gen. Merrill B. Twining USMC (Ret.)* (Novato, CA: Presidio, 1996), 15.
12 Lawrence E. Davies, "Bulkeley Back, Tells of Sinkings," *New York Times*, May 8, 1942, 5.
13 Smith, *MacArthur's Escape*, 247.
14 "Torpedo Boats Can Knock Out Japs: Bulkeley," *Chicago Tribune*, May 9, 1942, 2.
15 Stade, *Twelve Handkerchiefs*, 86.

Chapter 37

1 "Konko Narrative," 8.
2 "Glover, Offset and Napolillo Narrative," 7.
3 "Tisdale," http://www.history.navy.mil/research/histories/ship-histories/danfs/t/tisdale.html (accessed on March 14, 2015), 1.
4 Roscoe Creed, *PBY: The Catalina Flying Boat* (Annapolis, MD: Naval Institute Press, 1985), 95.
5 Ibid.
6 Donald J. Young, *Final Hours in the Pacific: The Allied Surrenders of Wake Island, Bataan, Corregidor, Hong Kong, and Singapore* (Jefferson, NC: McFarland & Company, 2011), 92.
7 "Trabajador," http://www.history.navy.mil/research/histories/ship-histories/danfs/t/trabajador.html (accessed on March 31, 2015), 1.
8 Norman, *We Band of Angels*, 112.
9 Brantingham, *Fire and Ice*, 34.
10 "Tisdale," 1.

11 Major Larry S. Schmidt, "American Involvement in the Filipino Resistance Movement on Mindanao During the Japanese Occupation, 1942–1945," master's thesis, (Fort Leavenworth, KS: U.S. Army Command and General Staff College, 1982, 77.
12 "Richardson Interview," 3.
13 Wolfert, *American Guerrilla*, 31.
14 Ibid, 45.
15 Frank Hewlett, "A PT Expendable Shows Up on Leyte," *New York Times*, October 28, 1944, 5.
16 Morton, *Fall of the Philippines*, 577.
17 Chun and Gerrard, *The Fall of the Philippines*, 87.

Chapter 38

1 "Navy Hero Opens Relief Fund Drive," *New York Times*, May 15, 1942, 21.
2 "New PT Boat Leaves the Ways," *New York Times*, May 17, 1942, 36.
3 "John Duncan Bulkeley," 3.
4 "Mosquito Boat Skippers to be Pine for Action," *Chicago Tribune*, September 4, 1942, 10.
5 Breuer, *Devil Boats*, 62.
6 "Medal of Honor Given Bulkeley," *New York Times*, August 5, 1942, 5.
7 Bachman, *Honorable Profession*, 43.
8 "John Duncan Bulkeley," 2.
9 "Stribling," http://www.history.navy.mil/research/histories/ship-histories/danfs/s/stribling-ii.html (accessed on April 21, 2015), 1.
10 Rachel L. Swarns, "Vice Adm. John D. Bulkeley, 84, Hero of D-Day and Philippines," *New York Times*, April 8, 1996, B12.
11 "John Duncan Bulkeley Vice Admiral, United States Navy," http://www.arlingtoncemetery.net/jdbulkel.htm (accessed April 25, 2015), 1–3.
12 "Commander Robert Bolling Kelly, U.S. Navy: Transcript of Record" in "Kelly Biographical Sketch and Service Record," 1.
13 Buckley, *Close Quarters*, 119.
14 "Officer Biography Sheet," in "Kelly Biographical Sketch and Service Record," 1.
15 "Irwin," http://www.history.navy.mil/research/histories/ship-histories/danfs/i/irwin.html (accessed on April 23, 2015), 1.
16 "Robert B. Kelly, Commander of PT Boat in WWII Dies," *Washington Post*, January 27, 1989, C8.
17 Buckley, *Close Quarters*, 456.
18 Smith, *MacArthur's Escape*, 212.

Chapter 39

1 Winslow, *The Fleet The Gods Forgot*, 82.
2 Buckley, *Close Quarters*, 26.
3 "POW List for MTBRON 3," http://www.west-point.org/family/japanese-pow/MTB-3.htm (accessed on October 28, 2013), 1–3.
4 "Statement of William Francis Konko Made to Lt. W.H. Wright 14 February 1945," World War II Interviews (College Park, MD: National Archives), 1.
5 "Missing for Three Years 'Expendable' Reaches U.S. to Phone Mother Here," undated newspaper article courtesy of Jeremy Konko.
6 "Comes Home to 'Dreamland' After Three years in Philippines," undated newspaper article courtesy of Jeremy Konko.
7 Hewlett, "A PT Expendable Show Up on Leyte," 5.
8 "Richardson Manuscript," 7.
9 Rafael Steinberg, *Return to the Philippines* (Alexandria, VA: Time-Life Books, 1979), 18.
10 "Ruperto K. Kangleon: 6th Secretary of National Defense, May 28, 1946 to August 31, 1950," http://www.dnd.gov.ph/DNDWEBPAGE_files/past-snd/kangleon.html (accessed on June 5, 2013), 1–3.
11 Douglas MacArthur, ed., *Reports of General MacArthur: The Campaigns of MacArthur in the Pacific, Volume 1* (Washington, D.C.: Center Of Military History, 1994), 317.
12 Joaquin Chung Jr, *For Love of Country: Saga of Ruperto K. Kangleon and the Leyte Guerrillas* (Philippines: Integrated Publishing House, 1989), 20.
13 "Richardson Interview," 10–11.
14 "Summary of Operations Motor Torpedo Boat Squadron Three," 5.
15 "Commander A. C. Jacobs to Mrs. Velma W. Goldsberry," in "Richardson Service Record."
16 "Mother Received Letters," *New York Times*, October 28, 1942, 5.
17 "Interview with Iliff D. Richardson, 4.
18 "Ensign Becomes Major," *New York Times*, October 28, 1942, 5.
19 "Richardson Interview," 35.
20 Donald A. Stauffer, "Behind Enemy Lines," *New York Times*, April 22, 1945, BR1, and Orville Prescott, "Books of the Times," *New York Times*, April 20, 1945, 17.
21 Oliver, "Iliff D. Richardson, 83, War Hero," 1–2.
22 Samuel Eliot Morison, *History of United States Naval Operations in World War II Volume VII: Aleutians, Gilberts and Marshalls* (Edison, NJ: Castle Books, 2001), 38.
23 "Douglas MacArthur," http://www.history.com/topics/douglas-macarthur (accessed April 24, 2015), 1.
24 Steinberg, *Return to the Philippines*, 116.

Epilogue

1 "William L. White, Writer, 73, Dead," *New York Times*, July 27, 1973, 34.
2 "Authors and Critics Select the Best Books of the Year," *Chicago Tribune*, December 6, 1942, G22.
3 "Heroine Identified in Expendable Epic," *New York Times*, January 19, 1943, 21.
4 John Miller and Lang Thompson, "They Were Expendable (1945)," http://www.tcm.com/tcmdb/title/2070/They-Were-Expendable/articles.html (May 4, 2015), 1.
5 Emily Smith, *The John Wayne Handbook: Everything You Need to Know about John Wayne*. (E-Book: Emereo Publishing, 2012), 250.
6 Crowther, Bosley, "Movie Review: They Were Expendable (1945)." http://www.nytimes.com/movie/review?res=9E01E5D71F38E333A05752C2A9649 D946493D6CF (accessed May 5, 2015), 1.
7 Tag Gallagher. *John Ford: The Man and His Films* (Berkeley, CA: University of California Press, 1986), 221.
8 "Wins $290,000 Suit," *New York Times*, December 4, 1948, 9.
9 "Army Nurse Who was One of the Angels of Bataan," http://articles.chicagotribune.com/1993-02-27/news/9303185498_1_bataan-corregidor-malinta-tunnell (accessed October 24, 2014), 1.
10 Miller and Thompson, 3.
11 Rottman, *US Patrol Torpedo Boats*, 8.
12 Buckley, *Close Quarters*, 491–509.

BIBLIOGRAPHY

Books

Abbott Hall: USNR 1940–1945. Chicago, IL: Abbott Hall Publications Committee, Nd.

Astor, Gerald. *Crisis in the Pacific: The Battles for the Philippine Islands by the men Who Fought There.* New York: Dell, 1996.

Bachman, Bruce M. *An Honorable Profession: The Life and Times of One of America's Most Able Seamen.* New York: Vantage Press, 1985.

Beck, John Jacob. *MacArthur and Wainwright: Sacrifice of the Philippines.* Albuquerque, NM: University of New Mexico Press, 1974.

Brantingham, Henry. *Fire and Ice.* San Diego, CA: ProMotion Publishing, 1995.

Brereton, Lewis H. *The Brereton Diaries: The Air War in the Pacific, Middle East and Europe.* New York: William Morrow and Company, 1946.

Breuer, William. *Devil Boats: The PT War against Japan.* New York: Jove Books, 1988.

Breuer, William. *MacArthur's Undercover War: Spies, Saboteurs, Guerrillas, and Secret Missions.* New York: J. Wiley and Sons, 1995.

Breuer, William B. *Sea Wolf: The Daring Exploits of Navy Legend John D. Bulkeley.* Novato, CA: Presidio Press, 1998.

Buckley, Captain Robert J. *At Close Quarters: PT Boats in the United States Navy.* Washington, DC: United States Government Printing Office, 1962.

Chesneau, Roger, ed. *Conway's All the World's Fighting Ships: 1922–1946.* London: Conway Maritime Press, 1980.

Chun, Clayton and Howard Gerrard. *The Fall of the Philippines 1941–42.* Oxford, UK: Osprey, 2012.

Chung Jr., Joaquin. For *Love of Country: Saga of Ruperto K. Kangleon and the Leyte Guerrillas.* Philippines: Integrated Publishing House, 1989.

Connaughton, Richard. *MacArthur and Defeat in the Philippines.* NY: Overlook Press, 2001.

Costello, John. *Days of Infamy: MacArthur, Roosevelt, Churchill – The Shocking Truth Revealed: How Their Secret Deal and Strategic Blunders Caused Disaster at Pearl Harbor and the Philippines.* New York: Pocket Books, 1994.

Costello, John. *The Pacific War.* New York: Rawson, Wade Publishers, Inc., 1981.

Craven, Wesley F. and James L. Cate. *The Army Air Forces in World War II: Volume One – Plans and Early Operations, January 1939 to August 1942.* Chicago, IL: University of Chicago Press, 1948.

Creed, Roscoe. *PBY: The Catalina Flying Boat.* Annapolis, MD: Naval Institute Press, 1985.

Dull, Paul S. *A Battle History of the Imperial Japanese Navy.* Annapolis, MD: Naval Institute Press, 1978.

Frank, Richard B. *Guadalcanal.* New York: Penguin Books, 1990.

Gallagher, Tag. *John Ford: The Man and His Films.* Berkeley, CA: University of California Press, 1986.

Gordon, John. *Fighting for MacArthur: The Navy and Marine Corps' Desperate Defense of the Philippines.* Annapolis, MD: Naval Institute Press, 2011.

Gorman, Robert, ed. *Great Events from History: The 20th Century, Volume I: 1941–1970.* Pasadena, CA: Salem Press, 2008.

Hayes, Grace P. *The History of the Joint Chiefs of Staff in World War II: The War Against Japan.* Annapolis, MD: Naval Institute Press, 1982.

Hersey, John. *Men on Bataan.* New York: Alfred A. Knopf, 1942.

Hibbs, Ralph Emerson. *Tell MacArthur to Wait.* New York: Carlton Press, 1988.

Holbrook, Stewart H. *None More Courageous*. New York: MacMillan Co., 1942.

Huff, Sidney. *My Fifteen Years with MacArthur*. New York: Lippincott, 1964.

Johnson, Frank D. *United States PT-Boats of World War II in Action*. Poole, England: Blandford Press, 1980.

Lee, Clark. *They Call it Pacific*. New York: Viking Press, 1943.

MacArthur, Douglas, eds. *Reports of General MacArthur: The Campaigns of MacArthur in the Pacific, Volume 1*. Washington, DC: Center Of Military History, 1994.

MacArthur, Douglas. *Reminiscences*. New York: McGraw-Hill, 1964.

Manchester, William. *American Caesar: Douglas MacArthur, 1880–1964*. Boston: Little, Brown & Company, 1978.

Miller, Edward S. *War Plan Orange: The U.S. Strategy to Defeat Japan, 1897–1945*. Annapolis, MD: Naval Institute Press, 1991.

Miner, LTC William D. *Surrender on Cebu: A POW's Diary – WW II*. Paducah, KY: Turner Publishing Company, 2001.

Morison, Samuel Eliot. *History of United States Naval Operations in World War II Volume III: The Rising Sun in the Pacific*. Edison, NJ: Castle Books, 2001.

Morison, Samuel Eliot. *History of United States Naval Operations in World War II Volume VII: Aleutians, Gilberts and Marshalls*. Edison, NJ: Castle Books, 2001.

Morison, Samuel Eliot. *History of United States Naval Operations in World War II Volume IV: Coral Sea, Midway and Submarine Actions*. Edison, NJ: Castle Books, 2001.

Morton, Lewis. U.S. *Army in World War II: The War in the Pacific: The Fall of the Philippines*. Washington, DC: Center of Military History, U.S. Army, 1989.

Nelson, Curtis L. *Hunters in the Shallows: A History of the PT Boat*. Washington, DC: Brassey's, 1998.

Norman, Elizabeth. *We Band of Angels: The Untold Story of American Nurses Trapped on Bataan by the Japanese*. New York: Random House, 1999.

Perret, Geoffery. *Old Soldiers Never Die: The Life of Douglas MacArthur*. New York: Random House, 1996.

PT Boats, Inc. *Knights of the Sea*. Dallas, TX: Taylor Publishing Co., 1982.

Quezon, Manuel L. *The Good Fight*. New York: Appleton – Century Company, 1946.

Robson, R.W. *The Pacific Islands Handbook*. New York: The Macmillan Company, 1946.

Rogers, Paul P. *The Good Years: MacArthur and Sutherland*. New York: Praeger, 1990.

Rottman, Gary. *US Patrol Torpedo Boats*. Oxford, UK: Osprey, 2008.

Sloan, Bill. *Undefeated: America's Heroic Fight for Bataan and Corregidor*. New York: Simon & Schuster, 2012.

Smith, Emily. *The John Wayne Handbook: Everything you need to know about John Wayne*. E-Book: Emereo Publishing, 2012.

Smith, George W. *MacArthur's Escape: John "Wild Man" Bulkeley and the Rescue of an American Hero*. St. Paul, MN: Zenith Press, 2005.

Spector, Ronald H. *Eagle Against the Sun: The American War with Japan*. New York: Vintage Books, 1985.

Stade, Joan Bulkeley. *Twelve Handkerchiefs: The Global Journey of Alice Wood Bulkeley through World War II and the Twentieth Century with an American Navy Hero*. Tuscan, AZ: Patrice Press, 2001.

Steinberg, Rafael. *Return to the Philippines*. Alexandria, VA: Time-Life Books, 1979.

Toland, John. *But Not in Shame: The Six Months After Pearl Harbor*. New York: Random House, 1961.

Tucker, Spencer, ed. *The Encyclopedia of World War II: A Political, Social, and Military History, Volume II*. Santa Barbara, CA: ABC-CLIO, 2005.

Twining, Merrill B. and Carey, Neil G. *No Bended Knee: The Battle For Guadalcanal: The Memoir Of Gen. Merrill B. Twining USMC (Ret.)*. Novato, CA: Presidio, 1996.

Van Der Vat, Dan. *The Pacific Campaign*. New York: Simon & Schuster, 1991.

Wainwright, Jonathan. *General Wainwright's Story: The Account of Four Years of Humiliating Defeat, Surrender, and Captivity.* Garden City, NY: Doubleday & Company, 1946.

Watts, Anthony J. and Brian G. Gordon. *The Imperial Japanese Navy.* New York: Doubleday & Company, Inc. 1971.

West, Howard F. *Iron Men Wooden Boats.* Westminster, MD: Heritage Books, 2005.

Whitcomb, Edgar D. *Escape from Corregidor.* Bloomington, IN: Author House, 2012.

White, William L. *They Were Expendable.* New York: Harcourt, Brace And Company, 1942.

Whitney, Major General Courtney. *MacArthur: His Rendezvous with History.* New York: Alfred A. Knopf, 1956.

Williford, Glen M. *Racing the Sunrise: The Reinforcement of America's Pacific Outposts, 1941–1942.* Annapolis, MD: Naval Institute Press, 2010.

Winslow, Walter G. *The Fleet The Gods Forgot: The U.S. Asiatic Fleet in World War II.* Annapolis, MD: Naval Institute Press, 1982.

Wolfert, Ira. *American Guerrilla in the Philippines.* New York: Simon and Schuster, 1945.

Young, Donald. *The Battle of Bataan: A Complete History.* Jefferson, NC: McFarland & Company, 2009.

Young, Donald J. *Final Hours in the Pacific: The Allied Surrenders of Wake Island, Bataan, Corregidor, Hong Kong, and Singapore.* Jefferson, NC: McFarland & Company, 2011.

Action Reports and Official Documents

Bulkeley, Lieutenant J.D. to Commander Allied Naval Forces Southwest Pacific. "Announces Destruction of PT-32 at Tagauyan Island, P.I. 13 March 1942 and Request Investigation of Circumstances." April 23, 1942.

Robert B. Kelly Biographical Sketch and Service Record. United States Navy: History & Heritage Command.

Commandant Sixteenth Naval District to CO MTNRON Three. "Operation Order." March 10, 1942.

CO MTBRON Three to CinC Allied Forces in the S.W. Pacific. "Report of Night Action off Cebu Island by PT's 41 and 34 off Cebu Island." April 21, 1942.

CO MTBRON Three to CinC U.S. Fleet and Chief of Naval Operations. "Summary of Operations Motor Torpedo Boat Squadron Three from 7 December 1941 to 10 April 1942." May 21, 1942.

CO MTBRON Three to Commandant, Sixteenth Naval District. "Narrative Report of Operations of PT-41 Night of 24 January 1942, Obtained Hit on Merchant Ship Anchored West of Sampaloc Point, Philippines." January 26, 1942.

CO MTBRON Three to Commandant, Sixteenth Naval District. "Night Operations, PT-35 and 41 off Subic Bay, the Night of 17–18 February 1942." February 17, 1942.

CO MTBRON Three to Commandant, Sixteenth Naval District. "Report of Action of U.S.S. PT-34 on the Night of January 22–23, 1942." February 27, 1942.

CO MTBRON Three to Commandant, Sixteenth Naval District. "Report of Attack of PT-32 on Enemy Cruiser-Type Surface Ship off Subic Bay." February 3, 1942.

CO MTBRON Three to Commandant, Sixteenth Naval District. "Report of Attack on Enemy Vessels in Port Binanga, 19 January 1942." January 20, 1942.

CO MTBRON Three to Commandant, Sixteenth Naval District. "U.S.S. PT-35 – Report of Condition of." January 13, 1941.

CO MTBRON Three to Commanding General U.S. Forces Far East. "Report of Night Action with Enemy Surface Ship off Cebu Island, By PT's 41 and 34." April 12, 1942.

CO MTBRON Three to Commanding General U.S.I.P. "Report of Trip to Dumaguette and Lift of President Quezon and Party to Oroquita by PT-41." April 15, 1942.

CO Permit to Commander, Submarines, U.S. Asiatic Fleet. "U.S.S. Permit (SS 178) – Report of Fourth War Patrol, Forwarding of." n.d.

CO PT-31. "Report of Circumstances of Loss of this Boat." January 23, 1942.

CO PT-32 to CO MTBRON Three. "Narrative Report of Engagement with Enemy Aircraft while Moored at Sisiman, Luzon." n.d.

CO PT-32 to Secretary of the Navy. "U.S.S. PT-32 – Report of Destruction of." March 15, 1942.

CO PT-33 to CO MTBRON Three. "Report of Circumstances of Grounding on a Coral Reef off Luzon during Night Action." December 30, 1941.

CO PT-34. "Report of Attack on Japanese Cruiser off Cebu Island and of Subsequent Loss of PT-34 to Japanese Air Attack while Attempting to Reach Cebu Harbor." n.d.

CO U.S.S. Seadragon to Commander Submarines, U.S. Asiatic Fleet. "War Patrol Number 2 – Report – Forwarding of." April 26, 1942.

CO U.S.S. Snapper to Commander Submarines, U.S. Asiatic Fleet. "U.S.S. Snapper – Report of No 2 War Patrol. Period from 6 March 1942 to 25 April 194." April 25, 1942.

Deck Log, *Guadalupe*.

"Iliff D. Richardson Service Record." National Personnel Records Center, St. Louis, MO.

Joint Army-Navy Assessment Committee. *Japanese Naval and Merchant Shipping Losses during World War II by All Causes*. Washington, DC: U.S. Government Printing Office, 1947

Muster Roll. Motor Torpedo Boat Squadron Three, October 1941.

"Narrative by Ensign D.L. Glover, Chief E.H. Offset & Chief F.J. Napolillo. Philippine Experiences." World War II Interviews. College Park, MD: National Archives.

"Narrative by Lieutenant Iliff D. Richardson, USNR. Guerilla Experiences in the Philippine Islands." World War II Interviews. College Park, MD: National Archives.

"Narrative by William F. Konko, Warrant Electrician, USN: Philippines Guerillas." World War II Interviews. College Park, MD: National Archives.

Office of Public Relations, U.S. Navy. *Navy Department Communiques 1–300 and Pertinent Press Releases*. Washington, DC: U.S. Government Printing Office, 1943.

Rockwell, Rear Admiral F.W. to CinC U.S. Fleet. "Narrative of Naval Activities in Luzon Area, December 1, 1941 to March 9, 1942." August 1, 1942.

Rockwell, Rear Admiral F.W. "Supplement of Narrative for December 1, 1941 to March 9, 1942." (Four Volumes.)

Secretary of the Navy. *Register of the Commissioned and Warrant Officers of the Navy of the United States, Including Officers of the Marine Corps.* Washington, DC: Government Printing Office, 1941.

Special Staff Military History Section, Fat East Command. *Imperial Japanese Navy in World War II: A Graphic Presentation of the Japanese Naval Organization and List of Combatant and Non-Combatant Vessels Lost or Damaged in the War, Part 2.* Washington, DC: U.S. Government Printing Office / BiblioGov, 2013

"Statement of William Francis Konko Made to Lt. W.H. Wright 14 February 1945." World War II Interviews. College Park, MD: National Archives.

War Diary, Sixteenth Naval District.

Articles

"Anthony B. Akers, Ran for Congress." *New York Times*, April 2, 1976.

"Army Nurse Who was One of the Angels of Bataan." http://articles. chicagotribune.com/1993-02-27/news/9303185498_1_bataan-corregidor-malinta-tunnell (accessed October 24, 2014)

"Authors and Critics Select the Best Books of the Year," *Chicago Tribune*, December 6, 1942, G22.

Crowther, Bosley. "Movie Review: They Were Expendable (1945)."http:// www.nytimes.com/movie/review?res=9E01E5D71F38E333A-05752C2A9649D946493D6CF (accessed May 5, 2015).

December 21, 1945

Bulkeley, John and Jack Ryan. "MacArthur's Closest Call." *Family Weekly*, May 27, 1962.

Cabral, Steve. "Floatplanes in Second World War at Sea." http://www. avalanchepress.com/floatplanes.php (accessed February 18, 2015).

"Coma Noel Richardson." http://www.legacy.com/obituaries/houston-chronicle/obituary.aspx?pid=154924215 (accessed January 22, 2014).

Davies, Lawrence E. "Bulkeley Back, Tells of Sinking's." *New York Times*, May 8, 1942.

"Douglas MacArthur." http://www.history.com/topics/douglas-macarthur (accessed April 24, 2015).

"Douglas MacArthur." http://www.history.army.mil/faq/mac_bio.htm (accessed December 3, 2013).

"Ensign Becomes Major." *New York Times*, October 28, 1942.

"Fifty Years of Naval District Development, 1903–1953." http://www.history.navy.mil/library/online/navy_dist.htm (accessed January 7, 2014).

"Films: US Naval Reserve Midshipmen's School, WWII." http://www.library.northwestern.edu/node/2082 (accessed January 15, 2014).

"George Cox Jr., Whose PT-Boat Evacuated MacArthur, is Dead." *New York Times*, January 11, 1972.

"Heroine Identified in Expendable Epic." *New York Times*, January 19, 1943.

Hewlett, Frank. "A PT Expendable Shows Up on Leyte." *New York Times*, October 28, 1944.

Hitt, Colonel Parker. "Amphibious Infantry: A Fleet on Lake Lanao." http://1-22infantry.org/history3/lanao.htm (accessed January 24, 2015).

Hlava, Chuck. "Rich Memories." Undated Newspaper Article. http://www.cnac.org/emilscott/richardson01.html (accessed May 30, 2013).

Hurst, Michael. "The Story of the Bombing of the Enoura Maru." http://www.powtaiwan.org/archives_detail.php?THE-STORY-OF-THE-BOMBING-OF-THE-ENOURA-MARU-17 (accessed August 8, 2014).

"Inventory of the Charlotte Ellen Martin Papers." http://www.oac.cdlib.org/findaid/ark:/13030/c8xw4mhj/entire_text/ (accessed February 27, 2015).

"John Duncan Bulkeley Vice Admiral, United States Navy." http://www.arlingtoncemetery.net/jdbulkel.htm (accessed April 25, 2015).

Jurika, Louis. "A Philippine Odyssey." http://corregidor.org/crypto/intel_01/A%20Philippine%20Odyssey%20-%20Louis%20Jurika.pdf (accessed February 25, 2015).

"M'Arthur Denies Brereton Report." *New York Times*, September 28, 1946.

"Medal of Honor Given Bulkeley." *New York Times*, August 5, 1942.

"Message of Support to the Philippines." http://www.presidency.ucsb.edu/ws/?pid=16076 (accessed June 30, 2014).

Miller, John and Lang Thompson. "They Were Expendable (1945)." http://www.tcm.com/tcmdb/title/2070/They-Were-Expendable/articles.html (May 4, 2015)

"Mosquito Boat Skippers to be Pine for Action." *Chicago Tribune*, September 4, 1942.

"Mother Received Letters." *New York Times*, October 28, 1942.

"Navy Hero Opens Relief Fund Drive." *New York Times*, May 15, 1942.

"New PT Boat Leaves the Ways." *New York Times*, May 17, 1942.

"New Yorker Leads Daring Raid on Foe." *New York Times*, January 21, 1942.

Oliver, Myrna. "Iliff D. Richardson, 83, War Hero." http://articles.latimes.com/2001/oct/23/local/me-60625 (accessed May 30, 2013).

Prescott, Orville. "Books of the Times: Hero's or Author's Work? Perilous Adventures on Leyte." *New York Times*, April 20, 1945.

"Quezon Plans Trip in Latin America." *New York Times*, May 20, 1942.

"Robert B. Kelly, Commander of PT Boat in WWII Dies." *Washington Post*, January 27, 1989.

Sayre, Francis B. "War Days on Corregidor." *Life*, April 20, 1942.

"Ships Constructed at the Brooklyn Navy Yard." http://www.columbia.edu/~jrs9/BNY-Ships.html (accessed October 30, 2013).

Stauffer, Donald A. "Behind Enemy Lines." *New York Times*, April 22, 1945.

Swarns, Rachel L. "Vice Adm. John D. Bulkeley, 84, Hero of D-Day and Philippines." *New York Times*, April 8, 1996.

"The Spanish-American War, 1898." http://history.state.gov/milestones/1866-1898/spanish-american-war (accessed December 2, 2013).

"Torpedo Boats Can Knock Out Japs: Bulkeley." *Chicago Tribune*, May 9, 1942.

"Tydings–McDuffie Act." http://www.princeton.edu/~achaney/tmve/wiki100k/docs/Tydings-McDuffie_Act.html (accessed December 2, 2013).

"Wife is Pleased." *Chicago Tribune*, January 21, 1942.

Wilkins, H. Ford. "Admiral at Cavite Narrowly Escapes Bomb; Filipino as His Side in Shelter Ditch is Killed." *New York Times*, December 15, 1941.

"William L. White, Writer, 73, Dead." *New York Times*, July 27, 1973.

"Wins $290,000 Suit." *New York Times*, December 4, 1948.

Other

"An Administrative History of PT Boats in World War II." http://www.gdinc.com/AN_Admin_History_of_PTs-001.pdf (accessed November 13, 2013).

Imperial Japanese Navy Page. http://www.combinedfleet.com/bb.htm. (accessed on various dates).

"Interview with Iliff D. Richardson." Denton, TX: Admiral Nimitz Museum and University of North Texas Oral History Collection, 1997.

John L. Tuggle Collection (AFC/2001/001/4840), Veterans History Project, American Folklife Center, Library of Congress, Washington, DC

National Archives Website. http://aad.archives.gov (accessed on various dates).

Naval History and Heritage Command Website. http://www.history.navy.mil (accessed on various dates).

NavSource Online: Service Ship Photo Archive. http://www.navsource.org/archives (accessed on various dates).

"POW List for MTBRON 3." http://www.west-point.org/family/japanese-pow/MTB-3.htm (accessed on October 28, 2013).

"Ruperto K. Kangleon: 6th Secretary of National Defense, May 28, 1946 to August 31, 1950." http://www.dnd.gov.ph/DNDWEBPAGE_files/past-snd/kangleon.html (accessed on June 5, 2013).

Schmidt, Major Larry S. "American Involvement in the Filipino Resistance Movement on Mindanao During the Japanese Occupation, 1942-1945 [Master's Thesis]." U.S. Army Command and General Staff College: Fort Leavenworth, Kansas, 1982.

Tarkington, Col. Hiram W. "There Were Others." Unpublished Manuscript. http://www.west-point.org/family/japanese-pow/ThereWereOthers/ManuscriptLinks.htm (accessed on March 7, 2015).

Undated Manuscript. Iliff Richardson Collection. Nimitz Education and Research Center, National Museum of the Pacific War, Fredericksburg, Texas.

Undated Newspaper Articles Courtesy of Jeremy Konko.

INDEX

192nd Tank Battalion, 123

Agno River, 107
Ah Cheu, 206–207, 210, 215
Akers, Anthony, viii, 27, 50, 124–125,
    182, 202, 208, 216, 221, 229–230,
    249, 254, 303, 308, 312, 323–324,
    329, 337
Akin, Spencer, 213–214, 219–220
Aleutian Islands, 334
American Expeditionary Force, 37
American Guerilla in the Philippines, 334
American Volunteer Ambulance
    Corps, 27
Annapolis, Maryland, 5
Aparri, Philippines, 78–80
Apo Island (and Apo Pass), 209–210
Arnold, Henry H., 66
Arizona, 32
Army Air Corps, 6
Army-Navy Club Manila, xii, 124, 127
Asiatic Fleet, ix, 58, 60, 63, 76, 82, 129
Aso Maru, 154
Astoria, 23
Australia, 126, 130–131, 192–197,
    200–201, 202, 206, 225, 227, 234,
    237–240, 251, 253, 260, 262, 274,

275, 285, 291, 298–302, 207, 317,
    319–320, 325, 329, 331, 337–338

B-17 Flying Fortress, 42, 65–70, 77, 79,
    93, 202, 237–239, 300
Babcock, Hazel Mae, 328
Bacolod, 255
Bagac Bay, 159, 168, 176
Balikpapan, Borneo, 60
Ballough, Rudolph, 156, 162–163
Banshu Maru 52, 154
Baracoa, 5
Bataan Island, 78
Bataan Death March, 304–305, 330
Bataan Peninsula, xii, 60, 80, 93,
    96, 127–128, 132, 137, 142–145,
    152, 165–166, 169, 171–173, 176,
    178, 184, 186, 191, 194, 200–201,
    205, 231–232, 239, 255, 284, 308,
    314, 340
    American plans to defend, 39, 41, 44
    Fall of, 257–258, 272–274, 287
    Geography of, 134
    Retreat into, 105–108, 113–115,
        122–124, 133–135, 164
Batalan River, 159
Battle of Java Sea, 195

Belgium, 35
Beliveau, Clayton, 53
Bell, California, 46
Binanga Bay (also known as Port Binanga), 144, 150–151, 154, 158, 164, 326
Bittern, 48–50, 82, 85
Black Hawk, 61
Bohol Island, 255, 264, 272
Boise, 59, 61, 75
Bonhomme Richard, 4
Bombay, India, 9
Borneo, 195, 232
Brantingham, Henry, 11, 27, 50, 110, 116, 118–119, 141–142, 166, 208, 218, 235, 241–242, 244, 259, 264, 291–294, 311–313, 315–316, 324, 329
Brereton, Lewis, 45, 66–67, 70–71
Brooklyn Navy Yard, 3–4, 10
Brooklyn, New York, 323
Bulkeley, Alice, 9, 153, 276, 309
Bulkeley, Elizabeth, 4
Bulkeley, Fredrick, 4
Bulkeley, John D., viii–ix, xiii, 23, 29, 46, 51, 53, 72, 83, 93, 95–98, 119, 121, 128, 141, 164–166, 182, 200, 230–231, 238, 241, 253, 276, 302, 309–310, 332, 337–338, 340
    Action in Bagac Bay, 166–170
    Attack on Binanga Bay, 144–146, 149, 152–155
    Considers escape plan to China, 187–88
    Death of, 327
    During attack on Cavite, 86–87, 89
    Early life, 4–5
    Evacuation from Philippines, 299–300
    In Australia, 307–308
    Last battle in Subic Bay, 182–184
    Last days in Manila, 126–127

MacArthur evacuation, 195–197, 199–201, 202–204, 207, 209–210, 215–216, 219–220, 222–223, 227
    Medal of Honor, 325–326
    Navy career, 6–11
    On loss of *PT-32*, 234–235
    Physical description of, 3
    Quezon rescue, 245, 249, 251–252
    Rescue of *Corregidor* survivors, 99–100
    Return to the United States, 323–324
    Sea battle off Cebu, 263–265, 270–271, 275
    Subic Bay action, 173–176
Bulkeley, Jr., John, 276

Caballo Island, 138
Cabanatuan, Philippines, 135
Cabra Island, 209–210
Cagayan, Philippines, 203, 221, 226, 230, 233, 238, 243, 249, 263, 298–299
Caibobo Point, 171
Calumpit Bridges, 122–123
Camiguin Island, 78
Campbell, Alexander, 68
Camp John Hay, 67
Camp Murphy, 81
Camp O'Donnell, 305
Canacao Bay, 53, 72
Canopus, 112, 115, 137, 172, 181–182, 258
Canton Island, 309
Cape Cod, Massachusetts, 6
Caribbean Sea, 5, 10, 31
Casey, Hugh, 213–214, 216, 219–220
Catalina Island, 22
Cavite Navy Yard, viii, x, xiii, 50, 53, 58–61, 72, 73–75, 93–94, 154, 181
    Abandoned, 114
    Bombed by Japanese, 81–89
    Destruction of, 90, 92

Cebu, Philippines (and Cebu City), 184, 198, 231, 255–256, 258–260, 263–265, 270–272, 275–282, 284–285, 286–289, 291–294, 297, 299–300, 304, 312–313, 330–332
Chalker, Joseph, 87
Champlin, Malcolm, 73, 186
Chandler, Barron, 27, 101, 131, 140, 145, 148–149, 152, 166–169, 199
Chapple, Wreford, 219, 233–234
Chaumont, 7
Chelsea, Massachusetts, 327
Chicago, Illinois, 47–48, 324
China, 33–34, 187, 198
Chungking, China, 187–188
Chynoweth, Bradford, 232, 284–285
Clark Field, 44, 66, 68–70, 73, 77–78, 81, 93
Cleland, Morrison "Dad," 258–259, 262, 293
Clement, William, ix,
Cleveland, Ohio, 331
Cockburn, George, 162
Colombian Steamship Line, 5
Commandantia, ix, x, 73, 88, 90
Compton Junior College, 46
Cook, John, 289–290
Cornell, Theodore, 290
Corregidor, 98–99
Corregidor, xii, 96, 98–99, 101, 103, 109–111, 113, 115, 124, 126–127, 132, 138, 140, 143–144, 164–166, 170, 176, 181–182, 185–186, 191–197, 199, 202–208, 219, 232, 234, 237, 239, 260–261, 274–275, 284, 287, 294, 310, 313–314, 330, 338, 340
    As part of American strategy to defend Philippines, 39, 43, 105
    Description of, 135–136

Fall of, 306–307, 321
Final days, 304–305
Cotabato River, 299
Cox, George, 27, 50, 125, 164–165, 173–175, 182, 202, 206, 211, 249, 253, 264, 266, 271, 300, 302–303, 308, 312, 324, 329, 337
Culp, James, 156, 158, 160–162
Cuyo Islands, 202–203, 215–217

Darwin, Australia, 239, 313
Davao, Philippines, 59, 65, 73, 203, 231–232, 284, 298
Dean, William, 156, 162–163
Dedham, Massachusetts, 328
Deisher, Jacob, 318
Del Carman Field, 81
Del Monte Airfield, 44–45, 68, 71, 93, 227, 231–232, 235, 237–239, 298, 300, 302, 311–312, 318–319
DeLong, Edward, 26, 94, 117–118, 145, 152, 155–162, 173–176, 178–180, 200, 314–315, 330
Denver, Colorado, 46
Dewey, 137, 181, 258
Dewey, George, 31
Diana, HMS, 8
Don Esteban, 237
Dorsey, Jimmy, 324
Dumaguete, Philippines, 250–251, 255
Dutch East Indies, 30, 35, 62, 195, 239, 321

Earlham College, 27
East China Sea, 30, 79
Edsall, 26
Egypt, 9
Eichelberger, Paul, 242
Eisenhower, Dwight D., 38
Electric Boat Company, 17, 324
Emporia, Kansas, 337

Empire of Japan, 29, 33, 334
Endicott, 327
Engadine, 98
Enoura Maru, 163

Fee, Dode, 99–100
Fee, Elton "Jack," 99–100
Fertig, Wendell, 331
Flight Gridiron, 313, 315
Floyd, Nat, 188, 205
Formosa, 30, 45, 63, 65, 76, 78–79, 203
Fort Stotsenburg, 43, 70, 106
Fort William McKinley, 43
Fortune Island, 185
France, 27, 33, 35, 326
Fredericksburg, Texas, 334

Germany, 27, 30, 33, 35, 41
Gerow, Leonard, x
Gibraltar, 9, 135
Gingoog Bay, 243
Glassford, Jr., William, 60, 75–76
Glover, DeWitt, 119, 235, 265, 301–302, 311–313, 316–318, 331
Goodman, David, 217, 281
Grande Island, 184
Great Britain, 27, 33, 35–36
Great Depression, 6, 37
Greenwalt, Beulah "Peggy," 101, 128, 205–206, 261, 278, 304, 314, 337–339
Guadalcanal, 309
Guadalupe, 3–4, 12, 22–23, 25, 46
Guam, 62, 64, 92
Guantanamo Bay, Cuba, 327

Hackettstown, New Jersey, 5
Hanoi, Vietnam, 58
Hart, Thomas, ix, 51, 58–59, 61, 73, 76, 87, 90, 92, 103, 111, 113, 124, 129
Hayo Maru, 103

Harris, David, 267, 271, 281, 286, 293
Hibbs, Ralph, 81
Hitler, Adolph, 41
Holland, 33, 35
Homma, Masaharu, 63, 122, 136, 143, 176, 232, 257, 274, 284, 297, 304–305
Hong Kong, 8, 58, 62, 81, 92, 143, 187
Honolulu, Hawaii, 22
Hopkins, Harry, 193
Hornet, 163
Houlihan, John, 87, 253
Houston, 59, 61, 75, 195
Houston, Texas, 47
Huff, Sidney, 195–197, 205, 207, 219, 224–225
Hunter, Velt, 266, 282

Iba Field, 68, 73
Ilinin Point, 155
Indianapolis, 6–7
Indochina, 30, 35, 60, 260
Iowa, 3
Irwin, 328
Isabel, 82
Italy, 41

Japanese Fourteenth Army, 63
John D. Ford, 82
Jones, Albert, 123
Johnson, Cone, 50, 140–141, 208, 234, 329
Jurika, Tom, 286–288

Kangleon, Ruperto, 331
Kaye, Danny, 324
Kelly, Robert B., xii–xiii, 52, 75, 82–83, 87, 93, 95, 97–98, 145, 162, 167–168, 182, 185, 198, 200, 236, 239–240, 244–245, 259, 277–282, 308–309, 323–324, 337–340

Death of, 329
Early life and naval career, 26
Escape from Cebu, 286, 293–296, 301
Evacuation from Philippines, 302–304
MacArthur evacuation, 202, 205,
  208, 212–213, 216–217, 222–223,
  225–226, 228
Navy career, 327–328
On Corregidor, 101, 127–128,
  165–166
Sea battle off Cebu, 263–270, 275–276
Kennedy, John F., 324, 329
Key Biscayne, Florida, 338
Key West, Florida, 10–11, 27
Kalamazoo, Michigan, 26
Kiji, 266, 269, 275
King, Edward, 273–274, 284
King, Ernest J., 10, 193, 325
Knox, Frank, 61
Konko, William, 229–230, 250,
  252–254, 311–312, 314,
  316–318, 331
Korea, 33–34
Kuma, 265–268, 275

LaGuardia, Fiorello, 323
Lake Lanao, 254, 297, 299, 301–302,
  309, 313, 316, 330
Lamon Bay, 105
LaMonja Island, 176, 180
Langley, 76
Lee, Clark, 124, 187, 205
Legaspi, 185
Lewis, John, 331
Leyte, 231, 320–321, 332
Leyte Luck, 320–321
Light, James, 253
Lingayen Gulf, 79, 103–106, 132
Long Beach, California, 9
Long Island City, New York, 9, 153
Longoskawayan Point, 171–172

Los Angeles, California, 22, 46
Luzon, Philippines, xii, 30, 43–45, 58,
  62, 65, 67, 76, 78, 102, 104, 106,
  109–110, 132, 134, 199–200, 231,
  255, 304, 313, 330
Luzon Point, 169, 178

MacArthur, Arthur, 197, 206–207,
  211, 215
MacArthur, Douglas, x, xiii, 36, 60–61,
  67, 70–71, 77, 92, 113, 125, 134,
  178, 191–193, 202, 232, 274–275,
  298–300, 303, 308–309, 319,
  324, 340
  Background and early army career,
    37–38
  Evacuation from the Philippines,
    193–197, 199–201, 206–209, 215,
    219, 222, 224–225, 227, 237–240
  Plans to defend the Philippines,
    39–44, 104–105
  Requests reinforcements, 129–131
  Return to Philippines, 333–335
  Visits Bataan, 136
  Withdraw to Bataan, 106–108
MacArthur, Jean, 196, 205–207,
  211, 215
Mactan, 126
Mactan Island, 277
Malalag Bay, 65
Malaya, 60, 62, 92, 143, 171, 195, 284
Malinta Tunnel, 135, 165, 306
Manchuria, China 34
Manila Bay, viii, x–xi, 29, 31, 39–40,
  43, 53, 60, 72, 75–76, 80, 83–84, 87,
  91, 94, 103, 106, 109, 113, 116, 128,
  132, 135, 138, 164–165, 185–186,
  202, 209, 234
Manila Hotel, x, 38, 126
Manila, Philippines, vii, 25, 29–31, 40,
  43–44, 58, 62, 64–67, 70, 76, 80, 84,

90, 92, 96–97, 104, 106, 109, 112, 122, 138, 163, 203, 232, 307
Declared open city, 108, 113–114
Location, 32
Occupied by the Japanese, 123–126
Under attack by air, 81–83
Manila Yacht Club, 50, 53
Marblehead, 52, 61
Mariana Islands, 23, 30
Mariveles Mountain, 152, 178, 208, 273
Mariveles, Philippines (and Mariveles Harbor), x, xii–xiii, 59–60, 73–75, 82, 88, 90, 93, 101–102, 110–111, 119, 136, 137–138, 152, 162, 169–171, 176, 178, 208, 234, 274, 330
Marshall, George C., 42, 130, 193–194
Marshall, Richard, 125, 208
Martin, Cecil John, 288
Martin, Charlotte, 288
Martino, John, 151, 269, 281
Maryanne, 173, 176, 178, 180
Mayagao, Philippines, 158
Maywood, California, 46
McMicking, Joseph, 208
Melbourne, Australia, 239, 274
Mexico, 22
Miami, Florida, 328
Mindanao, 82
Mindanao, Philippines, 44, 59, 65, 68, 93, 193, 197, 203, 219–223, 226, 227, 230–231, 238, 241, 243, 250–251, 253–255, 259, 271, 276, 291, 293–294, 301, 309, 312–313, 315, 318–321, 330–331
American plans to defend, 232
Japanese invasion of, 284, 297–299, 303
Location of, 32
Mindoro, 110, 203–204, 209, 219, 229
Minglanilia, Philippines, 278
Minneapolis, 27
Misamis, 241–243

Misamis Bay, 271, 276
Missouri, 3, 335
Moore, George, 207
Morhouse, Charles, 207
Moron, Philippines, 158–159, 171
Montgomery, Robert, 338
Morton, Louis, 42
Motor Torpedo Boat Submarine Chaser Division One, 26
Motor Boat Submarine Chaser Squadron One, 10
Motor Torpedo Boat Squadron Two, 326
Motor Torpedo Boat Squadron Three, viii, 26, 54, 90, 229, 304, 310, 337
Motor Torpedo Boat Squadron Seven, 326
Motor Torpedo Boat Squadron Nine, 327
Motor Torpedo Boat Squadron Forty, 329
Motor Torpedo Boat Squadron Training Center, 324
Mount Natib, 134
Mount Samat, 258, 273
Murray, Bond, 208, 254, 312, 330

Niagara, 129
Nanking, China, 34
Naples, Italy, 9
Napo Point, 161
Napolillo, Francis, 331
Nashville, 333
Negroes, Philippines, 226, 231, 233, 238, 249, 254–255, 263–266, 292, 308
New Britain, Connecticut, 26
New Georgia, 328
New Guinea, 321, 324, 334
New York, New York, 3–5, 8, 10–11, 23, 26, 309, 323
Niagara Falls, New York, 27

Nichols Field, 44–45, 76–77, 81, 127
Nielson Field, 66, 68, 80–81
Nimitz, Chester, 48
Noel, Coma, 47–48
Northwestern University, 47
Norden bombsight, 42
Norfolk, VA, 6

Office of Naval Intelligence, 7
Olongapo, Philippines, 58, 60, 102, 142, 144, 184
Opan Shipbuilding and Slipway Corporation, 255–256, 258
Otus, 82
Owen, Paul, 331

P-35 Fighter, 81, 320
P-40 Warhawk, 54, 69–70, 79–80, 84–85, 139, 172, 178, 196, 209
Panama Canal, 35
Panay, Philippines, 203, 221, 231, 233, 235, 237, 284, 297
Panay Incident, 7
Parker, George, 43–44, 106, 134, 142
Pasig River, 49
Patrol Wing 10, 60, 76
Payne, Earl D., 85
PBY Catalina, 60, 85, 113, 254, 311, 313, 315–317, 330
Pearl Harbor, Hawaii, viii, xi–xii, 23, 36, 43, 61, 64, 89, 129
Peary, 96, 115, 128
Pedro Miguel Locks, Panama Canal Zone, 22
Pensacola, 129–130
Pensacola, Florida, 9
Perth, 195
Permit, 194, 203, 219–221, 233
Pete Floatplane, 280
Petross, Lynn C., 49
Philippines, viii, ix, 3, 8, 11, 24–25, 32, 36, 38, 47, 60, 200, 216, 219–220,

237, 239, 254, 259, 300, 308, 310, 325, 335, 339–340
American plans to defend, 40–43
Geography of, 32
Japanese plan to attack, 62–63
Japanese invasion of, 78–80, 102–103
Strategic location, 30
Philippine Scouts, 43–44, 106, 142, 273
Phillips, Jim, 84
Phillips, Tom, 61, 92
Phoenix Islands, 129
Pierson, Ernest, 111, 118–119
Pigeon, 82, 111, 115
Pillsbury, 96, 115–116, 128
Plant, William, 50, 156, 162–163
Point Santiago, 117
Pope, 110
President Cleveland, 48
President Coolidge, 23
Prince of Wales, HMS, 61, 92
PT-31, 11, 83, 87, 110, 112, 116–119, 121, 167, 173
    Attack on Binanga Bay, 144–148, 152–153
    Loss of, 155–157, 162–163
PT-32, 99–100, 121, 138–141, 166, 173, 181, 329
    Battle of the Points, 178–180
    Loss of, 233–235
    MacArthur evacuation mission, 208, 213–214, 218, 219–221
PT-33, 54, 72, 83, 85–87, 94–95, 97, 110–111, 128, 291
    Loss of, 116–119, 121
PT-34, 52, 97–98, 101, 121, 138, 141, 181, 185–186, 198, 236, 240–241, 245, 254, 259, 261, 263, 276–280, 286, 293, 300, 324
    Action in Bagac Bay, 166–171
    Attack on Binanga Bay, 144–152, 154
    Loss of, 282–284

MacArthur evacuation mission,
208–209, 212–213, 216–217,
220–223, 225
Sea battle off Cebu, 263–269, 275
PT-35, 11, 27–28, 50, 83, 86–87, 141,
173, 181, 254–256, 259, 261–262,
264, 291, 293, 311–312
Last battle in Subic Bay, 182–184
MacArthur evacuation mission, 208,
216, 219–221, 229–230
Quezon rescue, 249–250, 252
Scuttled, 295
PT-41, 11, 27, 53, 112, 119–121,
126–127, 164, 166, 173, 176,
185–186, 196, 253–254, 259–261,
276, 283
Final disposition, 299, 301–302,
311–312
Last battle in Subic Bay, 182–184
MacArthur evacuation mission,
205–212, 214, 219, 222–226, 230
Quezon rescue, 249–250, 252
Sea battle off Cebu, 264–265,
267–268, 270
PT-109, 329
Purnell, William, 58

Quail, 82, 172
Quezon, Manual L., 33, 38–39, 105,
108, 125, 136, 191–192, 237–238,
245, 249–253, 308
Quinauan Point, 178–179
Quincy, 26

Radio Tokyo, 125
Rainbow Three, 40
Rainbow Five, 41, 60, 105
Ranger, 131
Ray, Harold (Herbert), x, 96, 144, 197,
207, 214, 216
Reed, Albert, 9
Reed, Donna, 338

Rendova Island, 328
Repulse, HMS, 61, 92
Revolutionary War, 4
Reynolds, Willard, 168, 267, 271–272,
277, 281–282, 287, 293
Richardson, Carl, 147, 181
Richardson, Iliff, 49–50, 52–53, 72, 73,
82, 94, 96–97, 99, 109–112, 138–141,
145, 162, 185, 187, 200, 235–236,
241–245, 255–256, 258–261,
277–279, 282–283, 319–321, 340
Action in Bagac Bay, 166–167, 169
Attack on Binanga Bay, 145–152
Death of, 334
During attack on Cavite, 85–87,
89–90
Early life & naval career, 46–48
Escape from Cebu, 286–290, 292–294
Loss of PT-33, 116–121
MacArthur evacuation mission, 198,
208, 217–218, 222–226
Member of Philippine Guerilla
movement, 331–334
Sea battle off Cebu, 263–272
Rockwell, Francis, viii, ix, xiii, 53, 59,
61, 74, 83–85, 88–89, 96–97, 103,
113–115, 121, 128, 137–138, 144,
152, 164, 188, 202–204, 208, 212,
216–217, 219–221, 223, 225–226,
239, 334
Rogers, Paul, 208, 229–230
Roosevelt, Franklin D., 6, 35, 38, 41,
130, 191–192, 307, 324–325
Ross, Albert, 217, 266–267, 271, 281
Russia, 33, 35
Ryujo, 65

S-38, 103
Sacramento, 7–9
Sampaloc Point, 184
Sanuki Maru, 280
San Antonio, Texas, 6, 27

San Bernardino Strait, 23, 102
San Felipe, 75
San Francisco, California, 48, 130, 309
San Pedro, California, 26
Sanders, Morgan G., 5
Santa Cruz, California, 26
Saratoga, 9
Sayre, Francis B., 61, 89, 105, 192
Schumacher, Vincent, 26, 138–140, 176, 178–179, 202, 208, 213–216, 220–221, 233–234, 329
Scott, Norman, 129, 131
Seadragon, 82, 84, 260–261
Sealion, 82, 84, 114
Shanghai, China, 7–8, 58, 143
Shark, 115
Sharp, William, 43–44, 227, 232, 297–299, 302–303, 321–322
Shell Island, 260–261
Shepard, George, 242, 281
Silver Spring, Maryland, 327
Singapore, 58, 61, 64, 81, 192, 195
Si Kiang, 100, 110
Siquijor Island, 264, 271
Sisiman Cove, 75, 93, 97–98, 100–101, 110, 131, 138–139, 141, 146, 152, 164, 166, 174–176, 180, 182, 195–196, 198, 202, 205–206, 208
Sixteenth Naval District, viii, 59
Snapper, 260
Solomon Islands, 327
Soriano, Don Andres, 238, 249–250, 252
South China Sea, 41, 82, 132, 187
Spanish-American War, 31–32
Stark, Harold, 59
Subic Bay, 58, 60, 144, 153–154, 173–175, 178–180, 184, 199, 202–204, 266, 314
Surabaya, Java, 219

Sutherland, Richard, x, 38, 66–67, 70–71, 197, 200, 207, 209, 216, 219–220, 230, 239
Suva, Fiji, 129
Stanley Point, viii, ix, 53, 72, 73, 76, 82–85, 87–88, 102–103, 114
Statue of Liberty, 3
Stimson, Henry, 41
Stingray, 103
Stivers, Charles, 208
Stribling, 327
Subic Bay, 102, 137, 142, 165–166, 182
Swatow, China, 8, 187
Swordfish, 192, 237

Tagauayan Island, 202, 215, 219, 229–230, 233
Takao, Formosa, 163
Tanon Point, 263–264
Tarakan, Borneo, 60
Task Force Five, 60, 75
Tenryu, 266
Tennessee, 26
Ternate, Philippines, 164–165
They Were Expendable, 338–339
Third Naval District, 49
Thurber, Harry B., 4
Tills, Robert G., 65
Tisdale, Ryland, 283, 313, 316–317
Tokyo, Japan, 58
Tokyo Rose, 194
Trabajador, 200, 314
Treaty of Paris, 31
Tripartite Pact, 35
Tsushima Straits, 33
Tuggle, John, 12, 331
Twining, Merrill, 309
Tydings–McDuffie Act, 32

United States Naval Academy, 5, 26
University of Houston, 48

University of Rochester, 27
University of Texas, 28
U.S. Army Forces in the Far East
  (USAFE), 40, 45
Utter, Harmon T., 85

V-7 United States Naval Reserve
  Midshipmen's School, 47
Verde Island Passageway, 109, 116,
  128, 185
Vietnam, 30
Vigan, Philippines, 78–80
Virginia Beach, Virginia, 4
Visayan Islands, 231–232, 284

Wagner, Frank, 76
Wainwright, Jonathan, 43–44, 79,
  105–106, 122–123, 132, 134, 136,
  172, 194, 200–201, 250, 257–258,
  273–274, 299, 306–307, 314, 319,
  321–322, 335
Wake Island, 62, 64, 92
War Plan Orange, 39–40, 105–106

Washington, DC, x, 6, 9, 41, 45, 59–60,
  90, 129–130, 191–192, 196, 199, 225,
  324, 333
Watertown, New York, 27
Wayne, John, 338–339
West Point, New York, 5, 37
Wetherington, Thomas, 88
Whitcomb, Edgar, 69–70
White, William L., 337
William B. Preston, 65
Wilmington, California, 22
Wolfert, Ira, 334
Wood, Hilda Alice, 8
World War I, 7, 27, 30, 37, 46, 98

Yaeyama, 179–180
Yangtze River, 7
Yokohama, Japan, 207
Yorktown, 59

Zamboanquita, Philippines, 249
Zero Fighter, 62, 65, 68–70, 80–81,
  85–86, 254